DATE DUE

NOV 2 8 1994	

MICROCOMPUTER INTERFACING:

An experimental approach using the Z-80

Mike Cavenor

John Arnold

Department of Electrical Engineering
University College
University of New South Wales
Australian Defence Force Academy

PRENTICE HALL

New York   London   Toronto   Sydney   Tokyo

Prentice Hall, Inc., *Englewood Cliffs*, New Jersey
Prentice Hall of Australia Pty Ltd, *Sydney*
Prentice Hall Canada, Inc., *Toronto*
Prentice Hall Hispanoamericana, SA, *Mexico*
Prentice Hall of India Private Ltd, *New Delhi*
Prentice Hall International, Inc., *London*
Prentice Hall of Japan, Inc., *Tokyo*
Prentice Hall of Southeast Asia Pty Ltd, *Singapore*
Editora Prentice Hall do Brasil Ltda, *Rio de Janeiro*

Typeset by: Keyboard Wizards, Harbord, NSW.
Printed and bound in Australia by:
  Macarthur Press Sales Pty Limited, Parramatta, NSW.

Cover design by: Kim Webber

1 2 3 4 5 93 92 91 90 89
ISBN 0 7248 0794 2 (paperback)
ISBN 0-13-580952-5 (hardback)

National Library of Australia
Cataloguing-in-Publication Data

Cavenor, M.C. (Michael C.), 1940-
   Microcomputer interfacing.

   Includes index.
   ISBN 0 7248 0794 2.

   1. Computer interfaces. 2. Microcomputers.
   I. Arnold, John Fredrick. II. Title.

004.6

Library of Congress
Cataloguing-in-Publication Data

Cavenor, M.C., 1940-

   Microcomputer interfacing: an experimental approach / M.C.
   Cavenor & J.F. Arnold.
        p.   cm.

   ISBN 0-13-580952-5
   1. Computer interfaces. 2. Microcomputers--Circuits. 3. Computer
   interfaces--Experiments. 4. Microcomputers--Circuits--Experiments.
   I. Arnold, J.F. (John F.), 1954- II Title.

TK7868.158C38 1988
621'.398--dc 19   88-19805

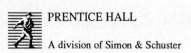

PRENTICE HALL

A division of Simon & Schuster

Contents

Preface   *xi*

Chapter 1   Fundamental Concepts   1

1.1 Number Systems and Codes   1
        Negative numbers   2
        Octal, Hexadecimal and BCD Representation   4
1.2 Microcomputers   6
        The Microprocessor   8
        Read-Only and Read-Write Memory   12
        Input-Output Devices   16
1.3 Analog to Digital and Digital to Analog Converters   16
        Analog to Digital Conversion   16
        Digital to Analog Conversion   18
        Selecting ADCs and DACs   20
     Problems   23

Chapter 2   Hardware Aspects of the Zilog Z80 Microprocessor   28

2.1 Theory of Operation of the Z80 Microprocessor   28
        The Arithmetic and Logic Unit   28
        Flag Register   29
        The CPU Registers   32
        The Control Unit   35
2.2 Information Transfer in a Microprocessor System   37
        Z80 CPU Pin Descriptions   37
        CPU Timing   41
        Instruction Opcode Fetch   43
        Memory Read or Write   45
        Input and Output Cycles   47
        Bus Request/Bus Acknowledge Cycle   49
        Interrupt Request/Interrupt Acknowledge Cycle   50
2.3 Summary   50
     Problems   51

Chapter 3   The Z80 Instruction Set   54

3.1 Z80 Addressing Modes   55
        Implied Addressing   55
        Immediate Addressing   55
        Immediate Extended Addressing   55
        Register Addressing   56

v

Register Indirect Addressing   56
Modified Page Zero Addressing   56
Relative Addressing   56
Indexed Addressing   57
Bit Addressing   57
Combined Addressing Modes   57
3.2   Z80 Instructions   57
Data Transfer Instructions   57
Data Processing Instructions   62
Test and Branch Instructions   64
Input-Output Instructions   66
CPU Control Instructions   67
3.3   Assemblers   68
Field 1: Label Field   68
Field 2: Opcode Mnemonic Field   69
Field 3: Operand Field   69
Field 4: Comments Field   70
Assembler Directives   70
ORG   70
EQU   70
DEFB   71
DEFW   71
DEFM   71
END   71
3.4   A Selection of Sample Program Segments   71
System Routines   71
Example Programs   73
Problems   76
Laboratory Exercises   78
Exercise 3.1   An Introduction to Input/Output using the VDU   78
Exercise 3.2   Monitoring Keyboard Status   79
Exercise 3.3   ASCII to Hexadecimal and Decimal Conversion   80
Exercise 3.4   Decimal Multiplication   81
Exercise 3.5   Multiplication Quiz   83
Exercise 3.6   Relocation of Blocks of Data in Memory   85
Exercise 3.7   Adding Machine   86
Exercise 3.8   Sum of Integers   87

Chapter 4   Simple Parallel Input/Output Using the Intel PPI   88

4.1   Introduction   88
4.2   The Intel 8255 Programmable Peripheral Interface   89
Mode 0: Basic Input/Output   89
Addressing the PPI   91
4.3   Using the PPI for Unconditional Data Transfer   92
4.4   Handshaking Input/Output   94
4.5   The PPI in Mode 1   96

Mode 1: Strobed Input   96
Mode 1: Strobed Output   98
4.6   Strobed Bi-Directional Input and Output   98
Bi-Directional: Input to the Microcomputer   100
Bi-Directional: Output from the Microcomputer   100
4.7   The Bit Set-Reset Facility   101
4.8   PPI Pin Allocations   104
Problems   107
Laboratory Exercises   110
Exercise 4.1   The Monophonic Organ   110
Exercise 4.2   The Double Pulse Generator   111
Exercise 4.3   The Arbitrary Waveform Generator   113
Exercise 4.4   The Seven Segment Display   116
Exercise 4.5   The Multi-Digit Seven Segment Display   118
Exercise 4.6   Numeric Display Using a Cathode Ray Tube   120
Exercise 4.7   Interfacing a Keyboard   122
Exercise 4.8   The Successive Approximations ADC   125
Exercise 4.9   The Digital Storage Oscilloscope   127
Exercise 4.10 Graticules, Cursors and Digital Readout   130

Chapter 5   Z80 Interrupts and the Intel PPI   133

5.1   The Z80 Interrupt Request Line   134
Interrupt Mode 0   136
Interrupt Mode 1   138
Interrupt Mode 2   138
Return from Interrupt   140
5.2   The Z80 Non-Maskable Interrupt Line   140
5.3   Use of the PPI in Mode 1 to Facilitate Interrupt Handling   142
Combined Modes of Operation   145
5.4   Interrupt Software   145
CPU and PPI Initialization   146
Initialization of Data Storage and Counters   147
The Interrupt Service Routine   148
Problems   150
Laboratory Exercises   152
Exercise 5.1   Data Acquisition under Interrupts   152
Exercise 5.2   Interrupt Driven Reaction Timer   154
Exercise 5.3   The Logic Analyzer   156
Exercise 5.4   Interrupt Driven/I/O with Joystick Controller   158
Exercise 5.5   Signal Averaging using Interrupts   160
Exercise 5.6   Output to a DAC using Interrupts   163
Exercise 5.7   Output under Interrupt Control to a Printer   164
Exercise 5.8   Traffic Light Controller   167

Chapter 6   The Zilog Z80 PIO and Multi-Level Interrupts   169

6.1   The Zilog Z80 PIO   169
The Microprocessor Interface   169

The Interrupt Control Section 171
The Peripheral Interface Ports 172
The Internal Control Logic 174
6.2 Zilog Z80 PIO Port Operation 174
Mode Control Register 175
Input/Output Select Register 176
Mask Register 176
Mask Control Register 176
Data Input, Data Output Registers and Handshake Control
Logic 176
6.3 Programming the Z80 PIO for Basic Input/Output 176
6.4 The Zilog Z80 PIO under Interrupt Control 178
Port Initialization 182
6.5 Programming the Z80 to Handle Multi-Level Interrupts 183
Define the Position in Memory of the Table of Vectors 184
Load the I Register with the Most Significant 8-bits of the
Address of the Table of Vectors 184
Load the Table of Vectors with the Starting Addresses of All
Interrupt Service Routines 184
Set the Interrupt Mode to Mode 2 185
Enable Interrupts 185
6.6 Examples 186
Problems 193
Laboratory Exercises 195
Exercise 6.1 Data Acquisition under Interrupt 195
Exercise 6.2 Signal Averaging under Interrupt 197
Exercise 6.3 Introduction to Multi-Level Interrupts 200
Exercise 6.4 Reaction Timer 202
Exercise 6.5 The Logic Analyzer 204
Exercise 6.6 Intruder Alarm Controller 206
Exercise 6.7 Bi-Directional Data Acquisition
and Display using Interrupts 207
Exercise 6.8 File Transfer 209

**Chapter 7   Serial I/O Using the Intel 8251 and Zilog Z8530 Serial
Communication Devices 211**

7.1 The RS 232-C Interface Standard 211
Use of the RS 232-C Interface Standard 213
7.2 The Intel 8251 PCI 216
The Microprocessor Interface 216
Modem Control 218
Transmit Buffer and Control 219
Receive Buffer and Control 220
Programming the 8251 PCI 220
Command Instruction 222
Status Register 223
7.3 The Zilog Z8530 SCC 224
Baud Rate Generator 224

        Z8530 SCC Registers   225
        Initialization Procedure   226
        Status Information   229
    Problems   231
    Laboratory Exercises   232
        Exercise 7.1 Serial Communications to Keyboard and Screen   232
        Exercise 7.2 File Transfer via a Serial Link   234
        Exercise 7.3 Interrupt Driven Keyboard for Program Control   236

Chapter 8   Designing a Simple Stand-Alone System   238

    8.1 Introduction   238
    8.2 Z80 CPU Input and Output Signals   238
        A_0 - A_{15}, D_0 - D_7 and Unused Pin Connections   239
        $\overline{MREQ}$, $\overline{IOREQ}$, $\overline{RD}$ and $\overline{WR}$ 239
        Clock Input $\overline{(CLK)}$ 239
        Reset Input $\overline{(RESET)}$ 240
        $\overline{M1}$ and the Reset of the Z80 PIO   241
        $\overline{INT}$ 242
    8.3 Interfacing ROM and RAM Memory   242
        Memory Speed Requirements   242
    8.4 Interfacing the parallel and Serial I/O Devices   247
        Addressing   247
        PPI Output Buffer   247
        PCI Level Shifting Devices   248
        Interrupts   248
    Problems   250
    Laboratory Exercises   251
        Exercise 8.1 Simple Parallel and Serial I/O Experiment   251
        Exercise 8.2 Data Acquisition and Display   252
        Exercise 8.3 Traffic Light Controller   254

    Appendix A: ASCII Code Conversion Table   255

    Appendix B: Data Sheet for the Zilog Z80 Microprocessor
                    Including the Z80 Instruction Set   257

    Appendix C: Data Sheet for the Intel 8255A Programmable
                    Peripheral Interface   289

    Appendix D: Data Sheet for the Zilog Z80® PIO Parallel
                    Input/Output Controller   311

    Appendix E: Data Sheet for the Intel 8251A Programmable
                    Communication Interface   325

    Appendix F: Data Sheet for the Zilog SCC Serial
                    Communications Controller   343

    Index   367

Preface

With the Z80 having been around for the best part of ten years, one might be excused for asking why do we need another text book on such a well established microprocessor? We feel that the highly practical approach that we are advocating to the study of the highly practical topic of microcomputer interfacing is unique and that the Z80 is the best microprocessor to use to teach the fundamentals of this very important subject. Once they have learnt the basic interfacing techniques employed with the Z80, it is our experience that students have little difficulty in progressing to more complex microprocessors and peripheral devices.

In common with many topics in electrical engineering, microcomputer interfacing is most effectively learnt by students when they are given ample opportunity to reinforce the theoretical concepts with interesting and relevant laboratory exercises. A cursory inspection of the many exercises following each chapter of this book will reveal that the instructor has several experiments to choose from based directly on topics discussed in the preceding chapter. This allows the instructor to use different experiments to reinforce the same theoretical material from year to year. In addition, experience of using relatively complex devices in their simpler modes of operation is obtained before the full capabilities of the devices are discussed. This step-by-step approach, combined with first hand practical experience, has been shown to dispel much of the mysticism surrounding the introduction of a new complex chip. Each chapter ends with a number of problems which also help to reinforce the theoretical material covered earlier.

Chapter 1 briefly reviews the concepts in digital systems which form the foundation for later chapters. We expect that most students undertaking a course in microcomputer interfacing will already be familiar with this material but it is included in order to provide a ready source of reference when needed.

The next two chapters describe the Z80 microprocessor in terms of its hardware (Chapter 2) and instruction set (Chapter 3). The early part of Chapter 2 contains all the hardware information needed in order to be able to program the Z80. This text aims, however, to take students beyond just being able to program the Z80. After working through it, they should be able to design simple stand-alone microcomputer systems including the Z80 CPU, together with memory and peripheral chips. For this reason, a large amount of material is included on the timing of Z80 operations. This is probably more detailed than is really needed at this stage of the student's study. The instructor is therefore free to include as much or as little of the material in section 2.2 as is desired. This material does, however, form the basis of work in Chapter 8 on the design of stand-alone systems and must be covered by that stage. Chapter 3 provides a complete description of the addressing modes and instruction set of the Z80. A brief description of the features provided by a standard assembler is also included as well as several sample program segments. The student is now ready to begin to use the Z80. Eight programming exercises of graded complexity are therefore included at the end of this chapter so that the student can become familiar with programming the Z80 as well as with using the experimental system.

In Chapter 4, the topic of transferring information between the microprocessor system and other peripheral devices is introduced for the first time. The Intel 8255 Programmable Peripheral Interface (PPI) is used to carry out this function. This is an industry standard device which is still used extensively with more complex microprocessor systems. The student starts by examining the device in its most simple modes of operation and progresses to the point of being able to use the device for bi-directional data transfer. A number of interesting and informative laboratory exercises are included to give the student practice in using the PPI. These range from a monophonic organ to a simple digital storage oscilloscope.

An important topic when using microprocessors is the concept of interrupts. This is dealt with extensively in the next two chapters. In Chapter 5, the Z80 interrupt modes are considered in some detail. Again, detailed timing diagrams for interrupt response are included and the consideration of these can be left to a later stage if so desired. The method of performing an interfacing task using a PPI under interrupt control is then described. Several laboratory exercises are included to reinforce these concepts covering applications such as data acquisition, a simple logic analyzer and DAC output under interrupts.

Chapter 6 introduces the parallel input/output device designed specifically for the Z80, the Z80 PIO. The main advantage of the PIO is that it is able to use the mode 2 interrupt response of the Z80 in order to implement a multi-level interrupt structure. The procedures needed to successfully implement such a structure are described. Actual program segments required to carry out the initialization of the microprocessor and the Z80 PIO for a number of applications are included as are several laboratories which employ multi-level interrupts. These range up to interrupt-driven bi-directional data transfer.

Up to this point, only parallel input/output has been considered. Serial input/output is considered in Chapter 7. The first section describes the RS 232-C interface standard and then follows a description of two commonly used serial input/output peripheral chips. These are the Intel 8251 Programmable Communication Interface and the Zilog Z8530 Serial Communications Controller. Several laboratory exercises are provided in order to allow the student to experiment with serial input/output.

The final chapter (Chapter 8) attempts to draw together all of the hardware information contained in the earlier chapters by describing the design of a simple stand-alone Z80 microprocessor system.

The appendices provide a tabulation of the ASCII code as well as data sheets on every device used in the text. This means that even after completing the course, the text will provide a useful reference manual when using systems which use any of the devices described.

The book has been designed for a 54 hour course to be run during the second, third or fourth years of a course in engineering or computer science. If used as a course for computer scientists, the instructor may find it appropriate to leave out much of the detailed hardware material.

We are grateful to many people whose efforts have gone into the making of this textbook: the staff at Prentice Hall Australia who supported it, the reviewers who helped to improve it, our students who helped us to refine the material over the past few years and Steve Dick of this department who expertly drew all of the illustrations.

Mike Cavenor
John Arnold
Canberra, Australia

1 Fundamental Concepts

Several aspects of number systems, coding and digital logic will be briefly reviewed in this chapter. This will form the basis of work in later chapters. It is anticipated that most readers will already have encountered these topics in introductory texts on digital systems. The present treatment, however, is biased towards their use in microcomputer systems and, as such, will provide a useful reminder and reference section.

1.1 NUMBER SYSTEMS AND CODES

Positive numbers are represented in binary form in the standard positional notation in which the weighting of each binary digit, or bit, increases by a factor of two in moving one place to the left. Thus the binary number 1001.11_2 represents in decimal form:

$$\text{Binary } 1001.11_2 = 1*2^3 + 0*2^2 + 0*2^1 + 1*2^0 + 1*2^{-1} + 1*2^{-2} = 9.75_{10}$$

Conversion from binary to decimal is carried out as above, using the definition of standard positional notation. Conversion from decimal to binary proceeds separately for the integer and fractional parts, requiring repeated division by two for the integer conversion and repeated multiplication by two for the fractional conversion. This is illustrated in the following example.

Example 1.1

Convert 14.333_{10} to binary.

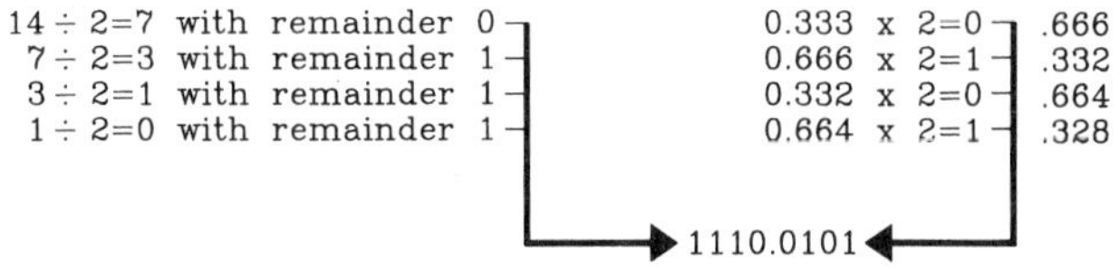

```
14 ÷ 2=7 with remainder 0          0.333 x 2=0   .666
 7 ÷ 2=3 with remainder 1          0.666 x 2=1   .332
 3 ÷ 2=1 with remainder 1          0.332 x 2=0   .664
 1 ÷ 2=0 with remainder 1          0.664 x 2=1   .328

                        1110.0101
```

Figure 1.1 Decimal to binary conversion

Example 1.1 illustrates several aspects of number representation that the microcomputer user will need to bear in mind. First, no provision is made within the binary numbers held in the computer for the binary point separating the integer from the fractional part. Mixed numbers would most likely be stored in the microcomputer with one or more 8-bit words, or bytes, representing the integer part with a further byte, or bytes, representing the fractional part. It is then the responsibility of the programmer to organize the storage and manipulation of these bytes in the correct manner. With addition, for example, fractional parts must only be added to fractional parts having the same weighting.

Second, not all fractions can be represented exactly in binary form. When, as is shown in Example 1.2, an integer has been divided into three equal parts, the sum of the parts will not necessarily return the original integer.

Example 1.2

Represent the number 1.0 as an 8-bit integer and an 8-bit fractional part and carry out division by three. Multiply the result by three and comment on the result.

```
Representation:  00000001.00000000
Divide by 3
                 00000000.01010101
            11 | 00000001.00000000
                 11
                 0100
                   11
                   0100
                     11
                     0100
                       11
                       01

Multiply by 3
                 00000000.01010101
                               11
                 0000000001010101
                 0000000001010101
                 0000000011111111

               =00000000.11111111 = 255/256 ₁₀
```

Figure 1.2 Division and multiplication by three

Clearly, the final result is not identical to the original number due to the limited precision to which certain decimal numbers are represented when stored in binary form.

Negative numbers

The eight bits that go to make up a word in a microcomputer may represent either positive numbers only or both positive and negative numbers. In the first case, the numbers range from 0 to 255, whereas when negative numbers are included, an 8-bit word allows numbers in the range -128 to +127 to be represented. Which of these two interpretations is placed upon a number stored within the microcomputer is entirely under the control of the programmer and both interpretations can co-exist simultaneously.

It is customary for negative numbers to be represented in microcomputers in their so called 'complements' form rather than in a 'sign and magnitude' form. The reason for this becomes clear when one attempts to subtract two signed numbers. Depending upon the signs and relative magnitudes of the two numbers, the correct answer is found by performing one or other of six different operations. By contrast, the operation of subtraction is consistent regardless of the sign or magnitude of the operands if the numbers are expressed in complement form.

Two forms of complement notation may be used, namely 1's complement and 2's complement. The 1's complement of an n-bit number, representing -x, is formed by subtracting +x from the number 2^n-1. Thus, -21 represented as an 8-bit number in 1's complement is formed by subtracting +21 (00010101) from 2^8-1 (11111111).

$$
\begin{array}{rcl}
2^8-1 & = & 11111111 \\
+21 & = & \underline{00010101} \\
& & 11101010 \quad = \quad \text{-21 in 1's complement form}
\end{array}
$$

By inspection, it is clear that the 1's complement of a number is formed by simply inverting all the bits in the corresponding positive number.

The 2's complement of an n-bit number -x is formed by subtracting +x from the number 2^n. Since 2^n is only one greater that 2^n-1, it is clear that a short cut method for forming the 2's complement of a number is to invert all the bits and then add 1. Figure 1.3 is a table showing the range of 8-bit numbers possible in the two complement notations discussed. The table shows that with both schemes, a negative number is indicated by a 1 in the most significant bit position. The 1's complement notation results in one fewer number than for 2's complement since the 11111111 codeword in 1's complement notation represents the redundant minus zero. If complement representation of negative numbers is used, the operations to be performed for addition and subtraction, and hence for multiplication and division, are always the same regardless of the signs and magnitudes of the operands. These rules, however, are different from the normal rules of addition and subtraction as will be apparent from the following examples.

1's Complement	2's Complement

Addition

	1's Complement		2's Complement
1.	Add the two numbers	1.	Add the two numbers
2.	Perform end-around-carry if a carry bit is produced in step 1	2.	Discard any carry bit produced in step 1

Subtraction

	1's Complement		2's Complement
1.	Form the 1's complement of the number to be subtracted	1.	Form the 2's complement of the number to be subtracted
2.	Add the number formed in step 1 to the other number	2.	Add the number formed in step 1 to the other number

3. Perform end-around-carry if a carry bit is produced in step 2

3. Discard any carry bit produced in step 2

1's Complement	Number	2's Complement
0111 1111	+127	0111 1111
0111 1110	+126	0111 1110
invert 0000 0001	+1	0000 0001 invert bits
bits 0000 0000	0	0000 0000 & add 1
1111 1110	−1	1111 1111
1000 0000	−127	1000 0001
not allowed	−128	1000 0000

Figure 1.3 Table showing 1's complement and 2's complement representation of 8-bit numbers

Example 1.3

Perform the following calculations in binary using both 1's complement and 2's complement notation.

(a) -37 + 45   (b) 67 - 103

Solution

1's Complement

+37 = 00100101
-37 = 11011010
+45 = 00101101
      1 ←00000111
           →1
      00001000 = +8$_{10}$

+103 = 01100111
- 103 = 10011000
+ 67 = 01000011
       11011011
Negative →
Invert Bits →00100100 = -36$_{10}$

2's Complement

+37 = 00100101
-37 = 11011011
+45 = 00101101
       ✗←00001000 = +8$_{10}$

+103 = 01100111
- 103 = 10011001
+ 67 = 01000011
       11011100
Negative
11011011 ∴ Subtract 1
00100100   and invert
=-36$_{10}$

Figure 1.4 Solution to Example 1.3

Octal, Hexadecimal and BCD Representation

Expressing numbers of even moderate size in binary form is cumbersome, difficult to read and error prone. A common practice to overcome these difficulties is to group the binary digits in threes or fours and write down the resulting octal, hexadecimal or binary coded decimal (BCD) notation. A conversion table is shown in Figure 1.5.

The method for converting a binary number to octal and hexadecimal form is illustrated in Figure 1.6. In this text, hexadecimal numbers will be indicated by the suffix H, octal numbers by the suffix Q and binary numbers by the suffix B. Numbers with no suffix will be standard decimal numbers. Thus, in Figure 1.6, the three alternative representations of the number are D19.7H, 110100011001.0111B and 6431.34Q.

Decimal	Natural Binary	Octal	Hexadecimal	Binary Coded Decimal
0	0000	00	0	0000 0000
1	0001	01	1	0000 0001
2	0010	02	2	0000 0010
3	0011	03	3	0000 0011
4	0100	04	4	0000 0100
5	0101	05	5	0000 0101
6	0110	06	6	0000 0110
7	0111	07	7	0000 0111
8	1000	10	8	0000 1000
9	1001	11	9	0000 1001
10	1010	12	A	0001 0000
11	1011	13	B	0001 0001
12	1100	14	C	0001 0010
13	1101	15	D	0001 0011
14	1110	16	E	0001 0100
15	1111	17	F	0001 0101

Figure 1.5 Conversion table from decimal to natural binary, octal, hexadecimal and binary coded decimal

D	1	9	.	7	Hexadecimal
1 1 0 1	0 0 0 1	1 0 0 1	.	0 1 1 1	Natural Binary
6	4	3 1	.	3 4	Octal

Figure 1.6 Conversion of a natural binary number to octal and hexadecimal

BCD appears at first sight to be similar to octal and hexadecimal as simply a means of expressing long strings of binary digits in a more readable form. It is, however, much more than just a shorthand representation of binary numbers. It is an essential intermediate step between the microcomputer and its two most common peripheral devices, namely the keyboard and visual display unit (VDU). Consider the basic problem of displaying the result of some calculation that has been performed using binary arithmetic in the computer. Assume, for example, that the calculation resulted in the binary number 00101010B.

Most microcomputer users would expect this result to be displayed on the screen of the VDU in decimal form, in this case the number 42. The computer communicates with the VDU one character at a time via the ASCII code in which each keyboard and screen character is assigned a unique 7-bit codeword. A copy of the ASCII code is included in Appendix A. It is necessary, therefore, to convert the 8-bit binary number into, in this case, two numbers, one representing the 10s and the other representing the units. Since only four bits are required to represent the decimal numbers 0 to 9, an 8-bit word may be used to accommodate two decimal digits as shown in Figure 1.7.

4	2	Decimal
0 1 0 0	0 0 1 0	Binary Coded Decimal (BCD)

Figure 1.7 BCD representation of the number 42

Thus BCD represents in the first four bits a number between 0 and 9 with a weighting of 10 while the remaining four bits represent a number between 0 and 9 with a weighting of one. In order to display the two-digit number 42 on the screen it is necessary to convert first the 10s digit and then the units digit to their equivalent ASCII codewords and then transmit each codeword in turn to the screen. This is shown in Figure 1.8.

1.2 MICROCOMPUTERS

The design of logic circuits from first principles using Boolean algebra, or in an ad hoc manner using the medium scale building blocks available in the early 1970s, allowed many useful digital instruments, data acquisition systems and controllers to be constructed. A limitation of such approaches, however, is that modifications to the planned use of a circuit can often lead to the need for a complete redesign. Hardwired logic circuits are most inflexible and if, during the development or use of a product, a superior mode of operation is devised then such changes usually await the launch of a new model. A solution to these problems appeared with the arrival of the microcomputer. With much, if not all, of the digital processing being carried out by the execution of a program, changes could be incorporated into the product even after the instrument had been delivered to the customer. Providing the designer has included hardware necessary to meet all conceivable uses, within the limitations of cost, then last-minute changes can be implemented by a change in the controlling program. The use of a microcomputer in the design of a product thereby imparts a degree of flexibility that is unavailable in a dedicated, hardwired design.

1. Binary to B.C.D. Conversion

00101010 → 0100 0010

2. BCD to ASCII Conversion

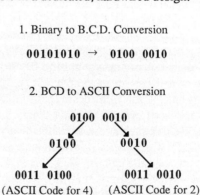

3. Serial Transmission to VDU

Figure 1.8 BCD to ASCII conversion for display on a VDU

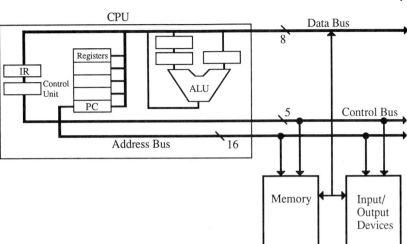

Figure 1.9 Basic microcomputer system

A further significant advantage of including a microcomputer is that several operations that previously had been performed by special-purpose hardware could now be performed by the microcomputer thereby reducing component cost, printed circuit board area, assembly time and power consumption. These advantages are apparently achieved at almost no cost since large capacity memory chips are only a little more expensive than their smaller counterparts. There is, however, a non-trivial cost to the development of reliable software. As the code increases in size when more and more functions are implemented in software, the problem of fully testing all aspects of the program escalates. The cost of developing, documenting and maintaining good software must therefore be balanced against the savings in hardware mentioned above. The trend, however, is inexorably towards the greater use of microcomputers.

The three essential parts that go to make up a basic microcomputer system, as illustrated in Figure 1.9, are the microprocessor or central processing unit (CPU), memory and input-output devices. The interaction between these components is best illustrated by following through the execution of a typical instruction, for example, loading a number from memory into one of the CPU's internal registers.

For the purpose of this explanation it is necessary to assume that the previous instruction has just been executed and that a register, namely the program counter (PC), contains the address in memory of the next instruction to be executed. The contents of the program counter are placed onto the address bus and a control signal is issued by the CPU to command the memory device to put the digital word contained at that address onto the data bus. This digital word is interpreted by the CPU as an instruction to perform some task and, as such, is latched into the instruction register (IR). The instruction is decoded in a manner that will be described in more detail in the next chapter and various control signals are generated to allow the tasks specified by the instruction to be carried out. At this stage, the program counter is automatically incremented and thus 'points' to the next location in memory. Depending upon the exact form of the instruction, the CPU may now be in possession of all the information needed to perform the required task and may thus commence the execution phase. Alternatively, it may still be necessary for the CPU to continue fetching additional parts of the instruction from memory at successive locations. Once the address in memory at which the data item is located is known to the CPU, this address is asserted onto the address bus and the resulting data from memory is placed onto the data bus for subsequent latching into the selected register. This concludes the execution phase of the instruction after which the program counter is again incremented and the next instruction is fetched from memory. It is now instructive to consider the hardware aspects of the various components featured in Figure 1.9 and in the above explanation.

The Microprocessor

As implied in the above description of the execution of an instruction, the microprocessor, or CPU, is the focus of all activity within the microcomputer. It is the CPU that provides the address and control signals that allows data to be transferred from place to place within the computer. Furthermore, it is within the CPU that all of the arithmetic and logical manipulations on the data are performed in accordance with the sequence of instructions that comprise the microcomputer's program. In spite of the importance of this device, the internal architecture of an 8-bit microprocessor, such as the Zilog Z80, is comparatively simple. The CPU consists essentially of a number of registers providing temporary storage for several operands, the arithmetic and logic unit (ALU) and the instruction decoding register and control unit. Many aspects of the component parts of the CPU will be familiar to readers who have studied combinational and sequential logic design as part of an introductory course in digital systems. These topics will be briefly reviewed in the next few sections with attention being drawn to the non-ideal behavior of practical devices that may not have been covered in earlier studies.

Registers
A register is simply a group of D-type flip-flops that share a common clock input but have separate D inputs and Q outputs. It will be recalled that a D-type flip-flop captures the logic signal that is present at the D input at the time of the rising edge of the clock and retains this signal at the Q output until it is replaced on the next clock pulse. Eight such flip-flops are contained within the 74HC374 octal register, as shown in Figure 1.10, thus allowing for the storage of one 8-bit data word.

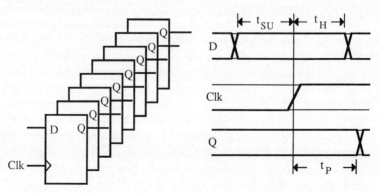

Figure 1.10 The 74HC374 register and its timing requirements

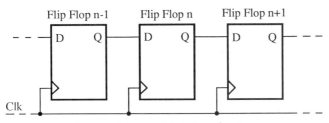

Figure 1.11 Serial shift register

Constraints on the ideal mode of operation, as implied by the above description, occur in the form of minimum time periods, both before and after the clock pulse, during which the data inputs must remain stable to ensure reliable operation. In the case of the 74HC374, High speed CMOS register, a minimum set-up time (t_{SU}) of 20ns prior to the arrival of the clock pulse and a minimum hold time (t_H) of 5ns after the pulse must be allowed for guaranteed operation. Typical devices will, however, operate satisfactorily with t_{SU} and t_H values of 10ns and 0ns respectively. In addition, a propagation delay t_p of some 30ns following the clock pulse must be allowed for the Q outputs to take on the values clocked into the D inputs.

Since much of the activity within a computer involves transferring data from one register to another, it is of interest to ask how rapidly such a transfer can take place. Is it possible, for example, to transfer data into a register while at the same time transferring previously stored data from that register to a second register? The ability to operate in this manner is an essential requirement of the serial shift register shown in Figure 1.11. The extent to which such a configuration will operate reliably using a 74F374, Fairchild Advanced Shottky TTL register is analyzed in the following example.

Example 1.4

A 1-bit serial shift register, such as that shown in Figure 1.11, is to be made from a 74F374 octal register. The clock is running at a frequency of 50 MHz with a 1:1 mark:space ratio. Using the timing information provided, determine whether the shift register will operate reliably under worst-case conditions.

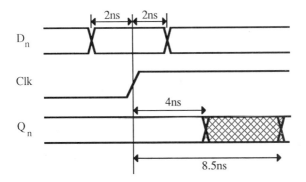

Figure 1.12 Timing diagram for 74F374 octal register

Data

		Min	Typ	Max	Units
Set-up time	t_{SU}	2.0			ns
Hold time	t_H	2.0			ns
Propagation delay	t_P	4.0	6.5	8.5	ns

The circuit is more readily analyzed when this information is transferred to a timing diagram as in Figure 1.12.

Set-up Time

The output from stage n-1 of the shift register, which is the input to stage n, will have settled to its final value not later than 8.5ns after the rising edge of the clock pulse. The D inputs of each stage are thus stable for the remainder of the 20ns period up to the arrival of the next rising clock edge. This 11.5ns (20ns - 8.5ns) period is in excess of the minimum set-up time (2.0ns) requirement.

Hold Time

The Q outputs start to change no earlier than 4ns after the rising edge of the clock and so the previous contents of each stage are held constant for this time period. With the 74F374, it is sufficient that the input to each stage is held for a minimum of 2ns (t_H) and so the hold time requirement is satisfied.

It may be concluded, therefore, that the 74F374 will operate reliably as a serial shift register at this clock frequency.

Buses and Three-state Buffers

An inspection of any machine code program for a microcomputer will reveal that the majority of instructions involve simply transferring data from one location to another. For example, transferring operands from registers to the ALU and transferring the result back to a register. While it is possible to provide separate data paths from all possible sources to all possible destinations such a complicated solution is rarely implemented. The more usual practice is to provide a data bus, as shown in Figure 1.13, to which the inputs and outputs of all registers are directly connected.

The data bus is just a collection of conductors connecting together all D_n register inputs and Q_n register outputs for each of the n-bits in the computer word. A transfer from one register to another then takes place by the source register placing its contents onto the bus which then gets loaded into the destination register by a suitably timed latching pulse. It is apparent from the above discussion that the output pins of several digital registers are connected together. This is a situation that under normal circumstances must never be allowed to happen. If, in connecting any two logic outputs together, the output of one device were asserted high while the output of the second were asserted low, then the common connection would assume some indeterminate voltage level and an excessive current would be drawn from the power supply. In the case of high speed CMOS devices, two interconnected gates with outputs in contention give rise to an output voltage of approximately half the supply voltage with a current drain of approximately 40mA.

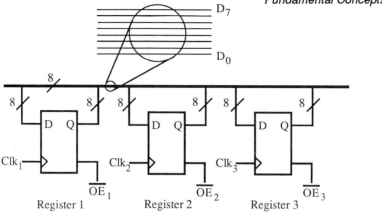

Figure 1.13 Bus arrangement for a series of registers

This problem is overcome with the three-state output stage in which an additional logic input signal has the ability to render the output inactive or high-impedance. This allows many outputs to be joined together provided only one device is active and all others are in their high impedance state. Devices that are often connected directly to data buses, such as the 74HC374 octal register, are provided with three-state outputs, however, all other devices may be so connected by the use of a three-state buffer such as the 74HC245 octal bus transceiver.

When a device with three-state outputs is being enabled while another device connected to the same bus is being inhibited, some care needs to be exercised to ensure that both devices are not active simultaneously during the brief change-over period. Information concerning such contentions may be deduced from the parameter t_{PZA} (propagation delay from high impedance to active) and t_{PAZ} (propagation delay from active to high impedance) shown in the output timing diagrams of the type illustrated in Figure 1.14. The device chosen to illustrate this feature is the 74HC374 octal register.

If one device changes from a high impedance state to an active state before the active device changes to a high impedance state then the potential exists for a peak surge current amounting to approximately 320mA for HC devices connected to an 8-bit bus. While the current pulse may only be a few nanoseconds in duration, if ignored it can lead to spurious behaviour in other sensitive devices. As will be seen later, this problem is also encountered within the microcomputer and overcome by suitably delaying the high impedance to active transition.

The Arithmetic Logic Unit
The ALU is a combinational circuit whose output Z depends upon the logic signals applied to the operand inputs A and B as well as to the instruction input I as shown in Figure 1.15. The range of instructions that the ALU incorporated into most 8-bit microprocessors can perform is extremely limited consisting of addition, subtraction and the logic operations of AND, OR, exclusive OR and complement. In addition to the primary 8-bit output of the ALU, a further output is provided in the form of a flag register. This register contains a series of 1-bit indicators or flags that relate to the outcome of the previous instruction. If the previous instruction resulted in an answer of zero or a negative number or an overflow then this information is made available to the control unit and to the programmer by way of the flag register.

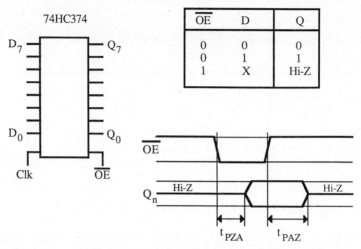

$\overline{OE}$	D	Q
0	0	0
0	1	1
1	X	Hi-Z

Figure 1.14 Output enable timing diagram

In order that the ALU can accept operands from the internal CPU data bus and return the result to the data bus, it is necessary that two further registers, namely A Temp and Temp R, be associated with the ALU as shown in Figure 1.15. In executing the instruction A plus B, the contents of register B are transferred to Temp R while the contents of the accumulator are transferred to A Temp. The two operands are now acted upon by the ALU and, following a propagation delay, the sum of the accumulator and register B appears at the output Z and hence on the internal data bus. This result is now latched into the accumulator, thus completing the execution of the instruction.

The Control Unit

The various registers within the microprocessor assert their contents onto the data bus or latch a new item of data from off the data bus under the command of suitably timed signals emanating from the control unit. An approach that has been taken since the early days of computer design is to store these signals in a memory and simply step through the memory generating each combination of control signals in turn. Such an approach has been taken in the case of the Z80 microprocessor and a discussion of its control unit is contained in the next chapter.

Read-Only and Read-Write Memory

Memory provides two essential functions in the operation of a microcomputer. First, the sequence of instructions that directs the operation of the computer is stored in memory where it can be readily accessed one instruction at a time by the microprocessor. Second, data that is acquired from some input device or data that is generated by the microprocessor to be sent to some output device often needs to be stored in memory. Small amounts of data, comprising no more than a few bytes, may be stored temporarily within the CPU's working registers. Large amounts of data, however, need to be stored in the computer's read-write

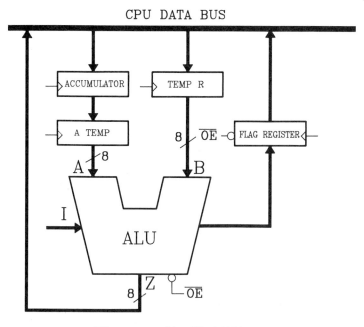

Figure 1.15 Simplified ALU

memory. This implies, as is indeed the case, that read-write memory is just an extension of the microprocessor's register set.

In the case of microcomputers that are incorporated into stand-alone instruments, it is necessary that the microcomputer commence executing its controlling program at the time that power is applied to the instrument. This program must therefore reside in a non-volatile form of memory such as a read-only memory (ROM) that retains its contents when the power is switched off. Personal computers and laboratory based computers, on the other hand, contain mostly read-write memory and the controlling program is loaded into memory from some secondary storage medium such as disk or magnetic tape. Even in these machines, it is still necessary to have a small program residing in non-volatile memory so that following a power-down situation, the computer has sufficient intelligence to allow it to communicate with the operator's console and thus allow the loading of programs from disk.

It is sufficient, for the purpose of the current discussions, to describe both read-only memory (ROM) and read-write memory by way of their terminal characteristics, as indicated in Figure 1.16. It should be noted that both ROM and RAM are, in fact, random access devices in that any sequence of addresses may be applied in a random fashion. It is traditional to abbreviate read-write memory with the letters RAM, standing for random access memory. Memory which may be written to, as well as read from, however, is more correctly referred to as read-write memory.

In both cases, an n-bit address is applied to the memory device to signify one location out of the 2^n possible locations that is being referenced. Provided that the chip has been selected and the output is enabled, the data residing at the selected address will then appear on the data lines at a time equal to the memory's access time following the assertion of an address. In the case of the read-write memory, data is written to a selected address by

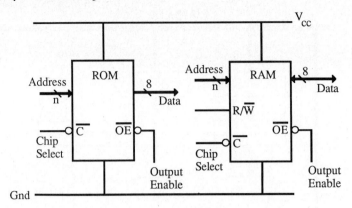

Figure 1.16 Connections to read-only and read-write memory

asserting the data onto the data lines and then pulsing the read/write line $R/\overline{W}$ low. When writing to a read-write memory device, it is necessary for the chip to be selected but for the output to be inhibited. Detailed timing diagrams for both reading from, and writing to memory devices will be considered in the chapter where the design of computer systems from individual devices will be discussed.

External Organization of Memory Chips
A review of manufacturers' data sheets for memory devices will reveal that memories of a given capacity may be obtained in a variety of different organizations. For example, a 16Kbit RAM (1K = 1024) may be organized so as to provide 16,384 locations each storing a 1-bit word or 4,096 locations each storing 4-bit words or 2,024 locations each storing 8-bit words. Each configuration has a particular advantage with the application for which the memory is to be used dictating which configuration is the optimum. The following considerations influence this choice.

The 16Kbit RAM when organized as a 2K by 8-bit device requires 11 address pins, eight data pins, two pins for power, a read/write pin and a chip select pin. This makes a total of 23 pins and thus the device is made up in a 24 pin dual-in-line (DIL) package. The spare pin is usually defined as a second chip select input to facilitate address decoding. This will be discussed more fully in a later section.

When the same capacity RAM is organized as a 16K by 1-bit device, four fewer pins are required since there is now a requirement for 14 address lines but only one data line. This results in a smaller package, higher manufacturer's yield and hence lower cost. One disadvantage, however, is that a minimum of eight devices are needed to provide a usable memory for an 8-bit microcomputer system. One philosophy that may be adopted, therefore, is to use byte-wide devices for systems requiring small amounts of memory and bit-organized devices where large amounts of memory are to be installed, thus taking advantage of the lower-cost devices. Systems employing 12-bit word lengths are clearly required to use 4-bit wide devices to implement memory in an efficient manner.

Address Decoding
It is customary for even the most basic microcomputer system to comprise several memory

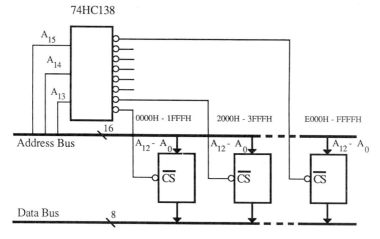

Figure 1.17 Address decoding scheme

devices, some of which will be read-only while others will be read-write. When an address is issued by the CPU, it is essential that only one of these devices responds by placing data onto the data bus. All other devices remain deselected. This is achieved using address decoding logic. A Z80 microprocessor, for example, generates a 16-bit address allowing it to address 2^{16}, or 65,536 (64K) unique memory locations. If the available memory chips have fewer than these maximum number of locations, then clearly several chips will need to be used to provide the full memory space. For example, eight 8K by 8-bit chips would be needed to provide a 64Kbyte memory, each chip having 13 address lines. The remaining three address lines (i.e. the most significant lines, A_{13}, A_{14} and A_{15}) are then used to determine which of the eight chips is to be selected in order to provide the data. A simple decoding scheme, using a 3-line to 8-line decoder such as the 74HC138, may then be used as shown in Figure 1.17.

Addresses falling within one of the listed 8K ranges causes an asserted low signal to appear at the selected output resulting in one of the memory chips being selected while all remaining chips are inhibited. As the size of individual memory chips increases, the complexity of the address decoding logic decreases, until the situation depicted in Figure 1.18 is arrived at in which only two chips are used, one ROM and one RAM.

When the number of essential pins required by a memory device of a given size is odd, as in the case of the 2K by 8-bit RAM considered in an earlier section, the remaining spare pin on the DIL package is usually dedicated to a second chip select input. If the two chip select inputs are of opposing assertion levels, a particularly simple address decoding scheme based only on the most significant address line may be implemented as shown in Figure 1.18. With A_{15} asserted low, corresponding to addresses 0000H to 7FFFH, the ROM is selected, whereas with A_{15} asserted high (i.e. 8000H to FFFFH) the RAM is selected.

This simple address decoding scheme can be used even when something less than the full 64Kbyte of memory is required. If, for example, it is sufficient to provide only 8Kbytes of ROM and 8Kbytes of RAM, the above addressing scheme can be used as long as the ROM occupies the region from 0000H to 1FFFH and the RAM occupies from 8000H to 9FFFH in the microcomputer's memory map. It must be noted that, with this simple addressing scheme, the ROM is selected for all addresses for which A_{15} is zero and not just the addresses

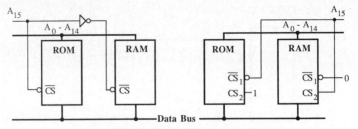

Figure 1.18 Two chip memory systems

0000H to 1FFFH. A similar situation applies for the RAM which will be addressed whenever A_{15} is set to one. This addressing scheme is therefore non-unique and so addresses 2000H, 4000H and 6000H would all cause location 0000H to be accessed.

Input-Output Devices

The basic concepts involved in having a microprocessor communicate with a peripheral device closely follow those for writing to and reading from memory. The microprocessor issues the address of the peripheral device and then asserts a control signal informing an output peripheral to accept output data from the data bus or an input peripheral to place input data onto the data bus. The detailed manner in which such data transfers are achieved is the central feature of this book and will be covered in some depth in succeeding chapters. To assist in these later discussions, however, it is appropriate that the reader should have a knowledge of the way in which typical peripheral devices provide input data and accept output data. Examples of input and output devices in the form of analog to digital and digital to analog converters will now be considered.

1.3 ANALOG TO DIGITAL AND DIGITAL TO ANALOG CONVERTERS

While this book is concerned primarily with processing digital signals, it is a well-established fact that most signals have their origins in the analog domain. Physical quantities such as force, velocity and sound intensity are analog in nature, meaning that they can take on any value from a continuous range of values. These physical quantities are then converted into analog voltages and currents by transducers, such as strain gauges and microphones. An essential step in the design of computer-based acquisition and control systems is, therefore, the conversion of the various input analog quantities to digital form prior to processing and the conversion of output results to analog form for display or control purposes. Some basic information concerning the mode of operation and the terminal characteristics of analog to digital converters (ADCs) and digital to analog converters (DACs) is included in support of the many useful experiments involving these devices that appear later in the book.

Analog to Digital Conversion

Conceptually, the simplest form of analog to digital converter is the simultaneous converter

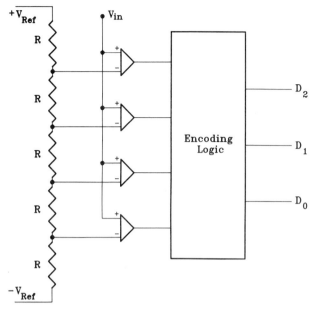

Figure 1.19 The simultaneous converter ADC

shown in Figure 1.19. A series of identical resistors connected between two reference voltages establishes a linear sequence of voltage decision levels against which the input voltage is compared. For a given input, V_{in}, the comparators with inputs from the resistor chain less than V_{in} produce an output of logic 1 whereas the remainder produce an output of logic 0. The encoding logic then converts this 'barograph' pattern into naturally weighted binary code.

As its name implies, the simultaneous converter is an extremely fast ADC. The time required to perform a conversion is simply the propagation delay through the comparators and encoding logic. Conversion rates of 100 MHz and beyond are common for this type of converter. It should be noted, however, that for an n-bit converter, 2^n resistors and comparators are required and this makes such converters expensive.

Rather than comparing the input voltage with 2^n voltages simultaneously, a more usual and much less expensive approach is to generate a sequence of voltages comparing each in turn with the input voltage. For example, if a voltage is generated for each of the 2^n possible combinations of an n-bit digital word in ascending order, then the codeword corresponding to the voltage at which the digitally generated voltage just exceeds the input voltage represents the required analog to digital conversion. Such a converter is called a digital ramp and comparator ADC and is illustrated in Figure 1.20. From the diagram, it is clear that the digital codeword corresponding to the analog input voltage is only valid at the time that the comparator changes from logic 1 to logic 0. This transition is used to capture the correct digital codeword into the latch.

A faster approach to the digital ramp and comparator ADC is the successive approximations ADC which is illustrated in Figure 1.21. Each bit in the n-bit converter is set to logic 1 in turn, commencing with the most significant bit. The resulting analog voltage, as generated by the digital to analog converter, is then compared with the input voltage V_{in}.

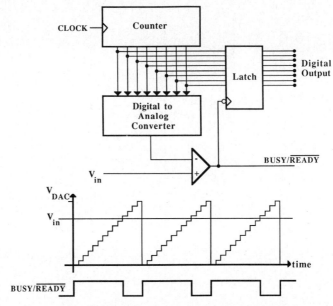

Figure 1.20 Digital ramp and comparator ADC

If the input voltage exceeds the output of the DAC then the bit remains set to logic 1 and the next bit is tested. If V_{in} falls below the output of the DAC, the bit is reset to logic 0 and the next bit is tested. When all n bits have been tested, the output of the DAC will have successively converged on the input voltage and the conversion is complete. The digital codeword corresponding to the input analog voltage may then be read from the successive approximations register.

It is evident from the above description that during the time that the conversion is taking place, the ADC is unable to provide a valid representation of the input voltage. As indicated in Figure 1.21, there is a period following the START command that the ADC is busy. Data should only be read from the converter at the end of this busy period when the ADC indicates that conversion is complete.

Digital to Analog Conversion

Digital to Analog conversion is a much simpler process than its inverse covered in the previous section. A DAC is a device that is always ready to accept input data words for conversion to analog output voltages. It is not necessary, therefore, to enquire by way of testing a status flag as to whether the DAC is busy. A DAC may not be able to change fully from its minimum output to its maximum output in the time between two successive input words, but it will accept the words and change as much as the intervening time will allow.

Conversion is usually performed by the R-2R ladder network shown schematically in Figure 1.22. Digital input words are applied to the switches causing either +V volts (for a logic 1) or zero volts (for a logic 0) to be applied to each of the resistors of value 2R ohms. The ladder has the property that the resistance to ground of the circuit to the left of any of

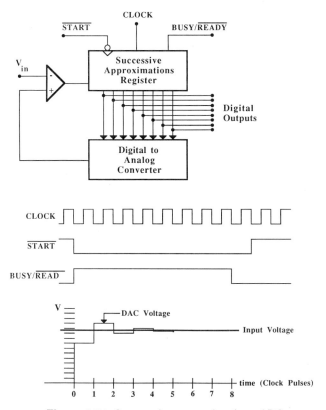

Figure 1.21 Successive approximations ADC

the nodes marked W,X,Y or Z is equal to R ohms. This is clearly evident for the node W where there are two resistors in parallel each of value 2R ohms connected either directly to ground, or via an ideal voltage supply having a negligible internal resistance.

Replacing these two resistors by a single resistor of value R ohms now reveals that the situation described above for node W also applies for node X and hence for all nodes in the ladder. If the digital input 1000 is now applied to the 4-bit DAC, the ladder circuit may be simplified to that shown in Figure 1.23(a) in which all resistors to the left of node Y have been replaced by a single resistor of value R ohms. The voltage appearing at node Z, and hence at the output of the voltage follower, is clearly $\frac{1}{2}$V volts.

With an input code of 0100, the situation just described now applies to node Y. If the circuit to the left of node Y is replaced by its Thevenin equivalent, as shown in Figure 1.23(b), then it is evident that the output voltage now becomes $\frac{1}{4}$V volts. Similar manipulation of the circuit for input codes of 0010 and 0001 result in output voltages of $\frac{1}{8}$V and $\frac{1}{16}$V volts respectively. As the circuit is linear, the principle of superposition applies and therefore digital inputs ranging from 0000 to 1111 produce output voltages increasing linearly from 0 volts to $\frac{15}{16}$V volts in steps of $\frac{1}{16}$V. It should be noted that in the above explanation it has been assumed that no load is ever connected directly to node Z of the ladder. It is essential, therefore, that a buffer, such as that provided by the operational amplifier voltage follower, be connected to node Z of the R-2R ladder.

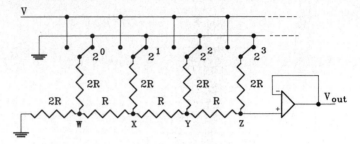

Figure 1.22 R-2R ladder digital to analog converter

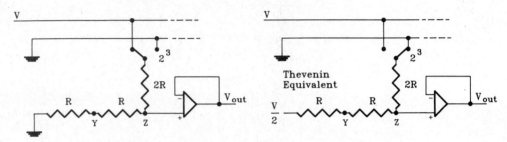

Figure 1.23   (a) Equivalent circuit   (b) Equivalent circuit
for input code 1000   for input code 0100

Selecting ADCs and DACs

When ADCs and DACs are to be selected for a specific task, a number of important decisions need to be taken which have a strong bearing on the component cost and ease of implementation of the proposed solution. A brief overview of the principal specifications for converters is given below allowing the wide range of commercial devices to be narrowed down to just a few contenders.

Resolution

Usually, the easiest decision which can be made about the desired converter is its resolution. The resolution is determined by the number of bits applied to a DAC or provided by an ADC following a conversion. It determines the smallest change that can be discerned. Thus 8-bit resolution allows a change of one part in 256 or 0.4 percent to be detected while 12-bit resolution allows for a change of one part in 4,096 or 0.025 percent to be detected. While it is possible to interface 8-bit converters to an 8-bit bus relatively easily, 12-bit converters require two data transfers in order to pass information to or from an 8-bit microcomputer. Figure 1.24 shows how a 12-bit ADC and a 12-bit DAC might be connected to an 8-bit data bus.

Following an analog to digital conversion, the 12-bit result is latched into two output buffers by the READY output of the ADC being asserted low. The microcomputer must then instruct each buffer in turn to present its data to the data bus so that it can be read in by the microcomputer. A somewhat more complex arrangement is required for the 12-bit DAC where an 8-bit word is first accepted by latch 1 with the following 4-bit word being accepted

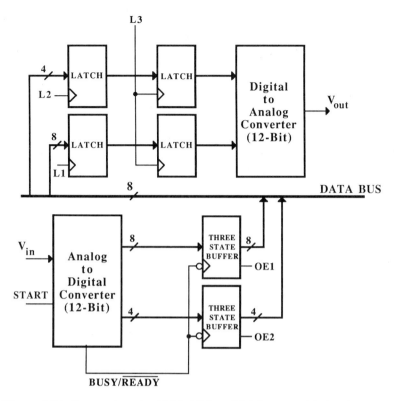

Figure 1.24 Connection of a 12-bit ADC and DAC to an 8-bit data bus

by latch 2. The full 12-bit word is then transferred into a second level of latch for presentation to the DAC. A total of five synchronized control signals, comprising two output enables and three latch signals, are required to allow the ADC/DAC system described above to operate correctly. Several commercially available ADCs and DACs have the latches or buffers described above incorporated into single chips. This considerably eases the interfacing problem. The decision to exceed 8-bits for either the ADC or the DAC is, however, not to be taken lightly.

Accuracy

Accuracy and resolution are often confused since both can be expressed in percentage terms. They are, however, two quite separate parameters that must be considered independently. The accuracy of a DAC, for example, indicates how close to the stated voltage the output will be for a given input codeword. A 6-bit DAC may generate output voltages ranging from 0 to 6.3V with a resolution of 0.1V (i.e. 1.5 percent) and an accuracy of 0.1 percent of full scale. This means, for example, that if an output of 3.0V is demanded then the actual voltage will lie within the range 2.994V to 3.006V (3.000 ± 0.1 percent of 6.3V).

Speed of Conversion

All ADCs will have a clearly stated conversion time indicating what time period will elapse

UNIPOLAR		BIPOLAR			
STRAIGHT BINARY		OFFSET BINARY		2's COMPLEMENT	
Code	Voltage	Code	Voltage	Code	Voltage
00000000	0.00V	00000000	-5.00V	00000000	0.00V
01000000	2.50V	01000000	-2.50V	01000000	+2.50V
10000000	5.00V	10000000	0.00V	01111111	+4.96V
11000000	7.50V	11000000	+2.50V	10000000	-5.00V
11111111	9.96V	11111111	+4.96V	11000000	-2.50V

Figure 1.25 Coding of 8-bit DACs and ADCs

following the application of a START signal before a valid digital codeword is generated. Generally, the shorter the conversion time, the more expensive the converter. With digital to analog converters, however, some care is needed in comparing competing devices since not all manufacturers express the relevant parameter, namely settling time, in an identical manner. The settling time is the time that will elapse following a change from zero to full scale deflection for the output to attain the stated voltage to within a specified degree of accuracy. This accuracy is usually expressed as a percentage of the full scale conversion range. A converter that settles to within 0.1 percent of full scale deflection in a given time is clearly superior to and hence more costly than, one that is only guaranteed to be in error by no more than 1 percent of full scale deflection in the same time. The application for which the converter is to be used will often dictate what maximum settling time can be tolerated. For example, a DAC used in the deflection circuit of a cathode ray tube display will require a brief settling time in order to give a sharp trace which is free from smearing.

Coding Format
Unipolar converters invariably employ straight binary encoding where a zero input or output voltage corresponds to an all-zero codeword. With bipolar converters, it is customary to provide both offset binary and 2's complement encoding since the two are identical except for the state of the most significant bit. A typical coding format for an 8-bit DAC that can be configured for both unipolar and bipolar operation is given in Figure 1.25.

PROBLEMS

Problem 1.1
Convert the following decimal numbers to binary:

(a) 94   (b) 0.6275   (c) 67.375   (d) 121.21

Problem 1.2
Convert the following numbers from their existing base to decimal:

(a) 11011001.1011B   (b) 13411_S

(c) 6A2B.12AH   (d) 10010011.10000111_{BCD}

Problem 1.3
Convert the following numbers to binary and perform the operations indicated:

(a) 63.125 - 47.5   (b) 18.625 x 5

(c) 5.6875 + 3.25   (d) 9AF2H - BCDH

Problem 1.4
Perform the following subtractions by converting the decimal numbers to binary and using:

(i) 1's complement notation;
(ii) 2's complement notation.

(a) 123 - 69   (b) 16.25 - 7.5

Problem 1.5
Perform the following conversions.

(a) 327.978 to binary, octal and hexadecimal.

(b) 110101101.001101B to octal and hexadecimal.

(c) 3AF.D2H to binary and octal.

(d) 327.25Q to binary and hexadecimal.

Problem 1.6
An ideal rectangular pulse of 20ns duration is applied to the input (A) of the circuit shown in Figure 1.26. Sketch the waveform appearing at the output (C) if the propagation delay through the inverter and NAND gate are both equal to 10ns.

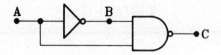

Figure 1.26 Circuit for Problem 1.6

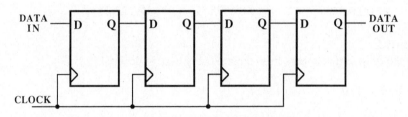

Figure 1.27 Circuit for Problem 1.8

Problem 1.7

Repeat Problem 1.6 using the following non-ideal data for the inverter and NAND gate propagation delays.

	Min	Typ	Max	Units
Propagation delay t_p	5	10	15	ns

Calculate the minimum and maximum pulse width of the waveform now appearing at the output (C).

Problem 1.8

A serial shift register is to be made from a 74F374 octal register as shown in Figure 1.27. The clock is running at a frequency of 100 MHz with a 1:1 mark space ratio. Using the timing information given, deduce whether the shift register will operate reliably under worst case conditions.

74F374			Min	Typ	Max	Units
	Set-up time	t_{SU}	2.0			ns
	Hold time	t_H	2.0			ns
	Propagation delay	t_p	4.0	6.5	8.5	ns

Problem 1.9

Deduce the maximum clock frequency at which the shift register described in Problem 1.8 will operate reliably.

Problem 1.10

Repeat Problem 1.9 using the high speed CMOS version of the 74374 octal register, 74HC374, with the following timing data:

74HC374			Min	Typ	Max	Units
	Set-up time	t_{SU}	20	10		ns
	Hold time	t_H	5	0		ns
	Propagation delay	t_P		18	36	ns

What minimum propagation delay must the 74HC374 have in order to ensure reliable operation?

Problem 1.11

It is customary to insert a gate between the clock input of each device and the master system clock, as shown in Figure 1.28, to provide a 'clock enable' control input. EN1 and EN2 enable the clock to register stages 1 and 2 respectively. Using the timing information given in Problem 1.8 for the 74F374 octal register, together with the following data on the 74F08 AND gate, determine the combination of propagation delays in the AND gates and register that are least favourable to the correct operation of the shift register. Hence, arrive at a conclusion as to whether the shift register will operate reliably under these worst-case conditions. In what way might your conclusions differ if it were assumed that both the AND gates came from the same package and hence had identical propagation delays?

		Min	Typ	Max	Units
74F08 Propagation delay	t_P	2.5		6.6	ns

Problem 1.12

Two 74F374 octal registers are connected to a common data bus as shown in Figure 1.29. The signal that enables register 2 is asserted at the instant that the signal enabling register 1 is removed. To what extent is there a contention on the data bus?

74F374			Min	Typ	Max	Units
	Set-up time	t_{SU}	2.0			ns
	Hold time	t_H	2.0			ns
	Output enable time	t_{PZA}	2.0	9.0	11.5	ns
	Output disable time	t_{PAZ}	2.0	5.3	7.0	ns
	Propagation delay (Clock to Output)	t_P	4.0	6.5	8.5	ns

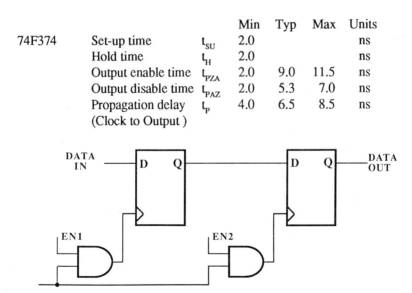

Figure 1.28 Circuit for Problem 1.11

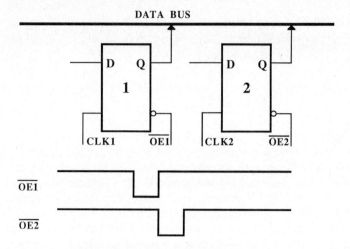

Figure 1.29 Circuit for Problem 1.12

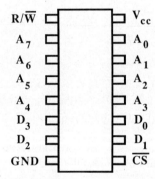

Figure 1.30 Read-write memory chip for Problem 1.13

Problem 1.13

Figure 1.30 shows the pin connections for a read-write memory. From the diagram deduce the following parameters:

(a) The storage capacity of the memory in bits.
(b) The external organization of the memory.
(c) How many such devices would be needed to produce a 4K by 8-bit read-write memory and how are these to be connected to a microcomputer's address lines?

Problem 1.14

A Z80 microcomputer system is to be provided with 64Kbytes of memory using the devices illustrated in Figure 1.31. The lowest 16Kbytes is to be implemented in ROM while the remaining 48Kbytes is to be implemented in RAM. Devise an address decoding scheme to support this configuration and draw a detailed schematic diagram for your proposed system.

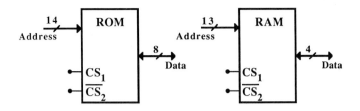

Figure 1.31 ROM and RAM chips to be used in Problem 1.14

2 Hardware Aspects of the Zilog Z80 Microprocessor

In the preceding chapter, the advantages of using a microprocessor to replace hardwired logic circuits have been clearly stated and the components that go to make up a typical microcomputer system have been described in general terms. This introduction to microcomputer architecture will be extended in the present chapter with an in-depth study of the Zilog Z80 microprocessor. This detailed treatment of the Z80 is intended to allow the reader to proceed beyond the stage of interfacing peripheral devices to already functioning Z80 microcomputer systems. It provides, in addition, the necessary timing details and explanations that allow the reader to design microcomputer systems from their component parts. This topic is taken up in the final chapter of this book and relies heavily on the details provided in the present chapter. Readers wishing to concentrate first on interfacing techniques are advised to skim over the sections on the Z80 pin assignments and timing, postponing a detailed study of these topics until venturing into the realms of microcomputer system design.

2.1 THEORY OF OPERATION OF THE Z80 MICROPROCESSOR

The Zilog Z80 microprocessor, in company with most other 8-bit microprocessors, is comprised of an arithmetic and logic unit, a number of general purpose and special purpose registers and a control unit as shown in Figure 2.1. Data and instructions are moved around within the microprocessor via an internal data bus. In the following sections, the configuration adopted for the Z80 will be examined and the role of each register will be explained.

The Arithmetic and Logic Unit

Figure 2.2 shows the block diagram of the Z80 ALU and its associated registers. The ALU accepts up to two operands at a time and produces an output in accordance with the function code that is determined by the instruction to be executed. Both operands presented to the ALU and the result achieved are of word width. For the 8-bit Z80 microprocessor, these are 8-bit quantities.

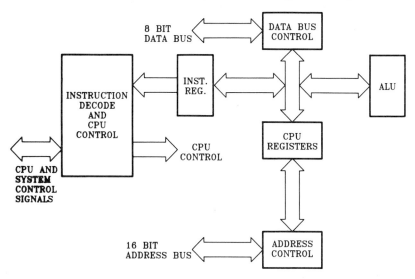

Figure 2.1 Block diagram of the Z80 microprocessor

The functions which the ALU incorporated in the Z80 microprocessor can perform include:

(a) binary addition and subtraction;
(b) logical AND, OR, exclusive OR, NOT and 2's complement;
(c) left or right shifts and rotates;
(d) increment and decrement;
(e) compare; and
(f) bit set, reset and test.

More complex operations, such as binary multiplication and division, are not provided by the Z80 ALU. Users who wish to use these more complex functions are faced with implementing them in software (i.e. by writing a program that achieves the complex function in several more basic steps).

Flag Register

In addition to the result output of the ALU, several 1-bit status signals are generated indicating specific attributes of the most recent result produced by the ALU. These status signals, called condition flags, are grouped together to form the flag register. The format of the flag register for the Z80 is shown in Figure 2.3. The register contains a total of six flags of which four can be tested by the programmer while the other two are used by the microprocessor in carrying out BCD arithmetic. The four testable flag bits and their functions are:

(a) **Carry flag (C)** This flag is set (i.e. C=1) if there is a carry from the most significant bit of the accumulator as might occur during an addition instruction. The flag is also set during a subtraction operation if a borrow is generated from the most significant accumulator bit. It can also be affected by some shift and rotate operations.

CPU DATA BUS

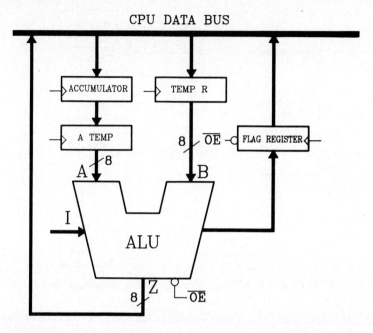

Figure 2.2 Block diagram of a typical ALU and its associated registers

(b) **Zero flag (Z):** The zero flag is set if the result of any ALU operation is zero.
(c) **Sign flag (S):** The sign flag is set if the sign of the last result was negative. The Z80 assumes 2's complement notation. Thus a negative number has a logic 1 as its most significant bit. The sign flag therefore reflects the state of the most significant bit of an ALU result.
(d) **Parity/Overflow flag (P/V):** This flag register bit has a double purpose, serving as both a parity and an overflow flag in different circumstances. In addition, it can also give the state of the CPU interrupt enable flip-flop, a topic that will be covered in Chapter 5. For logical operations, it represents the parity of the result, being set if the parity is even (i.e. the number of logic 1's in the result is even) and reset otherwise. For 2's complement arithmetic operations, the overflow flag indicates that a result greater than the maximum positive number (+127) or less than the minimum negative number (-128) has been produced. This can be best illustrated by some examples.

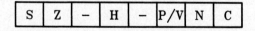

Figure 2.3 Format of Z80 flag register

Example 2.1

Deduce the state of the carry and parity/overflow flags at the conclusion of the following operations:

(a) 75 + 63

+75		01001011
+63		<u>00111111</u>
result	0	10001010

The binary addition of these two numbers gives 10001010 with no carry from the most significant bit. This corresponds to +138 if only positive numbers are considered. If the operands were considered to be 2's complement numbers, however, then the addition of the two positive numbers has given rise to a negative result (-118)! This error situation is correctly indicated by the parity/overflow flag being set.

(b) -1 + (-2)

-1		11111111
-2		<u>11111110</u>
Result	1	11111101

The binary addition of these two numbers gives 11111101 with a carry from the most significant bit. As the operands are 2's complement numbers, however, the addition of the two negative numbers has given rise to the correct negative result (i.e. -3). In this case, the parity/overflow flag will not be set.

The overflow flag is set whenever :

(i)   two positive numbers are added and the result is negative;
(ii)   two negative numbers are added and the result is positive;
(iii) a negative number is subtracted from a positive number and the result is negative;
(iv)   a positive number is subtracted from a negative number and the result is positive.

Overflow can never occur when numbers of opposite sign are added or numbers of the same sign are subtracted. By checking for the four circumstances listed above, overflow will always be accurately indicated by the overflow flag.

The two non-testable bits in the flag register and their functions are:

(a) **Half Carry Flag (H):** This flag is used to indicate a carry or borrow from the least significant four bits of an operation.
(b) **Subtract Flag (N):** This flag indicates that the last operation performed was a subtract operation rather than an add.

Both of these flags are used by the microprocessor in handling BCD arithmetic. Consider the addition of the two BCD numbers 23 and 39:

23	0010	0011	
<u>39</u>	<u>0011</u>	<u>1001</u>	
62	0101	1100	(5CH)
	<u>0000</u>	<u>0110</u>	
	0110	0010	(62H)

The decimal adjust accumulator instruction (**DAA**) examines the H and N flags (in this case they would both be reset) and then adjusts the result to reconvert it to BCD. In this example, six needs to be added. The method by which this adjustment to the accumulator takes place is by no means trivial. Interested readers are encouraged to consult the *Zilog Z80 CPU Assembly Language Programming Manual* for a detailed description.

The CPU Registers

General Purpose Registers

All bus-structured microprocessors require at least three registers closely associated with the ALU for the temporary storage of input operands and as a destination for the result. Such an arrangement is depicted in Figure 2.2. The provision of more registers within the microprocessor for the temporary storage of intermediate results increases the performance of the microcomputer by reducing the extent to which data must be transferred between the CPU and off-chip memory. Studies have shown that having a few registers located in the CPU reduces the number of relatively slow data fetches from memory from around two per instruction to only one in every five instructions.

As well as registers which can temporarily hold data, it is also necessary to provide a means of specifying an address in memory at which data is to be retrieved or stored. These registers are called index registers and must be of sufficient length to be able to specify any address. In the case of the Z80, the address space is specified by a 16-bit word (i.e. there are $2^{16} = 65,536$ bytes of memory) and so the index registers, of which there are two, are 16 bits wide.

The register set of the Z80 CPU is shown in Figure 2.4. The Z80 has two alternate sets of main CPU registers. Each consists of an accumulator, six general purpose 8-bit registers and a flag register. The general purpose registers can be used as simple 8-bit registers (B,C,D,E,H,L) for data storage or alternatively be combined to form 16-bit registers (BC, DE and HL) for both data and memory reference purposes. The CPU can access only one of the two alternate register sets at a time. It is possible, however, to swap from one set of general purpose registers to the other in only a single instruction. Similarly, the accumulator and flag registers can be swapped in another single instruction. As will be shown in a later chapter, the alternate register set provides an extremely convenient way of handling single level interrupts in an efficient manner.

Special Purpose Registers

In addition to the above general purpose registers, the CPU has a number of special purpose registers. Foremost amongst these is the program counter. The program counter always contains the address of the next instruction byte to be fetched from memory. Following the fetch of one instruction byte, the program counter is automatically incremented to point to the next byte in memory. When a programmed jump occurs, the contents of the program counter are replaced with the address of the instruction from which program execution is to continue. Execution will then resume at that address.

Another important special purpose register is the stack pointer. As previously stated, when the CPU executes a jump instruction, the contents of the program counter are replaced

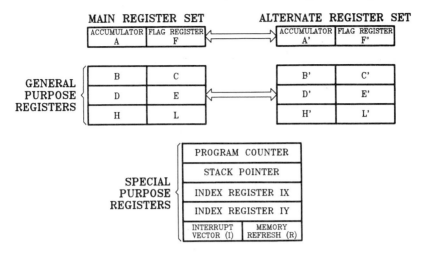

Figure 2.4 Z80 register set

by the address at which execution is to continue. Program execution then continues sequentially from that point. Another way in which a program can continue execution at other than the next sequential instruction is when a subroutine call is performed. As with the jump, the contents of the program counter need to be altered to the address at which program execution is to continue (i.e. the address of the first instruction of the subroutine). There is, however, one important difference. When execution of the subroutine is complete, the CPU must then return to the main program to continue from the instruction immediately following the subroutine call. It is therefore necessary to store the address of this instruction (called the return address) when the subroutine call occurs so that it is available when the return from subroutine occurs.

In the case of the Z80, as indeed with most microprocessors, this is achieved by using a last-in/first-out memory called a stack. Having fetched the subroutine call instruction, the program counter will have been incremented and therefore contains the address of the next instruction to be executed. This address is stored (in computer terminology 'pushed') onto

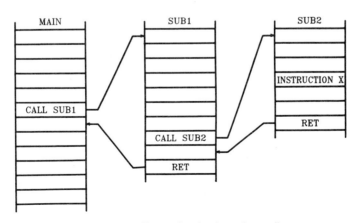

Figure 2.5 Example of subroutine calls

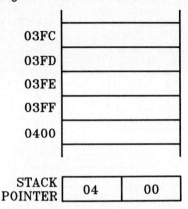

Figure 2.6 Stack initialized at 0400H

the stack. In the case of the Z80, the stack is simply a reserved area of external memory. When the return instruction is executed, the address saved on the stack is retrieved (in computer terminology 'popped') from the stack and placed in the program counter thus achieving the desired return from subroutine. The stack pointer register regulates the flow of data to and from the stack by maintaining the address of the last item placed on the stack. The whole process of calling and returning from subroutines can be best illustrated by way of an example. Consider Figure 2.5 which shows a program (MAIN) which calls a subroutine (SUB1) which in turn calls another subroutine (SUB2). It is essential that before any data transfer to or from the stack can take place, the position of the stack within memory is defined. This is achieved by loading the stack pointer register with an address that specifies the upper bound to the stack. In the following example, it has been assumed that the stack pointer register has been loaded with the address 0400H. Thus memory locations below 0400H form the stack as shown in Figure 2.6.

The steps involved when a subroutine call occurs are:

1. The contents of the stack pointer are decremented by 1.
2. The upper byte of the address stored in the program counter is stored at the memory location pointed to by the stack pointer.
3. The contents of the stack pointer are again decremented by 1.
4. The lower byte of the address stored in the program counter is stored at the memory location pointed to by the stack pointer.

Thus, by the time that instruction X, which occurs halfway through the innermost subroutine, is executed, the stack and stack pointer register will contain the addresses indicated in Figure 2.7. When a return instruction is executed, the steps that take place in retrieving the return address are:

1. The contents of the memory location pointed to by the stack pointer are fetched and placed in the lower byte of the program counter.
2. The value in the stack pointer is incremented.
3. The contents of the memory location pointed to by the stack pointer are fetched and placed in the upper byte of the program counter.

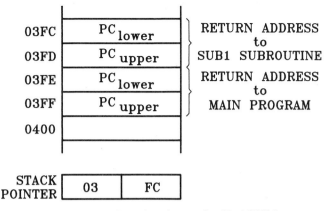

Figure 2.7 Stack pointer and stack at instruction X of SUB2

4.   The value of the stack pointer is again incremented.

From the above discussion it should be clear that the stack pointer must be loaded with an address prior to the first subroutine call or push instruction and space must be left for the stack to grow into. If insufficient space is reserved for the stack, it will grow in any case and may overwrite program instructions or data with unpredictable (and usually disastrous) results. In addition to subroutine calls, data can also be directly pushed to or popped from the stack using the Z80 **PUSH** and **POP** instructions.

As mentioned earlier, two 16-bit index registers (IX and IY) are also provided within the Z80 register set and are used to generate base addresses for indexed addressing modes. Instructions using the IX or IY registers to address memory contain an 8-bit byte to specify a 2's complement displacement from the base address in the appropriate index register. This mode of addressing is particularly useful when addressing tables of data, as will be demonstrated in the next chapter which describes the Z80 instruction set.

The last two special purpose registers are both 8-bit registers. The interrupt page address register (I) is used as part of the servicing of mode 2 interrupts and will be discussed in greater detail later.   The memory refresh register (R) contains a 7-bit counter which is automatically incremented after each instruction fetch. The data in the refresh counter is automatically placed on the lower half of the address bus while the CPU is decoding and executing an instruction. Together with a refresh control signal provided by the microprocessor, the signals provided on these address lines are all that are needed to carry out the refresh of dynamic RAM. Thus, dynamic RAM can be used with the Z80 with almost the same ease as static RAM.   Further details on interfacing static and dynamic RAMs to the Z80 microprocessor are contained in Chapter 8 which concentrates on the design of a stand-alone system.

The Control Unit

A computer system operates by sequentially fetching instructions from external program memory, decoding the instruction and then performing the function specified. Thus, the steps involved in a computer carrying out an instruction can be divided into a fetch cycle and an execute cycle.

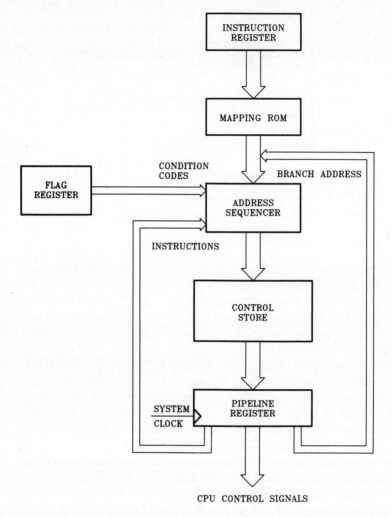

Figure 2.8 Microprocessor control section

During the fetch cycle, the address of the next instruction (which is contained in the program counter) is sent to memory and the data obtained from that location is placed into the instruction register of the CPU. This data contains two types of information relevant to the execution of the instruction. The first, namely the operation code or opcode, specifies the type of instruction to be performed. Examples of possible instructions include load, add, subtract, compare and so on. The second piece of information is the address which specifies the source and destination operands. An example of this is the instruction **LD A,B** which means load (the instruction) the contents of register B (the source) into the accumulator (the destination). Not all instructions are of the same length. Upon decoding the first instruction byte of a multi-byte instruction, the control unit knows that a further byte or bytes is required and can proceed to sequentially fetch them from memory. In the case of the Z80, the number of bytes required to specify an instruction can range from one to four.

Once the instruction has been placed into the instruction register, it is interpreted by the control unit as a command to generate various control signals that, for example, output enable source registers, instruct the ALU as to which operation is to be performed and finally latch the result into the destination register. These control signals are contained in a read-only memory called the control store. The relationship between the instruction register and the control store is illustrated in Figure 2.8. As each instruction is latched into the instruction register, the bit pattern comprising the instruction opcode is decoded into a starting address within the control store at which the control signals are located. This decoding is performed by the mapping ROM with the output of the mapping ROM being applied to the address inputs of the control store by the address sequencer at the start of each instruction execute cycle. Subsequent control signals are then located in successive locations within the control store. These control signals are latched into a pipeline register where they remain stable for one period of the system clock. During this period, the address sequencer applies the address of the next control word to the control store in readiness for the selected control word to be latched into the pipeline register on the next clock pulse.

In addition to stepping through the control store one location at a time, the sequencer can obtain the next address from an address field contained within the control word itself. This situation occurs primarily in the case of instructions that execute in different ways depending upon the state of the ALU flags. For example, control words may be in successive locations when a flag is reset but continue in some other part of the control store when the flag is set. Decisions as to which control word is to be selected next are made by the address sequencer in response to the condition code inputs.

There is a high degree of similarity between the way in which the address sequencer steps through the control store in generating the control signals for an instruction and the way that the CPU steps through the program memory in executing a program. The control unit is indeed a 'computer within a computer'. The contents of the control store are referred to as microinstructions or microcode thus further reinforcing the computer-like nature of the control unit.

2.2 INFORMATION TRANSFER IN A MICROPROCESSOR SYSTEM

Up to this point, the discussion has concentrated upon the way that the Z80 microprocessor works internally. In a practical system, of course, it is necessary for the microprocessor to communicate with external memory and input/output (I/O) devices. In order to do this, it must provide signals which allow these communications to proceed in an orderly and synchronized manner. In this section, the signals provided by the microprocessor will be looked at and discussions held on the ways in which they allow the microprocessor to perform both memory and I/O data transfers.

Z80 CPU Pin Descriptions

Figure 2.9 shows the signals associated with the Z80 CPU chip and the pin numbers on which these signals appear. The function of each pin or group of pins is described below. Signal names with an asterisk (*) appended have three-state outputs:

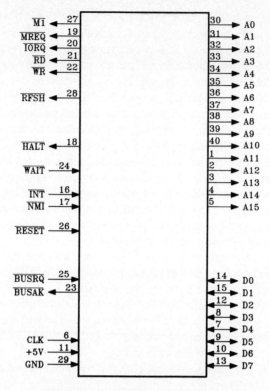

Figure 2.9 Z80 CPU pin configuration

(a)   *Address Bus*

A0-A15*   These output lines provide the 16-bit address for external memory. The
             CPU can therefore address 65,536 (64K) bytes of memory. The lower eight
             bits of the address bus (A0-A7) are used to address I/O devices. This allows
             a total of 256 I/O ports to be accessed. During an I/O instruction, the most
             significant eight bits of the address bus (A8-A15) have either the contents
             of the accumulator or the contents of register B placed on them depending
             on the instruction being executed. The lower eight bits of the address bus
             (A0-A7) have the contents of the memory refresh register (R) placed on
             them during a dynamic memory refresh cycle. Remember that the least
             significant seven bits of the R register are incremented after each instruc-
             tion fetch cycle. During a refresh cycle, the most significant eight bits of
             the address bus carry the contents of the interrupt page address register (I).

(b)   *Data Bus*

D0 - D7*   The eight input/output data lines which form the data bus are used to
             exchange data between the CPU and memory or I/O devices.

(c)   *Control Bus*

The signals which make up the control bus can be divided into three categories as shown in

Figure 2.9. The first of these is system control which deals with the synchronization of data transfers, the second is CPU control and the third bus control. Each group will now be discussed in more detail.

(i)   System Control

$\overline{M1}$ This output signal indicates that the current operation is an opcode fetch cycle. All Z80 instructions have one or two opcode bytes. In the case of instructions with two opcode bytes $\overline{M1}$ is asserted for both bytes. Note that data assembled with an instruction does not count as an opcode byte. Thus the instruction:

LD   IX,1234H

which causes the hexadecimal number 1234 to be loaded into the index register IX would be assembled (in hexadecimal) as:

DD   21   34   12.

The first two bytes are the opcode bytes and so $\overline{M1}$ would be asserted as each was fetched. The last two bytes are data and so $\overline{M1}$ would not be asserted while they were fetched.

$\overline{IORQ}^*$ $\overline{IORQ}$ is an output line which indicates that the lower eight bits of the address bus hold the address of an I/O device for an input or output operation.

$\overline{MREQ}^*$ This output signal indicates that the address bus holds the address of a memory location for a read or write operation.

Clearly, $\overline{M1}$ and $\overline{MREQ}$ will occur together every time an opcode is fetched from memory. It would appear, however, that $\overline{M1}$ and $\overline{IORQ}$ can never occur together since the former is associated with an opcode read from memory while the latter occurs in association with I/O read or write operations. In fact, $\overline{M1}$ and $\overline{IORQ}$ are asserted together by the CPU to acknowledge the receipt of an interrupt. More will be said about this in Chapters 5 and 6 which deal with interrupts.

$\overline{RD}^*$ This output line indicates that the CPU wishes to read data either from memory or from an I/O port. Upon receipt of this signal, the addressed device should place the appropriate data onto the CPU's data bus lines.

$\overline{WR}^*$ The $\overline{WR}$ signal is an output which indicates that the CPU has placed information onto its data bus which is to be stored at the memory or I/O port address held on the address bus.

$\overline{RFSH}$ This asserted low output signal indicates that the lower seven bits of the address bus hold a refresh address and that the current $\overline{MREQ}$ signal should be used to refresh dynamic memories.

(ii)   CPU Control

WAIT
This input line indicates to the CPU that the specified memory location or I/O port is not ready for a data transfer. This allows memory and I/O devices of any speed to interface to the Z80. The CPU simply marks time until the WAIT input is released.

HALT
The HALT output signal indicates that the CPU has executed a **HALT** instruction and is therefore waiting for an interrupt or reset in order to resume execution. While halted, the CPU continues to execute no operation (**NOP**) instructions so that the refresh of dynamic memory will continue.

NMI
This negative edge triggered input generates a non-maskable interrupt (i.e. the interrupt cannot be inhibited by the user). The Z80 CPU will restart execution from location 0066H after completing the current instruction. More details will be provided in later chapters dealing with interrupts.

INT
This input signal allows I/O devices to interrupt the current program of the CPU in order to obtain service provided that an internal CPU interrupt enable flip-flop has been set. The CPU can respond to interrupts in one of three modes. More details will be provided in the chapters on interrupts.

RESET
A logic low on this input line forces the program counter to zero and initializes the CPU by:

1. disabling the interrupt enable flip-flop;
2. setting registers R and I to 00H;
3. setting the interrupt mode to 0.

While RESET is asserted, the address and data buses go to the high impedance state and all other control signals become non-asserted.

(iii)   CPU Bus Control

BUSRQ
This input signal provides a means for other devices to take control of the address, data and control buses. Upon receiving an asserted BUSRQ signal, the CPU completes the current machine cycle (note that an instruction can consist of several machine cycles) and then places the address bus, data bus and three-state control bus signals into the high impedance state. Control signals which are not three-state are placed into the non-asserted state. This allows several processors to time-share use of the system buses or alternatively can allow a peripheral direct access to another peripheral or memory using direct memory access (DMA) techniques.

BUSAK
The BUSAK signal is used to signal to a device requesting use of the system buses via a BUSRQ signal that the CPU has released the buses and so it can proceed to make use of them.

In addition, there are three pins used to provide the system clock and DC power to the chip.

CLK   This pin is used to accept a single phase TTL clock to synchronize CPU operation.

+5V, GND   These pins accept DC power for the chip.

CPU Timing

A detailed consideration of the timing of Z80 CPU operations follows. The Z80 CPU executes a program using only a very limited set of operations. These are:

1.   memory read or write;
2.   I/O port read or write; and
3.   ALU operation.

All instructions are simply a series of these operations. In looking at the timing of an instruction, each of these basic operations is called a machine (M) cycle. Each M cycle in turn, is made up of three to six basic clock periods (T cycles). This is illustrated in Figure 2.10. The first machine cycle in any instruction is the opcode fetch which always consists of four to six T cycles. This can be lengthened using the $\overline{\text{WAIT}}$ signal. As long as $\overline{\text{WAIT}}$ is held low, the CPU will insert extra T cycles (called wait states) before completing a given M cycle. This allows the CPU to interface easily with low-speed memory and peripherals. If the instruction opcode consists of more than one byte, further opcode fetches will follow. After the entire opcode has been retrieved, the remainder of the machine cycles consist of memory or I/O port read/write operations or internal ALU operations and these take between three and five T cycles (which again can be lengthened using the $\overline{\text{WAIT}}$ signal). Methods for achieving these wait states are given in Chapter 8.

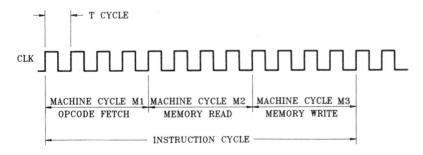

Figure 2.10 Timing associated with a single CPU instruction

Example 2.2

Describe what operations the CPU is performing during each T cycle for the instructions given.

(a) Increment (add 1 to) the contents of the accumulator.

Mnemonic:	**INC A**	
Assembled code:	3C	

Machine cycle	Function	T cycles
1	Memory read (opcode fetch)	4

This instruction consists of only a single machine cycle in which the opcode byte is fetched from memory. The increment of the accumulator occurs during this single machine cycle.

(b) Load the accumulator with 50H.

Mnemonic:	**LD A,50H**	
Assembled code:	3E 50	

Machine cycle	Function	T cycles
1	Memory read (opcode fetch)	4
2	Memory read	3

This instruction consists of an opcode fetch followed by the retrieval from memory of the data (in this case 50H) to be placed in the accumulator. Two machine cycles are therefore required.

(c) Increment the memory location pointed to by the HL register pair.

Mnemonic:	**INC (HL)**	
Assembled code:	34	

Machine cycle	Function	T cycles
1	Memory read (opcode fetch)	4
2	Memory read	4
3	Memory write	3

The first machine cycle is the opcode fetch. The value contained in the HL register pair is then placed on the address bus and the data stored at that memory location is retrieved and incremented (machine cycle 2). The result is then written back to the same memory location (machine cycle 3).

(d) Load the contents of the accumulator into memory location 4000H.

Mnemonic:	**LD (4000H),A**	
Assembled code:	32 00 40	

Machine cycle	Function	T cycles
1	Memory read (opcode fetch)	4
2	Memory read	3
3	Memory read	3
4	Memory write	3

The first machine cycle is the opcode fetch. The next two machine cycles are memory read cycles which fetch the bytes which define the memory address at which the data is to be stored (00H and 40H). Finally, the data in the accumulator is written to memory location 4000H in the fourth machine cycle.

(e)   Load register C with the data at the address given in the contents of the IX register plus one.

Mnemonic:	**LD C,(IX+01H)**	
Assembled code:	DD 4E 01	

Machine cycle	Function	T cycles
1	Memory read (opcode fetch)	4
2	Memory read (opcode fetch)	4
3	Memory read	3
4	Internal addition	5
5	Memory read	3

This instruction has a 2-byte opcode and so both of the first two machine cycles are opcode fetches. In the third machine cycle, the displacement to be added to the index register IX is fetched and then in the fourth machine cycle this displacement is added to the contents of register IX. Finally, in machine cycle 5, the data at the address calculated during machine cycle 4 is fetched from memory and placed into register C.

(f)   Increment the contents of the memory location given by the contents of index register IX plus 10H.

Mnemonic:	**INC (IX+10H)**	
Assembled code:	DD 34 10	

Machine cycle	Function	T cycles
1	Memory read (opcode fetch)	4
2	Memory read (opcode fetch)	4
3	Mcmory rcad	3
4	Internal addition	5
5	Memory read	4
6	Memory write	3

Again, this instruction has a 2-byte opcode and so the first two machine cycles are opcode fetches. The displacement to be added to the contents of index register IX is then fetched in the third machine cycle and the sum of the contents of IX and the displacement is formed in the fourth machine cycle. Then follows a memory read (machine cycle 5) where the data at the memory location calculated in machine cycle 4 is fetched and incremented and then finally (machine cycle 6) the incremented data is written back to memory.

Instruction Opcode Fetch

Figure 2.11 shows the timing of an opcode fetch cycle assuming that no wait states need to be added. The steps involved in the process are:

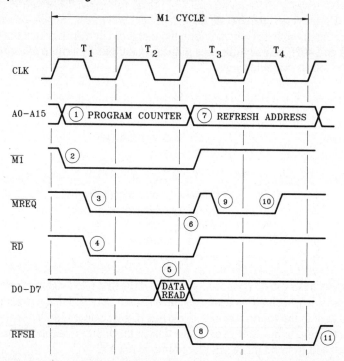

Figure 2.11 Timing diagram for an instruction opcode fetch cycle

1. The contents of the program counter are placed onto the address bus.
2. The $\overline{M1}$ signal is asserted to indicate an opcode fetch cycle.
3. The $\overline{MREQ}$ signal is asserted half a clock cycle later. By this time, the address lines will have had time to reach stability and so $\overline{MREQ}$ can be used to enable data directly onto the data bus.
4. The $\overline{RD}$ signal is asserted to indicate that the current cycle is a memory read cycle.
5. The contents of the data bus are read into the instruction register on the rising edge of clock cycle T3.
6. The $\overline{MREQ}$ and $\overline{RD}$ signals are released. Note that the data has been read prior to the read line being released.
7. Clock cycles 3 and 4 are used to refresh dynamic memories. The first step of this process is that the refresh address is placed in the lower seven bits of the address bus.
8. The $\overline{RFSH}$ line is asserted to indicate that a refresh cycle is under way.
9. The $\overline{MREQ}$ line is asserted to indicate that the refresh address is valid. By the time that $\overline{MREQ}$ is asserted, the refresh address will have had time to become stable on the address bus and so the falling edge of $\overline{MREQ}$ can be used to initiate the refresh cycle. Note that the $\overline{RD}$ line is not asserted. This prevents several dynamic RAM devices from placing data onto the data bus simultaneously.
10. $\overline{MREQ}$ is released.
11. The refresh address is removed from the address bus and the $\overline{RFSH}$ line is released.

Figure 2.12 illustrates the change in an opcode fetch cycle when wait states are added. Wait states are added to lengthen the read/write cycle in order to accommodate slow memory

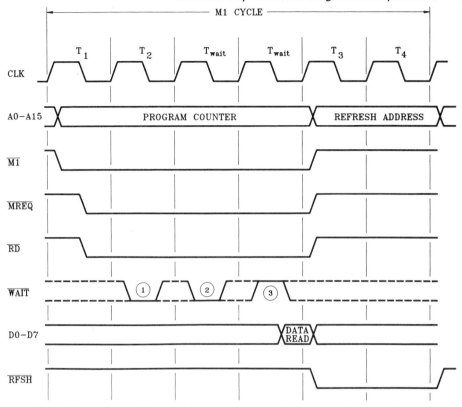

Figure 2.12 Timing diagram for instruction opcode fetch cycle with wait states

or slow peripheral devices. In the case of an opcode fetch, of course, only slow memory devices are being considered. Wait states are added if the WAIT signal is asserted on or before the falling edge of the second clock cycle. The full process is described below.

1. The CPU WAIT line is monitored on the falling edge of the second clock cycle. If WAIT is asserted then the next clock cycle becomes a wait state and all output signals maintain their current level.
2. The WAIT line is again monitored on the falling edge of the wait state clock cycle. If WAIT is still asserted then another wait state is added for the next cycle.
3. When WAIT is found to be released on the falling edge of the clock cycle during a wait state then the cycle continues and the opcode is read into the instruction register.

Memory Read or Write

Figure 2.13 gives the timing diagram for a memory-read cycle (other than an opcode fetch) followed immediately by a memory-write cycle. The memory-read cycle is, not surprisingly, very similar to an opcode-fetch cycle. The steps are:

1. The address of the memory location to be accessed is placed on the address bus.

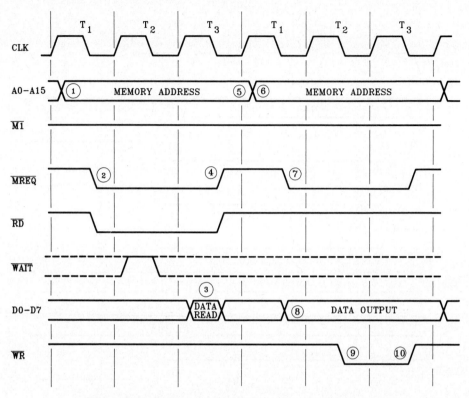

Figure 2.13 Timing diagram for a memory-read/write cycle

2. One half clock period later, the $\overline{\text{MREQ}}$ and $\overline{\text{RD}}$ signals are asserted as for an opcode fetch. Note that since this is not an opcode fetch cycle, $\overline{\text{M1}}$ is not asserted.
3. Provided that $\overline{\text{WAIT}}$ is not asserted on the falling edge of the second clock period, the CPU reads the data into the appropriate register on the falling edge of the third clock period. Note that this is half a clock period later than in the case of an opcode fetch. It is therefore the opcode fetch which determines the access time of memory which must be interfaced to the Z80. (If $\overline{\text{WAIT}}$ is asserted on the falling edge of the second clock period then wait states will be added until $\overline{\text{WAIT}}$ is released.)
4. MREQ and RD are released.
5. The memory address is removed from the address bus.

It is now appropriate to consider the memory-write cycle. In this case both address and data information are provided by the microprocessor. The steps involved are:

6. The address of the memory location into which data is to be written is placed onto the address bus.
7. One half clock period later when the address information has had time to stabilize, the $\overline{\text{MREQ}}$ signal is asserted to indicate that a valid address is on the address bus. Thus, $\overline{\text{MREQ}}$ can be used directly as a chip enable for memory devices.
8. The Z80 places the data to be written to memory onto the data bus.

9. When the data bus has had time to stabilize, the $\overline{WR}$ signal is asserted and so provides a $R/\overline{W}$ pulse to the memory chips.
10. WR and $\overline{MREQ}$ are released a half a clock period before information on the address or data bus is altered.

Again, the CPU tests the $\overline{WAIT}$ line on the falling edge of the second clock cycle and inserts wait states if it finds it asserted until such time as $\overline{WAIT}$ is not asserted on a falling clock edge when normal cycle execution continues.

Input and Output Cycles

The Z80 has a separate I/O space for communicating with peripherals. Figure 2.14 shows the timing diagram for an I/O-read cycle. The steps involved in an input cycle are:

1. The I/O port address is placed on the lower eight bits of the address bus. The upper eight bits of the address bus hold the contents of either the accumulator [e.g. **IN A,(00H)**] or register B [e.g. **IN r,(C)**] depending on the particular instruction being executed.
2. After the address bus has had time to stabilize, the $\overline{IORQ}$ and $\overline{RD}$ lines are asserted to indicate an input cycle. The $\overline{RD}$ line can be used to enable the addressed device to place data onto the data bus as was the case with the memory read cycle.
3. A wait state is automatically inserted after clock cycle 2. Without this, there may be insufficient time for an I/O device to decode its address and then assert the $\overline{WAIT}$ line prior to the CPU sampling the $\overline{WAIT}$ line on the falling edge of clock cycle 2.

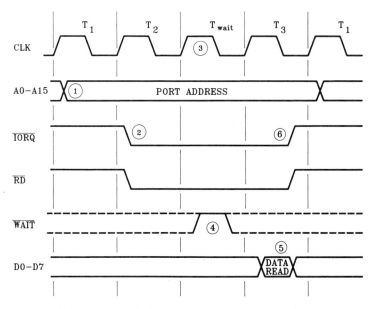

Figure 2.14 Timing diagram for an input cycle

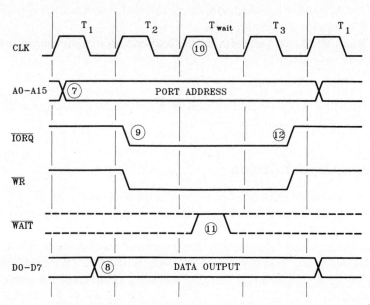

Figure 2.15 Timing diagram for an output cycle

4. The $\overline{\text{WAIT}}$ line is sampled during the first wait state. If $\overline{\text{WAIT}}$ is asserted, further wait states are added. If $\overline{\text{WAIT}}$ is not asserted, then the execution of the instruction continues normally.

5. The data bus is sampled on the falling edge of clock cycle 3 and the data acquired is placed into the appropriate register.

6. The $\overline{\text{IORQ}}$ and $\overline{\text{RD}}$ lines return to their non-asserted state and the input cycle is complete.

Now consider the output cycle shown in Figure 2.15. The differences here are similar to the differences between a memory read cycle and a memory write cycle, namely that the $\overline{\text{WR}}$ signal is asserted instead of the $\overline{\text{RD}}$ signal and also that the data bus is driven from the microprocessor. The steps involved are:

7. The I/O port address is placed on the lower eight bits of the address bus (the upper eight bits of the address bus hold the contents of either the accumulator or register B depending on the particular instruction being executed).

8. The data to be transmitted to the peripheral device is taken from the appropriate CPU register and placed on the data bus.

9. After the address bus and data bus have had time to stabilize, the $\overline{\text{IORQ}}$ and $\overline{\text{WR}}$ lines are asserted to indicate an output cycle. $\overline{\text{WR}}$ can also be used to clock data into the peripheral device.

10. A wait state is automatically inserted after clock cycle 2 for the same reasons as the input cycle.

11. The $\overline{\text{WAIT}}$ line is sampled during the first wait state. If $\overline{\text{WAIT}}$ is asserted, further wait states are added. If $\overline{\text{WAIT}}$ is not asserted then the execution of the instruction continues normally.

12. The $\overline{\text{IORQ}}$ and $\overline{\text{WR}}$ lines return to their non-asserted state and the input cycle is complete.

Bus Request/Bus Acknowledge Cycle

Earlier in this chapter, the role of the $\overline{\text{BUSRQ}}$ and $\overline{\text{BUSAK}}$ lines in allowing devices other than the microprocessor to take complete control of the address, data and control buses were discussed. Figure 2.16 shows the timing diagram for a bus request/bus acknowledge cycle. The steps involved in the process are:

1. The $\overline{\text{BUSRQ}}$ line is asserted by the device that wishes to take control of the buses.
2. The Z80 samples the $\overline{\text{BUSRQ}}$ line on the rising edge of the last clock cycle of every machine cycle and recognizes the request at the completion of the machine cycle. This means that for instructions which require more than one machine cycle, a bus request can be accepted in the middle of the execution of an instruction.
3. The Z80 asserts the $\overline{\text{BUSAK}}$ line to indicate to the device requesting mastership of the buses that it has released control and at the same time sets its address, data and three-state control output lines, such as $\overline{\text{MREQ}}$, $\overline{\text{IORQ}}$, $\overline{\text{RD}}$ or $\overline{\text{WR}}$ to the high impedance state. Other control lines, such as $\overline{\text{M1}}$ and $\overline{\text{RFSH}}$, which do not have a high-impedance state, are left non-asserted.
4. The Z80 continues to monitor the $\overline{\text{BUSRQ}}$ line on the rising edge of every clock cycle.

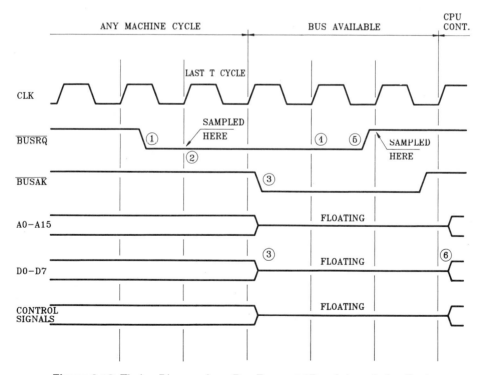

Figure 2.16 Timing Diagram for a Bus Request / Bus Acknowledge Cycle

5.   Upon detecting that $\overline{\text{BUSRQ}}$ has been released, the Z80 releases $\overline{\text{BUSAK}}$.
6.   The Z80 resumes control of the buses and continues with the first clock cycle of the next machine cycle.

It is worth noting that while the Z80 is not the bus master, no memory refresh will be carried out. Thus, if another device is to assume bus control for a significant period of time, that device must also take on the memory refresh function. In addition, the Z80 will not respond to interrupts while another device is the bus master.

Interrupt Request/Interrupt Acknowledge Cycle

The last important type of microprocessor response cycle is the response to interrupts. The use of interrupts is a major topic of this book. Accordingly, the detailed consideration of this subject will be left to Chapters 5 and 6.

2.3 SUMMARY

This chapter has attempted to give an overview of the hardware aspects of the Z80 microprocessor both from the point of view of a programmer and also that of a hardware designer. Without software, however, a microprocessor system cannot do anything at all. The instruction set of the Z80 together with information on programming form the basis of the next chapter.

PROBLEMS

Problem 2.1

Determine the value in the accumulator and the state of all flags in the Z80 flag register after execution of the instructions given below. The initial register contents are shown.

(a)   **DEC**   **A**   (Decrement accumulator)

with:

(i)	accumulator	=	00H
(ii)	accumulator	=	01H

(b)   **ADD**   **A,B**   (Add register B to accumulator)

with:

(i)	accumulator	=	10H	and	register B	=	20H
(ii)	accumulator	=	77H	and	register B	=	64H
(iii)	accumulator	=	95H	and	register B	=	52H
(iv)	accumulator	=	9AH	and	register B	=	66H
(v)	accumulator	=	99H	and	register B	=	9FH

(c)   **SUB**   **B**   (Subtract register B from accumulator)

with:

(i)	accumulator	=	2CH	and	register B	=	1BH
(ii)	accumulator	=	41H	and	register B	=	62H
(iii)	accumulator	=	53H	and	register B	=	99H
(iv)	accumulator	=	9FH	and	register B	=	21H
(v)	accumulator	=	ABH	and	register B	=	62H
(vi)	accumulator	=	CCH	and	register B	=	90H

Problem 2.2

The Z80 microprocessor has no multiply instruction. Draw a flowchart which describes an algorithm which will allow two unsigned 8-bit numbers to be multiplied to produce a 16-bit result using addition operations.

Problem 2.3

The Z80 microprocessor executed the following two instructions:

> **ADD**   **A,B**
> **DAA**

What is the value in the accumulator after each instruction, given that before either instruction is executed the register contents are as given below ?

(a)	accumulator	=	23H	and	register B	=	34H
(b)	accumulator	=	27H	and	register B	=	36H
(c)	accumulator	=	41H	and	register B	=	49H
(d)	accumulator	=	54H	and	register B	=	62H

Problem 2.4

Listed below are several Z80 instructions together with the number of machine cycles required to execute each. Describe what operation the CPU is performing during each machine cycle.

(a) **ADD   A,B**   (Add register B to the accumulator)
    Assembled code: 80
    Number of machine cycles: 1

(b) **LD   A,(HL)**   (Load the accumulator with the contents of the memory
                                                location pointed to by the HL register pair)
    Assembled code: 7E
    Number of machine cycles: 2

(c) **JP   2000H**   (Jump to location 2000H)
    Assembled code: C3 00 20
    Number of machine cycles: 3

(d) **RET**   (Return from subroutine)
    Assembled code: C9
    Number of machine cycles: 3

(e) **LD   IX,2000H**   (Load index register IX with 2000H)
    Assembled code: DD 21 00 20
    Number of machine cycles: 4

Problem 2.5

Draw timing diagrams which show the fetch and execute phases of each of the following instructions. Your timing diagram should show all relevant CPU signals.

(a) **LD   A,B**   (Load the contents of register B into the accumulator)
    Assembled code: 78
    Number of machine cycles: 1
    T cycles in each M cycle: 4

(b) **IN   A,(40H)**   (Load the accumulator with data from I/O port 40H)
    Assembled code: DB 40
    Number of machine cycles: 3
    T cycles in each M cycle: 4,3,4

(c) **CALL   2000H**   (Call the subroutine at location 2000H)
   Assembled code: CD 00 20
   Number of machine cycles: 5
   T cycles in each M cycle: 4,3,4,3,3

(d) **INC   (HL)**   (Increment the memory location pointed to by the HL
                                               register pair)
   Assembled code: 34
   Number of machine cycles: 3
   T cycles in each M cycle: 4,4,3

3 The Z80 Instruction Set

The instruction set of a microcomputer is simply a list of the basic operations that the microprocessor can perform. In the case of the Z80 microcomputer, there are approximately 150 different instructions. This makes the selection of just the right instruction for each problem a formidable task for the novice programmer. This problem is eased, however, by the grouping together of instructions that perform similar functions. The five main categories of instructions are:

(a) data transfer;
(b) data processing;
(c) test and branch;
(d) input-output; and
(e) CPU control.

What follows is not an exhaustive list of the Z80 instructions, but a coverage of a selection of instructions likely to be used in the exercises and experiments in later chapters of this book. A number of examples showing some common techniques used for handling particular programming situations are given, many of which can be modified for adoption in the laboratory exercises. Before examining these five different classes of instruction, it is important to note that there are several ways the location of the operand (or operands) on which the instruction is to act can be specified. These are called the 'addressing modes' of the microcomputer.

With a student's limited experience of assembly language programming, it is difficult enough to find a single instruction that appears to perform the task at hand. To be then told that there are upwards of ten variations of that instruction that, with more or less elegance, will achieve a similar result, is somewhat daunting. Such is the case with the various addressing modes of the microcomputer as can be demonstrated with a simple example. Suppose that it is necessary to load the accumulator with a number. This is clearly a most basic and frequently required task. The approach to be taken depends on whether the number is a constant or the result of some previous calculation. In the case of loading the accumulator with a constant, it is most likely that the constant (e.g. the number 80H) would be included within the instruction, (e.g. **LD A,80H**). This would assemble to 3E, 80. The constant forms the second byte of the instruction in what is termed immediate addressing.

If, however, the number to be loaded into the accumulator had resulted from a calculation and had previously been stored in some location in memory, an alternative approach would be appropriate. The address of the memory location would first be loaded into, say, the HL register pair, after which an instruction such as **LD A,(HL)** would cause the accumulator to be loaded with the desired number. This is an example of register indirect addressing. In most cases, the appropriate addressing mode to be used is relatively easy to decide following a consideration of the task at hand, as indicated in the two examples above. It is worthwhile, however, to scan the following addressing modes from time to time to see if the task can be performed in a more efficient way by using the full capabilities of the Z80 CPU.

3.1 Z80 ADDRESSING MODES

In general, a Z80 instruction specifies both the operation to be executed and the location of the data on which the operation is to be performed. Thus, the instruction **LD A,B** specifies that a LOAD instruction is to be executed and that the contents of the source register, register B, are to be loaded into the destination register, the accumulator. Data, on which the instruction is to operate, can either be stored in the various registers within the CPU, in external memory or in the input-output ports. The methods of specifying the address at which the data to be operated on is located are called addressing modes.

Implied Addressing

This mode refers to operations for which the instruction automatically implies that the data will be in a particular register (usually the accumulator) and that the result will appear in the same register.

NEG	(Negate the accumulator)
RRA	(Rotate the accumulator one position to the right)

Immediate Addressing

In this mode of addressing, the data byte is located in program memory immediately following the instruction.

LD A,55H   (Load accumulator with the number 55H.)

This would be assembled and loaded into memory as 3EH and 55H in successive locations.

Immediate Extended Addressing

This addressing mode is the same as the previous mode with the exception that the data is now 16 bits or two bytes. More often than not, the 16-bit quantity is an address pointing to some further location in memory.

LD HL,135EH   (Load HL register pair with the 16-bit quantity 135EH.)

After assembly and loading, this would give 21H, 5EH and 13H in three successive memory locations. Note that the address 135EH is loaded into memory in reverse order (i.e. the least significant byte first).

Register Addressing

Instructions that refer to data contained in registers within the CPU employ register addressing. Such instructions require little memory and execute quickly as no memory accesses beyond the instruction fetch are required.

LD C,B   (Load contents of register B into register C.)

Register Indirect Addressing

This type of addressing specifies a 16-bit register pair as a pointer to a location in memory in which the data is to be found.

LD C,(HL)   (Load register C with the contents of the memory location whose address is held in the HL register pair.)

If the HL register pair contains the value 75A1H and memory location 75A1H contains the data byte 5BH, then the above instruction would result in 5BH being placed into register C.

Modified Page Zero Addressing

Page zero is the area of memory for which the upper byte of the addresses is zero, that is, the 256 locations having the addresses 00XXH. The Z80 has a special subroutine call instruction to any one of eight locations in page zero of memory. These instructions take the form RESTART n (**RST n**) and set the program counter to n (n = 00H, 08H, 10H, 18H .... 38H).

RST 30H   (Push contents of program counter onto the stack, load the address 30H into the program counter and continue execution from that address.)

Relative Addressing

Relative addressing uses the byte following the instruction opcode as a displacement, in 2's complement form, to be added to the value of the program counter to form the address of the next instruction to be executed. It will be recalled that in executing the current instruction the program counter has already been incremented and points to the start of the next instruction. The displacement is, therefore, calculated from the address at the start of the next instruction.

HERE: JR HERE   (Execute an endless loop at the address having the label HERE.)

This would assemble to 18, FE. This is a 2-byte instruction and therefore the program counter is instructed to add minus 2, which in 2's complement notation is FE.

Indexed Addressing

Indexed addressing adds the byte following the 2-byte opcode to one of the two index registers (IX or IY) and forms a pointer to memory. It is, therefore, a simple extension to register indirect addressing.

LD B,(IX+25H)   (Load register B with the contents of the memory location whose address is found by adding 25H to the address contained in the index register IX.)

Bit Addressing

The Z80 instruction set contains several bit set, bit reset and bit test instructions. These allow any register or memory location to be specified for a bit operation using register, register indirect or indexed addressing. Three bits in the opcode specify which of the eight bits is to be set, reset or tested.

SET 3,(HL)   (Set to logic one bit 3 of the memory location pointed to by the HL register pair.)

Combined Addressing Modes

Many instructions, notably loads or arithmetic operations, specify more than one operand or address. In these cases, two types of addressing mode may be combined in a single instruction.

LD (HL),34H   (Load the memory location pointed to by the HL register pair with the number 34H.)

This is a combination of the register indirect and immediate addressing modes.

3.2 Z80 INSTRUCTIONS

Data Transfer Instructions

A surprisingly high percentage of the CPU processing time in any application is spent in the mundane task of moving data from one location to another. The main reason for this is that certain registers have specific roles to play in some of the CPU's instructions and must therefore be loaded with the appropriate operands before those instructions can be executed. One operand for 8-bit arithmetic and logic instructions, for example, must appear in the accumulator. Several instructions require the HL register pair to contain the address of an operand. Many instructions must therefore be devoted to making sure that data is in the right place before the 'important' data processing instructions can be carried out.

Load Register or Memory Location

The format for all 8-bit and 16-bit load instructions is:

$$\textbf{LD} \qquad \textbf{destination,source}$$

Examples of 8-bit load instructions:

LD	B,C
LD	A,(DE)

In the first example, the contents of register C are copied into register B. In the second example, the contents of register pair DE form an address in memory. A copy of the 8-bit number found at that address is written into the accumulator.

Examples of 16-bit load instructions:

LD	HL,(1500H)
LD	HL,TABLE

In the first example, the contents of memory location 1500H are loaded into register L and the contents of memory location 1501 are loaded into register H. TABLE is used, in the second example, as a label, indicating the address of a location in memory at which the first entry in a table of data appears. The assembler, which is a program which translates Z80 source code into Z80 executable machine code, will evaluate the memory address corresponding to 'TABLE' (say wxyzH, representing a 16-bit number) producing the code 21, yz, wx. This, and other aspects of the assembler will be considered in detail later in this chapter. However, labels are an important factor in improving the readability of assembly language programs and will be used extensively in the examples that follow.

Example 3.1

Write a program segment which adds 30H to each of the ten numbers in memory locations 1500H to 1509H and loads the new numbers in memory locations 1600H to 1609H.

Solution

```
      TABLE1  EQU   1500H         ;First entry in Table 1
      TABLE2  EQU   1600H         ;First location in Table 2
      ;
              LD    HL,TABLE1     ;Set HL to address of first number
              LD    DE,TABLE2     ;Set DE to address of first location
              LD    B,10D         ;Using B as counter, set to ten
      LOOP:   LD    A,(HL)        ;Get first (next ) number into A
              ADD   A,30H         ;Add 30H to it
              LD    (DE),A        ;Store it in first (next ) free location
              INC   HL            ;
              INC   DE            ;Point to next number & location
```

```
            DEC    B            ;
            JP     NZ,LOOP      ;Done all ten? No, go back to LOOP
  NEXT:                         ;Yes, continue with program
```

Transfers to and from the Stack

In the previous example, a number of data items were stored in memory at a known address allowing the data to be accessed at any time during the execution of the program. An equally common requirement is to store data in memory temporarily, for example, to make available the general purpose registers during the execution of a subroutine. In this case, the address in memory at which the data is stored is not important. What is important is the ability to restore the registers to their former condition at the end of the subroutine. A convenient method of achieving this is to store the register contents on the stack using the **PUSH** instruction and later recover the register contents using the **POP** instruction.

The stack plays an important role in the execution of many instructions in the Z80's repertoire. It is the cause of some confusion for the novice programmer, and above all, an ill-considered use of the stack is a common cause of strange, inexplicable happenings during program execution. Use of the stack has already been described in Chapter 2. It is worthwhile devoting some time at this stage, however, to re-emphasize the correct use of the stack in order to avoid future problems.

In a Z80 system, the stack is merely an area of memory, the limits of which are defined by the stack pointer register (SP). It is good practice to load the stack pointer register as the first statement in all programs, and reserve space for the stack at the end of the program as indicated in the following program segment.

```
            LD     SP,STACK     ;Load stack pointer register
                   :
                   :
                   :
            JP     OS           ;Last statement - back to system
            DEFS   40H          ;Reserve space for the stack
  STACK     EQU    $            ;Address of top of stack
```

In this program segment, and in all examples given in this book, the stack pointer register will be loaded with an address 40H locations on from the address of the last instruction. These 40H locations are thereby reserved for the stack to grow into as data and addresses are pushed onto the stack and later popped off the stack as program execution proceeds. If, for example, the above program results in STACK being set to address 0400H then the region of memory from 03C0H to 0400H constitutes the stack as shown in Figure 3.1(a).

Use of the Stack in Saving Registers

If registers B,C,D and E contained the numbers 21H, A2H, EFH, and 05H respectively, then the instructions

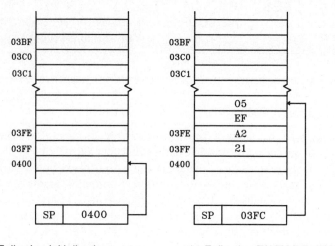

(a) Following initialization   (b) Following **PUSH BC, PUSH DE**

Figure 3.1 The stack

PUSH   BC
PUSH   DE

would result in the stack changing to that shown in Figure 3.1(b). The stack pointer register points to the address of the last entry on the stack. Having saved the contents of the four registers in memory, the registers may be used for other purposes, after which

POP   DE
POP   BC

would restore the registers to their former condition and SP would again contain 0400H. It should be noted that as data is pushed onto the stack, the stack expands into the reserved space in the direction of the program instructions. As data is popped off the stack, the stack contracts to its original size. Clearly, care needs to be exercised to ensure that sufficient space is set aside for the stack when expanded to its maximum size. It is also essential that every **PUSH** is matched with a **POP** or else the stack will continue to grow until it consumes the user's program or data. In addition, the last-in, first-out convention must be adhered to, otherwise the contents of registers will become swapped.

Use of the Stack in Calling Subroutines
When a segment of code is likely to be used several times, (e.g. a time delay routine) it is customary to write the code as a subroutine that is called from the main program. During the execution of the subroutine, the address at which the main program must resume after completing the subroutine needs to be stored in memory. In the case of the Z80 CPU, this return address is pushed onto the stack and later recovered. The high and low bytes of the program counter are saved in the next two free locations in the stack and the stack pointer is adjusted to point to the last entry. The program counter is then loaded with the address of the first instruction in the subroutine and execution resumes from that address. At the end

of the subroutine, execution is returned to the main program by the above operations proceeding in the reverse order.

Upon the execution of the return instruction, the program counter is restored to its former state prior to the subroutine **CALL** and the stack pointer register is suitably adjusted. For both the **RET** and **POP** instruction, the data previously pushed onto the stack remains in memory without being erased when it is no longer required. It does, however, get overwritten on the next occasion that data is written to that part of the stack.

16-bit Exchange Instructions

The Z80 microcomputer contains a set of eight registers in what is known as the alternate register set. These alternate registers duplicate the main register set but the two sets of registers cannot be used at the same time. In fact, the only operation that may be carried out using the alternate register set is to exchange their contents with the equivalent registers in the main register set. This is achieved by way of the following two instructions:

EXX		;BC↔BC',DE↔DE', HL↔HL'
EX	**AF,AF'**	;AF↔AF'

The principal use of the alternate register set is to allow some current calculation to be quickly put aside thus releasing the main register set for some urgent task. This is particularly relevant to the handling of interrupts, a topic that will be studied in some detail in Chapter 5. Four other 16-bit exchange instructions exist, allowing the DE register pair to be exchanged with the HL register pair, while any one of HL, IX and IY may be exchanged with the last two entries onto the stack.

Block Transfer and Search Instructions

Many applications for microcomputers occur in which data is handled in blocks rather than in single items. Analog to digital converters may be called upon to produce several consecutive samples of an input waveform, thereby defining the input voltage over a period of time. Alternatively, a single input item may need to be compared with a range of possible values in a look-up table to allow, for example, a non-linear conversion to be carried out. In both of these cases, and in many more instances, data or constants are best handled by way of a block or table. The Z80 instruction set includes a number of powerful instructions that allow blocks of data to be moved or systematically searched until a match is found. These instructions require a number of registers to be set to certain initial conditions, as indicated below.

> HL points to a SOURCE address;
> DE points to a DESTINATION address; while
> BC is used as a 16-bit COUNTER.

a)   **LDI** (load and increment)
      LDIR (load, increment and repeat)

The **LDI** instruction moves one byte of data from the memory location whose address appears in the HL register pair to the memory location whose address appears in the DE register pair. Register pairs HL and DE are both incremented whilst BC is decremented. **LDIR** carries out the **LDI** instruction repetitively until the counter BC becomes zero.

b)   **LDD** (load and decrement)
        LDDR (load, decrement and repeat)

These instructions behave much as the **LDI** and **LDIR** instructions except that HL and DE are decremented rather than incremented. Care must be exercised in selecting between **LDIR** and **LDDR** when the source and destination blocks overlap, to ensure that as the source block of data is moved it does not overwrite data that is yet to be moved.

c)   **CPI** (compare, increment)
        CPIR (compare, increment and repeat)

Data contained within the accumulator is compared with the contents of memory at the location pointed to by the HL register pair. HL is then incremented and the counter BC is decremented. With the **CPIR** instruction, the above comparison is repeated until either a match is obtained or until the BC register pair contents reaches zero. The **CPIR** instruction is particularly useful in comparing a character transmitted by a terminal with a table of characters held in memory for the purpose of deciding which of a series of options has been selected. Such is the situation that applies in menu-driven programs. Note that HL is incremented after the match is found and thus points to the following byte. This is shown diagrammatically in Figure 3.2.

Data Processing Instructions

The data processing capabilities of the Z80 microprocessor are severely limited. The assembly language programmer is restricted to the arithmetic functions of addition and subtraction; logic operations of AND, OR, exclusive OR, NOT and 2's complement together with a number of rotate and shift operations.

Arithmetic Instructions
The 8-bit arithmetic instructions are restricted to addition and subtraction with one operand contained within the accumulator. The second operand may be located in a register or in memory at a location pointed to by either the HL register pair or by one of the index registers.

```
ADD     A,r       ;A ← A + r, (r=A,B,C,D,E,H or L)
ADD     A,(HL)    ;A ← A + (HL)
ADC     A,r       ;Add with carry
```

Increment (**INC**) and decrement (**DEC**) instructions specify one register, register pair or memory location which is both the source and destination for the operation.

```
INC     (HL)      ;Increment the memory
                  ;location whose address is in HL
```

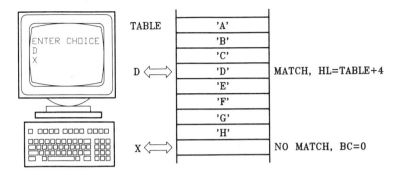

Figure 3.2 Use of the **CPIR** instruction in character matching

The 16-bit arithmetic operations include the addition or subtraction of operands contained within the BC, DE, or HL register pairs, or within the index registers. Similarly, the increment and decrement instructions refer to 16-bit operands contained within the same register pairs or index registers.

ADD	**HL,BC**	;HL ← HL + BC
INC	**HL**	;HL ← HL + 1

An instruction that may be used in conjunction with the above arithmetic operations for handling numbers in BCD format is the decimal adjust accumulator (**DAA**) instruction. Users of computers are most familiar with numbers expressed in decimal form and so demand that computers accept decimals as input numbers and print out decimals as output numbers. This is despite the fact that the computer performs calculations in binary. As an alternative to decimal to binary conversion following input and the reverse conversion prior to output, it is possible to store numbers within the computer in binary form in which the decimal weighting of groups of four bits is retained. Thus an 8-bit binary number can be considered as two 4-bit groups representing the 100 decimal numbers 00 to 99. When two such numbers are added together, or one number is incremented or decremented, an adjustment needs to be carried out when the sum of the least significant bits exceeds nine. This task is performed by the **DAA** instruction. For all arithmetic operations in which the result is required in BCD format, the **DAA** instruction must follow immediately.

Logical Instructions

The logical operations of AND, OR, exclusive OR and NOT are performed on a bit-by-bit basis using one operand in the accumulator and, where necessary, a second operand located in a register or in a memory location pointed to by either the HL register pair or by an index register.

AND	**B**	;If accumulator	=	10101010
		;and register B	=	00001111
		;then accumulator	=	00001010

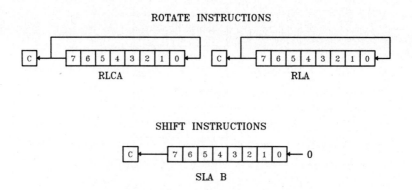

Figure 3.3 The rotate and shift instructions

The **AND** instruction performs the useful operation of 'masking off' unwanted bits. In the above example, the four most significant bits were removed without affecting the four least significant bits by applying the mask 0FH. Similarly, when a status word is read from a device in which each bit signifies some attribute (e.g. polarity, over-range, busy) a particular condition may be tested by first isolating the bit in question and then testing for a simple zero or non-zero condition.

Rotate and Shift Instructions

Any register or memory location may be rotated left or right or shifted left or right one bit position at a time. As indicated in the examples shown in Figure 3.3, the original bit pattern is retained during rotation but is lost when shifted. The carry bit in the flag register may be included in the rotation or not, as desired.

Test and Branch Instructions

The ability to continue execution at one of two different locations depending upon the result of some calculation or comparison gives the microprocessor most of its processing power. The test and branch instructions allow the state of peripheral devices to be tested, pulse trains to be generated and a myriad of other tasks to be performed in the monitoring and control of a wide range of electronic devices.

Unconditional Jump Instructions

JP wxyzH instructs the CPU to overwrite the program counter with the 16-bit address wxyzH and resume execution from that address. **JR** (jump relative) achieves the same result and is preferred for the following two reasons:

(a) **JR** is a two byte instruction whereas **JP** uses three bytes.
(b) **JR** gives rise to relocatable object code. (Jump to the location 20 bytes on from the current location will work at any position in memory, whereas jump to address 15D3H requires the program resumption point to remain at address 15D3H.)

The **JR** instruction does, however, require a longer execution time than a **JP** instruction. In addition, since the displacement from the current program counter value is defined by an 8-bit 2's complement number, the maximum change in address specified in the **JR** instruction relative to the address of the **JR** instruction itself is limited to the range -126 to +129 bytes and thus **JR** cannot always be used.

Conditional Jump Instructions

With both the **JP** and **JR** instructions, as set out below, a CPU condition flag may be tested to decide whether the jump will occur or if execution will continue at the next instruction. The conditional jumps are:

JP	**Z,address**	**JR**	**Z,address**	;Jump on zero
JP	**NZ,address**	**JR**	**NZ,address**	;Jump on non-zero
JP	**C,address**	**JR**	**C,address**	;Jump on carry
JP	**NC,address**	**JR**	**NC,address**	;Jump on no carry
JP	**PO,address**			;Jump on parity odd
JP	**PE,address**			;Jump on parity even
JP	**P,address**			;Jump on result positive
JP	**N,address**			;Jump on result negative

Example 3.2

Write a program segment which will cause a subroutine called ACQUIRE to be executed ten times. The program segment should commence at location 0200H.

Solution

```
0200 06 0A              LD    B,10D      ;Use B as a counter; set to ten
0202 CD XX XX LOOP: CALL  ACQUIRE     ;Routine to acquire 1 data item
0205 05                 DEC   B          ;Decrement counter
0206 20 FA              JR    NZ,LOOP    ;10 ? No, back to LOOP
0208          DISP:                      ;Yes, display data items
```

The object code has been included in this example to show the calculation of the offset in the jump relative instruction. Following the fetch phase of the **JR** instruction, the program counter contains the address of the next instruction, that is, the address associated with the label DISP namely 0208H. In order to return to the instruction **CALL ACQUIRE** when the condition is satisfied (i.e. when B is not zero) requires the program counter to change by minus six. Minus six in 2's complement is FAH and this becomes the second byte in the JR instruction. It should be noted that this calculation and encoding is all performed by the assembler program from the source code listing and is not directly the concern of the programmer. However, in the important debugging phase of program development, the programmer often uses the object code listing and should at least be aware of how this offset is calculated and how it will appear.

The Call and Return Instructions

The **CALL** instruction temporarily transfers program execution to a subroutine, at the end of which, the return instruction (**RET**) transfers execution back to the main program. The use of subroutines does much to improve the readability of assembly language programs and all programmers are encouraged to use subroutines wherever possible. Both the call and return instructions may be made conditional (e.g. **CALL NZ,DISPLAY**) with the same set of conditions as for the **JP** instruction.

Input-Output Instructions

The essential elements of microcomputer interfacing may be summarized in the simple block diagram shown in Figure 3.4. All peripheral devices wishing to provide data to the CPU, or accept data from the CPU, must be connected to the data bus by way of a buffer or a latch respectively. A logic analyser monitoring the activity on the data bus would reveal a continuous flow of data and instructions passing between the CPU and its memory. Peripheral devices wishing to engage in a dialog with the CPU must be capable of asserting their input data onto the bus and latching their output data off the bus at exactly the right time. Address decoding logic is required to discriminate between which of several peripheral devices is to provide or accept the data.

If the address decoding logic asserts the output from the buffer with an address of say C1H, and the latch responds to an address of say D3H, where these addresses were chosen arbitrarily then the input and output instructions take the following form:

IN	A,(0D3H)	;input from device D3H to accum.
OUT	(0C1H),A	;output from accum. to device C1H

It is useful to note that both instructions resemble the LOAD instruction, that is:

IN	**Destination,Source**
OUT	**Destination,Source**

Additional input-output instructions that are available include **INI** (in and increment), **INIR** (in, increment and repeat), **OUTI** (out and increment) and **OTIR** (out, increment and repeat). The repeat instructions are particularly useful for acquiring or transmitting blocks of data at high speed. Before using the **OTIR** instruction, it is necessary to load into the HL register pair the address in memory from which the data is to be taken. Furthermore, the address of the peripheral device must be loaded into register C and the number of data items to be moved must be loaded into register B. Similar requirements exist for the **INIR** instruction. A typical program segment would thus appear as:

LD	C,0C1H	;Address of output device in C
LD	HL,STORE	;HL points to start of data store
LD	B,100D	;Sending 100 data items
;		
OTIR		;Data is sent to latch at rate of
		;1 data point per 21 clock periods

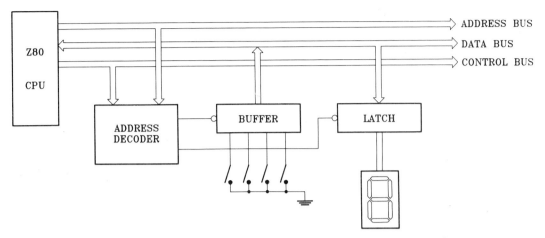

Figure 3.4 Interfacing peripheral devices using input buffers and output latches

CPU Control Instructions

The CPU control instructions refer primarily to the way in which the CPU responds to an interrupt. Interrupts are of major concern in interfacing applications since they provide an efficient way of handling peripheral devices that need to signal to the CPU that they are ready to transfer data. Such peripheral devices are provided with one or more 1-bit status signals, or flags, which indicate that they are busy or that their output lines do not, as yet, provide valid data. The CPU needs to monitor these flags to ensure that data is only taken from a device at a time when the output data is valid and stable. The CPU can monitor the status flags by executing an **IN** instruction on a regular basis and then performing a test to see whether the peripheral is ready to transfer its data. Alternatively, the CPU's attention may be drawn to the fact that a peripheral is now ready by the assertion of a logic signal on the interrupt input of the CPU chip. How the CPU responds to that logic signal, or indeed whether it will respond at all, depends upon which of the following CPU control instructions have been executed prior to the arrival of the interrupt.

EI (Enable Interrupts) and DI (Disable Interrupts)

The user has control over whether or not the CPU will respond to an interrupt on the $\overline{\text{INT}}$ input pin by way of the above two self-explanatory instructions. Following an interrupt, interrupts are automatically disabled to allow the programmer the option of taking care of the current interrupt before another one arrives. It is common, therefore, that interrupts will be re-enabled using the **EI** instruction near the end of the interrupt service routine and prior to returning to the main program. As explained in Chapter 2, the CPU will always respond to a logic signal applied to the $\overline{\text{NMI}}$ (non maskable interrupt) input on the CPU regardless of the use of the **EI** or **DI** instructions.

IM 0 (Interrupt Mode 0) IM 1 (Interrupt Mode 1) IM 2 (Interrupt Mode 2)

The interrupt mode of the CPU, which is set by the execution of one of the above three initializing instructions, dictates which instruction will be executed immediately following the arrival of the interrupt. Their effect will be described in detail in a later chapter. Interrupts play an extremely important role in microcomputer interfacing and will form a major part of Chapters 5 and 6. The true significance of interrupts only becomes apparent when other techniques for interfacing have been tried and their shortcomings exposed. For this reason, the treatment of the interrupt-related instructions has been brief. More details will follow at a time when the reader will be more receptive to the need for more sophisticated approaches to interfacing problems.

3.3   ASSEMBLERS

All of the instructions described in the above paragraphs have been written in the mnemonic form known as the Z80 assembly language. Ultimately, each instruction must be converted into binary and then loaded into the microcomputer's memory prior to execution by the CPU. This task is carried out by a translating program called an assembler. The input to the assembler is called source code whereas the output from the assembler is called object code. Assemblers ease the task of programming microcomputers in the following ways:

(a)   Assemblers allow instructions to be represented in mnemonic form, which is meaningful and easily remembered, rather than in binary form.
(b)   Addresses and displacements are calculated automatically by the assembler thus relieving the programmer of this task.
(c)   Registers, memory locations, variables and constants can all be referenced by name rather than by way of a binary number. This allows the resulting source code to be more readable and thus less prone to error.

Like all programming languages, assembly language has certain coding rules. Each line of source code consists of four fields, as shown below. It should be noted that fields are separated by at least one blank; however, the use of tabs to space fields into columns makes code easier to read. Continuation lines are not possible, but a line may consist entirely of comments.

```
LABEL:    OP-CODE  OPERAND    ;COMMENTS

LOOP:     JR       LOOP       ;Wait here
          XOR      A          ;Clear Accumulator
```

Field 1: Label Field

Labels, or names, are optional; however, careful choice of names at selected positions within the code invariably improves the intelligibility of the program. For example, the first statement in a subroutine should preferably start with a label that describes the action performed by that subroutine. When the subroutine is subsequently called from the main program there is then little doubt as to what processing is being performed at each stage. A main program might consist of nothing more than just a few **CALL** statements, that with little further comment adequately document that part of the program.

```
CALL    INITIAL     ;Initialize I-O ports
CALL    ACQUIRE     ;Acquire 256 data points
CALL    SQUARE      ;Square each value
CALL    DISPLAY     ;Output to oscilloscope
```

Field 2: Opcode Mnemonic Field

The opcode field contains the mnemonic for the Z80 instruction. Assembler directives, examples of which are given later, may also be located in this field.

Field 3: Operand Field

The operand field, which may require zero, one or two operands, identifies the data to be operated upon by the Z80 instruction. When no operand is specified, as for example in the instruction **RLA**, the data is located in the accumulator. When two operands are required, the first is the destination for the result of the operation, whereas the second operand specifies the data source.

```
LD      A,B         ;Copy reg. B to accumulator
ADD     A,C         ;Add C to acc with result in acc
LD      C,64H       ;Load reg. C with the number 64H
```

Immediate data appearing in the operand field, as is shown above, may be specified in several different ways. The decision as to which to use is often determined by a consideration of which method conveys the greatest meaning. If, for example, a device's status word has been read and it is desirable to select specific bits by way of an **AND** operation, then a mask specified in binary form makes good sense. The same mask, specified as a decimal number, would be most confusing. The options include:

(a)   Hexadecimal: **LD   C,64H**

(b)   Decimal: **LD   C,100D**
                     LD   C,100   ;Decimal is the default condition

(c)   Octal: **LD   C,144Q**

(d)   Binary: **LD   C,01100100B**

(e)   Location counter: The symbol '$' represents the address in memory at which the current instruction will be loaded after assembly. Thus:

                     JP $+6   ;Jump to address six bytes beyond
                                            ;first byte of this instruction

(f)   ASCII: **LD   A,'*'**   ;Load A with ASCII equivalent of *

(g)   Label: **LD**   **HL,TABLE**   ;Table represents start of data

(h)   Expressions: **IVCTR**   **EQU**   **((($/256)+1)*256)**

The above expression, which is evaluated at the time of assembly, equates the label IVCTR to the first address on the next 256 byte page of memory. For example, if the statement were to appear at address 15C3H, then $=15C3H, $/256 =15H and so IVCTR becomes 1600H. Expressions may include the four arithmetic operations, six comparative operations (<, >, etc.) and four logic operations.

Field 4: Comments Field

The optional comment field, which must be preceded by a semicolon, may contain much useful documentation. It is quite common for segments of code to be used in other programs, either by new authors or by the same author after a lapse of some time. If the code contains explanatory comments then there is less likelihood of it being used incorrectly or subjected to modifications that give rise to erroneous results. The importance of using comments to document code cannot be over-emphasized.

Assembler Directives

A brief perusal of a typical program written in Z80 assembly language code will reveal that, in addition to the opcodes described above, there are several additional statements that do not form part of the Z80 instruction set and in fact serve a quite different purpose. These are the assembler directives that instruct the assembler program to operate on the Z80 source code in a particular way. One example of an assembler directive is the **ORG** statement which tells the assembler at which address in memory the following instruction should be located. Different assembler programs use different directives and therefore it is unproductive to describe in detail the directives for any one assembler. A few of the more common directives will be described briefly, however, in order to allow the reader to make sense of the routines outlined later in this chapter and in other parts of the book.

ORG

This directive sets the value of the location counter, $, to the value specified in the operand field. The first instruction following the **ORG** statement will be assembled for loading at this address. The location counter then increments for each byte of instruction and data that appears in the source code. In the programs that follow an origin (**ORG**) of 100H has been used in accordance with the recommendations of the CP/M operating system.

                    ORG   **100H**   ;set program start to 100H

EQU

The equate directive is used to set the value of a label to an 8-bit number or a 16-bit number or address. This is a most useful facility for making a program understandable with a minimum of comments. The appearance of meaningful mnemonic labels throughout the source code assists the programmer to keep track of the logic and thus reduces programming errors. Labels for constants, input-output port addresses, control words and so on must first be defined by way of a series of equate statements.

```
BUFF      EQU      0D3H
LATCH     EQU      0C1H
```

DEFB
This directive defines the contents of a memory location at an address equal to the value of the location counter, $, to be the number specified in the operand field.

```
ZERO:      DEFB   00H
```

DEFW
This directive defines the contents of two memory locations to be the 16-bit number specified in the operand field. The least significant byte is located at the current value of the location counter, $, while the most significant byte is located at $+1.

```
ADDRS:      DEFW   1000H
```

DEFM
This directive defines the contents of n memory locations, starting at an address equal to the value of the location counter, to be the ASCII representation of the n characters making up the string.

```
MSG:       DEFM   'This is a message'
```

END
This directive signifies the end of the source program; any following statements will be ignored by the assembler.

3.4 A SELECTION OF SAMPLE PROGRAM SEGMENTS

The following routines illustrate many of the concepts raised in the preceding sections and should prove useful in performing the exercises and experiments in later chapters.

System Routines

Microcomputers require a small degree of intelligence in order to perform the basic tasks of communicating with a keyboard and visual display unit (VDU). This intelligence takes the form of a program in read-only memory which is executed as soon as power is applied to the computer. When the computer is provided with disks then the operating system is loaded into memory by the program in ROM allowing the user access to a wide range of programs.

Computers without disks are limited to a more elementary program in ROM that allows the user to monitor a few basic aspects of the computer's operation, such as viewing and modifying the contents of memory.

In either case, the ability to communicate with a VDU will have already been provided by the computer manufacturer. The program segments that allow the computer to accept characters from a keyboard and to send characters to a display form part of the computer's system routines. These routines are available for use by the programmer. Routines will vary between different microcomputers and therefore little is achieved by describing any one set of routines in great detail. The following four routines are, however, typical of those commonly provided and serve to illustrate how such routines are used.

(a) Print a Character on the VDU

```
            LD      A,'#'
            CALL    TTYOUT
```

The ASCII code for the character to be printed is loaded into the accumulator and a subroutine call is made to an address specified by the manufacturer. In the above example, this address has been replaced by the label TTYOUT.

(b) Print a String of Characters on the VDU

```
            LD      HL,MESS
            CALL    BUFOUT
    ;
    MESS:   DEFM    ' Enter next value '
            DEFB    '$'
```

The HL register pair are loaded with the address at which the message to be printed begins. A subroutine call is then made to invoke printing. All characters up to, but not including, a delimiting character (in this case assumed to be a $ symbol) are then printed.

(c) Input from VDU Keyboard

```
    LOOP:   CALL    TTYIN
            CP      '#'
            JR      NZ,LOOP
```

Following a call to TTYIN, the ASCII code for the key pressed on the keyboard is returned in the accumulator. In the above program segment, execution remains in the loop until the '#' key has been pressed.

(d) Keyboard Status

```
            CALL    TTYST
            JR      NZ,INPUT
```

In the previous example, the program would remain at the instruction **CALL TTYIN** waiting for a key to be pressed. As an alternative, it may be desirable to first test whether the keyboard has been struck and then read the key when the key press has been detected. This may be achieved by reading the keyboard status using the instruction **CALL TTYST**. If no key has been pressed, the zero flag is set, and so a test on this flag determines whether an input character is waiting.

In practice, the subroutines TTYIN, TTYOUT, TTYST and BUFOUT would need to be defined by way of four equate (**EQU**) statements to the four equivalent addresses in the monitor program as specified by the microcomputer manufacturer. In the case of the CP/M disk-based operating system, which has proved popular with many users of Z80 systems, an alternative approach has been adopted to achieve the same end result. This is the loading of register C with a function code, specifying which subroutine is to be called, and then jumping to a single address, usually location 0005H. Regardless of which system is available on your microcomputer, it is essential to spend some time becoming familiar with the built-in routines in order to avoid having to rewrite standard subroutines.

Example Programs

Example 3.3

Develop a program which accepts a string of characters from the keyboard, echoing each character as received and then echoes the entire string, having detected a # character.

Solution

```
CR        EQU    0DH        ;ASCII code for carriage return
LF        EQU    0AH        ;ASCII code for line feed
;
          LD     SP,STACK   ;Load stack pointer register
START:    LD     HL,BUFF    ;Set HL to start of character buffer
IN:       CALL   TTYIN      ;Get next input from keyboard
          CALL   TTYOUT     ;Echo it to screen
          LD     (HL),A     ;Store it in memory
          INC    HL         ;Point to next free location
          CP     '#'        ;Is character a '#' ?
          JR     NZ,IN      ;No-get next character
                            ;Yes-print out all characters again
OUT:      LD     (HL),'$'   ;BUFOUT needs last char. to be $
          LD     HL,BUFF    ;Set HL to start of string
          CALL   BUFOUT     ;Print string
          LD     A,CR       ;Tidy up - print carriage return
          CALL   TTYOUT     ;
          LD     A,LF       ;and line feed
```

```
              CALL    TTYOUT      ;
              JR      START       ;Return to START for new string
    BUFF:     DEFS    80D         ;Buffer to hold 80 characters
              DEFS    40H         ;Space for stack
    STACK     EQU     $           ;
              END
```

Comments

Example 3.3 contains a loop that is terminated only when a certain event, namely, input of the '#' character, is recognized. A person unaware of the escape character would have difficulty exiting the loop. A safer method to terminate a loop is to count the number of repetitions and exit after a specified upper limit has been reached. An example of this approach is given in Example 3.4.

Example 3.4

Develop a program which will print the first nine letters of the alphabet onto the VDU screen.

Solution

```
    OS        EQU     0000H       ;Operating system re-entry point
    ;
              LD      SP,STACK    ;Load stack pointer register
              LD      B,9         ;Using B as a counter
              LD      A,'A'       ;Load A with ASCII of first letter
    LOOP:     CALL    TTYOUT      ;Print character
              INC     A           ;Set up next letter in accumulator
              DEC     B           ;Decrement counter
              JR      NZ,LOOP     ;B reached zero? No-print next
              JP      OS          ;Yes-return to operating system
              DEFS    40H         ;Space for stack
    STACK     EQU     $           ;
              END
```

Comments

This program relies on the fact that the ASCII codewords for the alphabetic characters are numerically sequential. A similar, but slightly more complicated approach, is required in handling hexadecimal characters since the ASCII code for 'A' does not follow that for '9'.

Example 3.5

Write a program that accepts two single digit decimal numbers from the keyboard, forms the two-digit product and displays the answer on the VDU.

Solution

```
            LD      SP,STACK      ;Load stack pointer register
START:      CALL    TTYIN         ;Get first number
            SUB     30H           ;Convert from ASCII to binary
            LD      B,A           ;Store a copy in B
            CALL    TTYIN         ;Get second number
            SUB     30H           ;Convert from ASCII to binary
            LD      D,A           ;Store a copy in D
            XOR     A             ;Clear A
LOOP:       ADD     A,D           ;Add D to A
            DAA                   ;Require the result in BCD
            DEC     B             ;Decrement counter
            JR      NZ,LOOP       ;Finish? No, add D to A again
OUT:        LD      C,A           ;Yes, save copy in register C
            RRA                   ;TTTT UUUU to UTTT TUUU
            RRA                   ;UUTT TTUU   (T Tens)
            RRA                   ;UUUT TTTU   (U Units)
            RRA                   ;UUUU TTTT
            AND     0FH           ;0000 TTTT Isolate tens
            ADD     A,30H         ;Convert 4 bits to ASCII
            CALL    TTYOUT        ;Print tens
            LD      A,C           ;Get back TTTT UUUU
            AND     0FH           ;0000 UUUU Isolate units
            ADD     A,30H         ;Convert to ASCII
            CALL    TTYOUT        ;Print units
            JR      START         ;Start again
            DEFS    40H           ;Space for stack
STACK       EQU     $             ;
            END
```

Comments

The above program, while logically correct, suffers from a number of deficiencies. It assumes that the input will only be a number between 1 and 9. No checking of the input character is carried out to test for illegal characters and no account is taken of the first input being zero. The reader is encouraged to attempt Laboratory Exercise 3.4 and modify this program to allow for all contingencies.

PROBLEMS

Problem 3.1
Write a program segment which will cause your name to be typed on the screen of a VDU.

Problem 3.2
It is desired to find the first occurrence of the character 41H (ASCII A) in a block of data which extends from 1400H to 1500H. Write two program segments to carry out this task, one using the **CPIR** instruction and the other employing only basic operations.

Problem 3.3
An unsigned 16-bit number can represent decimal numbers in the range 0 to 65,535. Write a subroutine which will accept a 16-bit number in the HL register pair and print its decimal equivalent on the screen of the VDU. Ensure that the values of all registers are unaffected when the subroutine terminates.

Problem 3.4
Write a program segment which will take a pair of 2-digit BCD numbers in the range 0 to 50 stored in the B and C registers, compute their sum (in BCD) and display the result on the VDU.

Problem 3.5
Figure 3.5 shows the lighting pattern for a seven segment LED display for the decimal characters 0 to 9. Write a subroutine which will accept a number in the range 0 to 9 in the accumulator and return with the accumulator containing a 7-bit codeword which will indicate which LED segments are to be illuminated (logic 1 = illuminated). No other registers are to be affected. The accumulator bit corresponding to each LED segment is shown in Figure 3.6.

Problem 3.6
An 8-bit analog to digital convertor converts input voltages in the range ±5V to 2's complement format (i.e. +5V = 7FH, 0V = 00H, -5V = 80H). Write a subroutine which will accept a 2's complement number in the accumulator and display its equivalent decimal value (to one decimal point) on the VDU screen. Thus, if the 2's complement value is 40H, the value +2.5V should be displayed on the VDU.

Figure 3.5 7-Segment LED illumination patterns

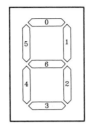

Figure 3.6 Accumulator bit assignment

Problem 3.7
An 8-bit digital to analog convertor converts 2's complement numbers into voltages in the range ±5V. Write a program segment which will accept a decimal number from the keyboard (to one decimal point) and displays on the keyboard the appropriate 2's complement number. Thus, if the value +2.5 is typed then 40H should appear on the VDU.

Problem 3.8
One method of generating pseudo-random numbers is to use the mixed congruential method. Random number n_{i+1} is generated from random number n_i using the following relationship:

$$n_{i+1} = an_i + c \text{ (modulus m)}$$

The modulus simply means that the number m is continually subtracted from n_{i+1} until it falls in the range 0 to m-1. It is therefore necessary to determine values for a, c, m and n_1. Using a modulus of 256 is particularly useful when 16-bit arithmetic is performed as the modulus operation corresponds simply to setting the upper eight bits to zero. Suitable values for the other constants are:

$$a = 5$$
$$c = 17$$
$$n_1 = 3$$

Using the method described above, write a subroutine which will return a random number in the range 0 to 15. This routine will prove useful for later laboratory exercises.

Laboratory Exercise 3.1

An Introduction to Input/Output using the VDU

Aim

The aim of this experiment is to introduce the student to the use of the VDU input and output routines provided by the manufacturer of the system being used.

Introduction

It is usual for the manufacturer of a microcomputer system to provide an operating system containing a number of system routines which the user can make use of in the development of programs. Amongst the earliest capabilities provided is the ability to communicate with the VDU connected to the system. In order to successfully complete this laboratory exercise, it is necessary to find out how these routines work and then use them to perform some simple operations.

Procedure

1. Write, debug and test a program that will type your name on the system VDU and then return to the operating system.

2. Write, debug and test a program that will accept a string of characters from the VDU keyboard and store them in system memory. Character input is to be terminated by a carriage return character. The characters stored should be compared with a copy of your name. If the comparison is exact then a message is to be printed and the program is to return to the operating system. If the comparison is not exact, the program is to ask for a new string of characters. (Note: This is the way that password checking is performed by a computer.)

3. Extend the program developed in part 2 so that after three unsuccessful attempts, your program types a sign-off message and returns to the operating system.

Laboratory Exercise 3.2

Monitoring of Keyboard Status

Aim

The aim of this experiment is to allow the user to control input from the VDU keyboard by monitoring the keyboard status flag.

Introduction

When a user program calls the system routine which brings in a character from the VDU keyboard, a loop is entered which will not be exited until a character is typed on the keyboard. While this is a satisfactory approach if the microcomputer cannot proceed without this information, it is far from satisfactory if the microcomputer could be carrying out some other task. A better approach is to monitor the status flag which indicates if a character is ready from the keyboard. If no character is ready, the microcomputer continues with its task. If a character is ready, the microcomputer calls the appropriate system routine to bring in the character and then performs the appropriate processing. The microcomputer manufacturer will usually provide a system routine to carry out this monitoring. This experiment aims to give experience in using this feature.

Procedure

1. Develop a program which will print the character '#' on the VDU at a rate of approximately ten per second. You will need to provide a delay routine to slow down the rate of output of characters.

2. Extend your program so that it continually monitors the keyboard and when a character is typed continues to print out the new character at the same rate as before.

3. Further extend your program so that if a '$' character is typed then the program returns to the operating system.

Laboratory Exercise 3.3

ASCII to Hexadecimal and Decimal Conversion

Aim

The aim of this experiment is to implement a scheme for carrying out ASCII to hexadecimal and decimal conversion.

Introduction

In writing programs, it is often necessary to accept characters from the keyboard (in ASCII code) and then to convert them into a form in which they can be used. For example, the decimal numbers 0-9 are represented in ASCII code by the hexadecimal numbers 30H-39H. Before they can be used in a numeric calculation, these ASCII codes must be converted to natural binary. This experiment is intended to reinforce an understanding of ASCII code.

Procedure

1. Develop a program which will accept an ASCII character from the keyboard of your VDU and then type onto the VDU screen the ASCII character together with its hexadecimal and decimal equivalents. A suitable format for the terminal output is shown.

ASCII CODE:	A
HEXADECIMAL:	41
DECIMAL:	65

Extension

1. Develop a program that accepts a two digit decimal number typed on the keyboard and then prints the character with the equivalent ASCII code on the VDU. The steps involved in carrying out this process are:

   (a) convert the two digit decimal number into an 8-bit binary equivalent. Careful thought needs to be given to the development of a simple algorithm to perform this conversion.

   (b) transmit this character to the VDU for display.

Laboratory Exercise 3.4

Decimal Multiplication

Aim

The aim of this experiment is to develop a program which will accept pairs of single digit decimal numbers from the keyboard and print out the product.

Procedure

This experiment builds on Example 3.5 of this chapter.

1. Extend the program given in Example 3.5 to allow for checking for illegal input characters (i.e. characters other than 0-9).   Also ensure that the program performs correctly when one or other of the input numbers is a 0. The form of the output should be:

```
                          6 * 7 = 42
                          3 * 3 = 09
```

If a character other than 0-9 is entered, an error message should be typed and the multiply problem should be repeated up to the error. A typical output would then be:

```
    6 * F  ** Illegal Character - only numbers in the range 0-9 allowed
    6 *
```

2. Further improve your program by only printing a single digit answer if the result is less than 10. The printout shown above would then become:

```
                          6 * 7 = 42
                          3 * 3 = 9
```

Extension

Extend your program so that it carries out the multiplication of single digit hexadecimal numbers. A typical result might then be as shown:

```
                      6 * 7  = 2A
                      A * A  = 64
```

Your program should still check that legal characters have been entered and flag any errors. In this case, the checking process is a little more complex since the numbers 0-9 and the letters A-F are not contiguous in the ASCII code.

Laboratory Exercise 3.5

Multiplication Quiz

Aim

The aim of this experiment is to develop a program which will generate a series of ten single-digit multiplication problems, accept an answer to each from the user, indicate whether the answer is correct or incorrect and finally give a score out of ten after each series of problems.

Introduction

Computer systems are making an ever-increasing impact in the area of computer-aided learning. In this experiment, a program will be developed which will help train a user in simple one-digit multiplication problems.

Procedure

1. Develop a program that will display a pair of randomly generated decimal numbers in the range 0-9 and display them in the format shown.

4 * 5 =

For details on generating random numbers, refer to Problem 3.8.

The program should then accept a two character input from the keyboard, check that the characters are decimal. If a non-decimal response is received, an error message should be typed and then the problem should be restated. The program should then check that the result entered is correct and a message indicating whether the result was correct or incorrect should be printed. When the answer is incorrect, the correct answer should be displayed. A typical VDU display would then be:

4 * 5 = 20	CORRECT
9 * 7 = 6S	ILLEGAL CHARACTER - TRY AGAIN
9 * 7 = 63	CORRECT
4 * 3 = 14	INCORRECT - CORRECT ANSWER IS 12
3 * 3 = 09	CORRECT

2. Further refine your program to force the user to press a carriage return before the answer is accepted. This will allow answers of less than 10 to be entered as a single number rather than with a preceding 0. The VDU display therefore becomes:

4 * 5 = 20	CORRECT
9 * 7 = 6S	ILLEGAL CHARACTER - TRY AGAIN
9 * 7 = 63	CORRECT
4 * 3 = 14	INCORRECT - CORRECT ANSWER IS 12
3 * 3 = 9	CORRECT

3. Incorporate the program developed so far into a multiplication quiz in which ten problems are posed and a score out of ten is given at the conclusion of the test.

Extensions

1. Modify the program developed in the above experiment so that it tests the multiplication of single digit hexadecimal numbers.

2. Modify the program developed in the above experiment so that it tests the multiplication of two digit decimal numbers (i.e. input numbers in the range 0-99 giving results in the range 0-9999).

Laboratory Exercise 3.6

Relocation of Blocks of Data in Memory

Aim

The aim of this experiment is to develop a program which will allow a block of data to be moved from one part of memory to another.

Introduction

When operating with a computer system, it is quite common to wish to move a block of data from one part of memory to another. When the two blocks of memory do not overlap, this is a straightforward task. When the blocks of memory do overlap, however, a more careful approach is necessary.

Procedure

1. Develop a subroutine which will load 256 successive memory locations starting at 1000H with the numbers 00H to FFH. Verify that the numbers have been loaded correctly using the memory display feature of your operating system.

2. Develop a program which will move a block of data from one part of memory to another. The program should accept the start and end address of the data to be moved and the start address at which the data is to be placed from the keyboard following suitable prompting messages. Test that your program works correctly by performing the following move operations after loading locations 1000H to 10FFH with the subroutine developed in the first part of this experiment and then examine the moved data again using the memory display feature of the operating system:

(a)   Move 1000H-10FFH to start at 2000H.
(b)   Move 1000H-10FFH to start at 800H.
(c)   Move 1000H-10FFH to start at 1080H.
(d)   Move 1000H-10FFH to start at 0F80H.

Laboratory Exercise 3.7

Adding Machine

Aim

The aim of this experiment is to write a program which adds together a series of decimal numbers. This type of function could be provided on cash registers and point-of-sale machines.

Procedure

1. Devise a program which will accept up to five decimal numbers in the range 0.00 to 99.99. The entry of each number is to be terminated by a carriage return. The numbers are to be added together and the result displayed either:

(a) when a blank line is entered (i.e. a line which consists only of a carriage return character);
    or
(b) after the fifth number has been entered.

A sample output is shown below.

34.25
17.1
0.12
4
TOTAL = 55.47

Extension

1. Extend your program so that it can handle negative as well as positive numbers.

Laboratory Exercise 3.8

Sum of Integers

Aim

The aim of this experiment is to develop a program which will sum the positive integers from 1 to N and display the result on the VDU.

Procedure

1. Develop a program which will accept a two digit decimal integer as an input and then calculate the sum of all integers from 1 to the integer entered. The result must then be displayed on the VDU. A sample output is shown below.

```
ENTER NUMBER:                                       12
SUM OF INTEGERS FROM 1 to 12 IS:                    78
```

Extension

Devise a program which will calculate the value of n! where:

$$n! = (n)(n-1)(n-2) \dots (2)(1)$$

in the range n=1 to 8. (Hint: You may prefer to perform the calculations entirely in binary form and then print the final result in decimal making use of the subroutine developed in Problem 3.3.)

4 Simple Parallel Input/Output Using the Intel PPI

4.1 INTRODUCTION

Having gained experience of assembly language programming techniques, it is now appropriate to deal with the main topic addressed by this book, namely, acquiring data from external input devices, processing the acquired data and finally transferring data to memory or to external output devices. As outlined in the previous chapter, data transfers between the CPU and external devices are performed during the execution of an **IN** or an **OUT** instruction. During such instructions, the data appear only briefly on the data bus and it is the responsibility of the interfacing hardware that output data is captured and that input data is asserted only during these brief times. At all other times the data bus carries instructions and data passing between the memory and the CPU.

It is essential, therefore, that the device supplying the input data be isolated from the data bus by a buffer and that the output data be captured in a latch. A typical arrangement embodying these concepts in which data are acquired from an analog to digital converter (ADC), processed and sent for display to a digital to analog converter (DAC), is shown in Figure 4.1.

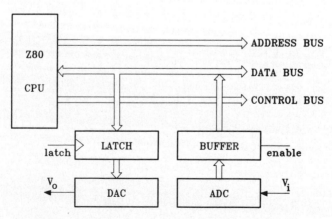

Figure 4.1 Simple data acquisition and display system

As the above requirements of buffering and latching input and output data are common to many interfacing applications, several integrated circuit manufacturers have produced devices that have been designed specifically to aid this task. The devices designed to work hand in hand with the Z80 microprocessor include the Intel 8255 Programmable Peripheral Interface (PPI) and the Zilog Z80 Parallel Input-Output device (Z80 PIO). A description of the first of these devices and how it is used for simple input-output of parallel data forms a major portion of this chapter. The Z80 PIO will be covered in Chapter 6.

4.2 THE INTEL 8255 PROGRAMMABLE PERIPHERAL INTERFACE

The PPI was designed to provide a solution to the problem of handling a diverse range of peripheral devices. As a consequence, it is a complex device with a set of detailed data sheets running to many pages. The complexity of the PPI can be made manageable, however, by adopting the approach of discussing initially only those aspects that will be needed to allow for simple I/O. In later chapters, when experience and confidence have been gained in using the device in its simplest mode of operation, these more advanced features can be explored.

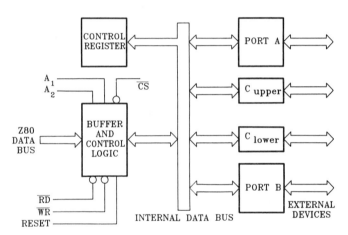

Figure 4.2 Block diagram of the 8255 PPI

Mode 0: Basic Input/Output

In its simplest mode of operation, the PPI provides three 8-bit ports, each of which can be programmed to act as an input port or as an output port. When a port is specified to be an output port, the output data is latched, and when designated an input port the input data is buffered. In simple terms this means that when the CPU writes data to an output port, that data remains there until the CPU writes some new data to the port. Alternatively, peripheral devices providing input data may be connected directly to a port set up for input and the CPU can be programmed to read that data at an appropriate time. As may be inferred from the block diagram of the PPI shown in Figure 4.2, one of the three ports, namely port C, may be treated as two 4-bit sub-ports. This splitting of port C is of particular significance when the

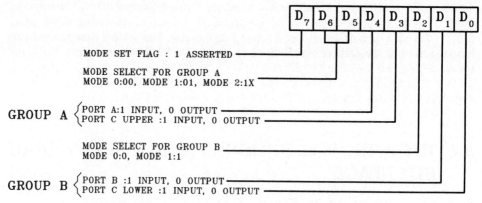

Figure 4.3 Mode control word format for 8255 PPI

PPI is used in mode 1, which will be discussesd later in this chapter. All combinations of input and output ports, and sub-ports may co-exist simultaneously as specified by the mode control word.

The mode control word is determined by the user by considering what function is required for each port and sub-port, as set out in Figure 4.3 This is sent by the CPU to the PPI's control register. As will be discovered shortly, other commands are sent to the control register as well as the mode control word. In order to identify the current command as a mode control word, the most significant bit, bit D_7, is set to logic 1. In addition, because port C upper is associated with port A and port C lower with port B in the PPI's more sophisticated modes of operation, these ports are grouped together imposing the same mode of operation on both ports in the grouping.

Example 4.1

Determine the mode control word required to set port A as an input port, port B as an output port with C upper as an output port and C lower as an input port.

Solution

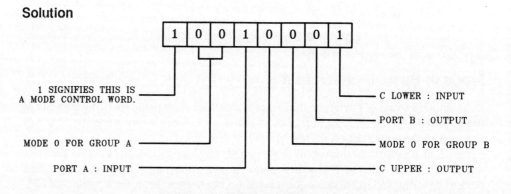

MODE CONTROL WORD = 91H

Figure 4.4 Mode control word for Example 4.1

While it is assumed that users will always attempt to do the right thing, that is, read from an input port and write to an output port, it is of interest to learn what happens when these simple rules are violated.

If a port has been configured as an input port and one attempts to write to that port, basically nothing happens. Logic signals connected to data input lines remain unchanged. If, however, the port has been configured as an output port and one reads from that port, the data transferred to the CPU will be a copy of the last data word sent to the port. If no previous output to the port has occurred, the port will return 00H when read by the CPU. In effect, each output port in the PPI acts as a register holding a copy of the last data word that was sent to it.

Addressing the PPI

The PPI is provided with two address pins, A_1 and A_0, to specify the address of one of the three ports or the control register within the device. The addressing scheme is shown in Figure 4.5.

If a system is to be constructed with just a single PPI, pins A_1 and A_0 of the PPI can be connected directly to lines A_1 and A_0 of the Z80 address bus and the chip permanently selected by connecting $\overline{CS}$ (Chip Select) low. Under these circumstances, the PPI occupies the address space from 00H-03H. When more than one PPI needs to be accommodated then the remaining six I/O address lines, A_7-A_2, need to be decoded to provide individual chip select signals for each PPI in the system. A particularly simple technique, known as linear selection, requires each chip select input to be connected to a separate address line, as shown in Figure 4.6. PPI A is then selected for the four port addresses for which the most significant bit, A_7, is a logic 0 and A_6 to A_2 which are set to logic 1 (i.e. addresses 7CH to 7FH). A similar situation applies for the six other possible PPIs that may be accommodated within this scheme. The price to be paid for the simplicity of both of the above schemes is that the addressing is non-unique. With the PPI permanently selected, as in the first situation, the device will recognize and respond to all port addresses and not just 00H-03H. A serious problem can arise with non-unique addressing when two or more PPIs are selected simultaneously. If one of the port addresses 00H-03H were asserted with the intention of reading data from PPI F in Figure 4.6, then in fact all six PPIs would attempt to place data onto the data bus. Should it be necessary for some reason to locate a PPI at some specific address, a complete address decoding scheme would need to be used.

$A_1 \; A_0$	LOCATION
0 0	PORT A
0 1	PORT B
1 0	PORT C
1 1	CONTROL REG.

Figure 4.5 Addressing scheme for the PPI

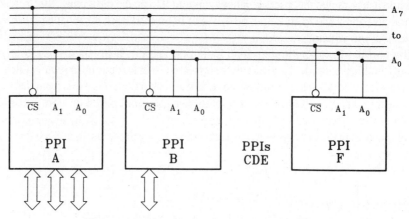

Figure 4.6 Linear selection for up to six PPIs

Example 4.2

Determine the addresses that must be used when communicating with the six PPIs shown in Figure 4.6 to avoid all possible bus contention problems.

Solution

	A_7	A_6	A_5	A_4	A_3	A_2	A_1	A_0	Port A	Port B	Port C	Cntrl Reg.
PPI A	0	1	1	1	1	1	A_1	A_0	7C	7D	7E	7F
PPI B	1	0	1	1	1	1	A_1	A_0	BC	BD	BE	BF
PPI C	1	1	0	1	1	1	A_1	A_0	DC	DD	DE	DF
PPI D	1	1	1	0	1	1	A_1	A_0	EC	ED	EE	EF
PPI E	1	1	1	1	0	1	A_1	A_0	F4	F5	F6	F7
PPI F	1	1	1	1	1	0	A_1	A_0	F8	F9	FA	FB

Figure 4.7 Port addresses for six linearly addressed PPIs of Figure 4.6

4.3 USING THE PPI FOR UNCONDITIONAL DATA TRANSFER

A number of peripheral devices are able to provide data or accept data at any time. Such data transfers are unconditional and take place when the appropriate **IN** or **OUT** instruction is executed in the running of the program. For example, if, as part of its overall task, a microcomputer is required to monitor a switch register or read the state of a counter, then these operations could be programmed to occur at a time convenient to the microcomputer rather than at a time dictated by the switch register or counter. Similarly, if the result of some

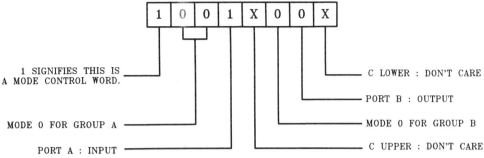

MODE CONTROL WORD = 90H

Figure 4.8 Mode control word for switch register and seven segment display

calculation is to be made available to a numeric display, then the data can be sent to the display at any time.

With only a rudimentary knowledge of the PPI acquired so far, it is possible to communicate with a wide range of peripheral devices. As an example, examine the steps necessary to read from a 4-bit switch register and display the binary number in hexadecimal form on a 7-segment display. The first requirement is to determine the mode control word for the PPI with the knowledge that one port (say port A) will be used to input data from the switch register while a second port (port B) will be used to output signals to the 7-segment display. Referring to Figure 4.3, the mode control word is as shown in Figure 4.8.

Following the format for writing Z80 assembly language programs outlined in Chapter 3, typical code for this problem would appear as follows.

```
MODE    EQU    90H         ;mode 0, A input, B output
SWTCH   EQU    00H         ;switch register to port A
DISPL   EQU    01H         ;display to port B
CNTRL   EQU    03H         ;control register of PPI
;
        ORG    100H        ;
INIT:   LD     SP,STACK    ;initialize stack pointer
        LD     A,MODE      ;set mode of PPI
        OUT    (CNTRL),A   ;
START:  IN     A,(SWTCH)   ;get input data
;
        CALL   CNVRT       ;convert it to 7 segment format
;
        OUT    (DISPL),A   ;send pattern to display
        JR     START
;
CNVRT:                     ;subroutine converting 4-bit
                           ;hex number into 7 seg. pattern
        DEFS   40H         ;reserve space for stack
STACK   EQU    $           ;
        END
```

4.4 HANDSHAKING INPUT/OUTPUT

Not all peripherals are able to transfer data at any time. Often a device needs to communicate to the computer that it is ready for the transfer to begin, or that it is still busy handling the previous data transfer. Such information is communicated by way of 1-bit status signals called flags. One peripheral that almost always needs to indicate its current status is the analog to digital converter (ADC) since ADCs require time to convert an analog input voltage into a digital codeword. Depending upon the conversion technique used, this time could be the equivalent of several, or several tens of instruction cycles of a microcomputer. The signals associated with a typical analog to digital converter together with its timing diagram are shown in Figure 4.9.

Upon receipt of a command to start, the analog input voltage is sampled, held constant and the conversion process is commenced. During the conversion time, the BUSY flag is set indicating that the data appearing at the digital output pins is not valid and should not be read by the microcomputer. The end of the conversion process is then indicated by the BUSY flag being reset or, using the alternative interpretation, by the $\overline{\text{READY}}$ flag being asserted.

It is clear from the above description that the microcomputer is required to continually monitor the ADC's BUSY flag and, on observing it going low, read the now valid data. An approach that is merely a simple extension to that described above, would be to connect the BUSY flag to one bit of port C, say C_7, and at the appropriate point in the program enter a loop to wait for the flag to go low before reading the data.

If the ADC is required to transfer a sequence of conversions to the microcomputer, then a second loop must be entered to wait for the BUSY flag to be set high at the start of the next conversion. This will ensure that only one item of data will be read for each conversion. A program segment which uses this technique to acquire and store in memory 200 data items is given below.

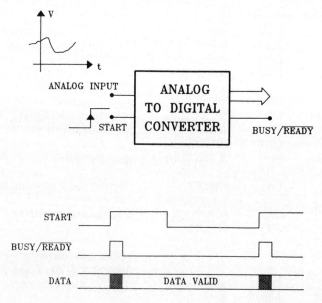

Figure 4.9 Analog to digital converter signals and timing diagram

```
              LD      HL,STORE      ;HL point to storage buffer
              LD      B,200D        ;use register B as counter
    ;
    WAITL:    IN      A,(PORTC)     ;read port C
              AND     80H           ;isolate C7
              JR      NZ,WAITL      ;busy?yes, look again
              IN      A,(PORTA)     ;no, data can be read
              LD      (HL),A        ;store data in memory
              INC     HL            ;point to next free location
              DEC     B             ;decrement counter
              JR      Z,CONT        ;acquired all data?yes, finished
    WAITH:    IN      A,(PORTC)     ;no, wait for  next conversion
              AND     80H           ;must now wait for BUSY flag
              JR      Z,WAITH       ;to go high before jumping back
              JR      WAITL         ;to wait for BUSY flag to go low
    ;
    CONT:                           ;remainder of program
```

One advantage of programming in an assembly language is that the programmer has a precise knowledge of how long each program segment will take to execute. For example, in the above program each waiting loop takes a time equivalent to 30 states. This comprises:

```
    WAITL:    IN      A,(PORTC)     ;11 states
              AND     80H           ;7 states
              JR      NZ,WAITL      ;12 states
```

With a 2 MHz clock, this corresponds to a loop time of 15 microseconds. The BUSY flag of the ADC is thus being sampled once every 15µs. The careful reader would appreciate that problems will occur with the above data acquisition system if the conversion time of the ADC, and hence the duration of the BUSY flag, is less than 15µs. Under these circumstances the microcomputer could miss the appearance of the BUSY flag altogether.

A simple solution to this problem, and one that can be applied to all peripherals that generate only a brief 'data strobe' pulse when they have data to transfer, is depicted in Figure 4.10. The brief status signal, or flag, may be extended in duration until the microcomputer has the opportunity to sample it. This technique requires the inclusion of an additional flip-flop. The effect of including the flip-flop is shown in the timing diagram illustrated in Figure 4.11. The falling edge of the BUSY flag sets the Q output of the flip-flop which is then sampled by the microcomputer every 15µs. Upon sensing the Q output to be at logic level 1, the program exits from the waiting loop, reads the data and then clears the flip-flop in readiness for the next conversion. The clearing of the flip-flop may be achieved either by writing an appropriate word to port C or by using the bit set/reset facility described in the next section. It will be apparent from the timing diagram that had the occurrence of the BUSY flag not been captured by the setting of the flip-flop, the microcomputer would have missed many of the data items.

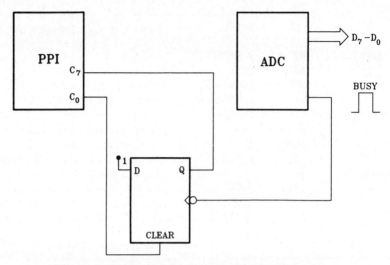

Figure 4.10 Flip-flop extends brief data strobe pulse

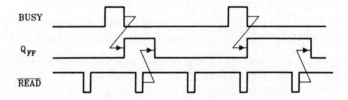

Figure 4.11 Flip-flop timing diagram

4.5 THE PPI IN MODE 1

While conditional I/O may be handled by the PPI in mode 0 using port C to monitor the status flags, a more elegant approach and one that offers a number of significant advantages is to use the PPI in mode 1. The most important of these advantages, namely the use of the interrupt facility, will be covered in detail in the next chapter. As a prelude to a study of interrupts, however, it is a worthwhile intermediate step to use the PPI in mode 1 for programmed transfer of data. This will reinforce the concepts involved in the handshaking process before adding the extra complexity of interrupts.

Mode 1: Strobed Input

It will be recalled that with the PPI in mode 0, input signals are buffered while output signals are latched. The peripheral device providing the input must therefore continue to assert the input signals until the CPU has passed the point in the program at which it reads from the input port. Furthermore, the peripheral must refrain from providing further input data until it is assured that the previous data has been accepted by the CPU. So, not only must the CPU monitor the peripheral to see if the input data is ready but the peripheral must also monitor the CPU to see if the previous data has been read and the CPU is ready to accept new data.

This two-way interchange of status information is conveniently handled by the PPI in the following manner. When a peripheral is ready to input data, it asserts the data onto the input pins of port A or port B of the PPI, which must previously have been designated as an input port operating under mode 1. At the time when the input data is valid, the peripheral generates a data strobe pulse which latches, or 'strobes', the data into the PPI's input latch. As the data enters the latch, the PPI responds with a status flag to indicate that the data has been accepted by the PPI. This signal has the mnemonic IBF indicating that its input buffer is full. Intelligent peripheral devices would then receive this signal as an indication that no more data should be transmitted to the PPI or it would merely overwrite previous data. In addition, upon receiving the signal that the PPI has accepted the data, the peripheral no longer need assert its data and is thus free to make ready for the next transfer.

The exchange of data and status signals described above have all taken place without any intervention, so far, on the part of the CPU. It is now the responsibility of the CPU to read the data from the input port of the PPI at the appropriate point in the program and store the data in memory, or act upon it in accordance with the aim of the program. The effect of reading the data from the port is to reset the IBF flag indicating to the peripheral that it may now transmit new data. As will be shown in the next chapter, the PPI can take one further step and send out an interrupt request to the CPU once data has been accepted in the input latch. For the present time, however, the information that valid data resides in the input latch waiting to be read must be discovered by the CPU by the execution of an **IN** instruction from port C, thereby allowing the CPU to check the condition of the IBF flag.

When the PPI is set to mode 1 with the receipt of the appropriate mode control word by the control register, two pins associated with port C are automatically designated as the data strobe input ($\overline{\text{STB}}$) and input buffer full output (IBF). In the case of port A being set to mode 1 input, C_4 becomes the ($\overline{\text{STB}}$) input and C_5 becomes the IBF output as indicated in Figure 4.12. For port B, the relevant pins are C_2 for ($\overline{\text{STB}}$) input and C_1 for IBF output. Even though the IBF pins are set to output lines, the CPU can read from port C and thereby ascertain the state of the IBF flag. Upon detecting the IBF flag to be set, the CPU can then read the data from the input port which then completes the transfer and cancels the IBF flag in readiness for the next transfer. The detailed timing diagram, indicating which signal initiates which action, is also given in Figure 4.12.

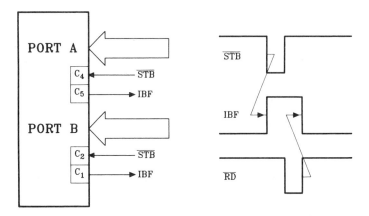

Figure 4.12 Pin designations and timing diagram for mode 1 input

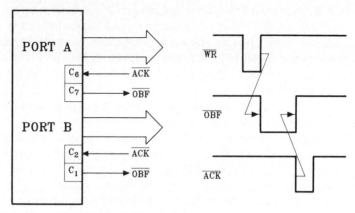

Figure 4.13 Pin designations and timing diagram for mode 1 output

Mode 1: Strobed Output

When the CPU is sending data to some output peripheral, such as a printer, it is clearly the computer that must initiate the transfer. This is achieved by the CPU writing data to a port of the PPI that has been designated as an output port operating in mode 1. Upon receiving the data in its output latch, the PPI indicates to the peripheral that data is available by asserting an Output Buffer Full flag ($\overline{OBF}$). The peripheral, upon sensing this flag, accepts the data and responds with an Acknowledge ($\overline{ACK}$) signal to indicate that the transfer is complete. Upon receipt of the $\overline{ACK}$ input, the PPI cancels the $\overline{OBF}$ flag thereby indicating that it is ready to accept new data. The CPU can determine when it is time to transmit another byte of data by monitoring the $\overline{OBF}$ flag. Once again, part of the handshaking process is carried out by the PPI without any intervention by the CPU. The CPU merely writes data to the output port; the PPI latches this data and generates the $\overline{OBF}$ flag. The timing diagram for a single output operation is shown in Figure 4.13.

Having designated one, or both ports of the PPI to be output ports operating in mode 1, specific lines in port C are automatically designated as the $\overline{OBF}$ output and $\overline{ACK}$ input lines. For port A, C_7 becomes the $\overline{OBF}$ output while C_6 becomes the $\overline{ACK}$ input. With port B, C_1 becomes the $\overline{OBF}$ output while C_2 becomes the $\overline{ACK}$ input.

4.6 STROBED BI-DIRECTIONAL INPUT AND OUTPUT

In the treatment of microcomputer interfacing thus far, only peripheral devices that are either input devices or output devices have been considered. A number of peripherals, however, both transmit and receive data over the same set of data lines. Such peripherals include bulk storage devices such as floppy disk drives or tape drives, or another computer system. Each requires data to be transferred in a parallel format. For reasons that have been fully discussed in Chapter 1, a convenient and efficient method of transferring data to, and from, such a device is by way of a bi-directional bus. All devices, between which data is to be passed, are connected to the bus with the source device enabled for output and the destination device enabled for input.

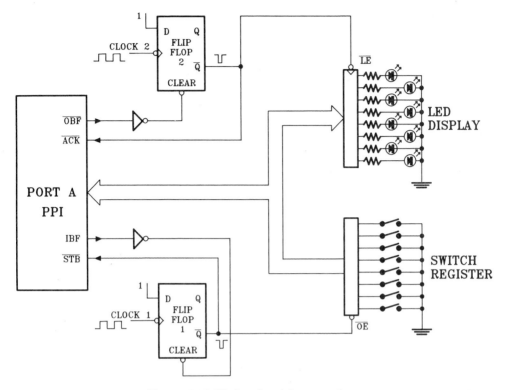

Figure 4.14 Bi-directional data transfer

The PPI, when initialized for mode 2 operation, can be connected directly to a bi-directional data bus and transfer data to, and receive data from other bi-directional peripherals connected to the bus, including a second PPI forming part of another microcomputer system. In mode 2, a port of the PPI behaves just like a mode 1 input port, and a mode 1 output port simultaneously, with one significant difference. This difference is that the I/O lines go to high impedance during the time that the port is neither receiving nor transmitting data. This allows other devices to be connected to a common bus without danger of output contention.

In Figure 4.14 a simple, 'contrived' bi-directional peripheral device is shown connected to a PPI for illustrative purposes. A three-state buffer, which isolates a switch register from the bi-directional bus, is enabled for transferring data to the computer, while a latch captures data sent by the computer for display on a series of LEDs. In this example experiment, the transfer of data to the computer occurs on the falling edge of clock 1, while the capture of data from the computer occurs on the falling edge of clock 2. The peripheral is clearly one for which data is transferred at a rate dictated by the peripheral device.

A further matter that deserves attention is the manner in which the handshake signals have been derived. As stated above, data transfer is to be initiated on specific transitions of two independent asynchronous clocks. This is more common than the situation described above for mode 1 operation of the PPI. Peripherals don't always provide the ideal data strobe (STB) or acknowledge (ACK) pulses as required by the PPI, and these pulses must often be fabricated from logic transitions, as is the case in this example. It is now appropriate to work through an input and output transfer for the circuit of Figure 4.14.

Bi-Directional: Input to the Microcomputer

With the 1 to 0 transition of clock 1, the peripheral is deemed to be ready to transfer data to the computer. Flip-flop 1 is clocked and the Q output goes low thus enabling the output of the three-state buffer. The same signal is applied to the strobe input of the PPI causing the data to be entered into the input latch of port A. With the input data captured in the input latch, the PPI issues its input buffer full signal (IBF) which clears the flip-flop, terminates the data strobe pulse and thus returns the three-state buffer to its high impedance mode. The CPU, upon sensing the IBF flag to be asserted, then reads from port A completing the data transfer. Having transferred the data to the CPU, the PPI then, automatically resets the IBF flag in readiness for the next data item.

Bi-Directional: Output from the Microcomputer

When sending data to an output device, it is the CPU that must first initiate the transfer and this it does by writing to port A of the PPI. The PPI latches the data and asserts its output buffer full flag ($\overline{OBF}$) to indicate to the peripheral that valid data is available. In the circuit of Figure 4.14, the assertion of $\overline{OBF}$ releases the CLEAR input of flip-flop 2. When the peripheral is ready to accept the data, as indicated by the 1 to 0 transition of clock 2, flip-flop 2 is clocked thereby causing $\overline{Q}$ to go low and the acknowledge signal ($\overline{ACK}$) to be asserted. The $\overline{ACK}$ input then enables the output buffer of the PPI placing the output data onto the data bus. With the output data made available, the output buffer full flag is reset thereby causing flip-flop 2 to be cleared and the $\overline{ACK}$ signal terminated. The rising edge of the $\overline{ACK}$ signal captures the data into the LED latch completing the output transfer.

In Figure 4.15 the arrangement whereby two PPIs, both operating in mode 2, can communicate with each other via a single bi-directional port is shown. Since of the four handshake signals only IBF is asserted high, a single inverter is required for each IBF output signal in order to generate the corresponding asserted low $\overline{ACK}$ signal. It is left as an

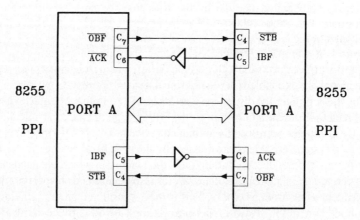

Figure 4.15 Interconnections for two PPIs operating as bi-directional ports

exercise for the reader to produce the timing diagram and explanations whereby a data item written to the port of the sending PPI by its host CPU will be latched into the port of the receiving PPI and subsequently read by the second computer (See Problem 4.13). The code necessary to allow messages typed on one keyboard to be displayed on the screen of both the sending microcomputer and the receiving microcomputer is given below.

```
IBFMSK      EQU      00100000B       ;IBF Mask = C5
ACK         EQU      01000000B       ;OBF Mask= C6
;
            LD       SP,STACK        ;
            CALL     INIT            ;Initialize PPI into mode 2
BACK:       CALL     TEST1           ;Test if ready for output
            CALL     TEST2           ;Test if ready for input
            JR       BACK            ;repeat
;
TEST1:      IN       A,(PORTC)       ;Input status word from PPI
            AND      ACK             ;Select C6, ACK
            CALL     NZ,SEND         ;If C6=1 Ready to send next char
            RET                      ;Otherwise return to main prog.
;
TEST2:      IN       A,(PORTC)       ;Input status word from PPI
            AND      IBFMSK          ;Select C5, IBF
            CALL     NZ,DISP         ;If C5=1 char. received. Display it
            RET                      ;Otherwise return to main prog.
;
SEND:       CALL     TTYST           ;Check keyboard status
            AND      A               ;Test zero flag
            RET      Z               ;Return if no character waiting
            CALL     TTYIN           ;Otherwise get character
            CALL     TTYOUT          ;Print on sending screen
            OUT      (PORTA),A       ;And send to other PPI
            RET                      ;Return to main prog.
;
DISP:       IN       A,(PORTA)       ;Get character from PPI
            CALL     TTYOUT          ;Print it
            RET                      ;and return
```

It should be noted that while both port A and port B may be operated in mode 1 as uni-directional ports, only port A may be operated in mode 2 as a bi-directional port. As indicated in Figure 4.15, specific lines of port C are automatically designated as $\overline{STB}$ and $\overline{ACK}$ inputs or IBF and $\overline{OBF}$ outputs. Two additional lines of port C are taken up as interrupt request lines, as will be explained in the next chapter. The remaining lines of port C may be specified as either input or output lines to monitor or generate additional 1-bit signals as required.

4.7 THE BIT SET-RESET FACILITY

The first part of this chapter has shown how it is possible to output 8-bit words using the PPI. It is necessary to configure one port as an output port, load the appropriate word into the accumulator and then execute an **OUT (PORT),A** instruction. There is, however, a frequent requirement to generate in addition several 1-bit signals. These may be used as a START signal for an ADC, a TRIGGER signal for an oscilloscope or, as in an earlier section, a flip-flop CLEAR signal. The PPI caters for such requirements in an elegant manner by way of the bit set/reset facility.

Any one of the eight bits of port C may be SET (i.e. produce a logic 1 output) or RESET (i.e. produce a logic 0 output) using a single **OUT** instruction. A control word, as set out below, is sent to the PPI's control register and the designated bit in port C is either set or reset as required.

D_7	D_6	D_5	D_4	D_3	D_2	D_1	D_0		
D_7-Bit set/reset flag 0	X	X	X	I	I	I	1 Set, 0 Reset		
D_7=0 Asserted				0	0	0	....	C_0
				0	0	1	....	C_1
				0	1	0	....	C_2
				0	1	1	....	C_3
				1	0	0	....	C_4
				1	0	1	....	C_5
				1	1	0	....	C_6
				1	1	1	....	C_7

It is essential that the appropriate half of port C, (i.e. port C upper or C lower), has already been specified as an output port via the mode control word before the bit set/reset facility is used.

Example 4.3

Using the bit set/reset facility, generate a brief START pulse suitable for use with an analog to digital converter connected to port A. The START pulse is to appear at the output pin C_1.

Solution (See Figure 4.16)

```
    MODE    EQU    90H         ;A input, C lower output
    ADC     EQU    00H         ;ADC connected to port A
    CNTRL   EQU    03H         ;control register of PPI
    SET     EQU    03H         ;
    RESET   EQU    02H         ;
    INIT:   LD     SP,STACK
            LD     A,MODE
            OUT    (CNTRL),A

    ;
    START:  LD     A,SET
            OUT    (CNTRL),A    ;C1 set to 1
            LD     A,RESET
            OUT    (CNTRL),A    ;C1 reset to 0
```

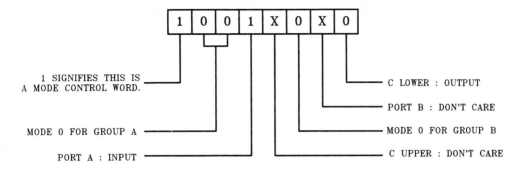

MODE CONTROL WORD = 90H

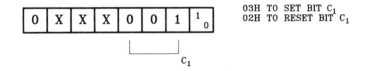

BIT SET / RESET WORD

Figure 4.16 Mode control word and set/reset word for Example 4.3

The ability to generate logic signals using the bit set-reset facility allows pulse trains of any arbitrary form to be produced with all parameters under software control. One example of such a waveform might be a burst of say 100 double pulses for which the period, second pulse delay and pulse width are all controlled via numbers loaded into the CPU's working registers.

It will no doubt occur to many readers that the waveforms illustrated in Figure 4.17 could have been generated simply by writing a succession of 8-bit words to port C in which a selected bit is first set and then reset repetitively. The approach of sending bit set-reset words

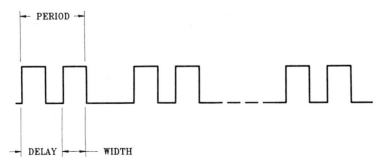

Figure 4.17 Burst of double pulses

to the control register is preferable, however, from the point of view of writing error-free code. The truth of this statement may be gauged by considering a situation in which several bits of port C are to be used for generating unrelated 1-bit signals. Assume, for example, that a particular application includes an ADC start signal, an oscilloscope trigger signal and an LED indicator. Each of these signals may be given a meaningful mnemonic label which is equated to a code word once a choice of output pin has been made.

STARTH	EQU	01H	;C_0 - ADC start high 0XXX 000-1
STARTL	EQU	00H	;C_0 - ADC start low 0XXX 000-0
TRIGH	EQU	05H	;C_2 - Trigger high 0XXX 010-1
TRIGL	EQU	04H	;C_2 - Trigger low 0XXX 010-0
LEDH	EQU	07H	;C_3 - LED high 0XXX 011-1
LEDL	EQU	06H	;C_3 - LED low 0XXX 011-0

At the appropriate time in the execution of the program, the above control words may be sent to the PPI's control register causing the selected signal to go high or low as required. Even with no additional comments, it is clear that when TRIGH is followed by TRIGL, a trigger pulse has been generated causing the oscilloscope time base to start a sweep.

The situation is considerably more confusing if one adopts the approach of sending an 8-bit word directly to port C. The word that must be sent in order to cause C_2 to go high depends on the current state of all the other bits that must appear at port C. In addition, this word is likely to be different at other times due to the changing nature of the other bits. The programmer is thus required to keep check of the state of the bits in the port at all times, so that in changing one bit he/she doesn't inadvertently change any of the others. The real difficulty comes, however, when the program is modified at some later time. Changes that are made to correct one problem can quickly lead to problems in apparently unrelated areas. The use of the bit set-reset approach has much to recommend it and should be used at all times for 1-bit control signals.

4.8 PPI PIN ALLOCATIONS

In the preceding sections of this chapter, information has been presented that allows a PPI forming part of a Z80 microcomputer system to be used for a variety of simple interfacing problems. By using a PPI as an intermediary between the Z80 microprocessor and its peripheral devices, interfacing has been reduced to a simple, straightforward task. In view of this statement, it is appropriate to enquire as to the ease with which a PPI, or perhaps an additional PPI, might be incorporated into an existing Z80 microcomputer system. This question is readily answered by an examination of the pin allocations of the 40 pin PPI package shown in Figure 4.18, and the interconnection diagram of Figure 4.19.

The three groups of eight pins shown on the right-hand side of the diagram in Figure 4.19 correspond to the now familiar A, B and C input-output ports that connect directly to the peripheral devices. A further group of eight pins, labeled D_0 - D_7, connect to the Z80's data bus allowing data and control words to pass between the CPU and the PPI. The two address pins, A_0 and A_1, together with the chip select input, $\overline{CS}$, allow the address of each port and the control register of the PPI to be specified, as for example in Figure 4.6 of this chapter.

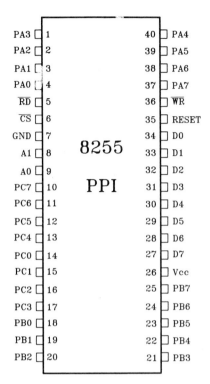

PA3 ☐ 1	40 ☐ PA4
PA2 ☐ 2	39 ☐ PA5
PA1 ☐ 3	38 ☐ PA6
PA0 ☐ 4	37 ☐ PA7
$\overline{RD}$ ☐ 5	36 ☐ $\overline{WR}$
$\overline{CS}$ ☐ 6	35 ☐ RESET
GND ☐ 7	34 ☐ D0
A1 ☐ 8	33 ☐ D1
A0 ☐ 9	32 ☐ D2
PC7 ☐ 10	31 ☐ D3
PC6 ☐ 11	30 ☐ D4
PC5 ☐ 12	29 ☐ D5
PC4 ☐ 13	28 ☐ D6
PC0 ☐ 14	27 ☐ D7
PC1 ☐ 15	26 ☐ Vcc
PC2 ☐ 16	25 ☐ PB7
PC3 ☐ 17	24 ☐ PB6
PB0 ☐ 18	23 ☐ PB5
PB1 ☐ 19	22 ☐ PB4
PB2 ☐ 20	21 ☐ PB3

8255 PPI

PIN NAMES

D0–D7	DATA BUS (BI–DIRECTIONAL)
RESET	RESET INPUT
$\overline{CS}$	CHIP SELECT
$\overline{RD}$	READ INPUT
$\overline{WR}$	WRITE INPUT
A0 A1	PORT ADDRESS
PA7–PA0	PORT A (BIT)
PB7–PB0	PORT B (BIT)
PC7–PC0	PORT C (BIT)
Vcc	+5 VOLTS
GND	0 VOLTS

Figure 4.18 8255 PPI pin allocations

The read ($\overline{RD}$) and write ($\overline{WR}$) inputs are controlled by the CPU and inform the PPI whether it should assert its data onto the data bus (CPU read) or whether it should accept data from the data bus (CPU write). These signals are usually derived from three control signals generated by the CPU in the manner shown in Figure 4.19. In this circuit, the CPU read and write signals are passed to the PPI only when the input/output request signal $(\overline{IOREQ})$ is asserted. These CPU signals, when combined, in effect become I/O read $(\overline{IOREAD})$ and I/O write $(\overline{IOWRITE})$.

Finally, the reset input of the PPI, which can be connected via an inverter to the asserted low reset input of the Z80 CPU, clears the control register and sets the three PPI ports to the input mode. The task of incorporating one or more PPIs into an existing Z80 microcomputer system is, therefore, quite simple and straightforward.

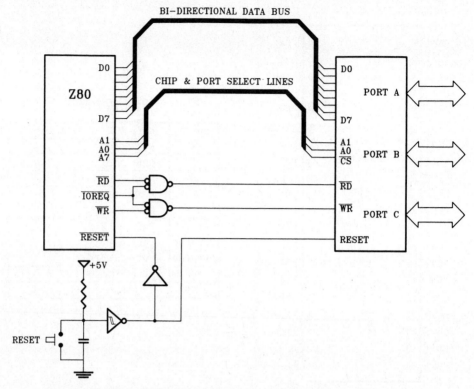

Figure 4.19 Interconnection between the Z80 CPU and the 8255 PPI

PROBLEMS

Problem 4.1

Determine the mode control word required by the 8255 PPI to set port A as an output port, port B as an input port with C upper as an input port and C lower as an output port.

Problem 4.2

A microcomputer system is to be constructed using 16 PPIs with a 74154, four line to 16 line decoder, to provide address decoding. Devise an address decoding scheme for this system, provide a schematic circuit diagram and determine the address of each of the 16 PPIs in the system.

Problem 4.3

A microcomputer system employing two PPIs uses the address decoding system shown in Figure 4.20. To what addresses will the two PPIs respond? What possible problems are averted in this scheme compared to linear selection with $\overline{CS}$ of PPI 1 connected to A_2 and $\overline{CS}$ of PPI 2 connected to A_3?

Problem 4.4

It is proposed to use bit C_6 of a PPI as an oscilloscope TRIGGER signal and C_7 as an ADC START signal in a data acquisition and display system employing both an ADC and a DAC. Determine the control words needed to establish the mode of the PPI and to produce pulses for both the ADC and oscilloscope.

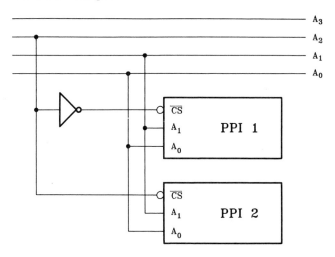

Figure 4.20 PPI connection for Problem 4.3

Problem 4.5
Write a segment of Z80 code that causes 100 data items, currently stored in memory at locations starting at BUFFER, to be transferred to an output device connected to port B of an 8255 PPI. The PPI is located at addresses 00-03 Hex.

Problem 4.6
Devise a method for searching a block of memory containing 100 data items and selecting the maximum and minimum values within that block. Write a program to fill the block of memory with 100 data items and include statements that allow both the maximum and minimum values to be selected. Modify your program to allow the address at which the maximum and minimum values are stored to be obtained and printed on the VDU.

Problem 4.7
Write a segment of Z80 code that causes 100 data items to be acquired from an input device and placed in memory at locations starting at STORE. The input data items are to be acquired at the rate of one every millisecond.

Problem 4.8
Draw a block diagram showing how a 64-key keyboard may be interfaced to a microcomputer when the keys take the form of an 8 x 8 matrix of normally open switches.

Problem 4.9
Microcomputers often perform the task of decoding one set of numbers into another either via an algorithm or via a look-up table. Use both of these techniques to convert a 4-bit binary number to its equivalent in which bits B_3 and B_0 are interchanged and bits B_2 and B_1 are interchanged as shown in Figure 4.21

Problem 4.10
Draw a block diagram showing how a microcomputer-based data acquisition and display system can convert a conventional oscilloscope into a digital storage oscilloscope. Identify and label all the signals needed to control the various components of your proposed system. Determine also the control words that need to be sent to the PPI.

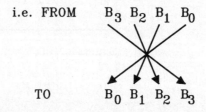

Figure 4.21 Bit interchange pattern for Problem 4.9

Problem 4.11

Using a look-up table in which the seven segment patterns shown in Figure 4.22 are stored, explain how an input binary number may be displayed on a seven segment display.

Problem 4.12

Write a segment of Z80 code that will detect when a logic signal has changed from a low level to a high level. The program should accept a logic signal from one port of a PPI and print out one character on the VDU each time a low to high transition occurs.

Problem 4.13

Draw a detailed timing diagram for the exchange of one data word from one Z80 CPU to another using the arrangement of two PPIs operating in mode 2 as shown in Figure 4.15. The exchange commences with a write from CPU 1 to PPI 1 and terminates with a read from PPI 2 by CPU 2.

Figure 4.22 Seven segment display patterns for the decimal digits

Laboratory Exercise 4.1

The Monophonic Organ

Aim

The aim of this exercise is to generate a series of periodic square waves that will produce musical tones when applied to a loudspeaker.

Procedure

1. Write a program that upon execution generates a continuous square wave at a frequency of 1 kHz. Apply the 1-bit output signal to a low pass filter, an audio amplifier and loudspeaker as shown in Figure 4.23 in order to demonstrate the presence of the signal. Incorporate into your program a delay routine that specifies the frequency of the audible tone.

2. Modify your program so that every half second the keyboard status is checked. If a key has been struck then the frequency of the tone should change to that specified by the input character. If no key has been struck, or a key other than those specified below, then the present tone should be maintained. The following table contains suggested output frequencies covering one octave of the acoustic spectrum.

C 1046 Hz.	D 1174 Hz.	E 1318 Hz.	F 1396 Hz.
G 1568 Hz.	A 1760 Hz.	B 1975 Hz.	C 2093 Hz.

3. As a final part of this exercise, enter a succession of notes into memory forming a well-known tune. Modify your program to accept these notes from memory rather than from the keyboard as in part 2.

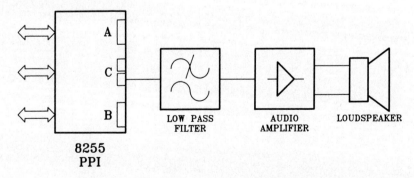

Figure 4.23 Block diagram of monophonic organ

Laboratory Exercise 4.2

The Double Pulse Generator

Aim

The aim of this exercise is to write a program that upon execution continuously provides periodic double pulses in which the delay time, t_d, progressively increases from period to period, as shown in Figure 4.24.

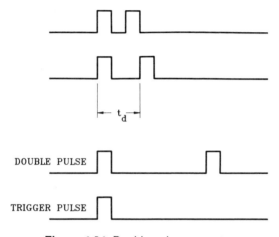

Figure 4.24 Double pulse generator output

Introduction

One of the major attractions of incorporating a microcomputer into an electronic instrument or controller is the flexibility that this approach brings to the way in which the instrument operates. In the specific case of a digital pulse generator, all time-related parameters may be varied simply by changing the numbers that specify the width, the delay and the repetition rate of the output pulse train. In the present laboratory exercise, this flexibility is emphasized by arranging for one of the above parameters, namely the delay time between two pulses to change over a period of several seconds during the execution of the program.

Procedure

1. Using the bit set-reset facility on the 8255 PPI, produce a pulse train of double pulses as shown in Figure 4.24. Include time delay routines into your program so that the width

of both pulses is 0.5ms, the delay time is 1.0ms and the repetition period is 10ms. An oscilloscope trigger pulse must also be generated coincident with the first of the double pulses. Observe the train of double pulses on an oscilloscope and adjust the sweep speed so that one complete period of the waveform fills the screen.

2. Modify your program so as to accept a single digit number from the keyboard in the range from one to nine that specifies, in milliseconds, a desired value of delay time between the two pulses. The pulse widths and repetition periods should be maintained at their previous values. Include checking for invalid keyboard entry. Verify the correct operation of your program by entering each number in turn and observing the second pulse to move in nine steps across the oscilloscope screen.

3. Further modify your program such that upon execution the second pulse appears to move uniformly from an initial position, with a delay time of 1ms, to a final position, with a delay time of 9ms, in a repetitive manner. An impression of uniform movement will be achieved if the delay time is increased from its initial value to its final value in 90 steps over a period of two seconds.

Laboratory Exercise 4.3

The Arbitrary Waveform Generator

Aim

The aim of this exercise is to generate an analog signal of some arbitrary waveform by applying a succession of numbers stored in the computer's memory to a digital to analog converter.

Introduction

Most electrical laboratories have many signal generators producing sinusoidal, square and triangular waveforms over a wide range of frequencies. However, when it is required to generate analog electrical signals having waveforms other than these three basic shapes, then some considerable difficulties are usually experienced. This is especially so if the waveform cannot be expressed as a mathematical function. Some examples might include the rainfall or hours of sunshine at a particular location on a day-by-day basis over a period of five years, or the terrain altitude along an aircraft's flight path. Such signals may be applied as inputs to electrical models of pastures or aircraft control systems.

A relatively recent approach to generating signals of some arbitrary waveshape has been to apply a sequence of numbers, representing a sampled version of the desired waveform, to a digital to analog converter. In the following experiment the basic concept of the arbitrary waveform generator will be demonstrated first with a regular waveform, namely a sawtooth, and then with more 'exotic' waveforms such as the sinc function.

Procedure

1. Write a program that reserves 256 memory locations and fills consecutive locations with the numbers 0 to 255. Output this block of memory continuously to a PPI to which is connected a digital to analog converter. Using the bit set-reset facility on port C of the PPI, generate an oscilloscope trigger pulse at the start of each output display loop. The resulting waveform should be displayed on an oscilloscope and should resemble Figure 4.25.

    It is suggested that you attempt this exercise in two ways. First, consult Chapter 3 and recall the procedures necessary for using the **OTIR**, (out, increment and repeat) instruction. Second, achieve the same result, i.e. to output all 256 numbers at the maximum rate, using more basic instructions from the Z80 instruction set. Measure the time taken to put out the ramp waveform using both methods and reconcile these measurements with the instruction execution times stated in the Z80 *Programming Manual*.

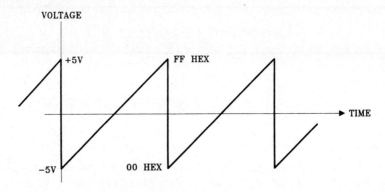

Figure 4.25 Sawtooth output

2. Re-run your program under the control of the system's debugging program (ZSID™ or similar) and execute up to a break point that is set at a position just prior to the output display routine. Using the substitute command, replace the numbers 00H to FFH with the following 256 hexadecimal numbers and continue execution.

22	22	21	21	21	20	20	20
20	20	20	20	20	21	21	21
22	22	23	23	24	24	25	26
27	27	28	29	2A	2B	2C	2D
2E	2F	30	31	32	32	33	34
35	36	36	37	38	38	39	39
3A	3A	3B	3B	3B	3B	3B	3B
3B	3B	3A	3A	3A	39	39	38
37	37	36	35	34	33	32	31
30	2F	2E	2C	2B	2A	29	28
27	25	24	23	22	21	20	1F
1E	1D	1D	1C	1B	1B	1A	1A
19	19	19	19	19	19	19	1A
1A	1B	1B	1C	1D	1E	1F	20
21	22	23	24	26	27	29	2A
2C	2D	2F	30	32	34	35	37
38	3A	3B	3D	3E	3F	40	42
43	44	44	45	46	46	47	47
47	47	47	47	46	46	45	44
43	42	41	40	3E	3D	3B	39
37	35	33	31	2F	2D	2A	28
26	23	21	1E	1C	19	17	15
12	10	0E	0C	0A	08	06	05
03	02	01	00	00	00	00	00
00	00	00	00	01	03	04	06
08	0B	0D	10	13	17	1A	1E
22	26	2B	30	36	3A	3F	45

4A	50	56	5C	62	68	6E	75
7B	82	88	8E	95	9B	A1	A7
AE	B4	B9	BF	C5	CA	CF	D4
D9	DD	E2	E6	EA	ED	F0	F3
F6	F8	FA	FB	FD	FE	FE	FE

3. Having completed the above exercise, it will be obvious that entry of data by way of the keyboard is both tedious and error prone. Where possible it is preferable to allow a computer to calculate the data points and then load them into memory directly. As an extension to this exercise, students may wish to write a short program in a high level language to generate a data file with 256 entries representing samples of the sinc function over a range from 0 to 3π radians. This data file must then be accessed by the Z80 program and converted into binary numbers for transmission to the DAC.

Laboratory Exercise 4.4

The Seven Segment Display

Aim

The aim of this experiment is to display the result of a calculation performed by the Z80 CPU on a 2-digit, seven segment numeric display.

Introduction

Seven segment displays are frequently incorporated into digital instruments in order to display the results of measurements or to indicate the current values of measurement parameters. In non-computer based equipment, decoding chips, such as the binary to seven segment decoder driver, are needed to convert the input binary numbers into signals appropriate for the seven segment displays. One of the many advantages of incorporating a microcomputer into an instrument is that decoding of binary signals prior to display can be performed by the microcomputer. This replacement of traditional hardware functions by software reduces the number of devices within the instrument, and hence its cost.

The light emitting diode (LED) seven segment display is not a device that lends itself to being driven directly by a PPI due to the nature of the load that it presents, namely a current of several milliamps per segment. A preferred method of driving a seven segment display is shown in Figure 4.26, in which a resistance tied to the +5V rail provides the current to illuminate each LED segment, while an open collector buffer is used to divert current away from the LED when that segment is to be extinguished. The traditional naming convention for each of the seven segments is shown in Figure 4.27.

Procedure

1. Write a program that generates a sequence of numbers that increment from 0 to 99 at a one hertz rate and displays the state of the count on the VDU.

2. Modify the program so that each digit of this 2-digit number is converted into the appropriate seven segment pattern and displayed on a 2-digit, seven segment display.

3. Further modify your program so that the count and display appears in hexadecimal rather than in decimal form.

4. Incorporate this program into the program written for Laboratory Exercise 3.4, the hexadecimal multiply program, so that the result of the hexadecimal multiplication is shown on the 2-digit seven segment display as well as on the VDU.

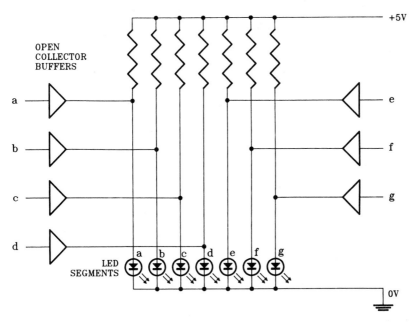

Figure 4.26 Seven segment display hardware

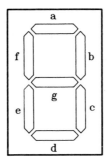

Figure 4.27 Seven segment display-segment naming convention

Laboratory Exercise 4.5

The Multi-Digit Seven Segment display

Aim

The aim of this experiment is to investigate the use of multiplexing in order to drive a multi-digit, seven segment display.

Introduction

In the previous exercise, a 2-digit number was displayed on two seven segment LED displays that required two ports of the PPI to provide the driving signals. Clearly, if it is necessary to display a 6-digit number, the simple approach adopted earlier would result in an excessive number of buffers and ports being used for what is in reality a simple task.

An alternative approach, using far less hardware, is to multiplex, or switch, the displays so that only one is activated at any time but with a sufficiently fast switching rate to avoid flicker. If all LED segments are connected in parallel, with the common cathode of each display connected to ground via a switching transistor, then a display of up to eight digits may be achieved using only two ports of the PPI. In effect, the same digit is sent to all displays but only that display for which the cathode transistor is switched on will actually light up. Provided each display is refreshed at a rate of greater than 100 Hz, the display will appear to be stable and free from flicker.

Procedure

1. Connect up three seven segment displays, as shown in Figure 4.28, and display the numbers from 000 to 999 in a continuous counting pattern.

2.. Modify your program so that the two leading zeros for numbers 0 to 9 and the single leading zero for numbers 10 to 99 are suppressed.

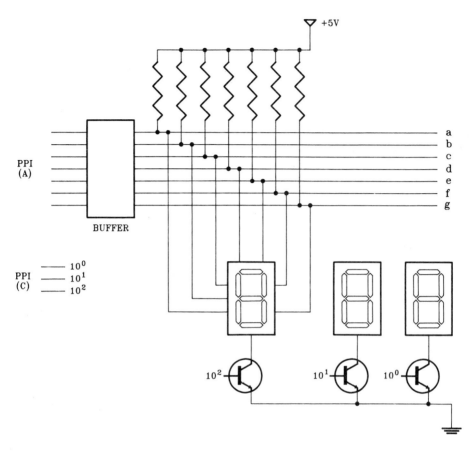

Figure 4.28 Hardware arrangement for multi-digit, seven segment display

---

Laboratory Exercise 4.6

Numeric Display Using a Cathode Ray Tube

Aim

The aim of this experiment is to display a multi-digit number on the cathode ray tube of an oscilloscope.

Introduction

Instrumentation that incorporates a cathode ray tube (CRT) display offers much greater flexibility than that using seven segment or dot matrix displays. Not only can alphanumeric data be presented, but line drawings, pull-down menus and the full range of text and graphics may be included. In this exercise, the CRT will become the display medium for the presentation of multi-digit numbers as shown in Figure 4.29.

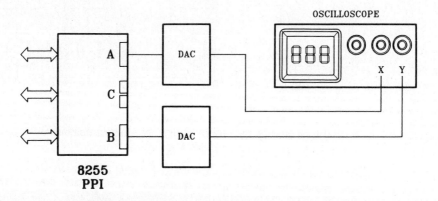

Figure 4.29 Use of an oscilloscope for multi-digit display

When numbers, that have previously been stored in memory, are presented to two digital to analog converters (DAC) connected to the X and Y inputs of an oscilloscope, the beam may be located at any position on the oscilloscope's screen. If a succession of numbers are sent to the DACs at high speed, the beam can be made to sweep out any desired pattern. A pattern of interest in the case of the current exercise is shown in Figure 4.30.

The beam of the oscilloscope must move uniformly along segments 1 to 7 of the first digit and then jump the space to the center of the second digit before tracing out the segments of the second digit. A 3-digit display may be obtained from an 8-bit DAC by arranging for each horizontal and vertical segment and inter-digit gap to have a length corresponding a change in the input code of 32 units.

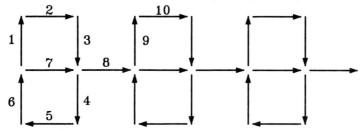

Figure 4.30 Multi-digit sweep pattern

Procedure

1. Write a program that generates a sequence of numbers, which when applied to two digital to analog converters, continuously traces out the seven segment pattern shown above.

2. Modify your program so that prior to tracing out each digit the computer checks the content of a storage location in which a number between 0 and 9 is located. This number is then decoded in order to decide which of the segments are to be displayed and which are to be omitted. In this way numbers from 0 to 999 may be displayed in sequence.

3. Further modify your program to suppress leading zeros and to provide a slight (say 1/4 width) slant to the digits.

Laboratory Exercise 4.7

Interfacing a Keyboard

Aim

The aim of this exercise is to interface an unencoded keyboard to a microcomputer by way of a PPI.

Introduction

An unencoded keyboard consists of a number of switches arranged in a matrix, as shown in Figure 4.31. In order to detect which key has been pressed, it is necessary to apply a sequence of logic signals to the row lines while monitoring the signals appearing on the column lines. This simple key identification technique is known as "row scanning", and the sequence of logic signals employed is the "walking one" or "walking zero" pattern.

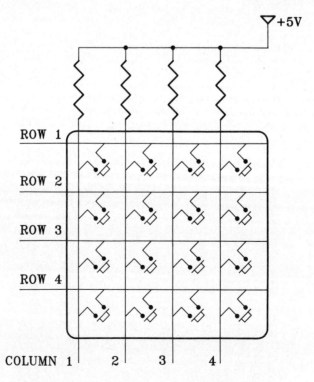

Figure 4.31 Arrangement of a simple hex keyboard

If, for example, the key at the intersection of Row 3 Column 3 has been pressed and the following walking zero pattern is applied to the row lines, then the outputs from the column lines will be as indicated. The fact that one of the column lines has changed to a logic 0 indicates that a key has been pressed while the combination of input code and output response enables the pressed key to be identified.

Time Period	Row	Col.	Row	Col.	Row	Col.	Row	Col.
1	0	1	1	1	1	1	1	1
2	1	1	0	1	1	1	1	1
3	1	1	1	1	0	0	1	1
4	1	1	1	1	1	1	0	1

All column lines will remain at logic 1 by virtue of their 'pull-up' resistors or, in the case of a key closure by the presence of a logic 1 on the connected row line, until the connected row line is set to logic 0.

Practical Considerations
While keyboards are essentially simple input devices, they do suffer from a number of operational problems that need to be considered. These include keybounce and simultaneous key presses. Techniques that may be used to overcome these problems are outlined briefly below.

Keybounce
If the act of striking a key causes the switch to close and then bounce open and close several more times, then many repetitions of the selected character will be transmitted to the computer. To avoid this keybounce problem, it is customary either to add debouncing hardware or, as in the present exercise, to solve the problem in software. Keybounce usually extends for a period of a few milliseconds, so if after detecting a key closure a delay of some 20 milliseconds is introduced before the key is finally identified, the multiple transmission of characters to the computer will be avoided.

Rollover
Rollover is the problem caused when more than one key is held down at the same time. In practice, it is essential to detect this situation and prevent erroneous output codes from being generated. Three main strategies used to resolve this problem are the two-key rollover, the N-key rollover and the N-key lock-out techniques.

Two-key rollover provides protection for the case in which two keys are pressed at the same time. The simplest scheme ignores the reading from the keyboard until only one key closure is detected. The last key to remain pressed is the correct one.

N-key rollover ignores all keys pressed until only one remains down, whereas N-key lock-out takes into account only the first key pressed and any additional keys which might have been pressed and released do not generate any codes.

Procedure

1. Using port C of a PPI interface the hexadecimal keyboard to the computer so that the selected character appears on the VDU each time a key is pressed.

2. Incorporate your keyboard program into your earlier program multiplying two hexadecimal numbers (Laboratory Exercise 3.4) and verify the correct operation of the combined program.

3. Modify your program so as to incorporate a two-key rollover strategy and test the operation of your scheme. An appropriate test is to press key 1, press key 2, release key 1, release key 2. Consider carefully the time at which it is appropriate to transmit the selected key to the computer.

Laboratory Exercise 4.8

The Successive Approximations ADC

Aim

The aim of this exercise is to use the computer as a successive approximations register which, together with a DAC, forms the basis for a successive approximations ADC.

Introduction

The successive approximations ADC has become well established as the leading analog to digital conversion process for most applications. It combines a relatively simple hardware realization with a short conversion time, thus making it a leading contender for audio frequency sampled data systems. In the present exercise, the microcomputer will be programmed to act as the successive approximations register, putting out a sequence of data words to a DAC. The resulting analog voltage is then compared with the input voltage in order to determine the next output from the computer. The hardware arrangement is shown in Figure 4.32.

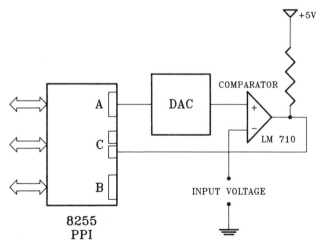

Figure 4.32 Hardware arrangement of successive approximation ADC

The successive approximations algorithm requires the computer to put out a data word in which the most significant bit (msb) is set (=1) and the remaining bits are reset (=0). When applied to the DAC, an analog voltage is developed, corresponding to half of full-scale-conversion. If the input voltage exceeds the output of the DAC, the msb is left unaltered and the next bit is set to 1. An output of 3/4 full scale conversion is thus generated. Alternatively, if the input voltage falls short of half full scale conversion then the msb is reset and the next bit is set. This gives rise to an output of 1/4 full scale conversion. This comparison is repeated for each bit in turn until all eight bits have been set or reset. The output of the DAC thus successively approximates the input voltage as each bit is tested.

Procedure

1. Construct the successive approximations circuit shown in Figure 4.32 and write a program to allow the Z80 CPU to act as a successive approximations register. Apply an input D.C. voltage and display the output codeword on the VDU, both in binary and hexadecimal.

2. Determine the transfer function of the DAC (i.e. the range of output voltages for input data words) and add a conversion routine to your program that allows the output to be displayed in volts.

   (*Note*: With the ADC running continuously, the output data for display on the VDU will be made available at a rate of approximately 1,000 readings per second. If the output numbers are followed by a carriage return without line feed, then the voltage will be displayed at the one position on the VDU screen.)

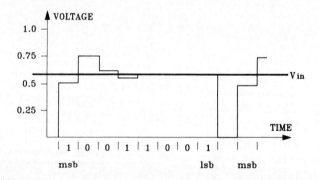

Figure 4.33 Successive approximation ADC - DAC output as a function of time

Laboratory Exercise 4.9

The Digital Storage Oscilloscope

Aim

The aim of this exercise is to acquire a series of samples from an input signal, store the samples in memory and then display the sampled waveform on an oscilloscope. This arrangement in effect converts a normal oscilloscope into a digital storage oscilloscope (DSO). A further aim of this exercise is to use the DSO to observe some simple input waveforms and hence investigate the phenomenon of aliasing.

Introduction

In an earlier exercise (Laboratory Exercise 4.3—The Arbitrary Waveform Generator), a sequence of numbers that had previously been loaded into memory were read out in turn to a digital to analog converter and the resulting waveform was displayed on an oscilloscope. With the current exercise, it is intended to acquire a set of samples of some analog input waveform, store these samples in memory and then read out the samples for display on an oscilloscope. What will effectively be built is a digital storage oscilloscope as shown in Figure 4.34. Having captured the input waveform, the waveform can be displayed at any desired repetition rate long after the signal has ceased to exist.

   In this first experiment involving an analog to digital converter (ADC), it is suggested that the interfacing problem be eased by using the CPU to initiate the conversion process. In this way the CPU has an *a priori* knowledge of when the ADC is ready to transfer the data; it does not have, therefore to monitor the ADC's BUSY flag. For example, if the ADC is required to perform conversions at a one kilosample per second rate (1 ksps), it is known that just prior to sending the next START pulse, the ADC will have had one millisecond to complete the previous conversion. This far exceeds the conversion time of most ADCs and therefore the data read by the CPU will be valid.

Procedure

1. Write a program that will cause the ADC to sample an input waveform on 256 occasions, one millisecond apart, with the 256 samples being stored in consecutive locations in memory. Having acquired the final sample, the program should then enter an endless display loop in which the samples are sent to a DAC and oscilloscope for display.

2. At the start of each display loop generate an oscilloscope trigger pulse such that the acquired waveform appears stable when displayed.

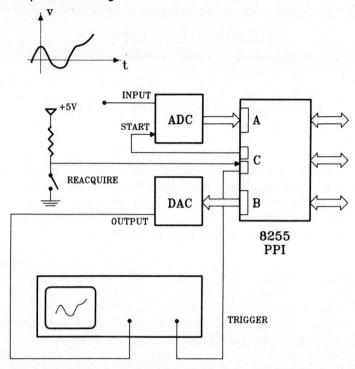

Figure 4.34 Hardware arrangement for simple digital storage oscilloscope

3. Modify your program so that at the end of each display loop the status of a logic switch is tested. If the switch is pressed, the program should branch out of the display loop in order to re-acquire a new set of 256 samples. If the switch is not pressed, the program should continue to display the currently stored waveform.

Using the Digital Storage Oscilloscope

Before moving on to the next exercise, it is worthwhile using your digital storage oscilloscope to record a few input waveforms in order to experience the delights and pitfalls of such an instrument.

Start by setting your input waveform to a sine wave of frequency 10 Hz. If your delay subroutine is accurate and you have a sampling rate of one thousand samples per second, you will observe just over two complete periods of the input sine wave. Compare this stable, flicker-free display with that obtained when you connect your analog oscilloscope directly to the input waveform. When the time-base is set to a speed that allows two complete periods to be displayed, it is difficult to see a sine wave at all! All you see is a spot oscillating up and down with a waveshape that is difficult to judge with any degree of certainty. The use of digital storage in order to capture, process and display slowly varying waveforms is a major advantage that digital oscilloscopes have over their analog counterparts.

Now set the input frequency to 1 kHz and acquire a new set of 256 samples. If this is the first time that you have used a digital oscilloscope you will no doubt be surprised to see a waveform having an apparent frequency of just a few Hertz. What is being displayed is an 'alias' of the input waveform brought about by an insufficient sampling rate. With a sample rate of 1 ksps, input signals must be restricted to frequencies of less than 500 Hz in order to avoid this misleading aliasing effect. It is quite informative to gradually increase the input frequency from 10 Hz, where the system is well behaved, to 1 kHz and above, where aliasing renders the system unusable. A variety of potentially confusing effects becomes apparent, which awakens the user to the possible pitfalls that accompany the use of digital storage oscilloscopes.

Laboratory Exercise 4.10

Graticules, Cursors and Digital Readout

Aim

The basic aim of this exercise is identical to that of the preceding exercise, namely to acquire a waveform by storing 256 samples in memory and then displaying the acquired waveform on an oscilloscope. It is proposed, however, to introduce some improvements to the system so as to extend your programming skills. These improvements include:

1. triggering the ADC by an external pulse generator; and
2. adding graticule and cursor lines to the display.

Introduction

1. *External Triggering of the ADC*
When it is important that a sample of an input waveform be taken at a precise time, or with a precisely known repetition rate, the START signal to the ADC is usually taken from a pulse generator rather than from the computer. Under these circumstances, the computer needs to be told when the ADC is BUSY carrying out a conversion or, alternatively, when it is READY to transfer data. It is necessary, therefore, for the computer to monitor the BUSY/READY flag of the ADC and to read one item of data each time the flag indicates that valid data is available. This is shown in Figure 4.35.

2. *Graticules and Cursor Lines*
When an input signal has been digitized by an ADC and converted back to an output analog signal by a DAC, the amplitude of the output waveform will not necessarily be the same as the amplitude of the original input waveform. Differences will arise when the voltage range for full scale conversion is different for the ADC and DAC devices. In order to display a waveform previously acquired by an ADC in such a way that accurate measurements of amplitude may be made, it becomes necessary to generate graticule lines of known voltage or, better still, to incorporate a user controlled cursor with numeric readout. A typical oscilloscope display is shown in Figure 4.36.

Procedure

1. Write a program that will allow 256 samples of an input waveform to be acquired from an externally triggered ADC. A pulse generator, set to a frequency of 1 kHz, provides the START pulses for the ADC while a logic switch is to be used to initiate acquisition of a new waveform. An oscilloscope trigger pulse is to be generated at the start of each display loop.

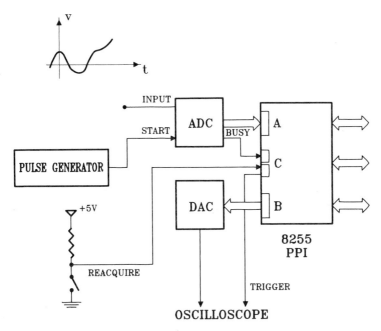

Figure 4.35 Hardware arrangement for digital storage oscilloscope with external triggering of ADC

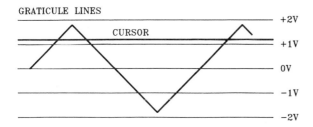

$$V_{max} = 1.7 \ \ VOLTS$$
$$V_{cursor} = 1.25 \ \ VOLTS$$
$$V_{min} = -1.7 \ \ VOLTS$$

Figure 4.36 Simple digital oscilloscope display with graticule lines and cursor

2. Modify your program in order to display five fixed graticule lines at positions corresponding to -2V, -1V, 0V, +1V and +2V respectively. Arrange for the acquired waveform to appear brighter than the graticule lines.

3. Arrange for your program to print out on the VDU the maximum and minimum values of the acquired waveform.

4. Add a further routine to your program that accepts an input, in volts, from the keyboard and displays a cursor line at the designated position. Arrange for this cursor to appear different from the existing graticule lines (e.g. brighter or thicker) and check its correct operation by entering the peak values displayed on the VDU.

The use of a microcomputer to improve the accuracy and ease of use of an instrument is a major trend in the design of modern test equipment. It will be evident that having acquired a waveform, there is virtually no limit to the data processing that may then be carried out on the sampled data points including peak detection, averaging, spectral analysis and much more. These concepts will be taken up in later exercises.

5 Z80 Interrupts and the Intel PPI

In Chapter 4, methods of exchanging information between the CPU and a peripheral using the Intel PPI were discussed and it was stated that not all peripherals are ready to exchange information at any point in time. Instead, some peripherals must signal to the computer that they are ready to exchange information. This can be done by having the computer monitor a 1-bit status signal called the READY flag and only transfer the information when the peripheral indicates that it is ready. While this works fine in principle, it has a number of limitations in practice:

1. The computer wastes a lot of time monitoring the READY flag. For example, the computer may test the READY flag hundreds of times before finding that the peripheral is able to begin a transfer. If there are other tasks that the computer can be carrying out, this leads to a significant decrease in efficiency.

2. If there are several peripheral devices to be checked, their READY flags will be tested sequentially or polled as shown in Figure 5.1. With such an arrangement, there may be a significant delay between the time that a peripheral indicates that it is ready to transfer data and the time that the processor detects this condition and initiates the transfer. For some peripheral devices, this delay would be unacceptable. In the case shown in Figure 5.1, if a flag becomes set just after it has been tested by the processor, the processor will not become aware that the device requires service until all other devices have been tested.

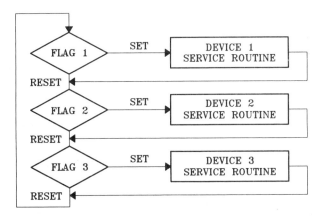

Figure 5.1 Polling of several peripheral device READY flags

133

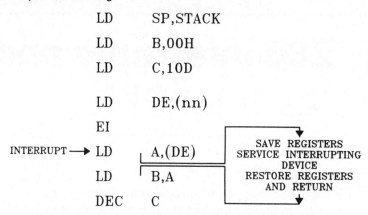

Figure 5.2 Sequence of events in servicing an interrupt

A more efficient approach is to allow peripherals which require service urgently to actively demand the attention of the processor rather than wait to be polled. When the processor receives this request for attention, it interrupts the process that it was carrying out and proceeds immediately to service the peripheral device which demanded attention. Such a request for attention initiated by a peripheral is called an interrupt. Figure 5.2 illustrates the sequence of events when an interrupt request occurs. Initially, the processor is executing a program when an interrupt request is received. Providing that the processor has been programmed so as to allow it to respond to interrupts, the processor will interrupt its program execution at the conclusion of the current instruction and branch to the appropriate interrupt service routine. The interrupt service routine should then save the current state of the processor (i.e. the values in the registers), service the peripheral device and then restore the state of the processor before resuming the interrupted program.

As mentioned briefly in Chapter 2, the Z80 CPU can accept interrupts on two pins. There is an interrupt request line (INT pin 16) and a non-maskable interrupt line (NMI, pin 17). The Z80 CPU responds quite differently to each of these, as is discussed in the next two sections.

5.1 THE Z80 INTERRUPT REQUEST LINE

The interrupt request line (INT) provides a maskable single level interrupt. That is, the Z80 CPU contains a software controlled interrupt enable flip-flop and the CPU will only respond to an interrupt on the INT line provided that this flip-flop is set. The state of the interrupt enable flip-flop is controlled by the enable interrupts (**EI**) and disable interrupts (**DI**) instructions. After a CPU reset, the interrupt enable flip-flop is reset. It is therefore the responsibility of the programmer to ensure that interrupts have been enabled before attempting any interrupt driven I/O. Note also that the programmer has the ability to disable interrupts during a part of a program when interrupts must not occur. This may be required, for example, during a particular part of the program that has timing constraints which cannot tolerate interrupts.

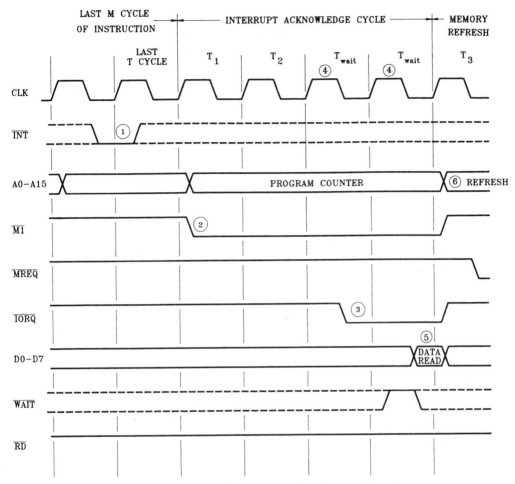

Figure 5.3 Interrupt request - interrupt acknowledge timing diagram

The CPU can respond to an interrupt in one of three ways, depending on whether it has been programmed to be in interrupt mode 0, 1 or 2 using the **IM 0, IM 1** or **IM 2** instructions respectively. The CPU is set to interrupt mode 0 following a reset. In each case, however, the first operation performed by the CPU is the generation of an interrupt acknowledge sequence, as shown in the timing diagram of Figure 5.3. The steps of the interrupt request - interrupt acknowledge process are as follows:

1. The state of the $\overline{\text{INT}}$ line is sampled on the rising edge of the last T cycle of every instruction. The interrupt will only be accepted if the internal interrupt enable flip-flop of the CPU is set.

2. A special $\overline{\text{M1}}$ cycle is commenced.

3. During the $\overline{\text{M1}}$ cycle, the $\overline{\text{IORQ}}$ line is asserted. Normally, $\overline{\text{IORQ}}$ is only asserted during

a peripheral read/write operation. It is not normally asserted during a machine cycle when $\overline{M1}$ is asserted since these cycles are opcode fetches which, by definition, must be memory fetches. The assertion of $\overline{M1}$ and $\overline{IORQ}$ together is therefore used to uniquely indicate an interrupt acknowledge cycle.

4. Two wait states are automatically inserted to give the interrupting device time to receive the interrupt acknowledge. Further wait states can be added by the interrupting device using the $\overline{WAIT}$ signal. If the $\overline{WAIT}$ input is not asserted during the second wait state, then this special $\overline{M1}$ cycle will terminate.

5. The interrupting device places an interrupt vector onto the data bus which is read by the CPU on the rising edge of T3. How this vector will be interpreted by the CPU depends upon the interrupt mode into which the CPU has been initialized. This is covered in greater detail below.

6. The execution of the interrupt service routine will commence immediately after the memory refresh part of the $\overline{M1}$ cycle.

When the CPU accepts an interrupt, the interrupt enable flip-flop is automatically disabled to prevent further interrupts being accepted until the user issues another enable interrupts instruction.

Interrupt Mode 0

When set to interrupt mode 0, the CPU completes the current instruction and then accepts a single byte or a series of bytes placed on the data bus by the interrupting device. It interprets this byte or bytes as an instruction. It is therefore the interrupting device which provides the first instruction to be executed as part of interrupt service rather than system memory. Instructions of any length can be executed in this way as the CPU will accept a multi-byte instruction from the interrupting device.

The most commonly used instruction returned by the interrupting device is a restart instruction. This is a single-byte instruction which causes the current value of the program counter to be saved on the stack and execution to continue from one of eight specific locations in the base page of memory. The **RST p** instruction can take values of p from 00H to 38H in steps of 08H. Execution continues from the memory location p. Thus:

>   RST 00H saves the PC and restarts from location 0000H
>   RST 08H saves the PC and restarts from location 0008H
>   RST 10H saves the PC and restarts from location 0010H
>   RST 18H saves the PC and restarts from location 0018H
>   RST 20H saves the PC and restarts from location 0020H
>   RST 28H saves the PC and restarts from location 0028H
>   RST 30H saves the PC and restarts from location 0030H
>   RST 38H saves the PC and restarts from location 0038H

Another useful instruction which could be placed onto the data bus by the interrupting device is a subroutine call. This performs the same function as a restart instruction in that the contents of the program counter are saved to the stack and, in addition, it provides the extra flexibility of allowing execution to continue from any address in memory. The subroutine call is, however, a 3-byte instruction and therefore the interrupting device must provide all three bytes. The first byte, that is the opcode fetch, must be present on the data bus at the time of the rising edge of T_3 as shown in Figure 5.3, whereas the second and third bytes must occur at the time of the falling edge of T_3 on subsequent input read cycles. Whether this additional hardware complexity in the interrupting device is worthwhile is doubtful, however, when it is realized that the same result can be achieved using a single-byte restart instruction together with an unconditional jump instruction at the address to which the restart instruction transfers control.

Multi-Level Interrupts
The above discussions have outlined the methods used to handle a single interrupting device. It is not unusual to wish to have more than one device which can generate interrupts. Two approaches are available:

1. In the first method, the READY flags of all interrupting devices are combined in a single OR gate to provide an interrupt when any device is ready to transfer data. The processor then branches to a single interrupt service routine regardless of which device is seeking attention, and proceeds by polling the peripheral devices to discover which has requested the interrupt. This approach does allow the CPU to carry out useful processing between requests for attention but some delay in servicing the interrupting device still remains while the processor works out which of the peripherals is ready.

2. A second, more efficient approach is to allow each interrupting device to generate a unique instruction during the interrupt acknowledge cycle. Using the restart instruction, it would be possible to handle up to eight interrupting devices using the hardware shown in Figure 5.4.

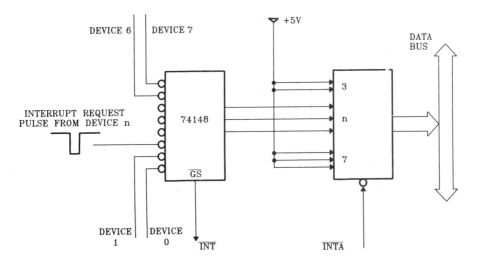

Figure 5.4 Multi-level interrupt implementation

The instruction **RST p** is assembled to the octal codeword 3n7Q, where n is in the range 0 ≤ n ≤ 7. The 74148 8-line to 3-line priority encoder produces at its 3-line output a 3-bit number which represents the highest priority input currently asserted (input 7 having the highest priority while input 0 has the lowest priority). The group select output ($\overline{GS}$) is also asserted when one or more inputs are asserted and can be used to directly drive the $\overline{INT}$ line of the Z80. The three output lines are fed directly to a three-state buffer to form the appropriate restart instruction code which is placed onto the data bus during an interrupt acknowledge cycle (M1 and $\overline{IORQ}$ both asserted). There are some limitations with this arrangement:

1. The system is limited to eight interrupting devices. Indeed, when it is remembered that the CPU begins execution from location 0000H after a system reset (the same address as a **RST 0** instruction), this may limit the number of interrupting devices to seven. Nevertheless, this will usually be more than adequate.

2. When two or more interrupts occur almost simultaneously, the highest will be serviced. As there is no memory in the interrupt priority determination, however, the others can be forgotten and so may not be subsequently serviced.

3. The hardware shown in Figure 5.4 will correctly respond to the highest of several interrupts which occur simultaneously when no other interrupts are being serviced. A problem arises, however, when an interrupt routine (say level 5) is entered. Using the hardware shown, if the programmer does not re-enable interrupts upon entering the interrupt service routine, then a higher priority interrupt (say level 7) which occurs during the lower priority interrupt will not be accepted. If interrupts are re-enabled, however, a lower priority interrupt (say level 1) will also be able to interrupt the higher priority one. It would be necessary to write careful software to overcome this difficulty and this would add a significant overhead to the service time for interrupts.

In Chapter 6, the Zilog Z80 PIO will be described. This is a parallel I/O device which handles up to 128 levels of interrupts in a way which overcomes the limitations described above.

Interrupt Mode 1

Interrupt mode 1 is really a subset of interrupt mode 0. Irrespective of what data (if any) the interrupting device places onto the data bus during the interrupt acknowledge cycle, the CPU performs a **RST 38H** instruction and so execution continues from location 0038H. Using this interrupt mode, the only way that multi-level interrupts can be accommodated is by polling within the interrupt service routine, as described above.

Interrupt Mode 2

This interrupt mode is the most powerful mode of interrupt response for the Z80 CPU. A single 8-bit byte of data is accepted from the interrupting device and is used to form an indirect subroutine call to any location in the Z80 memory space. The user maintains a table in memory which contains the 16-bit starting addresses of all interrupt service routines. A

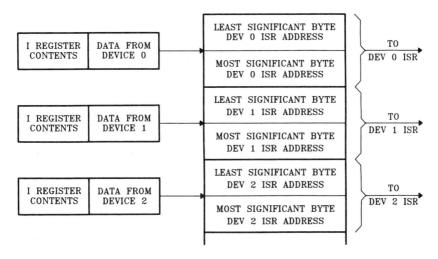

Figure 5.5 Interrupt service routine entry using interrupt mode 2

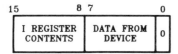

Figure 5.6 Format of the interrupt vector for mode 2 interrupts

pointer to one of these addresses is formed by combining the contents of the interrupt page address register (I) contained within the CPU, with the eight bits of data obtained from the interrupting device during the interrupt acknowledge cycle. Thus, if the I register contains 18H and the interrupting device places 40H onto the data bus during the interrupt acknowledge cycle, then the CPU will use the 16 bits of data contained in memory locations 1840H and 1841H as the 16-bit address of the interrupt service routine for the interrupting device. (In the above example, location 1840H would contain the least significant byte of the address and location 1841H would contain the most significant byte.) The 16-bit address formed by the contents of the I register together with the eight bits provided by the interrupting peripheral is called the interrupt vector. Figure 5.5 shows diagrammatically the interrupt service procedure for three interrupting devices.

In reality, the interrupting device needs only to provide seven bits of data as the CPU assumes that the least significant bit of the interrupt vector is zero. The interrupt vector pointing to the table of starting addresses is therefore made up as shown in Figure 5.6. This means that the address of the first byte of each entry in the table of starting addresses must be even. The I register contents defines a 256-byte page of memory (ii00H - iiFFH, where ii is the contents of the I register). Given that each table entry requires two bytes of memory, 128 interrupt service routine start addresses can be accommodated assuming that the start of the table is placed on a 256-byte boundary.

After the interrupting device has supplied the lower half of the address in the table of starting addresses, the CPU automatically saves the program counter on the stack before fetching the start address of the interrupt service routine from the table and then commences execution of the interrupt service routine. The total interrupt response time (assuming that no user inserted wait states are required) is 19 states, which equates to 4.75μs for a system driven by a 4 MHz clock. This time is made up of seven clock periods to fetch the lower eight bits of the table of starting addresses from the interrupting device, plus six clock periods to save the program counter contents to the stack plus a further six clock periods to obtain the address of the interrupt service routine from the table of starting addresses.

Interrupt Mode 2 Check List
In order to use this interrupt mode, the programmer must:

1. load the I register of the CPU with the most significant byte of the addresses of the table of start addresses. The I register is initialized to zero after a CPU reset;

2. determine the data to be provided by interrupting devices during the interrupt acknowledge cycle and then place the address of the appropriate interrupt service routine at the correct place within the table of starting addresses;

3. set the interrupt mode to mode 2 (set to mode 0 after a CPU reset);

4. enable interrupts.

Return from Interrupt

An interrupt service routine is normally ended with the return from interrupt (**RETI**) instruction. This causes the program counter to be loaded with the return address which was stored on the stack at the commencement of the interrupt and thus permits an orderly return to the interrupted program. In Chapter 6, it will be shown that the Z80 PIO looks for this instruction as part of its control of multi-level interrupt priority. The return from interrupt instruction does not cause the interrupt enable flip-flop of the CPU to be set. It is up to the user to issue an enable interrupt instruction to accomplish this. Note that an enable interrupt instruction sets the interrupt enable flip-flop only after the next instruction. This allows an interrupt service routine to be completed with the code.

```
            EI
            RETI
```

Thus the current interrupt service routine can be totally completed before another interrupt will be accepted by the CPU.

5.2 THE Z80 NON-MASKABLE INTERRUPT LINE

The non-maskable interrupt line ($\overline{\text{NMI}}$) is the highest priority Z80 interrupt. As the name implies, it cannot be disabled (masked) by the programmer and will be accepted by the CPU whenever a peripheral device makes an interrupt request. It is usually reserved for very

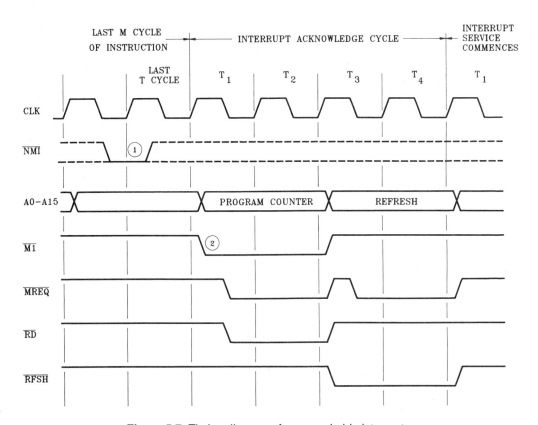

Figure 5.7 Timing diagram of non-maskable interrupt

important functions which must be attended to as soon as they occur. A typical example might be an impending power failure, when it may be desirable for system status to be saved to non-volatile memory. The CPU completes the current instruction after accepting a non-maskable interrupt, automatically saves the value of the program counter to the stack and then branches to location 0066H where the non-maskable interrupt service routine must commence. Figure 5.7 shows the timing diagram for a non-maskable interrupt.

The steps in the process are as follows:

1. The CPU samples the non-maskable Interrupt (NMI) input on the rising edge of the final T cycle of every instruction.

2. The remainder of the cycle is identical to an opcode fetch cycle (Figure 2.11) except that the data which appears on the data bus is ignored and the CPU proceeds to save the program counter to the stack and then restarts at location 0066H.

Notice that, in this case, the interrupt acknowledge provided by the M1 and IORQ lines for the maskable interrupt is not provided. Unlike the maskable interrupt, the non-maskable interrupt does not require the interrupting device to place a byte of data onto the data bus

OCCURRENCE	IFF_1	IFF_2
CPU RESET	0	0
DI	0	0
EI	1	1
LD A,I or LD A,R	■	■
ACCEPT INT	0	0
ACCEPT NMI	0	■
RETI	■	■
RETN	IFF_2	■

IFF_2 to
} PARITY/OVERFLOW
FLAG

■ = NO CHANGE

Figure 5.8 Effect of various instructions on interrupt enable flip-flop (IFF_1) and the interrupt enable temporary storage location (IFF_2)

during the interrupt acknowledge cycle in order to determine the interrupt service routine to be employed. As a consequence, the peripheral does not need to be aware that the interrupt acknowledge is occurring.

When a non-maskable interrupt occurs, the CPU interrupt enable flip-flop is automatically disabled to prevent maskable interrupts from being accepted. In many applications, it would be desirable to be able to know the state of this flip-flop prior to the non-maskable interrupt so that system status can be completely restored at the conclusion of the non-maskable interrupt service routine. The Z80 allows for this by providing a temporary storage location for the state of the interrupt enable flip-flop. The contents of the interrupt enable flip-flop (IFF_1) and the temporary storage location (IFF_2) are always identical except during a non-maskable interrupt when the interrupt enable flip-flop is reset while the temporary storage location contains the state of the interrupt enable flip-flop prior to the non-maskable interrupt. When a load accumulator with register I (**LD A,I**) instruction or a load accumulator with register R (**LD A,R**) instruction is executed, the contents of the temporary storage location is copied into the parity/overflow flag where it can be tested or stored for later use if this is desirable.

A second method of correctly retrieving the state of the interrupt enable flip-flop is to end the non-maskable interrupt service routine with a return from non-maskable interrupt instruction (**RETN**) as this causes the contents of the temporary storage location to be copied back to the interrupt enable flip-flop. Figure 5.8 gives a summary of the effect of various instructions on the interrupt enable flip-flop and the temporary storage location.

5.3 USE OF THE PPI IN MODE 1 TO FACILITATE INTERRUPT HANDLING

One of the major advantages of programmable devices is that they are able to operate in one of a variety of modes in order to match the current application. It was indicated in Chapter

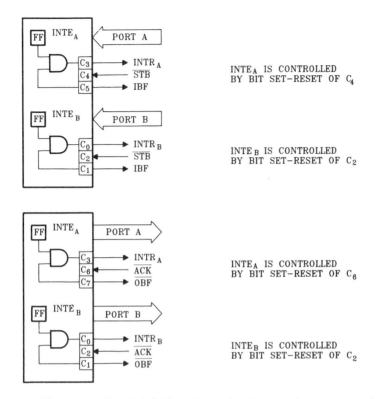

Figure 5.9 Signal definitions for mode 1 input and output

4 that the PPI has three modes of operation for data transfer, whereas in the previous section it was explained that the Z80 CPU also has three modes of interrupt response. It is a little unfortunate that in both cases these are listed simply as mode 0, mode 1 and mode 2, since a very real possibility for confusion and error exists when the PPI is used along with the Z80 for data transfer under interrupts. The user must make every effort to clearly distinguish between the operating modes of both devices.

In Section 4.5 the use of the PPI in mode 1 for programmed data transfer was described. In this mode of operation data is strobed into the PPI by way of a $\overline{STB}$ pulse generated by the peripheral. As shown in Figure 4.12, the falling edge of the $\overline{STB}$ pulse captures data into the input latch with the PPI signaling to the peripheral that it has accepted the data by raising its IBF (input buffer full) flag. At some later stage, as dictated by the program, the CPU reads from port C to ascertain the state of this IBF flag. Upon detecting that input data is available, the CPU then reads from the input port, the effect of which is to lower the IBF flag in readiness for the next input.

The main limitation of this approach is that the CPU must continually read from port C to know when data has been accepted by the input port. As has been shown in the earlier sections of this chapter, this information is more effectively conveyed to the CPU by the arrival of an interrupt, allowing the CPU to continue to perform useful processing until the time of arrival of the interrupt. The PPI, when used in mode 1, facilitates the generation of

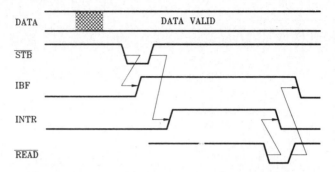

Figure 5.10 Timing diagram for input under interrupts

the interrupt in the following manner. Included within the PPI is a flip-flop known as the interrupt enable flip-flop (INTE). When this flip-flop is set AND the input buffer full flag (IBF) is asserted, a signal, known as the interrupt request (INTR), is generated at a specified output from port C as shown in Figure 5.9. Both ports A and B may be configured to generate the interrupt request signal with separate enabling flip-flops provided for each port.

The timing diagram for the acquisition of a single data item using interrupts is shown in Figure 5.10. The transfer is initiated by the peripheral generating a strobe signal when it has valid data to transmit. The falling edge of the strobe signal latches the data into the PPI which then responds by raising the input buffer full flag. With the interrupt enable flip-flop set, an interrupt request is then generated by the final, rising edge of the data strobe pulse. The interchange of control signals up to this point have all been handled by the PPI without any intervention by the CPU. If the CPU has been instructed to respond to an interrupt request by way of the enable interrupts instruction (**EI**), then it will enter the interrupt service routine and at some stage read the data captured in the PPI. As shown in Figure 5.10, the process of reading the input data cancels the interrupt request and resets the input buffer full flag. The peripheral device is thus made aware that the PPI is now ready to accept the next data item.

In the case of the CPU sending data to a peripheral device under interrupts, the CPU writes the first data item to the PPI and then returns to its main processing task. Subsequent data items are then written by the CPU following an interrupt generated by the peripheral when it has acknowledged receipt of the previous item. A timing diagram showing the first two interrupts of an output sequence is shown in Figure 5.11. The output sequence begins when the interrupt enable flip-flop (INTE) within the PPI is set. This immediately generates an interrupt for the CPU requesting an item of data to be written to the output port of the PPI. Having received the first data item in its output latch, the PPI cancels the interrupt request signal and informs the peripheral that data is waiting by asserting its output buffer full flag. At some later time, the peripheral accepts the data presented to it by the PPI, acknowledging the transfer by asserting and then canceling the signal on the $\overline{ACK}$ input of the PPI. This action resets the output buffer full flag and thereby generates a further interrupt request to the CPU.

A significant feature of both the input and output data transfers described above is that the CPU is only involved during the brief time that it takes to read data from the input port or write data to the output port. The exchange of control signals between the peripheral and the PPI is all handled by the PPI. This allows the CPU to continue with useful processing

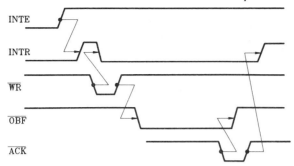

Figure 5.11 Timing diagram for output under interrupts

rather than having to monitor the status of the peripheral waiting for it to indicate that it is ready for the next transfer.

Whereas the **EI** and **DI** instructions provide control over the CPU as to whether it will recognize an interrupt originating from any source, the interrupt enable flip-flops within the PPI give the user a means of accepting an interrupt from one port of the PPI while ignoring interrupts from others. The interrupt enable flip-flops are controlled by setting or resetting the bits in port C as specified in Figure 5.9, using the bit set-reset facility described in Section 4.7.

Combined Modes of Operation

The signal definition diagrams of Figure 5.9 have been drawn with both ports A and B configured as input ports or output ports. Many other combinations of mode and direction are however possible to best suit the application. It is feasible, for example, to configure port A as a mode 1 input port acquiring data under interrupts, with port B operating as a mode 0 output port sending data to a digital to analog converter. With both ports A and B initialized to mode 1, it is clear from Figure 5.9 that six out of the eight lines of port C are used as control signals. The remaining two lines, C_6 and C_7 in one instance and C_4 and C_5 in the other, are available as two general purpose input or output lines. With one port configured in mode 1 and the other in mode 0, additional general purpose lines become available, some of which may be specified for input with the remainder configured for output.

5.4 INTERRUPT SOFTWARE

Interrupt software has essentially three components. These include a group of statements initializing the CPU and PPI, a further group of statements initializing the counters and storage areas to be accessed by the interrupt service routine, and finally the interrupt service routine itself. The exact composition of each of these components depends on the nature of the problem and thus is difficult to explain in general terms. As an alternative, a case study will be considered in which the requirements of each of these components will be addressed in such a manner that other problems can be attempted using a similar approach.

The case study consists of the design of a digital storage oscilloscope. Data is to be

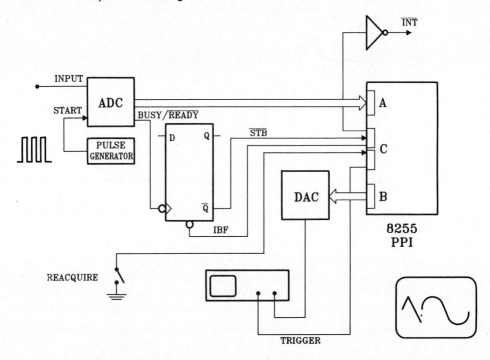

Figure 5.12 Interrupt driven data acquisition and display system

acquired from an analog to digital converter at a relatively slow rate, say one data point per second, stored in consecutive locations in memory and presented to an oscilloscope at a much faster rate to give a stable, flicker free display. In the main program, the CPU continuously accesses a block of 256 locations of memory, called STORE in the following code, and sends each data byte to a digital to analog converter for subsequent display on a normal, non-storage oscilloscope. At the start of each display sequence, a pulse is to be generated to trigger the time-base of the oscilloscope. Initially, STORE will be filled with zero bytes giving rise to a horizontal line on the display. With each interrupt, a data byte will be acquired, stored in memory and thereby included in the display. After 256 seconds a complete screen of acquired data will be displayed.

A schematic diagram of the proposed system is given in Figure 5.12, where it will be seen that the BUSY/READY output of the ADC is used to form the data strobe pulse for the PPI. This is exactly the same arrangement used in Chapter 4, where the PPI was configured in mode 1 for programmed transfer of data. The interrupt request signal, $(INTR_A)$, is generated from C_3 of the PPI, which requires inversion prior to its connection to the asserted low interrupt input ($\overline{INT}$) of the Z80 CPU. Additional 1-bit input and output signals have been assigned to a push-button switch, to initiate the acquisition of a new block of 256 samples, and to the oscilloscope time-base trigger signal.

CPU and PPI Initialization

The Z80 CPU is to be initialized for interrupts using the **IM 0** instruction to give the mode

0 response to an interrupt. That is, upon the arrival of an interrupt, the CPU finishes the current instruction, saves the program counter and restarts execution via an **RST p** instruction. Furthermore, it is assumed that hardware has been provided so that the restart instruction **RST 30H** occurs, giving rise to a jump to memory location 0030H. The choice of the above conditions was made in the following way. The PPI is not nearly as well suited to the Z80 mode 2 interrupt response as the Z80 PIO that will be treated in the next chapter. As stated earlier, interrupt mode 1 is just a particular case of Interrupt Mode 0 where a **RST 38H** instruction is executed rather than the more general **RST p** instruction. Finally, the choice of **RST 30H** rather than another of the restart instructions was purely arbitrary. The above conditions are therefore the least restrictive of those appropriate to the PPI.

The PPI is initialized for interrupts simply by setting the mode of the port designated to be the input port, say port A, to mode 1, input and by enabling the internal flip-flop. These actions are achieved by sending the appropriate mode control word to the PPI's control register and then by sending the bit-set word for C_4 (as set out in Figure 5.13) also to the control register.

Initialization of Data Storage and Counters

For the data acquisition and display system to operate in the desired manner, it is necessary that the main program and interrupt service routine both have access to the data storage area.

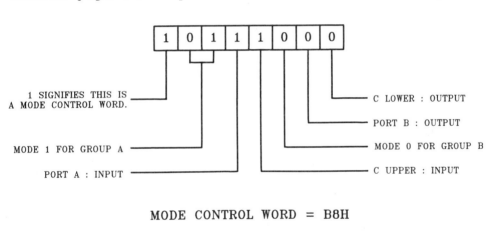

MODE CONTROL WORD = B8H

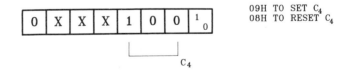

BIT SET / RESET WORD

Figure 5.13 Mode control word and flip-flop enable word

In the absence of an interrupt, the main program will simply bring the contents of each of the 256 memory locations into the accumulator in turn and then send them to the DAC via the PPI. At any time during this output sequence an interrupt may occur, at which time a new item of data is acquired and loaded into an appropriate location in the data storage area. Both the main program and the interrupt service routine require a 16-bit register pair pointing to the current memory location in their respective routines, and an 8-bit counter keeping track of how many data items have been displayed and how many have been acquired, respectively. Clearly, these registers and counters must not be changed by operations affecting the other routine.

The Z80 architecture, with its alternate register set and associated instructions, provides a particularly convenient way of handling this common problem. The registers in the main register set can be used to store the parameters associated with the main program and the registers in the alternate register set to store the parameters for the interrupt service routine. Upon the arrival of an interrupt, the execution of just two exchange instructions is all that is needed to save the contents of the entire main register set. It is necessary, however, to initialize the contents of the alternate register set at the start of the program so that when the interrupt service routine is entered for the first time, the 16-bit register pair is pointing to the first location in the data storage area and the 8-bit register contains the number of data items to be acquired. This is achieved using the following program segment.

```
INIT:       EXX                      ; Initialize HL' and B'
            LD      HL,STORE         ; for use in Interrupt
            LD      B,COUNT          ; Service Routine
            EXX
```

The Interrupt Service Routine

In this case study, as in many practical applications, the interrupt service routine is short and simple. All that has to be done after an interrupt is to acquire one item of data, store it away in memory and return to the main program. In addition, it must be ensured that, following the interrupt, a return is made to the same place in the main program and execution is continued without any of the registers having been changed by the interrupt. As indicated above, this latter requirement is taken care of by swapping the main register set for the alternate register set as the first and last task in the interrupt service routine. A further task, that is particular to this problem, is to determine whether all 256 data points have been acquired and, if so, return to the main program with interrupts disabled. In this way no further interrupts will be recognized by the CPU and the main program will continue to display the captured waveform. The acquisition of a new waveform can then be initiated once the CPU detects that the push-button has been pressed. It will be remembered that following the arrival of an interrupt, interrupts are automatically disabled. Further interrupts are only recognized following the execution of the enable interrupts instruction (**EI**).

```
INSR:     EXX                    ; exchange all registers
          EX      AF,AF'         ;
          IN      A,(ADC)        ; Get data point
          LD      (HL),A         ; store it in memory
          INC     HL             ; move to next free location
          DEC     B              ; decrement counter
          JR      Z,DONE         ; if finished, return without
          EX      AF,AF'         ; enabling interrupts.
          EXX                    ; otherwise,enable interrupts
          EI                     ; and return to main
          RETI                   ; program.
DONE:     EX      AF,AF'         ; return without enabling
          EXX                    ; interrupts to suspend
          RETI                   ; further data acquisition
```

It is of some importance to note that the enable interrupt instruction, **EI**, only takes effect following the completion of the next instruction. Often, the instruction following **EI** is the return from interrupts instruction **RETI**. By delaying the time at which interrupts are re-enabled, the CPU will have had time to recover the program counter from the stack, where it was deposited by the last interrupt, and return to the main routine.

Location of the Interrupt Service Routine
While in theory it is possible to locate the interrupt service routine at the memory location pointed to by the restart instruction, (location 0030H in the case of a **RST 30H** instruction) in practice this is rarely done. The reason for this is that the eight memory locations that separate the starting addresses of the **RST p** instructions provide too little space for even the most basic interrupt service routines. This problem is overcome simply by loading an unconditional jump instruction at the restart address and so transferring execution to some more convenient location in memory at which the interrupt service routine may be located. It will be left to the reader to devise a method by which this may be achieved. For further details see Problem 5.3.

PROBLEMS

Problem 5.1
Each of eight peripheral devices has a 1-bit READY flag connected to one bit of an input port on a PPI so that the status of all devices can be determined by a single **IN** instruction.

1. Write a program segment that enters a loop which reads these status flags continuously and branches out of the loop when any one of the devices indicates that it is ready to transfer data.

2. Assuming a system clock frequency of 4 MHz, determine the time that elapses between consecutive samples of the status flags.

3. Write an additional routine that is entered whenever one of the devices indicates that it is ready and branches to one of eight different locations depending upon which device is ready.

4. Calculate the worst case total elapsed time before a peripheral device is serviced.

Problem 5.2
The priority encoder shown in Figure 5.4 is to be used to provide one of eight restart instructions to the Z80 CPU following an interrupt request from one of eight interrupting peripherals. Devise a scheme and write the corresponding interrupt service routine (ISR) whereby a higher priority interrupting device may interrupt the ISR of a lower priority device, whereas a lower priority interrupting device will be recognized and serviced only after the ISR of the higher priority device has been completed. You may assume that the interrupt request signal ($\overline{INT}$ in Figure 5.4) persists for a time equivalent to the execution of several Z80 instructions.

Problem 5.3
Write a program segment that will allow the instruction **JP xxxxH** to be loaded during program execution into memory locations 0030H, 0031H and 0032H respectively. The 16-bit address xxxxH is to correspond to the start address of an interrupt service routine and should be defined in your program by the label **ISR:**.

(Note: It is not always possible to use the assembler directive **ORG 0030H** in order to locate the **JP ISR** instruction at the restart address of the instruction **RST 30H**. The CP/M operating system, for example, which is often used with the Z80 CPU in disk based systems reserves all memory locations below 0100H for use by the operating system. Locations 0030H et seq. must therefore be loaded during the execution of the user's program.)

Problem 5.4

Port B of a PPI is to be used to acquire data from an analog to digital converter and port A is to be used to output data via a digital to analog converter to an oscilloscope. Both data transfers are to take place under interrupt control at rates determined by two independent clocks. Data acquisition is to occur at a 10 Hz rate whereas the acquired data is to be displayed at a 10 kHz rate. The Z80 system is not provided with hardware to provide an interrupt vector and must therefore operate with a mode 1 interrupt response.

1. Determine the mode control word for the PPI.

2. Determine the control words that enable the interrupt enable flip-flops for both PPI ports.

3. Draw a circuit diagram of the ADC, DAC hardware and explain how the $\overline{\text{STB}}$, $\overline{\text{ACK}}$ and INT signals will be generated.

4. Decide which device will be of the higher priority and devise a flow chart for the interrupt service routine that will handle both interrupting devices.

Laboratory Exercise 5.1

Data Acquisition under Interrupts

Aim

The aim of this experiment is to acquire 256 samples of an input waveform at a rate determined by an external oscillator. The samples are to be stored in memory for subsequent display on an oscilloscope.

Introduction

In this laboratory exercise, the analog to digital converter is to derive its start-of-conversion pulses from an oscillator while the BUSY/READY output is to be used to generate an interrupt. This mode of operation allows samples to be acquired at precisely regular intervals, especially if the oscillator is crystal controlled. The generation of a precisely uniform pulse train is something that is difficult to achieve if the pulses are to be produced by the microcomputer because of the small variations in execution time that result when, for example, counters are reloaded on some loops and not on others.

The main program, which the CPU executes, unless interrupted by the ADC signaling that a new sample is available, simply displays the contents of memory in which the 256 samples are to be stored on an oscilloscope. Initially, the memory reserved for the storage of data should be filled with the numbers from 0 to 255 in consecutive locations, thereby giving rise to an initial display on the oscilloscope in the form of a sawtooth waveform. The hardware required for this experiment is shown in Figure 5.14.

Procedure

1. Write and test the main program which loads 256 locations in memory with the numbers 0-255 and displays them continuously, via a DAC, on the oscilloscope. Provide an oscilloscope trigger pulse that activates the time-base at the start of each display sequence.

2. Write an interrupt service routine which will acquire, and store in the display buffer, 256 samples from the ADC.

3. Modify the main program so that, at the end of each display sequence, the state of a push-button switch is monitored and data acquisition recommences if the button is pressed.

4. Further modify your program so that the display 'drifts' across the screen at a rate determined by the sampling rate of the ADC. In this continuous acquisition mode of

operation, a point on the display moves from the right-hand side to the left-hand side of the screen following 256 input samples. This is the so-called 'roll mode' of operation used in intensive care wards to monitor heart beat.

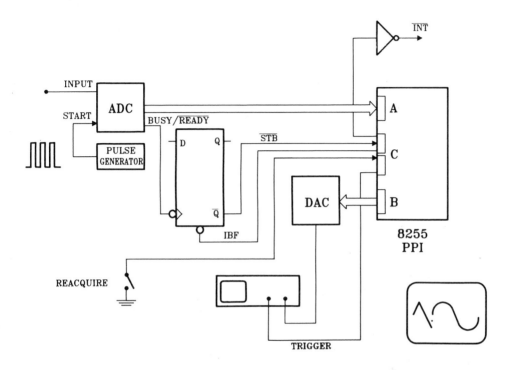

Figure 5.14 Hardware for data acquisition under interrupts

Laboratory Exercise 5.2

Interrupt Driven Reaction Timer

Aim

The aim of this experiment is to construct a timer that measures the average delay between the illumination of one of eight LED indicators and the pressing of the corresponding switch in a register of eight switches.

Introduction

The basic timing mechanism in this exercise takes the form of a 1 kHz oscillator that is used to generate an interrupt every millisecond. The mode of operation of the reaction timer is to be as follows.

Following a random delay of a few seconds, one of eight LED indicators is to be illuminated and the timing period commenced. The subject of the reaction time experiment is then required to press the switch located immediately below the illuminated LED. If the switch that has been pressed is the correct one, then the LED is extinguished and a further random waiting time occurs before another LED is illuminated. If an incorrect switch has been pressed, then the LED remains illuminated until the incorrect switch has been reset and the correct switch pressed. The timing continues throughout this period and, following a correct key press, the elapsed time for each test is to be displayed in milliseconds on the VDU screen. Following eight repetitions of the test, the average reaction time is calculated and displayed on the VDU.

Procedure

1. Write a program segment that generates a random sequence of 3-bit numbers in the range 000 to 111 and sends the numbers, in turn, to the output port of a PPI to which eight LEDs have been connected. Arrange for each of the random 3-bit numbers to illuminate the lower three bits of the port for a time of approximately two seconds. A method for generating random numbers was described in Problem 3.8.

2. Include in your program a subroutine which decodes the 3-bit number to a one-of-eight pattern in which only one of the LEDs is illuminated for the two second period.

3. Randomly illuminate one of eight LEDs while monitoring a set of eight logic switches. Upon detecting that the corresponding switch has been pressed, extinguish all LEDs for a two second period and then select a new LED to illuminate.

4. From one edge of the waveform generated by an oscillator running at 1 kHz, produce a narrow data strobe pulse that will give rise to an interrupt on the port of the PPI to which it is applied. A circuit for producing a brief $\overline{STB}$ pulse from the 1 to 0 transition of an input waveform is given in Figure 5.12.

5. Write an interrupt service routine that simply increments a 16-bit register pair with the arrival of each interrupt. Following the recognition by the computer that the correct switch has been pressed, interrupts are to be disabled and the decimal equivalent of the number stored in this register pair is to be displayed on the VDU. A subroutine to display a 4-digit decimal number corresponding to the 16-bit binary number contained in the HL register pair may already have been written in answer to Problem 3.3.

6. Convert all the above 'two second' delays into random delays ranging from two to five seconds, and finally compute the average of eight tests and display individual and average times, in milliseconds, on the VDU screen.

The basic principle of timing, illustrated by this exercise, is that commonly used by all computers having a 'real time' clock. Interrupts are frequently generated from the A.C. side of the power supply, giving a 20ms (50 Hz) or 16.667ms (60 Hz) resolution.

Laboratory Exercise 5.3

The Logic Analyzer

Aim

The aim of this exercise is to construct a basic logic analyzer capable of monitoring eight input lines. The analyzer must recognize a trigger word and display captured input words in a variety of different formats.

Introduction

The logic analyzer is used to monitor a number of digital lines and, upon the receipt of a suitable trigger signal, store the succession of digital words appearing on the digital lines for subsequent display in numeric form on the VDU or oscillographically. In the more useful forms of logic analyzer, it is possible to display:

1. the sequence of digital words that follow the trigger signal; or
2. the sequence of digital words that precede the trigger signal; or
3. the sequence of digital words that appear both before and after the trigger signal.

It is the last mode of operation that is to be employed in this exercise. Clearly, if input words which occur before the trigger word are to be displayed, all words must be stored in memory as they are acquired in the anticipation that the trigger word will occur next. A convenient method of achieving this requirement is to employ a 'ring buffer'. Data is written into an area of memory in a continuous manner. As the last location is filled the next data item overwrites the contents of the first location, and so on. As each data item is acquired, it is compared with the trigger word and acquisition is then stopped a given number of samples after the trigger word. The ring buffer thus contains data that was acquired both before and after the trigger word. In this exercise the sequence of digital words is to be provided by an analog to digital converter that performs conversions at a 100 Hz rate on a 1 Hz sine wave. The trigger signal is to be derived from the sequence of digital words from the ADC and corresponds to the time at which the input crosses the 0 volt axis in a positive direction. The display format to be used is illustrated in Figure 5.15.

Procedure

1. Connect an ADC to one port of a PPI and write a program that stores the samples, acquired under interrupt control, into 256 locations of memory. Connect a DAC to the PPI and output the 256 samples continuously for display on an oscilloscope. Generate an oscilloscope trigger signal that initiates the oscilloscope time-base at the start of each output sequence.

At this stage in the exercise the oscilloscope should be displaying a little more than two complete cycles of the input waveform with the displayed waveform being rewritten with a new waveform every two seconds.

2. Modify your program so that as each sample is acquired it is compared with the trigger word. When the trigger word is detected, acquisition should continue for a further 206 samples and then stop.

    The oscilloscope display should now appear stable; however, the start of the trace will bear no relationship to the time of arrival of the trigger word. Also, the final sample will be adjacent to the first sample at some random position on the trace.

3. Modify the display routine so that the oscilloscope trigger signal is generated 50 samples before the trigger word.

    The display should now comprise an ordered set of samples with the trigger condition, namely a zero crossing in the positive direction, appearing at a position approximately one-fifth the distance across the display.

4. Include in your program an additional routine that selects from the acquired data the trigger word together with ten words preceding the trigger word and ten words following the trigger word. Arrange for these 21 words to be typed out on the VDU in both binary and hexadecimal format.

(Note: The reader should be aware that a specific trigger word, such as 80H, may not always appear and thus an alternative test, such as the most significant bit changing from 0 to 1, may be more appropriate.)

OSCILLOSCOPE DISPLAY   VDU DISPLAY

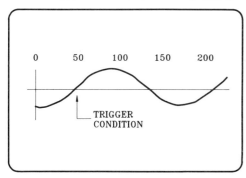

01011010	5A
01100000	60
01100110	66
01101011	6B
01110100	74
01111101	7D
10000001	81
10000110	86
10001110	8E
10010101	95
10011001	99
10011111	9F
10100011	A3

Figure 5.15 Logic analyzer display format

Laboratory Exercise 5.4

Interrupt Driven I/O with Joystick Controller

Aim

The aim of this experiment is to interface a joystick to the computer and use it to control the position of a sighting cross on an X-Y cathode ray tube display.

Introduction

In all previous experiments, the chief method used for communicating with the microcomputer was by way of the keyboard. Keyboards are relatively slow input devices, totally unsuited to real time control operations. A more recent approach has been to use light pens, digitizing tables, joysticks and 'rolling ball' input devices in an effort to enhance the ability of the operator to pass information quickly to a computer. In this exercise you will be using a joystick to enter numbers representing the position of a sighting cross on an X-Y cathode ray tube into the microcomputer.

The Joysticks
Joysticks are simply two potentiometers mounted at right angles to one another. Moving the joystick in the direction marked +Y → -Y, varies the output from the Y potentiometer only, over the range +5 volts to -5 volts, whereas moving the joystick at right angles varies the output from the X potentiometer over the same voltage range.

    The aim of the experiment is to enter the position of the joystick, as determined by two analog to digital converters, into the computer in digital form under interrupt control. To make the experiment interesting, this basic aim is to be incorporated into a game of skill involving hand-eye co-ordination.

    You are required to display a square and a cross on an oscilloscope. The square is to move around the screen in a random fashion while the cross is to move in response to the current position of the joystick. The program controlling the display of the square and cross is also required to compute the percentage time for which the center of the cross remains within the square and to print this out on the VDU after a period of approximately 60 seconds. The position of the joystick is to be sampled at a 100 Hz rate and the X and Y co-ordinates of the joystick entered into the microcomputer under interrupt control. The hardware required is shown in Figure 5.16.

Procedure

1. Generate a dot on the oscilloscope screen corresponding to the co-ordinates of the joystick, as entered into the microcomputer from the ADCs under interrupt control.

2. Generate a cross to replace the above dot. The horizontal and vertical dimensions of the cross should be equivalent to 16 DAC units. (i.e. one-sixteenth of full scale deflection

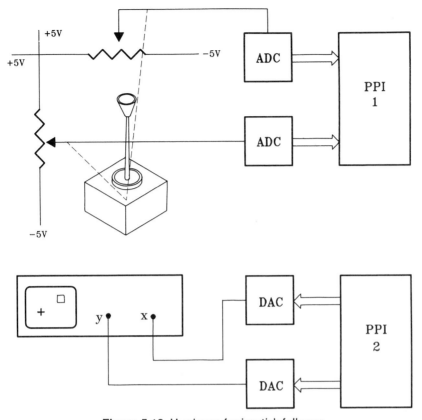

Figure 5.16 Hardware for joystick follower

of the DAC). Ensure that the cross moves around the screen in response to movement of the joystick.

3. Generate a square on the screen, in addition to the cross, of the same dimensions.

4. Write a routine that causes the square to move in a random manner, but in such a way that an operator can follow its movement both with the eye and with the cross. It is suggested that random signed numbers of limited range are added to the current co-ordinates of the square in order to generate the new co-ordinates. Care will be needed to handle the situation of the square approaching the limiting values of the X-Y DACs to avoid the square 'breaking up', with parts appearing simultaneously at the top and bottom of the display. A method of generating random numbers is described in Problem 3.8.

5. At the time of each interrupt determine whether the center of the cross lies within the square. At the end of the one minute test period, print out the number of occasions the cross was found within the square and the total number of samples.

6. Determine the percentage time the center of the cross remains within the square and display this on the VDU screen.

Laboratory Exercise 5.5

Signal Averaging Using Interrupts

Aim

The aim of this experiment is to perform signal averaging on a noisy waveform and hence produce a replica of the waveform for which the signal to noise ratio has been improved.

Introduction

Signal averaging is a technique whereby many repetitions of a noisy waveform are added together in phase. The amplitude of the desired signal progressively builds up whereas the noise amplitude diminishes due to the canceling out of the random fluctuations.

The requirement of phase coherence is crucial to the success of the method, and this limits the type of experiment to which signal averaging may be applied. One class of experiment for which the technique is particularly suited, is that in which a system is subjected to a stimulus (say a flash of light) and then the response (e.g. the resulting fluorescence) occurs a known time later. The responses, which are to be subjected to averaging, may be aligned in phase simply by their time relationship to the stimulus that caused them. In the present case, life will be made easy by using a signal generator that provides a second, digital output locked in phase to the main, analog output. To make the experiment work in a realistic manner it is necessary to first add noise to the analog output of the signal generator and then see to what extent the signal averaging can recover the original signal.

The noisy waveform, together with an in-phase 'stimulus' signal may be produced using the circuit given in Figure 5.17. The pseudo-random binary sequence generator produces a series of 8-bit parallel words in an apparently random fashion. A circuit for a simple pseudo-random binary sequence generator is shown in Figure 5.18 and uses an 8-bit shift register. The 8-bit words produced are applied to a DAC which then supplies a noise-like analog signal. Addition of this noise signal to the sinusoidal output from the signal generator using three resistors results in the noisy sine wave that acts as the input to the signal averaging system.

Procedure

1. Generate the noisy signal, as outlined above, and adjust the amplitudes of the noise and sine wave to give a signal to noise ratio of 0 dB and a peak amplitude below the full scale conversion input of the ADC. ($\pm$ 5 Volts).

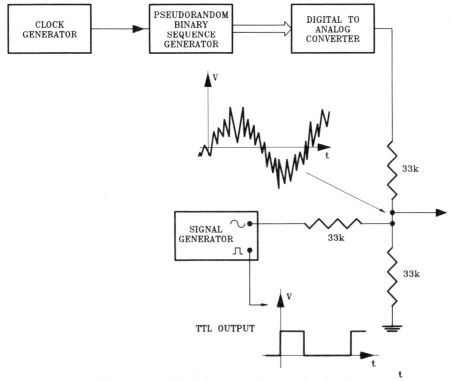

Figure 5.17 Circuit for generating a noisy signal

2. Set the frequency of the signal generator to 2 Hz and, under interrupt control, sample the waveform at approximately 100 samples per second until you have acquired 256 sample points. Display the acquired waveform on an oscilloscope at a rate that provides a bright, flicker-free trace. Arrangements should also be made to ensure that the oscilloscope is provided with a time-base trigger pulse at the start of each display sweep.

3. Repeat this burst of sampling a further 255 times adding the new sampled value to the previous total for each of the 256 sample points. You must ensure that on consecutive repetitions you are adding the samples together in phase. Determine the average value for each of the 256 samples and display this average value on the oscilloscope.

4. At this stage your signal averaging experiment is performing its designated task; it is, however, 'unfriendly' from a user's point of view. It will, for example, take several minutes to acquire all the data for the averaging process, during which time no output is being generated to inform the user that;

   (a) everything is progressing well; and
   (b) it has completed x% of its task.

Modify your program to provide regular 'bulletins' to the user as to what stage in the signal processing has been reached.

5. Further modify your program so that a 'running average' of the resulting waveform is maintained and presented for display on the oscilloscope.

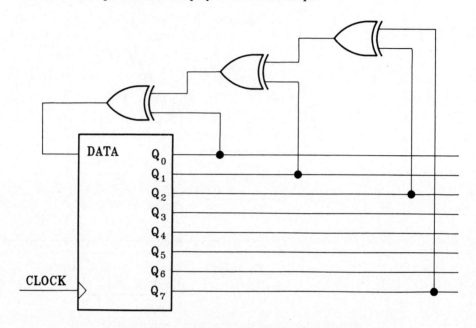

Figure 5.18 Simple pseudo-random binary sequence generator

Laboratory Exercise 5.6

Output to a DAC using Interrupts

Aim

The aim of this exercise is to output data from the computer at a uniform rate as determined by pulses emanating from an external oscillator.

Introduction

In several of the earlier experiments, data acquired from an ADC has been sent to a DAC for display on an oscilloscope. The resultant output waveform has the appearance of a uniform time sequence but, on closer inspection, is seen to be slightly irregular. The reasons for this non-uniform behaviour may be found in the slightly different execution times for the conditional jump instructions depending upon whether or not the condition is met and the extra instructions needed to reload registers used as counters.

When it is imperative that data points be presented to the DAC at a uniform rate, or where some degree of manual control be exercised over the output rate, then the data needs to be sent in synchronism with some external clock pulse generator. In the present laboratory exercise, a pulse generator is used to generate a sequence of interrupts which cause a new item of data to be sent to the DAC.

Procedure

1. Write an initialization routine that sets one port of the PPI to mode 0 output with the second port to mode 1 output. Reserve 256 memory locations and fill these with the numbers 0 to 255. Write a main program that simply outputs a rotating 1 pattern to a set of eight logic indicators at a speed that enables the rotating pattern to be readily discerned.

2. Devise an interrupt service routine that writes each of the above 256 numbers in turn to a DAC following the arrival of the rising edge of the external oscillator. Include a time-base trigger signal at the start of the output sequence to ensure that the oscilloscope provides a stable trace.

Laboratory Exercise 5.7

Output under Interrupt Control to a Printer

Aim

The aim of this exercise is to interface the computer to a printer using the 'Centronics' type parallel interface.

Introduction

One of the more common peripheral devices that is interfaced to microcomputers is the printer. Since printers are produced by many manufacturers, all of whom desire their printer to be chosen by the user regardless of the brand of microcomputer concerned, it is important that printers conform to a well known and well supported interface standard. One such standard is the Centronics type parallel interface. As it is unlikely that any microcomputer laboratory would have a batch of printers available for use in an interfacing experiment, the present experiment seeks to simulate the behaviour of a Centronics type printer by way of a simple circuit. The circuit generates all the handshaking signals normally generated by the printer while displaying on a seven segment display a series of 'print' characters. A single Centronics type printer could then be substituted for the circuit 'on demand' to test the correctness of the interface in a more realistic manner.

Printers are frequently equipped with input character buffers that allow two or three thousand characters to be transferred from the CPU at high speed to await printing. Brief documents can therefore be sent to the printer without the CPU having to wait for a slow printer to complete its task before moving on to some new task. Longer documents are transferred to the printer in blocks so that again the CPU can be engaged in some useful task while printing is proceeding. Timing diagrams for the printer interface standard are shown in Figure 5.19, first with the printer accepting characters at high speed to fill up the input buffer, and then when the input buffer is full. The Z80 CPU together with the 8255 PPI transmitting characters upon the receipt of an interrupt can handle both of these situations in an identical manner.

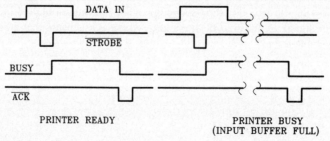

Figure 5.19 Timing diagrams for a Centronics type parallel interface

Upon receipt of an interrupt the PPI outputs the data and generates the data strobe pulse. The printer, or in this case the circuit simulating the printer, generates a BUSY pulse followed by an ACKNOWLEDGE pulse. This latter pulse is then used by the PPI to generate a further interrupt. In this interrupt driven configuration, it does not matter whether the duration of the BUSY pulse is the 500µs period between characters or the indefinite delay that occurs when the input buffer is full and printing is taking place.

Procedure

1. Write a main program that causes the eight logic indicators on the logic trainer to flash in some attractive pattern. Write an interrupt service routine that outputs the hexadecimal numbers 0 through F, while generating a data strobe pulse in accordance with the above specifications.

2. Design and build a circuit comprising a dual monostable flip-flop in which one flip-flop is triggered on the rising edge of the data strobe pulse and remains in this astable state for approximately one second. At the end of this 'printing' period a second monostable is triggered with a delay of 3.5µs representing the acknowledge pulse. This timing is shown in Figure 5.20.

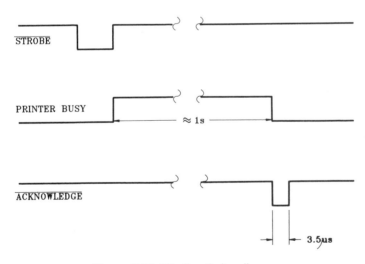

Figure 5.20 Flip-flop timing diagram

Verify the correct operation of this circuit by temporarily reducing the 1s delay period to a few tens of microseconds and observing the resulting waveforms on an oscillocope.

3. To the output port of the PPI, connect a seven-segment decoder driver latch (such as the Fairchild 9368) and a seven-segment display. Latch the output numbers from the PPI into the display using the data strobe signal. Printing is then taking place as each new character appears on the display.

4. Finally, connect a Centronics type printer to the output port and change the 16 hexa-decimal characters to their ASCII equivalents in order to verify the correct operation of your printer interface.

Laboratory Exercise 5.8

Traffic Light Controller

Aim

The aim of this exercise is to design a traffic light controller for a standard intersection, as shown in Figure 5.21.

Introduction

The traffic lights in each direction consist of the standard red, amber and green indicators, plus an indicator for pedestrians to *walk* or *don't walk*. [Note that *don't walk* can be derived from *walk* using an inverter.] These lights are to be driven from a PPI output port operating under interrupt control. A 1 Hz clock signal is available to generate the interrupts to the CPU in order to produce the light sequence and periods in Table 5.1.

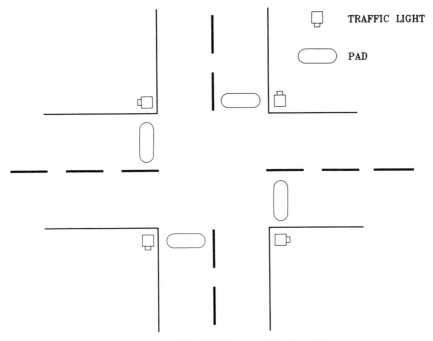

Figure 5.21 Standard intersection layout

Procedure

1. Using six LED logic indicators to represent the six traffic signal lights, write a program that implements the simple 'open loop', or timed system described above.

2. This is not a very good example of the use of interrupts since there is no function to be performed in the time outside interrupt service. Better use can be made of this time by installing four pressure pads in the road to count the number of cars passing along each road in each direction. Imagine that each pressure pad provides a logic high signal while a car is passing over it. Simulate the pressure pads by logic switches connected to a PPI input port and have your main routine collect data on the amount of traffic on each road. After each complete traffic light sequence, print the percent of traffic in each direction in the last five traffic light sequences.

3. The traffic light sequence described above gives each traffic direction an equal share of the available time. Use the data collected in part (2) to vary the share of total time that each road obtains. You should ensure, however, that each road receives not less than 20% of the total time irrespective of traffic conditions.

Table 5.1 Light sequence and periods for laboratory exercise 5.8

Direction 1		Direction 2		Period
RED	DON'T WALK	GREEN	WALK	20
RED	DON'T WALK	GREEN	DON'T WALK	5
RED	DON'T WALK	AMBER	DON'T WALK	3
RED	DON'T WALK	RED	DON'T WALK	3
GREEN	WALK	RED	DON'T WALK	20
GREEN	DON'T WALK	RED	DON'T WALK	5
AMBER	DON'T WALK	RED	DON'T WALK	3
RED	DON'T WALK	RED	DON'T WALK	3

6 The Zilog Z80 PIO and Multi-level Interrupts

In the previous chapter, the three modes of interrupt response of the Z80 CPU were discussed together with the features provided by the Intel 8255 PPI when used in conjunction with interrupting peripherals. The PPI, it will be recalled, handled all the handshaking signals associated with the peripherals and then generated an interrupt request signal that was passed to the CPU when some action by the CPU was required. In the case of several interrupting devices, additional hardware was required to specify exactly which device was demanding attention and at what memory location its interrupt service routine would be found.

A significant improvement in the way in which several interrupting devices of differing priorities may be handled by the Z80 CPU is achieved by the use of another programmable I/O device called the Zilog Z80 PIO. As will be seen in the following sections, the PIO can be loaded with an interrupt vector that allows the CPU to branch to any one of 128 interrupt service routines without additional hardware or the need for device polling.

6.1 THE ZILOG Z80 PIO

The Zilog Z80 Parallel Input/Output device (PIO) provides two 8-bit ports (A and B) with handshaking lines. Each port is controlled by a number of internal registers. A block diagram of the PIO is shown in Figure 6.1 in which the four major sub-sections of the device are clearly evident. Each of these will now be discussed in some detail.

The Microprocessor Interface

Data is transferred between the PIO and the Z80 by way of the data bus (D0-D7) whenever the chip enable signal ($\overline{CE}$) indicates to the PIO that it is being addressed by the Z80 microprocessor. Since each of the PIO ports (port A and port B) has a data register (D) and a control register (C), two signals need to be provided to specify which of the two ports is being addressed (B/$\overline{A}$) and whether it is the control or data register which is being accessed (C/$\overline{D}$). Figure 6.2 shows the microprocessor interface section of the PIO. It is usual to connect the port select line to line A0 of the address bus and the control/data select line to address line A1. When this is done, the two least significant bits of the I/O address specify

169

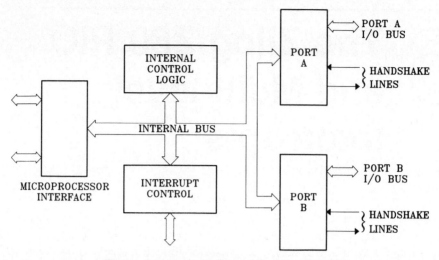

Figure 6.1 Block diagram of the Zilog Z80 PIO

the register to be accessed as, shown in Figure 6.3. The remaining six lines of the I/O address are then combined in the I/O address decoding logic to form the chip enable signal.

The final three signals which make up the microprocessor interface are $\overline{M1}$, $\overline{IORQ}$ and $\overline{RD}$. These signals are identical in name to three of the Z80 CPU signals discussed in Chapter 2. They are used to synchronize the transfer of information between the Z80 and the PIO. Table 6.1 lists the state of each of these lines for the various PIO functions.

Table 6.1 The state of PIO control lines for various functions

$\overline{CE}$	$\overline{M1}$	$\overline{IORQ}$	$\overline{RD}$	OPERATION
x	0	1	1	PIO reset
x	0	0	x	Interrupt Acknowledge Cycle
x	0	1	0	Opcode Fetch Cycle
0	1	0	0	Read from PIO register
0	1	0	1	Write to PIO register

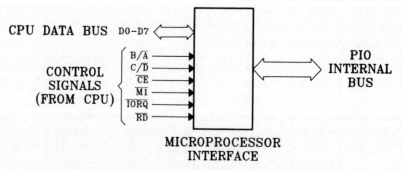

Figure 6.2 Microprocessor interface section of Z80 PIO

A1	A0	FUNCTION
0	0	PORT A DATA
0	1	PORT B DATA
1	0	PORT A CONTROL
1	1	PORT B CONTROL

Figure 6.3 PIO addressing scheme

Note:

1. The PIO is reset when its $\overline{M1}$ input is asserted in the absence of either $\overline{IORQ}$ or $\overline{RD}$. When a reset signal is applied to the Z80 CPU, all three of these control signals are released and so additional external hardware must be provided in order to perform a reset function on the PIO. This topic is discussed in more detail in Chapter 8.

2. The PIO needs to be able to detect interrupt acknowledge cycles and memory opcode fetch cycles because of the way that multi-level interrupts are handled. More will be said about this later in the current chapter.

3. Programmed transfers between the PIO registers and the CPU occur when $\overline{CE}$ and $\overline{IORQ}$ are both asserted. The state of the $\overline{RD}$ signal determines the direction of the transfer while the signals appearing on B/$\overline{A}$ and D/$\overline{C}$ define which port is being accessed and whether the transfer involves a PIO data or control register.

The Interrupt Control Section

The interrupt control section of the PIO involves three signal lines, as shown in Figure 6.4. The interrupt request line ($\overline{INT}$) is asserted by the Z80 PIO whenever it is requesting interrupt service from the Z80 CPU. The interrupt enable in (IEI) and interrupt enable out (IEO) signals are used to define the priority of a particular device when a series of devices are used in a multi-level interrupt application. The use of the PIO in its interrupt mode is discussed in considerable detail later in this chapter.

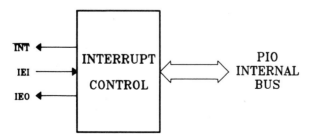

Figure 6.4 Interrupt control section of Zilog PIO

The Peripheral Interface Ports

The PIO provides two 8-bit data ports with appropriate control lines as shown in Figure 6.5. Ports A and B can be used as input ports, output ports and in a so called bit control mode, while port A can also be used in bi-directional mode. When configured into the bit control mode, the Z80 PIO continuously monitors the state of the signals connected to it and generates an interrupt when these signals take on predetermined values. In addition, port B is capable of supplying 1.5 mA @ 1.5V in order to drive Darlington connected transistors for applications which require higher currents. The functions of the four control lines $\overline{ASTB}$, ARDY, $\overline{BSTB}$ and BRDY depend upon the mode into which a particular port is configured as indicated in the following sections. With the exception of bi-directional mode, the functions performed by the port A and port B control signals are identical and so in the discussion which follows only port A will be considered. For the operating modes where either port A or port B could be used, $\overline{STB}$ is used to represent either $\overline{ASTB}$ or $\overline{BSTB}$ while RDY is used to represent either ARDY or BRDY.

Output Mode
The transfer of data from the PIO to the peripheral occurs in accordance with the timing diagram shown in Figure 6.6. When the CPU has written data to the port, the RDY line is asserted to indicate to the peripheral that the port has data ready to be transferred. The peripheral accepts the data by asserting the $\overline{STB}$ line. The rising edge of $\overline{STB}$ is interpreted by the PIO as acknowledgement from the peripheral that it has accepted the data. If the PIO interrupt enable has been set, a CPU interrupt will then be generated to request another byte of data from the Z80 CPU.

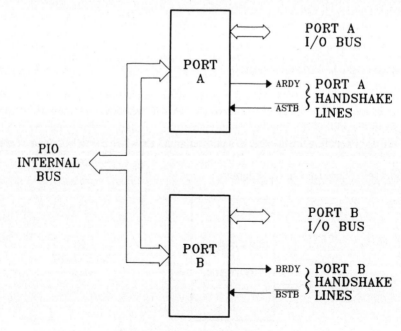

Figure 6.5 The PIO data ports

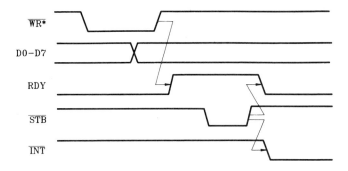

(WR* IS INTERNALLY GENERATED BY THE PIO FROM CE, IORQ AND RD)

Figure 6.6 Output mode data transfer

Input Mode

As shown in Figure 6.7, the transfer of data from the peripheral to the PIO is initiated by the PIO indicating that it can accept data by asserting RDY. The peripheral latches data into the input register of the PIO port using STB. Data is loaded into the PIO when STB is asserted while RDY is released on the rising edge of STB to indicate that the PIO port cannot accept further data. If the PIO interrupt enable has been set, a CPU interrupt is then generated on the rising edge of STB. When the Z80 CPU has read the data latched into the PIO, RDY will again be asserted to indicate that another byte of data can be accepted.

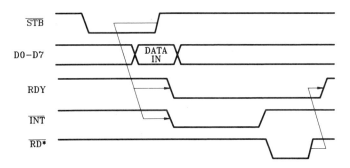

(RD* IS INTERNALLY GENERATED BY THE PIO FROM CE, IORQ AND RD)

Figure 6.7 Input mode data transfer

Control Mode

In Control Mode, neither STB nor RDY are used. The input STB is simply ignored while RDY is forced to the non-asserted state.

Bi-directional Mode

In bi-directional mode, the control lines of both ports A and B are required in order to synchronize bi-directional data transfers through port A. The timing diagram is shown in

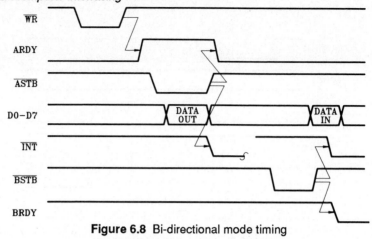

Figure 6.8 Bi-directional mode timing

Figure 6.8. The ASTB and ARDY signals synchronize transfers from port A to the peripheral while BSTB and BRDY synchronize transfers from the peripheral to port A. Each case will be considered separately.

1. Data Output
ARDY is asserted when data is available in the output register of port A. The peripheral device is required to respond by asserting ASTB. This causes the data in the output register to be asserted onto the port data lines. The rising edge of ASTB is used by the PIO as acknowledgment that the peripheral has received the data. A CPU interrupt will then be generated if the PIO interrupt enable flag has been set in order to fetch the next byte of data for transfer to the peripheral.

2. Data Input
BRDY is asserted by the PIO when the port input register is empty. The peripheral responds by latching data into the input register using BSTB. BRDY is released until the Z80 CPU has read the data held in the input register and a CPU interrupt is generated to force the CPU to carry out this read operation. Data is loaded into the port while the BSTB line is asserted and the interrupt is generated following the rising edge of BSTB.

The Internal Control Logic

The internal control logic receives the control words directed to each port and uses them to control the overall functions of the PIO. The control logic performs such functions as synchronizing the operation of each port, setting-up of ports and interrupt logic, determining whether a read or write operation is in progress and determining which port is being addressed.

6.2 ZILOG Z80 PIO PORT OPERATION

Figure 6.9 shows the block diagram of one of the Z80 PIO input/output ports. It can be clearly seen that each port consists of several registers which are used to define the way that the port operates. Each will now be considered briefly.

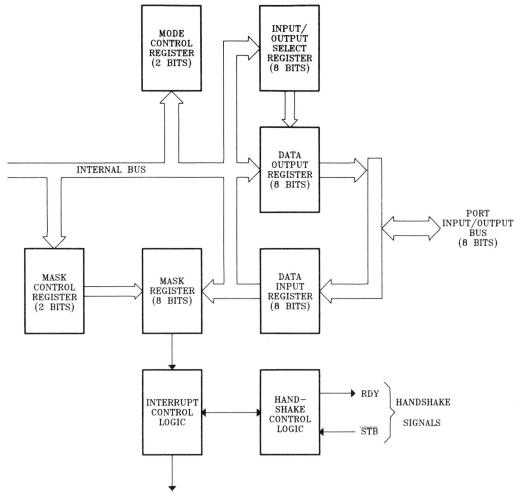

Figure 6.9 Block diagram of PIO input/output port

Mode Control Register

The 2-bit mode control register defines the mode in which a particular port will operate. These modes have already been mentioned in discussing the functions of the port handshake signals. More formally, the four modes of operation of a PIO port are:

Mode 0	Output
Mode 1	Input
Mode 2	Bi-directional (port A only)
Mode 3	Bit Control

The purpose of the first three modes should be clear. The fourth mode (bit control) allows each individual bit of the port to be defined as either an input bit or an output bit. The Z80 can read data through any lines set as inputs and write data to any lines set as outputs. Note that writing data to a line which is defined as an input will have no effect, while reading data from a line defined as an output will result in the last bit written to that line being returned. In addition, an interrupt can be generated if any input bit goes to a predefined level or if several inputs are all at some predefined level. The situations where interrupts will occur in this way are defined during port initialization. This mode of operation is particularly useful in applications where it is desirable that the microprocessor system monitor some operation. The PIO can be programmed to generate an interrupt if a specified condition is detected.

Input/Output Select Register

This 8-bit register defines whether a port line is an input or an output during mode 3 operation. It is programmed during initialization of the PIO.

Mask Register

The 8-bit mask register defines which lines will be monitored by the PIO during mode 3 operation. Monitored lines can cause the PIO to generate an interrupt when all are asserted or when any one is asserted as defined during PIO initialization.

Mask Control Register

The 2-bit mask control register is used during mode 3 operation to define whether all monitored input signal lines or any one monitored input signal line is able to generate an interrupt when asserted. Further, it defines the assertion level (i.e asserted high or asserted low) of the port data lines to be monitored. It is defined as part of the PIO initialization procedure.

Data Input, Data Output Registers and Handshake Control Logic

All data transfers between the PIO and a peripheral device occur via these registers. The Z80 can write data into the data output register or read data from the data input register at any time. As has already been demonstrated, the transfer of data between the PIO and a peripheral is synchronized by the port handshaking signals. The last block in Figure 6.9 is the interrupt control logic. The question of using the PIO under interrupt control is discussed a little later.

6.3 PROGRAMMING THE Z80 PIO FOR BASIC INPUT/ OUTPUT

Programming the PIO for simple, non-interrupt driven I/O requires the user to define the mode in which each port is to be used. This can be done by sending a single byte of information (called the mode control word) to the control register of each port. If mode 3

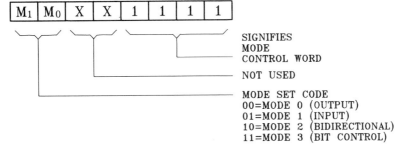

Figure 6.10 Format of mode control word

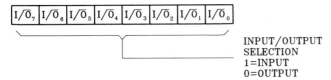

Figure 6.11 Format of input or output selection word for mode 3 operation

operation is selected (i.e. bit control mode), then a second byte of information must be supplied to define whether each port data line is an input or an output line. The format of the mode control word is shown in Figure 6.10.

The two most significant bits (D7 and D6) define the operating mode while the bit pattern 1111 in the least significant four bits identifies the word as a mode control word to the internal control logic of the PIO. If mode 3 operation is chosen, the next control word sent to the PIO port must define which lines are inputs and which are outputs. The format is shown in Figure 6.11. Thus, setting a bit to one defines it as an input while setting a bit to zero defines it as an output. Note that when a read operation is performed from a port set to mode 3, the data read will consist of input data from those port lines which are defined as inputs plus the contents of the output register for those lines defined as outputs.

Example 6.1

A PIO occupies the I/O addresses shown below. Write a segment of code which will initialize the PIO with port A as an input port and port B in bit control mode with data lines 0,1,4 and 5 as inputs and the remainder as outputs.

I/O Address	Function
80H	Port A Data
81H	Port B Data
82H	Port A Control
83H	Port B Control

Solution

The control words need to be defined first. For port A and port B, the mode control words are shown in Figure 6.12. The other control word to be defined is used to determine which lines in port B are inputs and which are outputs. This is shown in Figure 6.13.

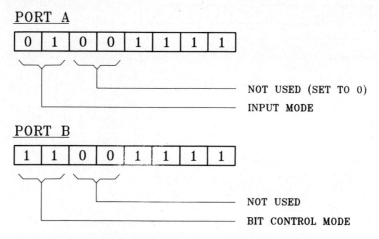

Figure 6.12 Mode control words for Example 6.1

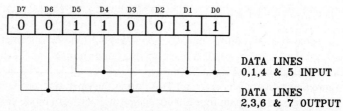

Figure 6.13 Port B input/output definition for Example 6.1

An example of a simple code segment to carry out the PIO initialization is given below.

```
PORTA    EQU    080H        ; Port A Data
PORTB    EQU    081H        ; Port B Data
CNTLA    EQU    082H        ; Port A Control
CNTLB    EQU    083H        ; Port B Control
MODEA    EQU    04FH        ; Port A Input
MODEB    EQU    0CFH        ; Port B Bit Control
IOB      EQU    033H        ; Bits 0,1,4 & 5 Input
;
         LD     A,MODEA
         OUT    (CNTLA),A    ;Define port A
         LD     A,MODEB
         OUT    (CNTLB),A    ;Define port B
         LD     A,IOB
         OUT    (CNTLB),A    ;Set I/O lines
```

6.4 THE ZILOG Z80 PIO UNDER INTERRUPT CONTROL

When used in conjunction with interrupts, the PIO is designed to make use of the Z80

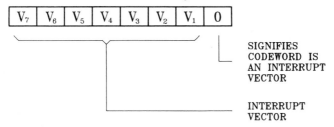

Figure 6.14 Format for loading interrupt vector

interrupt mode 2 response. In Chapter 5, it was shown that when the Z80 is operating in this mode, it expects to receive an 8-bit byte from the interrupting device, which, when combined with the contents of its own I register, will point to a pair of memory locations within a preset table of vectors, at which the address of the interrupt service routine of the interrupting device will be found.

The Z80 PIO provides a special register in each port into which can be loaded the vector to be placed onto the data bus during an interrupt acknowledge cycle for an interrupt generated by that port. The format of the required control word needed to load the interrupt vector is shown in Figure 6.14. The logic 0 in the least significant bit of the control word uniquely identifies it to the PIO internal control logic as an interrupt vector. The fact that the last bit of the interrupt vector must always be a zero does not represent a limitation as the Z80 CPU assumes that each interrupt service routine address will start at an even location (i.e. the least significant bit of the 16-bit address must always be a logic 0). During an interrupt acknowledge cycle for an interrupt from that port, the 8-bit byte of data placed onto the data bus will be in exactly the format shown in Figure 6.14.

Even with a single PIO, a separate interrupt can occur from each port. With more than one PIO, the possibilities for several interrupts increases. Thus, when an interrupt acknowledge cycle is underway, each port needs some method of determining whether the interrupt acknowledge cycle applies to it or not. This function is carried out by the interrupt priority daisy chain formed by the signals IEI and IEO mentioned briefly in Section 6.1. Figure 6.15 shows the daisy chain connection of the IEI and IEO lines for three PIOs. Notice also the internal connection of the IEI and IEO signals. Before a port will generate an interrupt, it first checks the state of the IEI signal. If IEI is asserted (logic 1), the port will proceed to generate the interrupt and will set IEO to the non-asserted (logic 0) level. If IEI is not asserted, the port will not generate an interrupt immediately but will continue to monitor the IEI line and will generate an interrupt when IEI next becomes asserted.

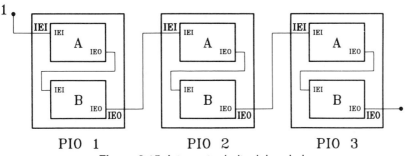

Figure 6.15 Interrupt priority daisy chain

Referring again to Figure 6.15, port A of PIO1 will always see IEI asserted and so will be able to generate an interrupt whenever it has an interrupt request pending. It is therefore the highest priority interrupt. Port B of PIO1 will be able to generate an interrupt whenever it has an interrupt request pending, providing that port A of PIO1 has no interrupt pending nor is it receiving interrupt service. It is therefore the second highest priority port. Continuing the argument, it is clear that the interrupt priority continues port A of PIO2, port B of PIO2, port A of PIO3 and port B of PIO3.

It is important to note also that under this scheme, a higher priority device will be able to interrupt the interrupt service routine of a lower priority device, providing that the Z80 has re-enabled its internal interrupt enable flip-flop. An example of this will be considered a little later.

When an interrupt acknowledge cycle is under way, each port checks two conditions. These are:

1. whether the port has an interrupt request pending;
2. whether the IEI signal to the port is asserted.

Only the highest priority interrupting port will satisfy both of these conditions and this port will place its interrupt vector onto the data bus. Figure 6.16 shows the timing diagram for an interrupt from the PIO. Notice in particular that the IEO signal goes to the non-asserted level in parallel with the port requesting an interrupt.

This scheme provides for the highest of several levels of interrupting devices to generate an interrupt and will permit a higher priority device to interrupt a lower priority one. A mechanism is needed to allow an interrupting port to realize that its interrupt service routine is complete thus causing it to reassert the IEO signal and so allow lower level devices to again generate interrupts. The PIO achieves this function by monitoring all opcode fetches on the

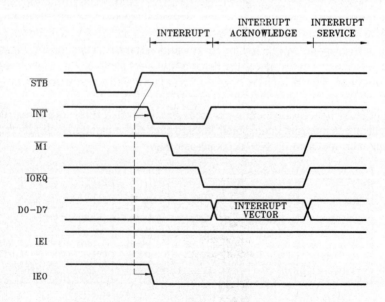

Figure 6.16 Timing diagram for a PIO interrupt

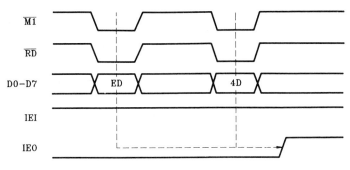

Figure 6.17 Timing diagram for PIO return from interrupt

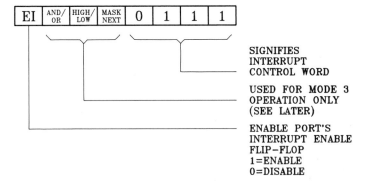

Figure 6.18 Format of interrupt control word

data bus, as indicated by $\overline{M1}$ and $\overline{RD}$ being asserted, and detecting a return from interrupt
(**RETI**) instruction. When a PIO port sees a **RETI** instruction (a 2-byte opcode EDH followed
by 4DH), it checks to see if it currently has IEI high and IEO low. If it does, it must be the
device being serviced and, as its interrupt service routine is now complete, it can re-assert
IEO. Figure 6.17 shows the timing diagram of an interrupting port upon detection of a return
from interrupt instruction.

When a return from interrupt instruction is executed, the next highest port with an
interrupt request will either commence (if it has not yet generated an interrupt) or resume (if
it was interrupted by the higher priority interrupt) interrupt service. It will hold its IEO line
low to ensure that lower priority devices will not generate an interrupt. The PIO is only able
to generate an interrupt if it has had its internal interrupt enable flip-flop set. This is done by
sending an interrupt control word to the appropriate PIO port. The format of the interrupt
control word is shown in Figure 6.18. Thus setting the most significant bit of the interrupt
control word will enable the internal interrupt enable flip-flop of a particular port. The next
three bits are used when bit control mode is selected; these will be discussed further in a
subsequent section. The last four bits identify the control word to the PIO internal control
logic as an interrupt control word.

It is possible to clear any pending interrupt from a PIO port by setting bit 4 (the mask
next bit) in the interrupt control word. It is then necessary, however, to send a mask word
to the control register of that port regardless of whether the port needs a mask or not. If it is

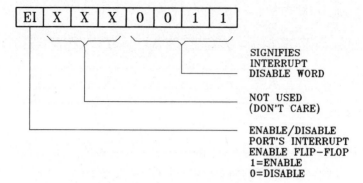

Figure 6.19 Format of interrupt disable word

required only to change the state of the PIO port's interrupt enable flip-flop, then this may be achieved using the interrupt disable word shown in Figure 6.19. Using this control word avoids any problems with masks and other features of mode 3 operation.

Port Initialization

It is now appropriate to consider the steps which must be taken in using the PIO under interrupts. The discussions will be divided according to the mode of the port under consideration.

Mode 0 - Output
After a reset operation, the port RDY line will be released. When the Z80 CPU writes a word to the output register, RDY will be asserted and so indicate to the peripheral that data is available. An output cycle can then proceed as discussed in Section 6.1.

Mode 1 - Input
After a reset operation, the port RDY line will be released. In order to start information transfer, therefore, the Z80 CPU must perform a 'dummy' read operation so that the RDY line to the peripheral becomes asserted so as to inform the peripheral that the PIO is able to accept a byte of data. Normal input cycles can then proceed as described earlier in this chapter.

Mode 2 - Bi-directional
Bi-directional mode is really a combination of Modes 0 and 1 using all four control lines as well as the eight I/O lines of port A. Output cycles can begin as soon as the CPU writes a byte of data to the PIO port while a 'dummy' read is required to correctly set the PIO for input operations.

Mode 3 - Bit Control
This mode is primarily intended for monitoring and control applications. The first control word after the mode control word which sets the port to mode 3 must be an input or output

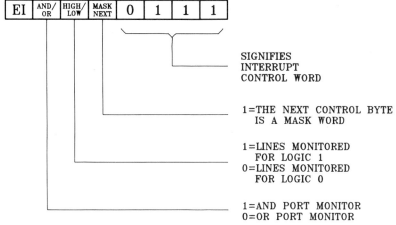

Figure 6.20 Format of interrupt control word

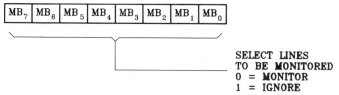

Figure 6.21 Format of mask word

selection word as shown in Figure 6.11. An interrupt can be generated when one or more of the port data lines go to a predefined state. This is defined when the interrupt control word is sent to the port. For convenience, Figure 6.20 again shows the format of the interrupt control word. Bit 4 informs the PIO port that the next control word received will define the lines to be monitored for generating an interrupt. Its format is shown in Figure 6.21. Only those lines with a logic zero in the mask bit will be monitored. It is worth mentioning again at this point that setting bit 4 of the interrupt control word will cause any pending interrupt from the port to be reset.

Bit 6 of the interrupt control word defines whether all input lines being monitored have to go to a given level before an interrupt is generated (the AND condition) or whether any one monitored input must go to a given level before an interrupt is generated (the OR condition). Bit 5 defines whether pins are to be monitored for a logic high or a logic low condition.

6.5 PROGRAMMING THE Z80 TO HANDLE MULTI-LEVEL INTERRUPTS

Various registers both within the CPU and the PIO together with specific memory locations must be initialized before a multi-level interrupt application can be commenced. It has already been shown that the following control words need to be sent to each port of the PIO:

1. mode control word (plus input/output selection word if mode 3 operation);

2. interrupt vector;
3. interrupt control word (plus mask if mode 3 operation and if called for by the interrupt control word).

The additional initialization procedures which the Z80 must perform are described briefly below.

Define the Position in Memory of the Table of Vectors

The table of vectors should preferably start on a 256 byte boundary (i.e. address xy00H). Imagine the situation where the table of vectors commences at location 13FEH. The memory locations containing the address of the first interrupt service routine would then be 13FEH and 13FFH (and so the I register must contain 13H). The memory locations containing the next interrupt service routine address would be 1400H and 1401H (and so the I register must contain 14H). The fact that the I register must be loaded with a constant value means that this situation cannot be allowed. By forcing the table of vectors to commence on a 256 byte boundary, up to 128 interrupting devices can be accommodated under Z80 interrupt mode 2. A single line of code which will locate the label IVCTR on the next available 256 byte boundary is

```
IVCTR        EQU      ((($/256)+1)*256)
```

where $ is the symbol representing the value of the location counter to the assembler. If:

$$\begin{aligned}
\$ &= 1325\text{H} \\
\text{then} \quad (\$/256) &= 13\text{H} \\
((\$/256) +1) &= 14\text{H} \\
(((\$/256) +1) *256) &= 1400\text{H} \quad \text{as required.}
\end{aligned}$$

Load the I Register with the Most Significant 8-Bits of the Address of the Table of Vectors

If IVCTR has been determined in the way described above then the I register can be loaded by the two lines of code shown below.

```
LD       A,IVCTR/256
LD       I,A
```

Load the Table of Vectors with the Starting Addresses of All Interrupt Service Routines

If there are three interrupting devices with starting addresses defined by the labels AISR,

BISR and CISR then a code segment to load the table of vectors (with starting address defined by IVCTR) is shown.

```
LD      HL,AISR
LD      (IVCTR),HL
LD      HL,BISR
LD      (IVCTR+2),HL
LD      HL,CISR
LD      (IVCTR+4),HL
```

This code will automatically place the interrupt service routines into the table of vectors in the correct, byte swapped (i.e. least significant byte first) order.

Set the Interrupt Mode to Mode 2

This is achieved simply using the following instruction:

```
IM      2
```

Enable Interrupts

An enable interrupt (EI) instruction must be executed by the Z80 before interrupts will be accepted. In a multi-level interrupt environment, however, there is another aspect which must be considered. If a higher priority device is to be able to interrupt a lower priority device, then the Z80 interrupt enable must be set. As the internal interrupt enable flip-flop is disabled when an interrupt is accepted by the CPU, interrupts must be re-enabled in the interrupt service routine. In fact, there is no reason why the very first instruction of the interrupt service routine should not be an enable interrupt instruction. This will mean that interrupts will be disabled for the execution of only two instructions (the enable interrupt instruction and its immediate successor). Strictly, it is not necessary to re-enable interrupts for the highest priority device as its interrupt service routine can never be interrupted. An enable interrupt would, of course, be necessary at the end of the interrupt service routine. However, as the PIO port which is communicating with this device cannot generate another interrupt request until the current one has been concluded by a return from interrupt instruction, there is no reason not to be consistent and begin all routines with an enable interrupt.

In a multi-level interrupt environment, it is possible that interrupt service routines will be interrupted by higher priority interrupts and then be resumed after those interrupts on a fairly frequent basis. It is important, therefore, to ensure that the interrupt service routine for one device does not affect the execution of the interrupt service routine of another device. At the very least, each interrupt service routine should save the contents of all the registers used in its execution. Providing that adequate space has been left, this information can most conveniently be stored on the stack. An example of the starting and concluding statements of a typical interrupt service routine is shown as follows:

```
AISR:       EI                      ; re-enable interrupts
            PUSH    AF              ; save registers
            PUSH    BC
            PUSH    DE
            PUSH    HL
                    :
                    :               ;perform interrupt
                    :               ;service
                    :
            POP     HL              ;restore registers
            POP     DE
            POP     BC
            POP     AF
            RETI                    ;return from interrupt
```

6.6 EXAMPLES

This chapter concludes with three examples of the software required to configure the Z80 and a single Z80 PIO for a multi-level interrupt task.

Example 6.2

The PIO, located at the addresses given in Example 6.1, is to be used under interrupt control, with port A working in input mode and port B in output mode. Write a code segment to configure the system to perform this task.

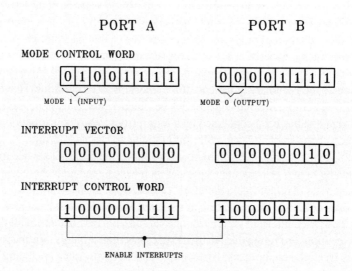

Figure 6.22 Control words for Example 6.2

Solution

Determination of Control Words
Figure 6.22 shows the mode control word, interrupt vector and interrupt control word. It is assumed that only two interrupting devices are being used in this system and so interrupt vectors of 00H and 02H have been chosen.

Z80 Software
A possible initialization procedure is given as follows:

```
PORTA    EQU    080H            ; Port A Data
PORTB    EQU    081H            ; Port B Data
CNTLA    EQU    082H            ; Port A Control
CNTLB    EQU    083H            ; Port B Control
MODEA    EQU    04FH            ; Port A Input Mode
MODEB    EQU    0FH             ; Port B Output Mode
IVECA    EQU    00H             ; Port A Interrupt Vector
IVECB    EQU    02H             ; Port B Interrupt Vector
ICWA     EQU    087H            ; Port A Enable Interrupt
ICWB     EQU    087H            ; Port B Enable Interrupt
;
START:   LD     SP,STACK
;
;               PIO INITIALIZATION
;
         LD     A,MODEA
         OUT    (CNTLA),A       ;Port A input
         LD     A,MODEB
         OUT    (CNTLB),A       ;Port B output
         LD     A,IVECA
         OUT    (CNTLA),A       ;Port A interrupt vector
         LD     A,IVECB
         OUT    (CNTLB),A       ;Port B interrupt vector
         LD     A,ICWA
         OUT    (CNTLA),A       ;Port A int. enable
         LD     A,ICWB
         OUT    (CNTLB),A       ;Port B int. enable
         IN     A,(PORTA)       ;Dummy read to set ARDY
;
;               Z80 INITIALIZATION
;
         IM     2               ;Interrupt Mode 2
         LD     A,IVCTR/256
         LD     I,A             ;Set I register
         LD     HL,AISR
         LD     (IVCTR),HL      ;A ISR address to table
         LD     HL,BISR
         LD     (IVCTR+2),HL    ;B ISR address to table
         EI
;
;               MAIN ROUTINE
```

```
;
                              :
                              :
                              :
                              :
;
;                   INTERRUPT SERVICE ROUTINE FOR PORT A
;
AISR:       EI
            PUSH    AF
            PUSH    BC
            PUSH    DE
            PUSH    HL
                    :
                    :
                    :
                    :
            POP     HL
            POP     DE
            POP     BC
            POP     AF
            RETI
;
;                   INTERRUPT SERVICE ROUTINE FOR PORT B
;
BISR:       EI
            PUSH    AF
            PUSH    BC
            PUSH    DE
            PUSH    HL
                    :
                    :
                    :
                    :
            POP     HL
            POP     DE
            POP     BC
            POP     AF
            RETI
;
            DEFS    40H                 ;Save space for stack
STACK:      DEFB    00H
;
IVCTR       EQU     (((($/256)+1)* 256)
            END
```

Example 6.3

Again, using the PIO of the previous two examples, write a code segment which will configure port A as a bi-directional port operating under interrupt control.

Solution

The configuration of the Z80 will be identical to Example 6.2. The A interrupt service routine (AISR) will handle the output of data to the bi-directional port while the B interrupt service routine (BISR) will handle input. As the code is identical to Example 6.2, it is not necessary to repeat it here. There are, however, differences in the PIO control words so attention is focused on that aspect.

Determination of Control Words
Figure 6.23 shows the control words for this application. The following points need special emphasis:

1. When port A is operating in bi-directional mode, port B must be set to bit control mode to free the lines BRDY and $\overline{\text{BSTB}}$ for use by port A.

2. As port B is set to bit control mode, the next control byte sent to the PIO must define which lines are inputs and which are outputs. No information is specified in the example on this point and so all have been set as inputs.

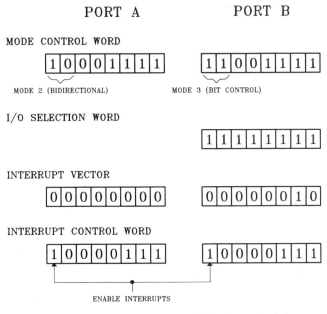

Figure 6.23 PIO control words for Example 6.3

Z80 Software

A possible code segment to initialize the PIO for this application is shown as follows:

```
        PORTA     EQU     080H        ; Port A Data
        PORTB     EQU     081H        ; Port B Data
        CNTLA     EQU     082H        ; Port A Control
        CNTLB     EQU     083H        ; Port B Control
        MODEA     EQU     08FH        ; Port A Bi-directional
        MODEB     EQU     0CFH        ; Port B Bit Control
        IOREGB    EQU     0FFH        ; All port B lines Input
        IVECA     EQU     00H         ; Port A Interrupt Vector
        IVECB     EQU     02H         ; Port B Interrupt Vector
        ICWA      EQU     087H        ; Enable Interrupt port A
        ICWB      EQU     087H        ; Enable Interrupt port B
        ;
        ;                 PIO INITIALIZATION
        ;
        LD        A,MODEA
        OUT       (CNTLA),A           ;Port A Bi-directional
        LD        A,MODEB
        OUT       (CNTLB),A           ;Port B Bit Control
        LD        A,IOREGB
        OUT       (CNTLB),A           ;All port B inputs
        LD        A,IVECA
        OUT       (CNTLA),A           ;Port A Interrupt Vector
        LD        A,IVECB
        OUT       (CNTLB),A           ;Port B Interrupt Vector
        LD        A,ICWA
        OUT       (CNTA),A            ;Port A Int. enable
        LD        A,ICWB
        OUT       (CNTLB),A           ;Port B Int. enable
        IN        A,(PORTB)           ;Dummy read to set BRDY
```

Example 6.4

The PIO of the previous examples is to be configured with both port A and port B used in bit control mode under interrupt control. Port A is to generate an interrupt if data lines 0, 1 and 3 are all high while port B is to generate an interrupt if either line 4 or line 5 or line 6 or line 7 is asserted low. All other port lines are to be used as outputs. Determine the code needed to correctly configure the Z80 system to perform this task.

Solution

Again, the Z80 initialization is identical to Example 6.2 and so once again, attention need only be given to the initialization of the PIO (Figure 6.24). The points to be noted on this occasion are:

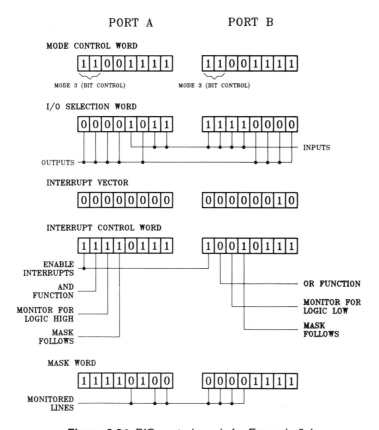

Figure 6.24 PIO control words for Example 6.4

1. since both ports are operating in mode 3, both require an I/O register control word;
2. both ports demand a mask control word by setting bit 4 in the interrupt control word. Strictly speaking, mask control words are not required in this application as, in both cases, all input lines are monitored for interrupts. They are, however, included for completeness.

Z80 Software

A possible code segment to initialize the PIO for this application is shown as follows:

```
PORTA    EQU    080H        ; Port A Data
PORTB    EQU    081H        ; Port B Data
CNTLA    EQU    082H        ; Port A Control
CNTLB    EQU    083H        ; Port B Control
MODEA    EQU    0CFH        ; Port A Bit Control
MODEB    EQU    0CFH        ; Port B Bit Control
IOREGA   EQU    00BH        ; Bits 0, 1 & 3 Inputs
IOREGB   EQU    0F0H        ; Bits 4, 5, 6 & 7 Inputs
```

```
IVECA       EQU     00H             ; Interrupt Vector port A
IVECB       EQU     02H             ; Interrupt Vector port B
ICWA        EQU     0F7H            ; Interrupt Control Word port A
ICWB        EQU     097H            ; Interrupt Control Word port B
MASKA       EQU     0F4H            ; Monitor Bits 0,1 & 3
MASKB       EQU     0FH             ; Monitor Bits 4,5,6 & 7
;
;                   PIO INITIALIZATION
;
            LD      A,MODEA
            OUT     (CNTLA),A       ;Port A Bit Control
            LD      A,IOREGA
            OUT     (CNTLA),A       ;Bits 0,1 & 3 inputs
            LD      A,MODEB
            OUT     (CNTLB),A       ;Port B Bit Control
            LD      A,IOREGB
            OUT     (CNTLB),A       ;Bits 4, 5, 6 & 7 inputs
            LD      A,IVECA
            OUT     (CNTLA),A       ;Port A interrupt vector
            LD      A,IVECB
            OUT     (CNTLB),A       ;Port B interrupt vector
            LD      A,ICWA
            OUT     (CNTLA),A       ;Port A int. control
            LD      A,MASKA
            OUT     (CNTLA),A       ;Monitor bits 0,1 & 3
            LD      A,ICWB
            OUT     (CNTLB),A       ;Port B int. control
            LD      A,MASKB
            OUT     (CNTLB),A       ;Monitor bits 4,5,6 & 7
```

PROBLEMS

Problem 6.1
Draw a table which shows the state (logic 0, logic 1 or don't care) of the six microprocessor interface control lines of a Z80 PIO (i.e. B/$\overline{A}$, C/$\overline{D}$, $\overline{CE}$, $\overline{M1}$, $\overline{IORQ}$ and $\overline{RD}$) during the following operations:
(a) a memory read cycle;
(b) a memory write cycle;
(c) a data read from port A of the PIO;
(d) a write to the port B control register;
(e) an interrupt acknowledge cycle;
(f) a hardware generated PIO internal reset.

Problem 6.2
A PIO port operating under interrupt control is to receive data from an ADC with a conversion time of 10µs. Design an interface between the PIO and the ADC to correctly synchronize the transfer using the RDY and $\overline{STB}$ signals.

Problem 6.3
It is desired to read data from a ROM into the memory of a Z80 system. The ROM address data comes from a counter which in turn is driven by an oscillator, as shown in Figure 6.25. Complete the hardware design which will allow data to be transferred to the Z80 via a PIO

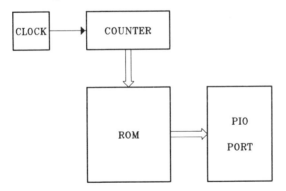

Figure 6.25 Hardware set up for Problem 6.3

port operating under interrupt control. Give careful consideration to the generation of the $\overline{STB}$ signal which is necessary to make the PIO port generate an interrupt.

Problem 6.4
The system described in Problem 6.3 will fail to operate correctly if the oscillator period is less than the time required for the Z80 system to fetch and store the ROM data byte. Develop a different hardware configuration making use of the PIO RDY line rather than an external oscillator to increment the counter.

Problem 6.5

A single PIO is used in a two-level interrupt application. Both ports are configured in mode 1 (input) and it can be assumed that both interrupt enable flip-flops are set and that each interrupt service routine begins with an enable interrupt (**EI**) instruction. The Z80 is initially executing the main program (i.e. not an interrupt service routine). Determine the interrupt being executed after each of the following chain of events:

(a) A byte of data is strobed into port B.
(b) A byte of data is strobed into port A.
(c) A second byte of data is strobed into port B.
(d) A second byte of data is strobed into port A.
(e) A third byte of data is strobed into port A.
(f) The current interrupt service routine finishes.
(g) The current interrupt service routine finishes.
(h) The current interrupt service routine finishes.
(i) The current interrupt service routine finishes.

Assume that, between each of these events there is sufficient time for the appropriate interrupt service routine to read the data held in the port.

Problem 6.6

A PIO is physically located on a different card to the CPU card which contains the Z80 microprocessor and 64Kbytes of RAM. When data from local memory is fetched by the Z80, it does not appear on the backplane which links the PIO card and the CPU card. Explain why the PIO cannot be used in interrupt mode. How can this problem be overcome?

Problem 6.7

A single PIO is to operate under interrupt control with port A in input mode and port B in bit control mode. Port B is to monitor three asserted low lines (D0,D1 and D2) and generate an interrupt when any one is asserted. Bit D4 of port B is also an input while the remainder of port B is used as output bits. Write the Z80 code necessary to correctly configure both the Z80 and the PIO ports for this task.

Problem 6.8

The three PIOs shown in Figure 6.15 are to be configured as follows:

1A	Bit control mode (interrupt if D7 or D6 is asserted high)
1B	Input mode
2A	Bi-directional mode
3A	Output mode
3B	Bit control mode (interrupt if D0, D4 and D5 are asserted low)

The user also requires another seven bits of input and six bits of output for miscellaneous purposes. Develop the Z80 code necessary to initialize the Z80 and the PIOs to perform this function. Include with your solution a diagram listing the function of each PIO port I/O line.

Laboratory Exercise 6.1

Data Acquisition under Interrupt

Aim

The aim of this experiment is to acquire 256 samples of an input waveform at a rate determined by an external oscillator. The samples are to be stored in memory for subsequent display on an oscilloscope.

Introduction

In this laboratory exercise, 256 samples of an input analog waveform are to be acquired from an analog to digital convertor (ADC) and stored in memory. The ADC is to derive its start of conversion pulse from an oscillator while the BUSY/READY output is to be used to generate an interrupt. This mode of operation allows samples to be acquired at precisely regular intervals, especially if the oscillator is crystal controlled. This is difficult to achieve if the start pulses are to be produced by the microcomputer. The main program, which the CPU will execute unless interrupted, is a routine which will display the contents of the memory in which the 256 samples are stored. Initially, this should be filled with the numbers 0 to 255 in consecutive locations, which will give rise to a sawtooth waveform.

Procedure

1. Write and test the main program which loads the 256 locations in memory with the numbers 0 to 255 and displays them continuously via a digital to analog convertor (DAC) on the oscilloscope. Use port B of the PIO to output the waveform values. Provide an oscilloscope trigger pulse that activates the time-base at the start of each display sequence. This will have to be done by using another PIO or, alternatively, a PPI port since port A of the PIO will be needed for data input.

2. Write an interrupt service routine which will acquire and store in the next location of the display buffer a sample from the ADC each time an interrupt is generated. After 256 values have been acquired, data acquisition is to stop.

3. Modify the main program so that at the end of each display sequence, the state of a push-button is monitored and data acquisition recommenced if the button is pressed. Again, the button will need to be monitored through another PIO or via a PPI.

4. Improve the system described in the previous section so that the switch is monitored by a PIO port in bit control mode. Upon detecting a logic high, the interrupt service routine for this port should cause reacquisition of data.

5. Further modify your program so that the display 'drifts' across the screen at a rate determined by the sampling rate of the ADC. In this mode of operation, data acquisition should be continuous (i.e. acquire 256 locations and then recommence data acquisition to the first buffer location, etc.). A point on the display will move from the right-hand side of the screen to the left-hand side after 256 samples. This is the so called 'roll mode' of operation used in intensive care wards to monitor heart beat and can be achieved by appropriate placement of the oscilloscope trigger pulse in each display cycle.

Laboratory Exercise 6.2

Signal Averaging under Interrupt

Aim

The aim of this experiment is to perform signal averaging on a noisy waveform and hence produce a replica of the waveform for which the signal to noise ratio has been improved.

Introduction

Signal averaging is a technique whereby many repetitions of a noisy waveform are added together in phase. The amplitude of the desired signal progressively builds up whereas the noise amplitude diminishes due to the canceling out of random fluctuations. The aim of this experiment is to perform signal averaging on a noisy waveform and hence produce a replica of the waveform for which the signal to noise ratio has been improved.

The requirement of phase coherence is crucial to the success of the method and this limits the type of experiment to which signal averaging may be applied. One class of experiment for which the technique is particularly suited is that in which a system is subjected to a stimulus (say a flash of light) and then the response, (e.g. the resulting fluorescence) occurs a known time later. The responses, which are to be subjected to averaging, may be aligned in phase simply by their time relationship to the stimulus that caused them. In this case, life will be made easy by using a signal generator that provides a second, digital output locked in phase to the main analog output. So that the experiment works in a realistic manner, it is first necessary to add noise to the analog output of the signal generator and then see to what extent the signal averaging can recover the original signal.

The noisy waveform, together with an in-phase 'stimulus signal' may be produced using the circuit given in Figure 6.26. The pseudo-random binary sequence generator (PRBSG) can be produced using a shift register. A pack of exclusive OR gates as shown in Figure 6.27.

The PRBSG produces a series of 8-bit words in an apparently random fashion. These are applied to the DAC which then produces a noise-like analog signal. Addition of this noise signal to the sinusoidal output from the signal generator using the three resistors shown results in the noisy sine wave that acts as the input to the averaging system.

Procedure

1. Generate the noisy signal in the method described above. Adjust the amplitudes of the noise and sine wave to give a signal to noise ratio of approximately 0 dB and a peak amplitude below the full scale conversion input of the ADC.

2. Set the frequency of the signal generator to 2 Hz and, under interrupt control, sample the waveform at approximately 100 samples per second until 256 sample points have

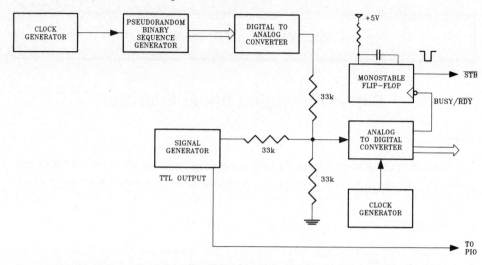

Figure 6.26 Generation of noisy input signal for Laboratory Exercise 6.2

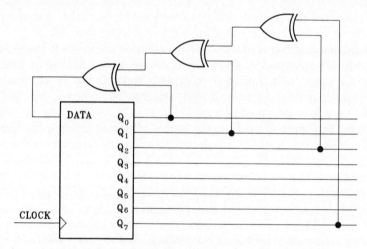

Figure 6.27 Pseudo-random binary sequence generator

been acquired. Display the acquired waveform on an oscilloscope at a rate that provides a bright, flicker-free trace. Arrangements should be made to ensure that the oscilloscope is provided with a time-base trigger pulse at the start of each display sweep. As one PIO port will be used to input the data under interrupt while the other is used for (non-interrupt driven) output, another PIO or a PPI will be required to generate this trigger pulse.

3. Repeat the burst of sampling a further 255 times adding the new sampled value to the previous summed total for each of the 256 sample points. By monitoring the digital output of the oscillator (again via another PIO or a PPI), ensure that you are adding samples together in phase. Determine the average value for each of the 256 data points and display this average on the oscilloscope.

4. At this stage, the signal averaging experiment is performing its designated task. It is, however, 'unfriendly' from the user's point of view. For example, it will take several minutes to acquire all the data for the averaging process during which time no output is being generated to inform the user that:

(a) everything is progressing well;
(b) the microprocessor has completed $x\%$ of the task.

Modify your program to provide regular 'bulletins' to the user as to the stage in the signal processing which has been reached.

5. Further modify your program so that a 'running average' of the processed waveform is displayed on the oscilloscope during the acquisition phase. This can be done in one of two ways:

(a) by continuously dividing the progressive sum in memory by 256 and thus watch the output waveform slowing grow from zero;
(b) by dividing the waveform by the number of acquisition cycles completed. This is more difficult (and a little slower) but far more dramatic as the noise can be seen to slowly diminish, leaving the desired signal.

Laboratory Exercise 6.3

Introduction to Multi-Level Interrupts

Aim

This experiment aims to introduce the use of multi-level interrupts by using manual push buttons to initiate each level of interrupt and the keyboard to terminate each interrupt service routine. By these means, the user can control the state of the multi-level interrupts.

Procedure

1. Connect two asserted low debounced push-button switches to the Z80 PIO $\overline{\text{ASTB}}$ and $\overline{\text{BSTB}}$ lines. Configure both ports as input ports and initialize them for interrupt response. Connect another PIO or PPI port to a series of eight LEDs. The main program is to cause the LEDs to be illuminated sequentially, one at a time.

2. Write the main program which will cause one LED at a time to be illuminated sequentially.

3. Add an interrupt service routine for each of the switches. When an interrupt is serviced, the interrupt service routine should:

   (a) print the message 'INTERRUPT FROM PORT A' or 'INTERRUPT FROM PORT B' as appropriate.
   (b) continue to print the letter A or B corresponding to the port whose interrupt is being serviced.
   (c) monitor the keyboard via a routine which indicates whether a key has been typed. The A interrupt service routine will be terminated by typing the letter A while the B interrupt service routine will be terminated by typing the letter B. If the appropriate letter is not typed then the processor will continue to print the letter corresponding to the interrupt being serviced.

   The screen should therefore look as shown below after the following events:

   (a) Generate level B interrupt.
   (b) Generate level A interrupt.
   (c) Level A interrupt terminated.

   INTERRUPT PORT B BBBBBBBBBBBBBBBBBBBBBBBBBBB
   INTERRUPT PORT A AAAAAAAAAAAAAAAAAAAAAAAA
   BBBBBBBBBBBBBBBBBB..................

4. Perform the following sequence of operations and explain the way that the system responds:

   (a) Generate a level B interrupt.
   (b) Generate a level A interrupt.
   (c) Generate a level A interrupt.
   (d) Generate a level B interrupt.
   (e) Hit A key.
   (f) Hit A key.
   (g) Hit B key.
   (h) Hit B key.

Laboratory Exercise 6.4

Reaction Timer

Aim

The aim of this experiment is to construct a timer that measures the average delay between the illumination of one of eight LED indicators and the pressing of the corresponding switch out of a register of eight switches.

Introduction

The basic timing mechanism takes the form of a 1 kHz oscillator that is used to generate an interrupt every millisecond. Following a random delay of a few seconds, one of eight LED indicators is to be illuminated and the timing period commenced. The subject of the reaction timer experiment is then required to press the switch located immediately below the illuminated LED. If the switch that has been pressed is the correct one, the LED is extinguished and a further random waiting time occurs before another LED is illuminated. If an incorrect switch has been pressed, the LED remains illuminated until the incorrect switch has been reset and the correct switch pressed. The timing continues throughout this period and, following a correct key press, the elapsed time for each test in milliseconds is to be displayed on the VDU screen. Following eight repetitions of the test, the average reaction time is calculated and displayed on the VDU.

Procedure

1. Write a program segment that generates a sequence of 3-bit pseudo-random numbers in the range 000 to 111 and sends the numbers in turn to the output port of a PIO or PPI to which eight LEDs have been connected. Arrange for each of the 3-bit numbers to illuminate the lower three bits of the port for a time of approximately two seconds.

2. Extend your program by including a routine which decodes the 3-bit number into a one-of-eight pattern in which only one LED is illuminated for each two second period.

3. Randomly illuminate one of eight LEDs while monitoring via a PIO input port a set of eight logic switches. Upon detecting that the corresponding switch has been pressed, extinguish all LEDs for a two second period and then select a new LED to illuminate.

4. From one edge of the waveform generated by an oscillator running at 1 kHz, produce a narrow data strobe pulse that will give rise to an interrupt on the port of a PIO to which it is applied. This can be done using either a monostable flip-flop or a D-type flip-flop, as described in Chapters 4 and 5.

5. Write an interrupt service routine that simply increments a 16-bit register pair with the arrival of each interrupt. Following the recognition by the computer that a correct switch has been pressed, the interrupt is to be disabled and the decimal equivalent of the number stored in this register pair are to be displayed on the VDU. (A subroutine to display a 4-digit number corresponding to the 16-bit binary number contained in the HL register pair may already have been written in answer to Problem 3.3.)

6. Configure the PIO port which monitors the switches into bit control mode and have it generate an interrupt when a switch is pressed. (Note that the switch pressed may not be correct and this will have to be checked in the interrupt service routine.) When the correct switch is detected, this interrupt must disable the one millisecond interrupts. The bit control port can then be configured to interrupt when all switches are reset. This can be used as the trigger to display the next random LED.

7. Convert all the above delays into random delays ranging from two to five seconds and finally compute the average of eight tests and display individual and average reaction times in milliseconds on the VDU screen.

The basic principle of timing, illustrated in this experiment, is that commonly used by many computers having a real time clock. Interrupts are frequently generated from the A.C. side of the power supply giving a 20ms (50 Hz) or 16.667ms (60 Hz) resolution.

Laboratory Exercise 6.5

The Logic Analyzer

Aim

The aim of this experiment is to construct a basic logic analyzer capable of monitoring eight input lines. The analyzer must recognize a trigger word and display captured input words in a variety of formats.

Introduction

The logic analyzer is used to monitor a number of digital lines and, upon receipt of a suitable trigger signal, store the succession of digital words appearing on the digital lines for subsequent display. In the more useful forms of logic analyzer, it is possible to display:

1.   the sequence of words that follow the trigger signal; or
2.   the sequence of digital signals that proceed the trigger signal; or
3.   the sequence of digital words that appear both before and after the trigger signal.

It is the last mode of operation that is to be employed in this exercise. The sequence of digital words is to be provided from an analog to digital convertor that performs conversions of a 1 Hz sine wave at rate of 100 samples per second. The trigger signal is to be derived from the sequence of digital words from the ADC and corresponds to the time at which the input crosses the 0V axis in a positive direction.

Upon receipt of the trigger word (0V = 80H), a total of 256 samples of the waveform are to be displayed on an oscilloscope via a digital to analog convertor. Fifty samples should proceed the trigger point. The display routine should give a bright, flicker-free display on the oscilloscope with stable triggering. In addition, a hexadecimal representation of the eight samples on either side of the trigger word are to be displayed on the VDU.

It should be noted that the trigger word 80H may not appear regularly and a more appropriate test might be the changing of the most significant bit of the ADC output from 0 to 1.

Procedure

1.   Write a routine which will give a flicker-free display of 256 memory locations on the oscilloscope. Data should be output through a PIO or a PPI port.

2.   Configure a PIO port to accept data from the ADC under interrupt control. Your interrupt service routine should place the data acquired into a 256 byte ring buffer (i.e. data is placed into memory in the order 1,2, ... 255,256,1,2, ... and so on).

3. Use a second PIO port configured in bit control mode to monitor the most significant bit of the ADC output and generate an interrupt when an appropriate zero crossing occurs. This interrupt should set up the display and acquire routines to display the acquired data in the method described in the specification above.

4. Add a push button switch to your device. A new acquire cycle is only to begin when the button is pressed.

5. Add a routine to display the 16 values required on the VDU.

Laboratory Exercise 6.6

Intruder Alarm Controller

Aim

The aim of this experiment is to design a controller for an eight station intruder alarm.

Introduction

This experiment involves the design of a controller for an intruder alarm to be installed in a house or business premises. The alarm is to send a signal to a central station if:

1.   any one of eight sensors returns an asserted high signal;
2.   a power fail is detected (this may indicate action by a burglar).

In this application, warning messages will be displayed on the VDU screen rather than transmitted to a central location.

Procedure

1.   Connect port B of a PIO to eight logic switches which will simulate the eight sensors. The port should be configured into bit control mode and generate an interrupt when any input is asserted high. The interrupt service routine will display a warning message on the VDU including a list of the sensor or sensors which have been detected.

2.   Connect a logic switch to port A of the same PIO. When this switch is asserted high, an interrupt is to be generated and an impending power-fail is to be reported on the VDU screen. Such a signal may initiate a changeover to battery operation in a real system.

Laboratory Exercise 6.7

Bi-directional Data Acquisition and Display using Interrupts

Aim

The aim of this experiment is to acquire and display digitized information through a single bi-directional PIO port.

Introduction

In this experiment, a data acquisition and display system which operates through a single bi-directional PIO port will be constructed. Since a bi-directional port is used, it is necessary to provide external circuitry to latch output data and prevent input data from appearing on the port I/O lines during an output cycle. Appropriate circuitry is shown in Figure 6.28. Both input and output transfers take place following a 0 to 1 transition in the corresponding clock waveform. Output transfers are entered into the external latch when the $\overline{ASTB}$ line is asserted by a monostable flip-flop pulse. This flip-flop is triggered providing the external buffer is not currently asserting data onto the bi-directional bus lines. Similarly, input transfers only take place if an output transfer is not taking place.

The microprocessor is to acquire data from an ADC which samples a 2 Hz waveform at 100 samples per second with the start of conversion signal being obtained from an external oscillator. The $\overline{BUSY/READY}$ signal of the ADC is to be used to generate interrupts to the Z80 CPU. It is required that data be continuously acquired and that the data be stored in a 256 byte ring buffer in the memory of the Z80 system. (A 256 byte ring buffer would store data into memory locations in the order 1,2,3...255,256,1,2,... and so on.)

A second external oscillator running at 10 kHz is to be used to generate interrupts to the output side of the bi-directional PIO port. Each interrupt causes the next byte in the ring buffer to be made available for display on the oscilloscope via the DAC. An oscilloscope trigger signal should be provided via the second PIO port to ensure a stable display. When operating correctly, the oscilloscope should show a stable display of the ring buffer with the newly acquired data being seen to overwrite the old data in the buffer.

Procedure

1. Write a program which causes eight LEDs connected to a PIO or PPI port to display a rotating one pattern. This will be the main program for this experiment.

2. Construct the hardware necessary to support the bi-directional data transfer via port A of a PIO and develop the necessary software to make the system operate.

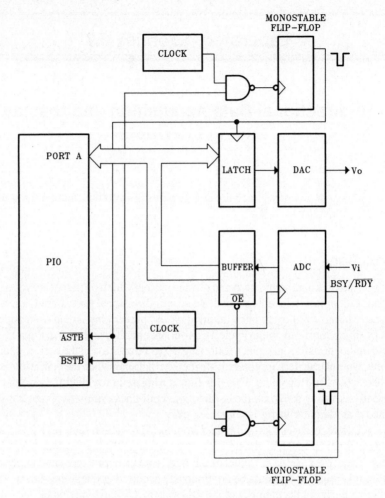

Figure 6.28 External circuitry for Laboratory Exercise 6.7

Laboratory Exercise 6.8

File Transfer

Aim

The aim of this experiment is to establish a parallel link between two microprocessors. Data transfer is to be carried out via bi-directional ports operating under interrupt control on two interconnected microcomputer systems.

Introduction

In this experimental session, a parallel link between two microcomputer systems will be established using a bi-directional PIO port on each machine. Both the input and output of data are to be carried out under interrupt control. Figure 6.29 shows a block diagram of the system hardware. When the left hand (LH) PIO is ready to output data, as indicated by ARDY being set high, the LH monostable will generate a brief ASTB pulse providing that:

1. the right hand (RH) PIO is not ready to output data; and
2. the RH PIO is ready to receive data (BRDY=1).

The ASTB pulse that outputs data from the LH PIO can also be used to strobe data into the RH PIO. The circuit is then repeated from the RH PIO to provide a two-way interchange of parallel data.

Procedure

1. Write a routine which causes the VDU to emit an audible tone. This will be the main routine for this experiment.

2. Construct the necessary hardware and develop the necessary software to facilitate data transfer. Use your system to:

   (a) cause characters typed on the keyboard of one machine to be displayed on the VDU of the other machine. A convenient scheme to achieve this would be to type characters on one VDU and have them entered into memory of the local machine and echoed to the VDU until a carriage return character is typed. Upon detecting this character, the entire string is then transmitted under interrupt control to the remote machine.
   (b) transfer a block of memory between one system and the other.

(c) transfer a disk file between one machine and another. (You may like to transfer the file in blocks of say 256 bytes including a checksum and then delay sending the next block until an acknowledge of the last block has been correctly received from the remote microcomputer.)

This experiment requires two microcomputer systems for its operation. It is suggested that individual students write the code for each machine and that they then link the machines and attempt to get the process operating.

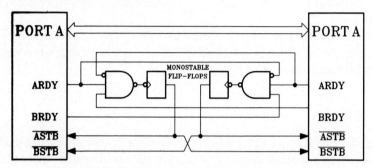

Figure 6.29 Hardware for bi-directional data transfer

7 Serial I/O Using the Intel 8251 and Zilog Z8530 Serial Communication Devices

In the case of the devices considered in earlier chapters, namely the Intel PPI and the Zilog Z80 PIO, data is transferred between the microcomputer and its peripherals in parallel form. It is necessary, therefore, that the peripheral be connected to the PPI, and that the PPI be connected to the microcomputer, via eight signal lines, with a further line providing a ground connection. One byte, or eight bits, of data is then transferred for each **IN** or **OUT** instruction. An alternative form of data transfer is often used for VDU screens and keyboards, for printers and for modems that allow microcomputers to exchange data via the public telephone network. This is serial transmission, where each data word is transmitted one bit at a time over a two-line channel. As the use of serial transmission is common to virtually all microcomputers, the major integrated circuit manufacturers have produced a number of specialized chips to simplify the problem of interfacing serial I/O devices. These are commonly referred to as universal synchronous asynchronous receiver transmitters or USARTs. They include the Intel 8251 Programmable Communication Interface (PCI) and the Zilog 8530 Serial Communications Controller (SCC) described in the following sections.

7.1 THE RS 232-C INTERFACE STANDARD

The RS 232-C interface standard, defined by the Engineering Industries Association (EIA), provides an interface between data terminal equipment (typically a computer, computer terminal or printer) and data communication equipment (typically a modem) employing binary data transfer in serial form. A similar standard, namely V.24, is defined by the International Telegraph and Telephone Consultative Committee (CCITT). RS 232-C is thus essentially an interface between an item of computer hardware and a modem. The modem then communicates with another modem and hence with another item of computer hardware. Modem communication can occur in one of three forms.

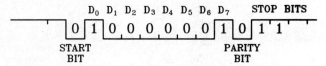

Figure 7.1 Serial bit stream for the keyboard character 'A'

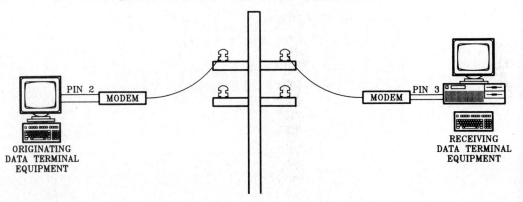

Figure 7.2 Terminal to terminal connection

Simplex mode:	Data is transmitted in one direction only.
Half-duplex mode:	Data may be transmitted in both directions but not simultaneously. The direction of data flow is altered to allow two-way transmission over a channel comprising a single pair of wires.
Full-duplex mode:	Data may be transmitted in both directions simultaneously, requiring two channels.

Normally serial data transmission is asynchronous, meaning that no synchronizing clock waveform needs to be transmitted to the receiver. Synchronism is achieved by the inclusion of a start bit at the beginning of the character bit pattern, one or more stop bits at the end, and adherence to an agreed bit transmission rate. A parity bit may also be included to allow for error checking by the receiver to ensure that the data has been received correctly. As will be discovered a little later, all of these additional bits are combined with the data bits automatically by the controller once it has been instructed by the CPU as to which mode of operation is required. The serial bit pattern used to transmit the keyboard character 'A' in ASCII with two stop bits and odd parity is shown in Figure 7.1.

Under the RS 232-C standard, all signals associated with the data terminal equipment, which will hereafter be referred to as DTE, or simply terminal, and with the data communication equipment, DCE or modem, appear on a 25 pin D-type connector. Data is sent by the transmitting terminal on pin 2 and is accepted by the receiving terminal on pin 3, as shown in Figure 7.2.

The terminal indicates to the local modem that it is able to handle information by asserting the Data Terminal Ready ($\overline{\text{DTR}}$) signal on pin 20. If the terminals at two interconnected modems both assert their $\overline{\text{DTR}}$ signals then the modems recognize that a connection is possible and inform their respective terminals of that fact by asserting the Data Set Ready (DSR) signal on interface pin 6. When a transfer of information has been completed, the connection is broken when either end releases DTR.

In a simplex or full duplex environment, the terminal wishing to transmit data can do so at any time and similarly data may be received at any time. The transmitting terminal issues a Request To Send (RTS) when it has data to transmit and this may be looped back to its own Clear To Send (CTS) input allowing transmission to proceed at once. With a half duplex connection, however, a possible contention for the communication channel exists which must be resolved to allow an orderly flow of two-way traffic. When a terminal has data to transmit, the originating terminal issues a RTS to the local modem on pin 4. This causes a signal to be sent to the far modem thereby causing it to send a Data Carrier Detect (DCD) signal to the receiving terminal. At the same time the local modem checks its own DCD signal on pin 8. If this signal is not asserted then clearly the far terminal is not about to transmit data and the modem can inform the local terminal that it is Clear To Send.

Having gained control of the communication line, the transmitting terminal continues to assert the RTS line and continues to receive the CTS response from the local modem. At the far end, Data Carrier Detect continues to be asserted throughout the transmission preventing that modem from issuing a Clear To Send signal to its terminal. When all information has been transmitted, the previously transmitting terminal releases its Request To Send causing the local Clear To Send to be released and the Data Carrier Detect signal to be released at the far end. Either terminal can then take control of the communication channel by asserting a RTS signal when it has data to transmit. A timing diagram showing this two-way interaction is given in Figure 7.3.

The last two important signal lines to be considered on the RS 232-C interface are the ground leads. The first of these is a frame ground (pin 1) which is used to prevent users receiving shocks in the case of electrical shorts or other problems. The other is the signal ground (pin 7) which establishes the common ground reference potential for all other signals except the frame ground. See Table 7.1 for a summary of major RS 232-C signals.

Use of the RS 232-C Interface Standard

Although RS 232-C was defined as an interface between terminal equipment on the one hand (a terminal, a computer or a printer), and a modem on the other, it is far more commonly used as a direct means of connecting items of computer hardware together, for example, in connecting a terminal to a computer and a computer to a printer, where no modems are required. The following sections will consider how this direct connection is made and what role the controller plays in facilitating the interconnection.

Even though in a direct interconnection between terminal and computer no modem is present, the RS 232-C interface must still receive the signals that the modem would have provided. The major signals of the RS 232-C interface may be divided into three categories, namely *grounds, data* and *control.* The cross-connection of each of these signals will now be considered.

Grounds
Since these lines are present for protection and signal reference only, they may be wired directly from one item of data terminal equipment to the other.

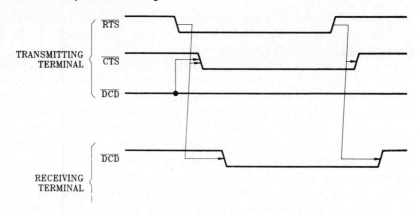

Figure 7.3 Timing diagram of RS 232-C handshaking signals

Table 7.1 Summary of major RS 232-C signals

Function	Pin	Signal Name	Direction
Data	2	Transmitted Data (TxD)	To Modem
Data	3	Received Data (RxD)	To Terminal
Control	4	Request To Send (RTS)	To Modem
Control	5	Clear To Send (CTS)	To Terminal
Control	8	Data Carrier Detect (DCD)	To Terminal
Control	6	Data Set Ready (DSR)	To Terminal
Control	20	Data Terminal Ready (DTR)	To Modem
Ground	1	Frame Ground	
Ground	7	Signal Ground	

Data
Each item of terminal equipment transmits data on pin 2 and receives data on pin 3. Thus pin 2 on one device must be connected to pin 3 on the other device, and vice versa.

Control
It has been shown that the control lines Request To Send (RTS) and Data Terminal Ready (DTR) are generated by the terminal, which in turn expects to receive Data Set Ready (DSR), Clear To Send (CTS) and Data Carrier Detect (DCD) from the modem. These latter three signals must be derived in some way from the signals generated by the terminal equipment.

Data Terminal Ready (DTR) and Data Set Ready (DSR)
DTR is asserted by the local terminal to indicate to its modem that it is turned on, while the modem responds with a DSR signal to indicate to the terminal that a connection with the remote station has been established. For the current application, a connection will be established as soon as both items of terminal equipment are turned on. It is sufficient, therefore, that the DTR generated by one terminal be used to provide the DSR signal for the other.

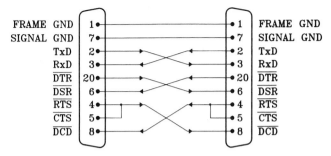

Figure 7.4 Terminal to computer connection for full duplex operation

Request To Send ($\overline{\text{RTS}}$), Clear To Send ($\overline{\text{CTS}}$) and Data Carrier Detect ($\overline{\text{DCD}}$)
With the simple direct connection that is being considered, either item of terminal equipment can transmit at any time. The transmitting terminal does, however, require a $\overline{\text{CTS}}$ signal to be asserted to allow it to send and it also needs to know that data will be arriving by having its incoming $\overline{\text{DCD}}$ line asserted. Both of these signals may be derived from the outgoing $\overline{\text{RTS}}$ signal as shown in Figure 7.4.

The RS 232-C implementation illustrated in Figure 7.4 is appropriate for a situation in which several terminals are connected to the input ports of a multi-user, time-shared computer. As each new user attempts to access the computer, the terminal server, or PACX, to which the terminals are connected, checks to see if a spare port is available and, if so, connects the above eight signal lines between terminal and computer port. If the terminal is subsequently unplugged or powered down, the terminal server would become aware of this fact via the released $\overline{\text{DTR}}$ signal and make the computer port available to a new user.

In a single-user environment, however, a very much simpler implementation, using only four interconnecting wires, becomes possible, as shown in Figure 7.5. The data terminal equipment at both ends is permanently cleared to send by holding the $\overline{\text{CTS}}$ input asserted, while the remaining control signals are dispensed with. Clearly, it is no longer possible to automatically check the status of the data terminal equipment, which must therefore be carried out manually by the user.

It will be apparent from many diagrams that have appeared in earlier chapters that data is transferred within the Z80 microcomputer in parallel form via the 8-bit wide data bus. In the previous section on transfer using the RS 232-C interface standard, however, it is clear

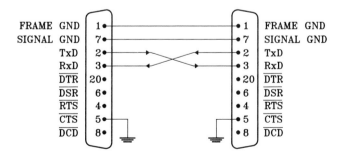

Figure 7.5 Simplified RS 232-C implementation

that data is transmitted and received by computers and terminals in bit serial form. A requirement exists, therefore, to convert the parallel data provided by the Z80 CPU into a serial bit stream, add the various start, stop and parity bits and transmit the resulting codeword at a standard data rate. A further requirement exists for a device performing the inverse of all of these functions. A number of devices exist from several manufacturers performing the functions of both transmitter and receiver in a single package. These devices are variously described as UARTs, USARTs, PCIs or SCCs standing for Universal Synchronous - Asynchronous Receiver Transmitters, Programmable Communication Interface or Serial Communications Controllers. The Intel 8251 PCI and the Zilog 8530 SCC are two such devices that will now be considered in sufficient depth to allow the reader to use the devices in their common asynchronous mode.

7.2 THE INTEL 8251 PCI

The Intel 8251 Programmable Communication Interface (PCI) is a universal synchronous/ asynchronous receiver/transmitter (USART) designed for serial data communication in microcomputer systems. The PCI is a peripheral device that can be programmed by the microprocessor to perform most serial transmission tasks. Although the 8251 can operate in a synchronous communication mode, only asynchronous communication will be considered here. It accepts data from the microprocessor in 8-bit parallel form and converts it to serial form for transmission. Simultaneously, it can receive serial data and convert it to 8-bit parallel form prior to passing the data to the microprocessor. Status signals are provided to allow the PCI to signal the CPU when it can accept a new character for transmission or when it has a character to pass to the CPU. A complete block diagram is shown in Figure 7.6. This block diagram can be divided into four sections, each of which will now be considered in turn.

The Microprocessor Interface

The microprocessor interface allows the microprocessor to communicate with the PCI. Data is transferred between the PCI and the microprocessor in 8-bit bytes. The PCI occupies two locations in the I/O address space of the Z80 (one for data and one for control) and so the Z80 transfers data using the **IN** and **OUT** instructions. The functions of the signal lines are given below.

D0 - D7	These three-state lines allow the 8251 to be connected directly to the data bus of the Z80. As well as the data to be transmitted or data received by the 8251, these lines also carry mode words, command words and status information as described below.
RESET	An asserted high signal on this input line will place the 8251 into idle mode. The 8251 will remain in this mode until its functions are reprogrammed by the Z80.

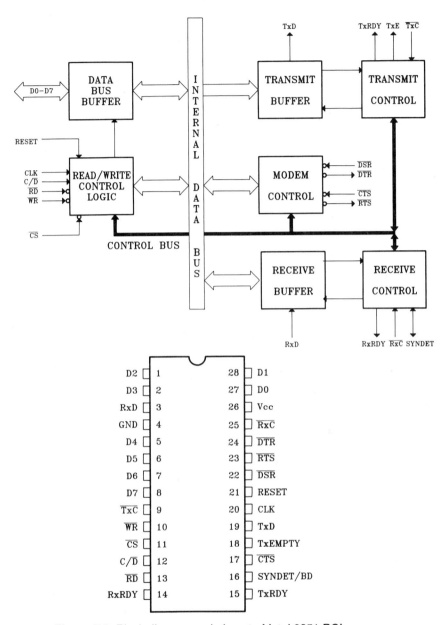

Figure 7.6 Block diagram and pin-out of Intel 8251 PCI

CLK

The CLK input is used to generate internal device timing signals for the 8251. The speed of data transmission and reception is not determined from this clock signal as the control sections of the transmit and receive buffers have their own clock inputs. It must, however, be at least 4.5 times the frequency of the transmit and receive clocks for correct operation.

$\overline{WR}$ An asserted low signal on this input line informs the 8251 that the Z80 is performing a write operation. The 8251, if selected, will accept the data as a control word or data to be transmitted.

$\overline{RD}$ An asserted low signal on this input line informs the 8251 that the Z80 is performing a read operation. The 8251 will place received data or status information onto the data bus providing that it is selected.

$C/\overline{D}$ This input line informs the 8251 whether the information being transferred in the current operation is data (logic 0) or status/control information (logic 1).

$\overline{CS}$ An asserted low signal on this input line enables the 8251. No data transfers will occur unless the 8251 is enabled.

Figure 7.7 gives the function performed by the 8251 for various combinations of the control lines.

$C/\overline{D}$	$\overline{RD}$	$\overline{WR}$	$\overline{CS}$	*Function*
x	x	x	1	Chip not selected-data lines to high impedance
0	0	1	0	8251 places received data onto data bus
0	1	0	0	8251 accepts data for transmission from data bus
1	0	1	0	8251 places status information onto data bus
1	1	0	0	8251 accepts control information from data bus

Figure 7.7 Effect of control lines on functionality of Intel 8251

Modem Control

The 8251 has four lines which can be used to control a modem. The signals have names which are familiar from the earlier consideration of RS 232–C. They are, however, general purpose in nature (with one exception) and can be used for functions other than modem control. The signal functions are outlined below.

$\overline{DSR}$ DSR is a general-purpose input signal which can be tested by the Z80 via a read of the 8251 status register. In modem control applications, it can be used to test the state of the Data Set Ready line from the modem.

$\overline{DTR}$ DTR is a general-purpose output line which can be set low by the Z80 setting the appropriate bit in a command instruction word to the 8251. In modem control applications, it can be used to signal Data Terminal Ready to the modem.

$\overline{RTS}$ RTS is a general-purpose output line which can be set low by the Z80 setting the appropriate bit in a command instruction word. In modem control applications, it can be used to signal Request to Send to the modem.

CTS $\overline{\text{CTS}}$ must be asserted if the PCI is to be allowed to transmit data. In modem control applications, it should be connected to the Clear to Send signal from the modem.

Transmit Buffer and Control

The Transmit Buffer accepts parallel data from the Data Bus Buffer, converts it to a serial bit stream, adds the appropriate start, stop and parity bits and then outputs the result on the TxD pin. While one character is being transmitted, another character can be loaded into the 8251 by the Z80. The operation is controlled by the Transmit Control section using three control signals. The functions of each of the signals in this section are given below.

TxD   Serial data is transmitted by the PCI via this pin.

TxRDY   An asserted high signal on Transmitter Ready (TxRDY) signals the microprocessor that the transmit section of the USART is ready to accept another character. As TxRDY is available as an output pin of the 8251, it can be used to generate an interrupt to the Z80. Alternatively, the Z80 can monitor the state of the TxRDY line via the 8251 status register. TxRDY is automatically cleared when a new character has been loaded from the Z80.

TxE   An asserted high signal on Transmitter Empty (TxE) signals the Z80 that the PCI has no further characters to transmit. It therefore indicates that transmission is complete as opposed to the TxRDY signal which indicates that the last character has been passed for transmission. As well as appearing as an output pin, TxE can be read by the Z80 via the status register. It can be used by the CPU as an indication to the Z80 to change the communication line from transmit to receive in half-duplex applications. TxE is automatically reset when a new character is received.

TxC   The Transmitter Clock ($\overline{\text{TxC}}$) input controls the rate at which bits are transmitted from the USART. The clock rate can be 1, 16 or 64 times the rate that bits are transmitted (often called the baud rate). The multiplier used is programmed into the 8251 during initialization. Data is shifted out on the falling edge of $\overline{\text{TxC}}$.

Example 7.1

a. The baud rate required for a given application is 300 baud. If the PCI internal multiplier factor is 16, what is the frequency of the transmit clock?

$$\overline{\text{TxC}} \text{ frequency} = 16 \times 300 = 4.8 \text{ kHz}$$

b. A 614.4 kHz clock is connected to the $\overline{\text{TxC}}$ input of a PCI. If the internal multiplier factor is 64, what is the resulting baud rate?

$$\text{Baud rate} = \overline{\text{TxC}} \div 64 = 9600 \text{ baud}$$

Receive Buffer and Control

The Receive Buffer accepts serial data from the RxD pin, converts this to parallel form after removing and checking all control bits and finally sends the received character to the microprocessor. Data reception is controlled by the two control lines discussed below. The SYNDET signal is only used in synchronous transmission modes and so is not discussed.

RxD	Serial data is received by the PCI on this pin.
RxRDY	An asserted high signal on this line indicates that the 8251 has a character ready for transfer to the microprocessor. The Receiver Ready (RxRDY) line can be used to generate an interrupt to the Z80. Alternatively, the Z80 can monitor the state of the RxRDY line by reading the 8251 Status Register. RxRDY is automatically reset by the 8251 when the character is read by the microprocessor.
$\overline{\text{RxC}}$	Receiver Clock ($\overline{\text{RxC}}$) controls the rate at which characters are received by the USART. As with the transmitter clock ($\overline{\text{TxC}}$), $\overline{\text{RxC}}$ can be chosen to be a 1, 16 or 64 multiple of the baud rate. This information is programmed into the 8251 by a mode instruction issued by the Z80. Data is clocked into the 8251 on the rising edge of $\overline{\text{RxC}}$. Note that the same multiplier applies to both the transmitter and the receiver clocks. In most communication applications, the PCI will be handling both transmission and reception of data on a single link. Thus, the transmit and receive baud rates will often be identical and hence so will the required transmitter and receiver clock frequencies. In these cases, it is permissible to tie both clocks to a single clock generator thereby simplifying the overall interface.

Programming the 8251 PCI

Before beginning the transmission or reception of data, the 8251 must be loaded with a set of control words which define amongst other things:

1. the transmit and receive baud rates;
2. the character length in bits;

3. the number of stop bits;
4. whether even, odd or no parity is to be employed;
5. the state of various pins of the 8251.

The control words are divided into two formats: the mode instruction and the command instruction. Each format will now be discussed.

The Mode Instruction

The first byte of data sent to the PCI control register after a reset is interpreted as a mode instruction. A reset occurs either when an asserted high signal is applied to the RESET pin of the 8251 (a hardware reset) or when a control instruction with an appropriate bit set is transferred to the 8251 (a software reset). More will be said about software resets in the next section. The format of the mode instruction is shown in Figure 7.8.

- S_2 and S_1 define the number of stop bits (either 1, 1.5 or 2).
- EP is set for even parity generation and checking and reset for odd parity.
- PEN enables parity generation and checking when set. Otherwise parity is neither generated nor checked.
- L_2 and L_1 define the length of each character in bits (either 5, 6, 7 or 8 bits).
- B_2 and B_1 define the factor by which the transmitter and receiver clock is divided in order to determine the transmitter/receiver baud rate.

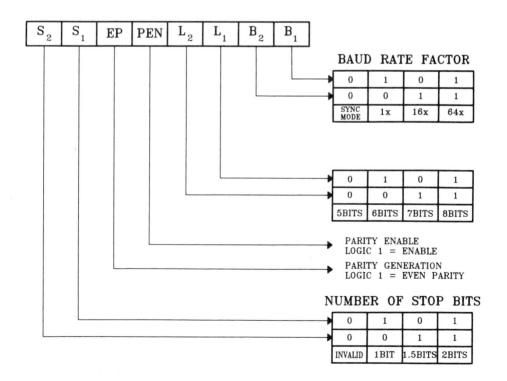

Figure 7.8 Mode instruction format

Example 7.2

Determine the mode instruction if the receiver/transmitter clock is to be divided by 16, the character length is eight bits, odd parity is to be used with two stop bits.

Solution

The appropriate mode instruction is shown in Figure 7.9.

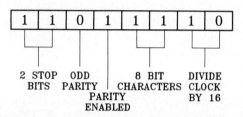

Figure 7.9 Mode instruction for Example 7.2

Command Instruction

All subsequent bytes of data sent to the 8251 control register following a mode instruction are treated as command instructions. The command instruction format is shown in Figure 7.10.

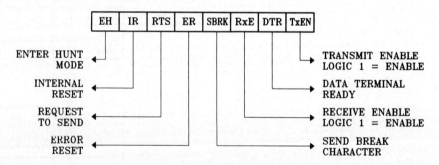

Figure 7.10 Command instruction format

EH   When set, this signal places the 8251 into hunt mode. It is not used for asynchronous communication.

IR   When set, this signal forces an internal reset of the 8251. After an internal reset, the next byte written to the 8251 control register will be treated as a mode instruction.

RTS   When set, this signal forces the $\overline{\text{RTS}}$ output pin to be asserted low.

ER	A logic one in this bit will reset all three 8251 error flags. The function of these error flags is discussed in the next section.
SBRK	When set, this bit causes the 8251 to continuously send break characters to be transmitted (i.e. TxD is forced low).
RxE	When set, this bit enables the 8251 to receive data on the RxD pin.
DTR	A logic one in this bit will cause the $\overline{\text{DTR}}$ output pin of the 8251 to be asserted low.
TxEN	When set, this bit enables the 8251 to transmit data on the TxD pin

The flow of information between the 8251 and the CPU after a reset is shown in Figure 7.11.

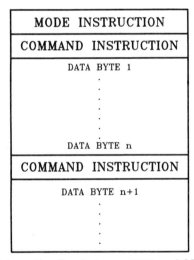

Figure 7.11 Information flow between 8251 and CPU after a reset

Status Register

The Z80 microprocessor can monitor the operation of the 8251 PCI by reading its status register. This is achieved by the microprocessor doing a read from the 8251 control register. The format of the status register contents is shown in Figure 7.12.

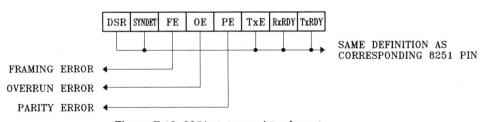

Figure 7.12 8251 status register format

The lines DSR (Data Set Ready), SYNDET (Sync Detect), TxE (Transmitter Empty), RxRDY (Receiver Ready) and TxRDY (Transmitter Ready) have the same definition as the 8251 pins of the same name (although not necessarily of the same logic assertion level) and so will not be discussed further. The other three status register bits define error conditions. These are:

PE   The parity error (PE) flag is set when a parity error is detected by the 8251 parity check circuitry.

OE   The overflow error (OE) flag is set when the CPU has not read the last character before the next one becomes available. The new character will overwrite the old character which will consequently be lost.

FE   The framing error (FE) flag is set when a valid stop bit is not detected at the end of a character.

None of these error conditions causes the 8251 to cease operations. All can only be detected by the user's software monitoring the appropriate status register bit. All error flags will be reset by a command instruction with the ER (Error Reset) bit set.

7.3 THE ZILOG Z8530 SCC

The Z8530 Serial Communications Controller (SCC) is a somewhat more complex device than the previously described 8251 PCI, providing additional functionality, particularly in support of synchronous serial transmission. In spite of the omission of any discussion of synchronous transmission, a description of the SCC for use in asychronous transmission is complicated by the need to consider the many control registers that are provided in this versatile device. One significant advantage of the SCC over the PCI for asynchronous transmission is the inclusion of a programmable baud rate generator which in many systems obviates the need for a separate oscillator to generate the standard transmission bit rates. This also allows any computer system employing an SCC to check the baud rate of its console terminal and to set the SCC to that speed without the necessity of an operator changing links or switches.

Baud Rate Generator

As stated in earlier sections, serial transmission takes place at one of a range of standard transmission data rates. A speed of 1200 bps is usual for modems connected directly to the public telephone network, whereas 9600 bps or 19200 bps are the preferred data rates for short computer to terminal links. With the 8251 PCI, a separate oscillator running at some multiple of the desired operating frequency must be provided and connected to the Receive Clock and the Transmit Clock inputs of the device. With the Z8530 SCC, the user may choose to use a separate oscillator or derive the receive and transmit clock inputs from the main system clock by way of the programmable baud rate generator. The generator consists of two 8-bit 'time constant' registers, a 16-bit down counter and a flip-flop on the output producing a square wave. The 16-bit time constant is counted down at a rate determined by the Z80's system clock and, upon reaching a count of zero, the flip-flop is toggled and the counter reloaded. The resulting output square wave then appears at a frequency given by:

$$\text{Baud Rate} = \frac{1}{2 \times (\text{Time Constant}+2) \times (\text{Baud Rate Clock Period})}$$

A further divider, introducing a factor of x1, x16, x32 or x64, as set by a command to write register 4, may also be included in order to obtain the desired baud rate. With a clock frequency of 4 MHz and a x16 clock mode, a time constant of 11 gives rise to a baud rate of 9615 bps, which is sufficiently well within the tolerance of 5 percent needed for reliable operation

Z8530 SCC Registers

Rather than describing the 8530 SCC in its entirety, much of which is of no interest to this book, the discussion will be limited to a brief description of those registers needing to be accessed for asynchronous serial transmission. Each of the SCC's two channels has its own set of 15 write registers that are programmed to initialize the SCC into its different modes of operation. In addition, there are eight read registers per channel from which the current status of the SCC may be obtained. The functions of these registers are set out in brief form in Figure 7.13.

Unlike many of the peripheral devices considered in earlier chapters, these control and status registers cannot be accessed directly by the CPU. Such an approach would require more than six bits of addressing information in order to allow each register to occupy one location in the Z80's port addressing field. An alternative approach used with the Z8530 SCC is to direct commands to all registers via a single control register for each channel. The commands are then two bytes in length with the first byte specifying which subsequent register is to be accessed, while the second byte contains the parameters to be passed to the selected register. The only exception to this rule is for write register 0 (WR0) and read register 0 (RR0), both of which may be accessed by a single write or read operation.

Register Commands
There are two types of bits in the write registers: mode bits and command bits. Write register 9, shown in Figure 7.14, is an example of a register that contains both types of bits. Bits D_7 and D_6 are command bits and are denoted as such by having boxes drawn around them, while the remaining bits are mode bits. Functions controlled by the mode bits are enabled when the appropriate bit is set to 1, or disabled when reset to 0. Functions controlled by the command bits can only be enabled. Various operating modes controlled by a single write register may be established by way of a single write to that register; however, only one command may be passed to the register at a time. For example, in the case of write register 9, two writes would be needed with D_7 and D_6 set to 10 and then 01 in order to reset both channels A and B. Care must be taken when issuing a command that the mode bits are not

READ REGISTER FUNCTIONS	
RR0	Transmit/receive buffer status and external status
RR1	Special receive condition status
RR2	Modified interrupt vector (channel B) Unmodified interrupt vector (channel A)
RR3	Interrupt pending bits (channel A)
RR10	Miscellaneous status
RR12	Lower byte of baud rate generator time constant
RR13	Upper byte of baud rate generator time constant
RR15	External/status interrupt information
WRITE REGISTER FUNCTIONS	
WR0	CRC initialize, mode initialization, register pointers
WR1	Transmit/receive interrupt and data transfer mode definition
WR2	Interrupt vector (accessed through either channel)
WR3	Receive parameters and control
WR4	Transmit/receive miscellaneous parameters and modes
WR5	Transmit parameters and control
WR6	Sync characters or SDLC address field
WR7	Sync character or SDLC flag
WR9	Master interrupt control and reset (accessed through either channel)
WR10	Miscellaneous transmit/receive control bits
WR11	Clock mode control
WR12	Lower byte of baud rate generator time constant
WR13	Upper byte of baud rate generator time constant
WR14	Miscellaneous control bits
WR15	External/status interrupt control

Figure 7.13 Function of SCC registers

changed inadvertently. A further complication arises from the fact that the order in which the various registers are accessed is important to ensure correct operation, as set out in the following section.

Initialization Procedure

The SCC initialization procedure occurs in three stages. The first stage consists of programming the operating modes and loading the constants. The second stage entails enabling the hardware functions, and finally, if required, interrupts are enabled in the third

Write Register 9

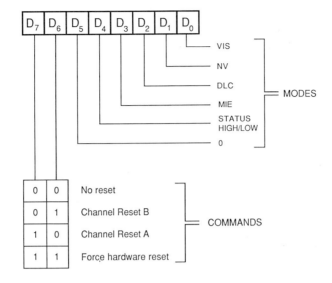

Figure 7.14 Command and mode bits

stage. Figure 7.15 shows the order in which the SCC registers are to be programmed. Those registers that need not be programmed are listed as optional in the comments column. The bits marked with an 'X' are to be selected by the user to suit the current application. The bits marked with an 'S' correspond to mode bits which have occurred earlier, at which time they will have been marked with an 'X'. These bits must therefore be set to the same value as selected previously.

Example 7.3

Initialize the SCC for asynchronous operation with eight bits per character, two stop bits, no parity, x16 clock mode which, with a 4 MHz clock input, allows transmission at a 9600 baud data rate.

Solution

	Reg.	Hex.	Comments
Modes			
	WR9	C0	Force hardware reset.
	WR4	4C	x16 clock mode, 2 stop bits, parity disabled.
	WR2	00	Interrupt vector.
	WR3	C0	Rx. 8 bits/char., Rx. en.(D_0) must be set to 0 at this time.
	WR5	E2	Tx. 8 bits/char., Tx. en.(D_3) must be set to 0 at this time.
	WR11	56	Rx. & Tx. clocks set to BR gen. TRxC = BR gen.

WR12	0B	Lower byte of time constant reg.=11.
WR13	00	Upper byte of time constant reg. = 00.
WR14	02	BR gen. source. BR en. (D_0) must be 0 at this time.

Enables

WR3	C1	Rx. enabled; all other bits as before.
WR5	EA	Tx. enabled; all other bits as before.
WR14	03	BR gen enabled; all other bits as before.

Register	Data	Comments
		Stage 1: Modes and constants
WR9	1 1 0 0 0 0 0 0	Hardware reset
WR0	0 0 0 0 0 0 X X	Select shift mode (Z8030 only)
WR4	X X X X X X X X	Transmit/receive control (selects synch or asynch)
WR1	0 X X 0 0 X 0 0	Select W/REQ (optional)
WR2	X X X X X X X X	Program interrupt vector (optional)
WR3	X X X X X X X 0	Selects receiver control. Bit 0 (Rx enable) must be set to 0 at this time
WR5	X X X X 0 X X X	Selects transmit control. Bit 3 (Tx enable) must be set to 0 at this time
WR6	X X X X X X X X	Program sync characters
WR7	X X X X X X X X	Program sync characters
WR9	0 0 0 X 0 X X X	Select interrupt control. Bit 3 (master interrupt enable) must be set to 0
WR10	X X X X X X X X	Miscellaneous control (optional)
WR11	X X X X X X X X	Clock control
WR12	X X X X X X X X	Time constant lower byte (optional)
WR13	X X X X X X X X	Time constant upper byte (optional)
WR14	X X X X X X X 0	Miscellaneous control. Bit 0 (BR generator enable) must be set to 0 at this time
WR14	X X X S S S S S	This register may require multiple writes if more than one command is used
		Stage 2: Enables
WR3	S S S S S S S 1	Set bit 0 (Rx enable)
WR5	S S S S 1 S S S	Set bit 3 (Tx enable)
WR0	1 0 0 0 0 0 0 0	Set TxCRC
WR14	0 0 0 S S S S 1	BR generator enable. Set bit 0 (BR generator enable). Enable DPLL.
WR1	X S S 0 0 S 0 0	Set bit 7 (DMA enable) if required
		Stage 3: Interrupt Enables
WR15	X X X X X X X X	Enable external interrupts
WR0	0 0 0 1 0 0 0 0	Reset external/status twice
WR0	0 0 0 1 0 0 0 0	Reset external/status twice
WR1	S S S X X S X X	Enable receive, transmit and external interrupt master
WR9	0 0 0 S X S S S	Enable master interrupt bit 3

1 - Set to logic one
0 - Set to logic zero
X - User's choice
S - Same as previously programmed

Figure 7.15 Order of setting 8530 SCC registers

If the SCC is to be used under interrupt control, additional commands, as given below, would be transmitted to the SCC as a final phase of the initialization procedure.

Enable Interrupts

WR15	00	All interrupts inhibited.
WR0	10	Reset ext/status interrupts.
WR0	10	Repeat second time!
WR1	10	Interrupt on all Rx characters.

Initialization of the SCC is achieved simply by sending each of the register addresses followed by its associated parameters to the selected control register. In the above example this requires a total of 30 writes to the control register for each channel. This is conveniently achieved by the following code segment which makes use of the out increment and repeat (**OTIR**) instruction.

```
INIT:      LD      HL,TABLE      ;Set HL to top of reg./parameter list.
           LD      C,ACTRL       ;C points to output port.
           LD      B,30D         ;Thirty data items to send.
           OTIR                  ;Send them.
           RET
;
TABLE:     DEFB    09H           ;Register 9
           DEFB    0C0H          ;Force hardware reset
           DEFB    04H           ;Register 4
           DEFB    4CH           ;x16 clock, 2 stop bits, no parity.
           DEFB

                     :
                     :
                     :
           DEFB    10H           ;Interrupt on all Rx characters
;
```

Status Information

All information concerned with the use of the SCC for asynchronous transmission may be obtained from read register 0 which may be accessed by a single read from the control register of the selected channel. Bit D_0 is set to 1 whenever a character has been received, while bit D_2 is set to 1 when the transmit buffer is empty. A segment of code that allows characters received by the keyboard to be echoed to the screen is given below.

```
BCTRL      EQU     0F0H          ;SCC addressed F0 to F3
ACTRL      EQU     0F1H          ;
BDATA      EQU     0F2H          ;
ADATA      EQU     0F3H          ;
;
```

```
START:      LD      SP,STACK    ;
            CALL    INIT        ;
RX:         IN      A,(ACTRL)   ;Read status word for Channel A
            BIT     0,A         ;Rx. character available?
            JR      Z,RX        ;No.Wait for keypress.
            IN      A,(ADATA)   ;Yes. Get character and
            OUT     (ADATA),A   ;echo it to screen.
TX:         IN      A,(ACTRL)   ;Check status word again.
            BIT     2,A         ;Tx. character gone?
            JR      Z,TX        ;No. Wait till transmission finished.
            JR      RX          ;Yes. Get next character.
;
```

A more efficient mode of operation, that does not involve the CPU continuously monitoring the status of the SCC, is to use interrupts. As may be seen from the above initialization procedure, provision is made for the loading of the interrupt vector into write register 2 and for specifying, in write register 1, the conditions under which an interrupt is to be generated. The use of interrupts in interfacing a keyboard via a serial port is particularly useful as it allows the user to maintain a tight control of the execution of any program. Rather than waiting for the program to test for a keypress, an interrupt driven keyboard will demand the attention of the CPU right away allowing, for example, the user to 'break in' in order to determine the state of various parameters at any time.

Much of the complexity of the SCC results from the synchronous transmission capabilities of the device which is not relevant to the present discussion. When used as an asynchronous receiver-transmitter, however, it differs from the simpler 8251 USART only in its more complex initialization procedure and in the inclusion of the useful baud rate generator.

PROBLEMS

Problem 7.1
Determine the mode control word and the frequency of the clocks used for both the transmitter and receiver for the 8251 PCI to allow the device to operate at 9600 baud, with two stop bits and no parity. Write a segment of code to initialize the PCI and to allow it to echo to the screen characters received from the keyboard.

Problem 7.2
The circuit shown in Figure 7.16 is to be used to generate the transmit and receive clocks for a 8251 PCI. Depending upon which link is in place, a baud rate of 2400 to 19200 is to be selected in factors of two as provided by the 74HC93 Binary Counter. Assuming the PCI to have been programmed with a x64 division factor, deduce the frequency of the crystal used in the oscillator.

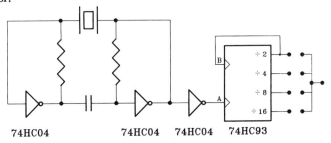

74HC04   74HC04   74HC04   74HC93

Figure 7.16 Clock circuit for Problem 7.2

Problem 7.3
A Zilog 8350 SCC is to be used with a crystal controlled oscillator running at 3.6864 MHz. If a division factor of x16 is used within the SCC, determine the numbers that must be loaded into the time constant registers in order to provide all the baud rates from 300 baud to 19.2 kilobaud, increasing in factors of two.

Problem 7.4
Determine the sequence of commands that need to be sent to a Zilog 8530 SCC in order to initialize it for asynchronous serial operation at a rate of 4800 baud with two stop bits and odd parity. The transmit and receive clocks are to be derived from the CPU's system clock which runs at 4 MHz.

Laboratory Exercise 7.1

Serial Communications to Keyboard and Screen

Aim

The aim of this experiment is to establish serial communications between a VDU and a microcomputer system.

Introduction

Most terminals are connected to their host computer via a serial communications link comprising one full duplex channel of a USART. The software used to initialize the USART and to allow basic communications with the screen and keyboard is usually contained within the boot ROM and is executed as soon as power is applied to the computer. In this experiment you are required to re-initialize the terminal USART and use it in a different mode to that established by the boot ROM.

Procedure

1. Consult the data sheets provided with your microcomputer and determine the port address at which the terminal USART is located. Also find the method whereby the operating parameters for your terminal can be changed (data rate, parity, etc.), but do not alter them at this stage. Terminal parameters are often set by way of a number of dual in-line switch registers; however, more sophisticated terminals may be set up from the keyboard once a set-up routine has been selected.

2. Determine the mode control words to initialize the terminal to operate at 110 baud with odd parity. Write an initialization routine and a main program that simply echoes the characters transmitted by the keyboard directly to the screen.
    (While you are writing and assembling the source code, your terminal must be set to the parameters expected by the boot ROM. Once you have given the command to execute your program you must then reset your terminal to the parameters expected by your program.)

3. As each character is received by the CPU, check to see if a control C has been typed and if so print a 'sign off' message and return control to the operating system.

4.* Modify your program so that characters are received from the keyboard at 9600 baud and echoed to the screen at 110 baud. Test the program for correctness by typing single characters and then observe the effect of typing characters faster than the rate at which they can be sent to the screen.

5. Further modify your program so that typed characters are stored in a buffer from which they are taken, in turn, for display on the screen.

While this use of a character buffer is somewhat contrived, the basic principle illustrated in this experiment is used with many systems to give a 'type ahead' facility. When a series of commands is used often (such as Exit Editor, Assemble, Link, Print List File, Execute, ...) these may be queued up in the type ahead buffer awaiting their turn. Such an arrangement does, however, require the receive side of the USART to be interrupt driven.

* Some systems may not allow this mode of operation.

Laboratory Exercise 7.2

File Transfer via a Serial Link

Aim

The aim of this experiment is to transfer data from one microcomputer to another by way of an RS 232-C serial link. Initially a block of data in the memory of one machine is to be transferred to the memory of the other machine while a similar process is continuing in the reverse direction. A more ambitious objective is then to transfer a file, held on disk, to the remote machine. Clearly you will need the co-operation of a fellow student in order to test your program. It is suggested that when you feel confident that your program is ready for testing, you load and run it on two interconnected machines. You will then make your machine available to your partner for testing purposes.

Procedure

1. Consult the data sheets provided with your microcomputer and determine the port address at which the second channel of the USART is located. Determine the mode control words to allow the USART to communicate with a similar device in a serial manner.

2. Write an initialization routine and a main program that transmits a series of printable ASCII characters contained in one region of memory while receiving and storing in another region of memory characters received from the remote microcomputer. In order to demonstrate that your transfer has taken place successfully, it is suggested that the receive character buffer be filled with ASCII space characters (20H) and that a header and footer be appended to the buffer. Your program should then print out this buffer before the transfer takes place and again following the transfer. The success, or otherwise, of the serial transfer will then be clearly evident.

    Some consideration will need to be given to the problem of initiating the transmission from each of the two machines. If one machine starts transmitting before the other machine is ready to receive, the message will be lost. One approach to overcome this problem is for each machine to transmit a 'start of transmission' character continuously until the remote machine responds with an acknowledge character. When this hand shaking process has been successfully completed, the main transfer can commence.

3. Consult the system manuals provided with your microcomputer and determine the format and system calls needed to load a file from disk into memory and to store a segment of memory onto disk. Include these routines into your program to allow a short file of known size to be transferred from disk storage on one machine to disk on the other machine.

4. Further modify your program to allow files of unknown length to be transferred with the file name being specified at run time once a communication link with the other machine has been established.

Laboratory Exercise 7.3

Interrupt Driven Keyboard for Program Control

Aim

The aim of this experiment is to operate a VDU under interrupt control.

Introduction

This experiment demonstrates the advantages provided by an interrupt driven keyboard in its ability to allow an operator to instantly regain control of a program from the keyboard. In many of the previous experiments, such as those involved with waveform acquisition and display, the program, once commenced, can only be aborted by pressing the system RESET button. With a little more effort, the program can be written so that control returns to the operator upon completion of a specified task. With this latter arrangement, the operator may detect that something has gone wrong immediately but must wait until a keyboard entry is requested before a change can be made. In the present experiment, a keypress generates an interrupt which suspends execution and allows the operator to change various parameters before execution is resumed.

Procedure

1. Using the procedure outlined in Laboratory Exercise 4.9, set up a waveform acquisition and display system. The system should allow 256 samples to be acquired from an input waveform and displayed continuously on an oscilloscope. The CPU must put out an oscilloscope trigger pulse at the start of each display cycle to provide a stable trace. In addition, it must also monitor a logic switch and acquire a new waveform when the switch is pressed.

    It is suggested that you reserve 'one page' of memory for waveform storage (i.e. from XX00 to XXFF = 256 bytes) so that in the display routine only the lower register in the register pair holding the memory address needs to be incremented.

2. Initialize the USART so that an interrupt is generated when any key on the keyboard is struck. The interrupt service routine must then prompt the user to enter a decimal number ranging from 0 to 255 which is then inserted into the program so as to specify the lower byte of the address from which the display sequence must start each sweep.

    In practice this means that having captured a waveform segment, any region of interest may be displayed immediately following the trigger point to allow for a more detailed inspection. Upon pressing the return key, the program must then return to the display routine and await a further keypress to change the trigger point, or a switch closure signaling a new waveform acquisition.

3. Make your program more professional by including the following:

   (a) Print the message 'Press any key to change trigger point'.
   (b) Include a character checking routine for out-of-range or illegal characters.
   (c) Provide the means whereby control may be returned to the operating system.

⑧ Designing a Simple Stand-Alone System

8.1 INTRODUCTION

The various problems and laboratory exercises that have been suggested at the end of each of the chapters so far are all intended to be carried out on a laboratory-based microcomputer system that has been provided with readily accessible parallel and serial interfacing devices, such as PPIs, PIOs and PCIs. The microcomputer will, no doubt, be equipped with a tape recorder or disks, for the storage of programs, together with a ROM-based monitor program or a disk based operating system for program handling and debugging. Such a system provides great flexibility and ease of use in what is primarily a learning environment.

Most student engineers and scientists wish to become proficient in the skills of microcomputer interfacing with the aim of practising these skills in a less sheltered environment. When it is decided that a microcomputer is to be designed into a new instrument, or employed in a data acquisition system for an existing experiment, the designer usually has in mind a dedicated system that has been optimized for the task at hand. Preferably, such a system should contain the very minimum of devices and should work without skilled attention, springing into action as soon as power is applied. The design of such a simple, stand-alone microcomputer system forms the basis for this final chapter. The system is to be provided with a PPI or PIO, for interfacing parallel devices, and a PCI for connection to a keyboard and screen. After development on a laboratory microcomputer system, the controlling program resides in EPROM, thereby allowing the system to operate in a stand-alone mode. Read-Write memory is also provided to allow the system to store data that has previously been acquired from an input port on the PPI. The system described in the following paragraphs has been used successfully by the authors in a number of simple microcomputer-based products in addition to its use as an instructional system.

8.2 Z80 CPU INPUT AND OUTPUT SIGNALS

As the principal component in any microcomputer system, it is appropriate that the connections and signals associated with the Z80 microprocessor should be dealt with first. It is inevitable, however, that decisions concerning these signals will have ramifications for other components in the system and vice versa. A design is therefore carried through with a knowledge of the requirements of all parts of the system and not just by taking each component in isolation. Considerable cross reference will be made to Chapter 2 in which the pin connections to the Z80 microprocessor and its timing diagrams have already been outlined.

A_0 - A_{15}, D_0 - D_7 and Unused Pin Connections

The 16 address lines and the eight data lines originating from the Z80 CPU are conceptually straightforward since these form the address bus and data bus of which much has been written in the previous chapters. The data lines connect directly to the bi-directional data pins of the ROM and RAM memory devices and similarly to the data pins of the PPI and PCI interfacing devices. How each of these devices connect to the address bus is postponed for a later section in which the address decoding requirements for each device are considered. A number of other pins on the CPU may be dealt with in an equally brief manner. The $\overline{\text{WAIT}}$, NMI and BUSREQ inputs have been described earlier and, for the sake of simplicity, are not to be used in this basic system. All of these functions must therefore be inhibited by means of pull-up resistors to +5 volts. Similarly, the $\overline{\text{HALT}}$, $\overline{\text{RFSH}}$, and $\overline{\text{BUSAK}}$ outputs are of no concern in the present system and therefore may be left unconnected. With the +5 volts and ground pins being self-explanatory, it is only necessary to concentrate on the eight pins that remain from the original 40.

$\overline{\text{MREQ}}$, $\overline{\text{IOREQ}}$, $\overline{\text{RD}}$ and $\overline{\text{WR}}$

The Z80 CPU generates these four control signals in order to synchronize the reading of data from, and the writing of data to, memory and I/O devices. The times at which these signals are asserted during the execution of an instruction may be deduced from the timing diagrams of Figures 2.11 to 2.15. An alternative set of four control signals may be derived from these Z80 signals (as shown in Figure 8.1), that prove to be more compatible with the control inputs required by both the memory and I/O devices. These signals are $\overline{\text{MREAD}}$ (memory read), $\overline{\text{MWRITE}}$ (memory write), $\overline{\text{IOREAD}}$ (I/O read) and $\overline{\text{IOWRITE}}$ (I/O write). The $\overline{\text{MREAD}}$ and $\overline{\text{IOREAD}}$ signals are connected to their respective OE·(output enable) or $\overline{\text{RD}}$ (read) pins on the memory or I/O devices causing the output buffer to be enabled. Data is thereby asserted onto the data bus to be read by the CPU. The $\overline{\text{MWRITE}}$ and $\overline{\text{IOWRITE}}$ signals are connected to the $\overline{\text{WR}}$ (write) input of the read-write memory or I/O device respectively, allowing the data provided by the CPU to be captured by memory or by a peripheral device.

Clock Input (CLK)

The Z80 CPU requires a single phase TTL clock operating at a frequency of up to 8 MHz depending upon the version of CPU chosen, as set out in Table 8.1.

Table 8.1 Maximum clock frequencies for the range of Z80 CPUs

	Z80	*Z80A*	*Z80B*	*Z80H*
Clock frequency	2.5 MHz	4 MHz	6 MHz	8 MHz
Clock cycle time	400ns	250ns	167ns	125ns

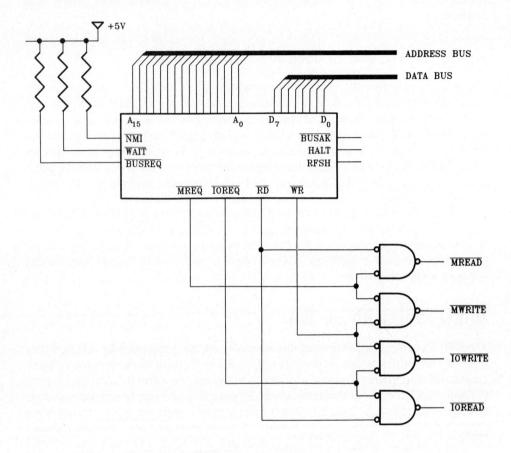

Figure 8.1 Signals associated with the Z80 CPU

A common method of generating this clock signal is illustrated in Figure 8.2. This consists of a crystal oscillator that employs two inverters together with a third inverter acting as a buffer. Since crystals of higher frequencies are smaller and cheaper than crystals of lower frequencies, it is common to employ a high frequency oscillator with a divider to produce the desired clock frequency. Some care must be exercised to ensure that the circuit oscillates reliably at the fundamental frequency of the crystal and not at some harmonic. For this reason an attractive alternative is to use a single chip hybrid oscillator.

Reset Input ($\overline{\text{RESET}}$)

It is essential that, when power is first applied to the microcomputer system, the CPU executes the program from the correct starting point, usually from memory location 0000H. This is achieved by holding the $\overline{\text{RESET}}$ input of the CPU asserted for a short period as the power supply stabilizes. A simple resistor-capacitor network with a rise time of a few

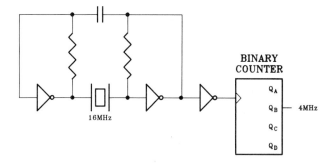

Figure 8.2 Common system clock circuit

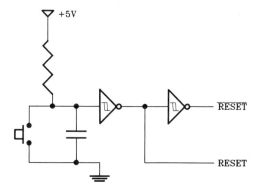

Figure 8.3 Z80 reset circuit

hundred milliseconds, followed by a Schmitt Trigger buffer to provide a well defined transition, provides a simple implementation of the power-on reset circuit. A manual reset may be provided at any time using a switch that momentarily discharges the capacitor and thereby asserts the RESET signal. In the circuit of Figure 8.3, a second inverter has been included to accommodate the different assertion levels required by the reset inputs of the CPU (asserted LOW), PPI and PCI chips (asserted HIGH).

$\overline{\text{M1}}$ and the Reset of the Z80 PIO

Unlike the Z80 CPU, the Intel PPI and the Intel PCI, the Z80 PIO does not have a separate pin performing the hardware reset function. Instead it is provided with internal logic that detects when $\overline{\text{M1}}$ is asserted in the absence of either $\overline{\text{IORQ}}$ or $\overline{\text{RD}}$ and uses this combination to perform the hardware reset.

It will be recalled from Chapter 2 that the appearance of $\overline{\text{M1}}$ normally signifies an instruction fetch and since instructions are fetched from memory, $\overline{\text{M1}}$ will normally occur along with $\overline{\text{RD}}$. The appearance of $\overline{\text{M1}}$ without $\overline{\text{RD}}$ therefore signals an abnormal occurrence. By including the $\overline{\text{IORQ}}$ signal from the Z80, two such unusual events may be signaled. $\overline{\text{M1}}$ together with $\overline{\text{IORQ}}$ is the signal combination used by the CPU to acknowledge that an interrupt has been recognized, whereas the signal $\overline{\text{M1}}$ in the absence of both $\overline{\text{RD}}$ and $\overline{\text{IORQ}}$

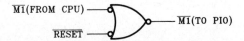

Figure 8.4 Circuit providing a hardware reset for the Z80 PIO

is used to reset the Z80 PIO. This signal combination is never generated by the Z80 CPU and so must be produced by a simple combinational logic circuit from the standard CPU control signals. Such an arrangement is shown in Figure 8.4. During normal operation when $\overline{\text{RESET}}$ is not asserted, the Z80's $\overline{\text{M1}}$ control signal is passed directly to the $\overline{\text{M1}}$ input of the PIO. During a CPU reset, however, all the Z80 control signals including $\overline{\text{M1}}$, $\overline{\text{RD}}$ and $\overline{\text{IORQ}}$ are released and thus with the circuit of Figure 8.4 the PIO appears to receive an $\overline{\text{M1}}$ signal from the Z80 in the absence of both the $\overline{\text{RD}}$ and $\overline{\text{IORQ}}$ signals. The PIO then performs a hardware reset.

$\overline{\text{INT}}$

The question of interrupt response using this system is discussed later in this chapter.

8.3 INTERFACING ROM AND RAM MEMORY

In an effort to minimize circuit complexity, the memory requirements of the stand-alone system may be met with just two chips, a 32Kbyte ROM (27256) and an 8Kbyte RAM (5564). The ROM occupies the lower half of the 64Kbyte address space of the Z80 while the RAM is located within the address range of 8000-9FFFH. As a result of this choice of addresses, a single address line, namely A_{15}, suffices to provide the chip select signal for both devices as shown in Figure 8.5.

Smaller capacity devices may be used for both the ROM and RAM; however, by always locating these devices at the addresses 0000H and 8000H, respectively, the same simple addressing scheme may be used regardless of size. The decision to use the largest possible ROM that could be accommodated with this arrangement was prompted by past experiences of finding even the simplest tasks growing in complexity as more and more features get added once the system is used.

Memory Speed Requirements

In just the same way that several versions of the Z80 CPU are available, so too are different versions of memory devices, each being characterized by a different access time. It will be recalled from Chapter 1 that the access time of a memory is the minimum time delay following the application of an address that must be allowed to ensure that the output data is stable and valid. Clearly, the shorter the access time of the memory the faster the CPU can operate. It is essential, therefore, that the memory and CPU clock speed be chosen with care. For the 27256 EPROM the access time may vary over a range of approximately three to one depending upon exactly which version is to be used, as set out in Table 8.2.

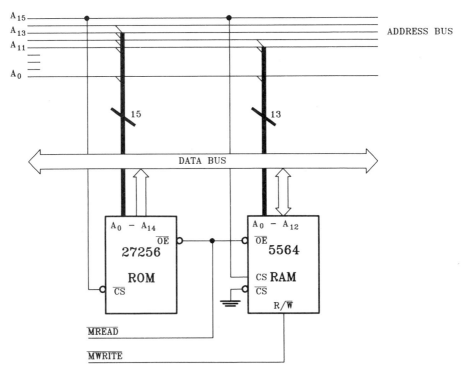

Figure 8.5 Circuit connections for the ROM and RAM memory

Table 8.2 Access times for the range of 27256 EPROMs

	27256-1	27256-2	27256	27256-3	27256-4
Access time	170ns	200ns	250ns	300ns	450ns

  With so many possible combinations of CPU speed and memory access time, it becomes confusing to write in general terms as to what combinations will operate reliably. As an alternative, a CPU will be selected, say the Z80A operating at a clock rate of 4 MHz. It is necessary to identify each delay path by which the memory might fail to provide valid data at the time that the CPU samples the data, and then indicate which of the above memories would fail to meet the critical delay. Similar calculations may then be carried out for each of the other CPUs in the Z80 range as an exercise by the reader.

Memory Read
It will be recalled from the timing diagrams of Chapter 2 that the most stringent requirements of memory access time occur during the $\overline{M1}$ cycle instruction fetch. The data provided by memory is sampled by the CPU on the rising edge of T_3 during the fetch, whereas it is sampled one half clock pulse later during a normal memory read. Data must therefore be available from the memory within two clock pulses or 500ns for a Z80A operating at 4 MHz. In the circuit of Figure 8.5, three separate signals must have stabilized before valid data will

appear at the output pins of the memory. These are the address lines, the chip select input and the output enable input. The delay time imposed by each of these signals will now be identified in order to calculate the critical delay time for the current system.

Access Time Delay

The address lines, A_0 - A_{15}, stabilize some 110ns, $t_{D(AD)}$, following the rising edge of the clock on the T_1 cycle. Data from the memory is therefore valid after a delay equal to the access time (t_{ACC}) following the application of this address. In order that the data is strobed reliably into the CPU on the rising edge of the T_3 cycle, the sum of $t_{D(AD)}$ and t_{ACC} must be less than two clock periods, or 500ns as indicated in Figure 8.6.

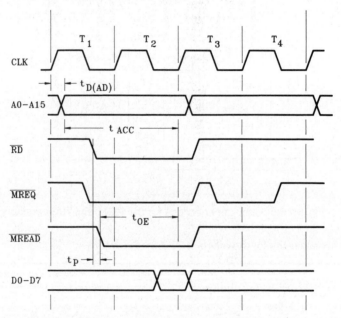

Figure 8.6 Timing constraints for an instruction fetch

Chip Select Delay

As the Chip Select input of the memory is connected to the A_{15} address line, it too will be subjected to an 110ns delay following the rising edge of T_1. For the 27256 EPROM, the Chip Select to Output Valid delay (t_{CS}) is identical to that of the access time and so the requirement that the chip is enabled before the rising edge of T_3 is the same as for the access time delay.

Output Enable Delay

As shown in Figure 8.5, the output enable signal for the memory is the $\overline{MREAD}$ signal produced by combining $\overline{MREQ}$ and $\overline{RD}$ in an AND gate. These latter signals appear some 85ns following the falling edge of T_1, $t_{DLØ(MR)}$, $t_{DLØ(RD)}$, (i.e. a total of 210ns from the rising edge of T_1). Following a delay of 15ns in the AND gate, a further Output Enable to Output Valid delay (t_{OE}) occurs within the memory chip. This output enable delay time must have terminated for the data to become valid before the rising edge of T_3.

From the table of delay times for the 27256 EPROM given in Figure 8.7, it is apparent that the output enable delay requirement is easily satisfied by all versions of the memory, whereas the access time and chip select delay requirements are met by all but the slowest device. It should be recognized that the simplicity of design of this basic system has done much to relax the speed requirements of the memory chips. Factors that are frequently present in more complex systems and absent in the present case can add significantly to the circuit delays and hence necessitate the use of faster memory chips. If, for example, several chips were used to make up the memory, a more complex address decoding scheme (such as that shown in Figure 1.17) would have to be used. The extra delay through the address decoder would reduce the time available for memory access and thus a faster memory chip would be needed. More significantly, if the memory were to be located on a separate board to that holding the CPU, it might well be necessary to provide buffers for both the address and data buses. The delays through these buffers, together with the delay in producing the buffer control signals, all reduce the time available for the memory to provide stable and valid data to the CPU.

Parameter	Description	Min Values All Types	Maximum Values					Units
			27256-1	27256-2	27256	27256-3	27256-4	
t_{ACC}	Address to output delay		170	200	250	300	450	ns
t_{CE}	Chip enable to output delay		170	200	250	300	450	ns
t_{OE}	Output enable to output delay		75	75	100	120	150	ns
t_{DF}	Output enable high to output float	0	60	60	60	105	130	ns
t_{OH}	Output hold from addresses, CE or OE (whichever occurred first)	0						ns

Figure 8.7 Timing specifications for the 27256 EPROM

The timing constraints referred to in the above paragraphs may be overcome in several ways. The decision to use high-speed memory chips or a low CPU clock frequency, or both, are obvious solutions to the problem but ones that impose a penalty of higher cost or lower operating speed. A solution that only marginally reduces the speed of execution is to include one or more WAIT states to each memory cycle. It will be recalled from Chapter 2 that the Z80 CPU has a $\overline{\text{WAIT}}$ input which, when asserted, maintains all CPU signals at their current levels. As the $\overline{\text{WAIT}}$ input is sampled on the falling edge of T_2, a shift register circuit clocked on the rising edge of the clock can be used to provide a WAIT time of 1, 2 or 3 clock periods to suit whatever memory is used. Such a circuit is shown in Figure 8.8.

On the first clock pulse after $\overline{\text{MREQ}}$ is asserted, a logic 0 is shifted into the first stage of the register. The $\overline{\text{WAIT}}$ input then becomes active holding $\overline{\text{MREQ}}$ low. After 1, 2 or 3 clock pulses, depending upon which link is inserted, the $\overline{\text{WAIT}}$ line is released and the T_3 cycle commences. The Z80 CPU is therefore able to accommodate memory of any speed, providing sufficient WAIT states are inserted between the T_2 and T_3 memory cycles.

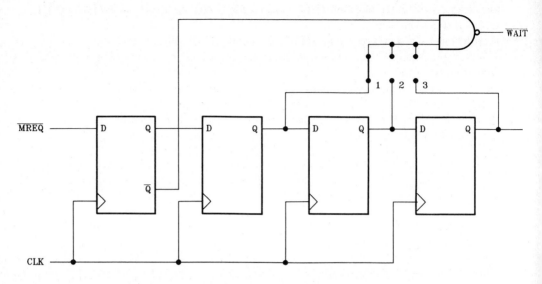

Figure 8.8 Circuit to add WAIT states to memory cycles

Memory Write

Data is written into the memory on the falling edge of T_3 and hence there is a requirement for the write cycle time of the memory to be no greater than two and one half clock periods less the CPU's address delay time, $t_{D(AD)}$, as shown in Figure 8.9. In addition, it is necessary that the write pulse width, t_{WP}, required by the memory be less than one clock period. This latter requirement results from the fact that the $\overline{WR}$ output from the CPU commences on the falling edge of T_2 and terminates on the falling edge of T_3. The write cycle of the CPU differs from the read cycle in that the write ($\overline{WR}$) signal is asserted for just one clock pulse whereas the read ($\overline{RD}$) signal is asserted along with the $\overline{MREQ}$ signal for two clock pulses. This ensures that the address lines to the memory, and the internal decoders within the memory, have had sufficient time to stabilize on the selected address, thereby avoiding data being written inadvertently into other memory locations.

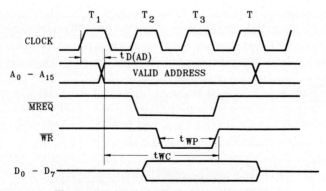

Figure 8.9 Write cycle timing requirements

8.4 INTERFACING THE PARALLEL AND SERIAL I/O DEVICES

Addressing

Since the stand-alone system is designed to accommodate one PPI and one PCI, a simple form of non-unique addressing may be used, requiring just a single inverter. The elements of this addressing scheme are shown in Figure 8.10. The PPI occupies four port addresses, from 00H to 03H, while the PCI adds a further two at locations 04H and 05H.

It should be remembered that the registers listed in the right-hand column of the table will respond to all I/O addresses having the least significant bits listed in the left-hand column. For example, port A of the PPI will respond to addresses 08H, 24H, 32H and so on, as well as address 00H. However, if the devices connected to these ports are given some meaningful name via the EQU equate statement, then difficulties with non-unique addressing are unlikely to occur. Both the PPI and PCI have $\overline{RD}$ and $\overline{WR}$ inputs whereby the CPU can read from the chip or write to the chip respectively. In both cases these are simply connected to the $\overline{IOREAD}$ and $\overline{IOWRITE}$ signals described earlier.

PPI Output Buffer

The peripheral ports of the Intel 8255 PPI have only a limited output current drive capability. The data sheets included in Appendix C indicate that the output voltage for a logic 1 output is only guaranteed to be greater than 2.4 volts if the port is called upon to source less than 200µA. Similarly, the output voltage for a logic 0 output is guaranteed to be less than 0.45 volts provided the port sinks less than 1.7 mA. This limited current output of the PPI can give rise to problems when a peripheral device is connected to the PPI by a cable of more than a few tens of centimetres in length. This is especially noticeable when the data is to be transferred at high speed. In essence, the PPI output and cable acts as an R-C network that charges and discharges with the familiar exponential growth and decay. If the receiving end

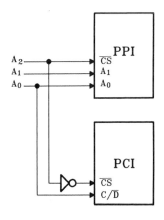

$A_2 A_1 A_0$	REGISTER
0 0 0	PPI PORT A
0 0 1	PPI PORT B
0 1 0	PPI PORT C
0 1 1	PPI CONTROL
1 0 0	PCI DATA
1 0 1	PCI CONTROL

Figure 8.10 Addressing scheme for the PPI and PCI

of such a transmission line, be it the PPI or the peripheral, samples the rising or falling waveform too early, it may receive some, or all, of the bits in error.

A solution to this problem may be found by either slowing down the rate of transmission or by reducing the cable length. If neither of these provide a remedy, it becomes necessary to enhance the output drive capability of the PPI with a line driver, such as the 74245 shown in Figure 8.11. When a stand-alone system is to be used for a specific purpose, such as a data acquisition system, it will have been decided which port is to be designated an input port and which is an output port. The direction inputs on the 74245 buffer can then be connected accordingly. If, however, the stand-alone system is to be used as an instructional system, so that all combinations of input and output ports can be accommodated, then the direction inputs of the buffer must be connected to two pins of port C to allow the direction of the buffer to be selected under software control. This latter arrangement is illustrated in Figure 8.11.

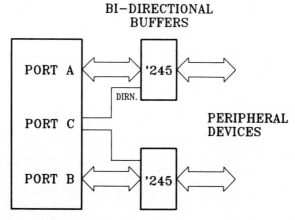

Figure 8.11 Bi-directional buffers to enhance output drive capability

PCI Level Shifting Devices

The PCI transmits and receives serial data conforming to the usual TTL unipolar voltage levels of approximately 0 volts and +5 volts. In order to communicate with serial devices complying with the RS 232-C recommended standard, it is necessary that these voltage levels be transformed into the bipolar range of -15 to -5 volts for a logic 1, and +5 to +15 volts for a logic 0. A new, and particularly simple, solution to this level shifting requirement is now available in the form of the MAX 232, TTL to RS 232-C transceiver. This monolithic integrated circuit contains two transmitters and two receivers in a single package operating from a single 5 volt supply.

The remaining requirement for the PCI is a clock circuit generating one or more of the frequencies that, following division within the PCI, translates into a standard data rate for serial transmission.

Interrupts

Much of the power of a microcomputer is wasted if the CPU is required to continuously monitor the state of a peripheral to determine when it is ready to transfer data. It is important, therefore, that the interfacing devices included on the stand-alone system be able to request attention via the process of generating an interrupt. In the case of the PPI, an interrupt request appears on output line C_3 for port A and on line C_0 for port B. With the PCI, an interrupt may be generated either by the receiver having accepted a new input character (RxRDY) or by the transmitter having finished transmitting the last output character (TxRDY). These four signals, which are all asserted high, may be inverted and combined to give an asserted low CPU interrupt signal ($\overline{\text{INT}}$) when any one device requires service, by way of the circuit shown in Figure 8.12. Provision has been included in this circuit to inhibit any of the interrupting devices by way of a movable link. Without such a facility the PPI output lines C_3 and C_0, for example, could inadvertently generate an interrupt resulting from data sent to port C. When more than one device can generate interrupts, polling will be needed to identify the actual interrupting device.

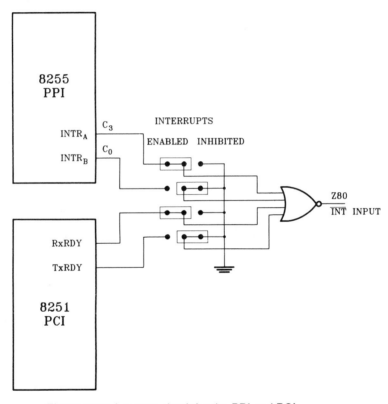

Figure 8.12 Interrupt circuit for the PPI and PCI

PROBLEMS

Problem 8.1
Using the information contained in Chapter 8, draw a complete circuit diagram of a stand-alone system comprising 32Kbytes of ROM, 8Kbytes of RAM, an 8255 PPI and an 8251 PCI.

Problem 8.2
Indicate the additional components needed to convert the system specified in Problem 8.1 to one containing 32Kbytes rather than 8Kbytes of RAM, all other specifications remaining unaltered. In answering this question assume that you have four separate 8Kbyte RAM chips.

LABORATORY EXERCISES

Virtually all of the experiments described in the earlier chapters may be performed using a stand-alone microcomputer system similar to that described in the above paragraphs. It is necessary, however, to have available a laboratory-based system on which the code may be developed together with PROM programming facilities. Having tested the code on a system that allows the changes that are an inevitable part of program development to be easily made, a PROM containing the debugged code may then be inserted into the stand-alone system. Since changes to programs that have been transferred to PROM are relatively time consuming, the laboratory exercises that follow have only moderately difficult objectives which may be achieved within a three to four hour laboratory session. The exercises, however, can be extended considerably in order to challenge the more advanced student.

Laboratory Exercise 8.1

Simple Parallel and Serial I/O Experiment

Aim

The aim of this experiment is to perform basic parallel and serial input-output data transfers to a stand-alone microcomputer system.

Procedure

1. Write a program that accepts an 8-bit binary number from a switch register, displays this number on a set of eight logic indicators and then proceeds to count down the display to zero at a rate of approximately one count per second. Upon reaching zero, the number on the switch register is to be re-entered and the count-down resumed.

2. Add to the above main program an interrupt service routine that is entered each time a key is pressed on a keyboard connected to the receive input of the PCI. Following a keypress, the selected character should appear on a VDU connected to the transmit output of the PCI.

3. Modify the above program so that the count proceeds at a rate determined by an external oscillator. On each high to low transition of the oscillator, an interrupt is to occur that has the effect of decrementing the displayed count by one. The main program should now become a routine that displays a 'pulsating' version of the count, that is one in which the illuminated logic indicators are made to turn on and off at a rate of approximately 10 Hz.

Laboratory Exercise 8.2

Data Acquisition and Display

Aim

The aim of this experiment is to produce a stand-alone data acquisition system in which the sampling rate may be altered via keyboard entry.

Procedure

1. Write and test the main program which loads 256 locations in memory with the numbers 0-255 and then continuously outputs the data to a DAC for display on an oscilloscope. Include an oscilloscope trigger pulse to give a stable output display.

2. Include an interrupt service routine that is entered each time an ADC connected to an input port of the PPI raises its READY flag. As each new sample is acquired, the data is to be loaded into the display buffer overwriting the previously loaded ramp waveform. Acquisition should be suspended when 256 samples have been obtained. Further acquisition cycles should commence following the pressing of a switch connected to one line of port C.

3. In the arrangement so far, the sampling rate for data acquisition is determined by the frequency of the external oscillator. Control over this data acquisition rate may be exercised by the microcomputer via the circuit shown in Figure 8.13. A four line to one line selector, controlled by a 2-bit address originating from port C of the PPI, allows one of four frequencies to be selected to drive the ADC.

4. Include a second interrupt service routine that is entered whenever the keyboard connected to the PCI is struck. This routine should examine the received character and ignore all but the four valid characters 1, 2, 3 and 4. When a valid character is received the sampling rate for the next acquisition cycle should then change to that indicated in Figure 8.13.

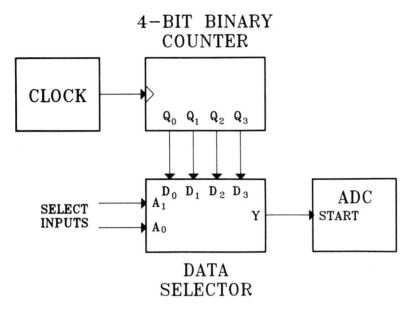

Figure 8.13 Frequency control circuit

Laboratory Exercise 8.3

Traffic Light Controller

Aim

The aim of this experiment is to design and build a traffic light controller that normally operates in a simple timed mode with, upon receipt of a command from a keyboard, priority being immediately granted to either the primary road (P) or the secondary road (S). Normal timed operation is then resumed upon receipt of a further command (N).

Procedure

1. Develop a main program that controls six logic indicators simulating two sets of traffic lights at an intersection of a primary road (P) and a secondary road (S). The lights should operate with a basic period of approximately two seconds thereby completing the following cycle in 12 seconds.

Primary	Secondary
Red	Green
Red	Green
Red	Amber
Green	Red
Green	Red
Amber	Red

2. Include an interrupt service routine that is entered each time a key on the keyboard connected to the PCI is struck. Initially, the service routine should filter out the two valid characters of P and S, freezing the display in favor of the primary road (P) or secondary road (S) if that road currently receives a green signal, or changing the display via a 2 second amber period to a constant green signal if the signal is currently red.

3. When normal timed operation is to be resumed, an 'N' character is to be entered after which time an amber signal restarts the normal sequence.

APPENDIX A: ASCII CODE CONVERSION TABLE

HEX	MSD	O	1	2	3	4	5	6	7
LSD	BITS	000	001	010	011	100	101	110	111
0	0000	NUL	DLE	SPACE	0	@	P	—	p
1	0001	SOH	DC1	!	1	A	Q	a	q
2	0010	STX	DC2	"	2	B	R	b	r
3	0011	EXT	DC3	#	3	C	S	c	s
4	0100	EOT	DC4	$	4	D	T	d	t
5	0101	ENQ	NAK	%	5	E	U	e	u
6	0110	ACK	SYN	&	6	F	V	f	v
7	0111	BEL	ETB	'	7	G	W	g	w
8	1000	BS	CAN	(	8	H	X	h	x
9	1001	HT	EM	)	9	I	Y	i	y
A	1010	LF	SUB	*	:	J	Z	j	z
B	1011	VT	ESC	+	;	K	[	k	{
C	1100	FF	FS	,	<	L	\	l	--
D	1101	CR	GS	—	=	M	]	m	}
E	1110	SO	RS	.	>	N	∧	n	≈
F	1111	SI	US	/	?	O	←	o	DEL

THE ASCII SYMBOLS

NUL	- Null	DLE	- Data Link Escape
SOH	- Start of Heading	DC	- Device Control
STX	- Start of Text	NAK	- Negative Acknowledge
ETX	- End of Text	SYN	- Synchronous Idle
EOT	- End of Transmission	ETB	- End of Transmission Block
ENQ	- Enquiry	CAN	- Cancel
ACK	- Acknowledge	EM	- End of Medium
BEL	- Bell	SUB	- Substitute
BS	- Backspace	ESC	- Escape
HT	- Horizontal Tabulation	FS	- File Separator
LF	- Line Feed	GS	- Group Separator
VT	- Vertical Tabulation	RS	- Record Separator
FF	- Form Feed	US	- Unit Separator
CR	- Carriage Return	SP	- Space (Blank)
SO	- Shift Out	DEL	- Delete
SI	- Shift In		

APPENDIX B: DATA SHEET FOR THE ZILOG Z80 MICROPROCESSOR INCLUDING THE Z80 INSTRUCTION SET

Z8400
Z80® CPU Central
Processing Unit

Zilog

Product Specification

April 1985

FEATURES

- The instruction set contains 158 instructions. The 78 instructions of the 8080A are included as a subset; 8080A software compatibility is maintained.

- Eight MHz, 6 MHz, 4 MHz, and 2.5 MHz clocks for the Z80H, Z80B, Z80A, and Z80 CPU result in rapid instruction execution with consequent high data throughput.

- The extensive instruction set includes string, bit, byte, and word operations. Block searches and block transfers, together with indexed and relative addressing, result in the most powerful data handling capabilities in the microcomputer industry.

- The Z80 microprocessors and associated family of peripheral controllers are linked by a vectored interrupt system. This system may be daisy-chained to allow implementation of a priority interrupt scheme. Little, if any, additional logic is required for daisy-chaining.

- Duplicate sets of both general-purpose and flag registers are provided, easing the design and operation of system software through single-context switching, background-foreground programming, and single-level interrupt processing. In addition, two 16-bit index registers facilitate program processing of tables and arrays.

- There are three modes of high speed interrupt processing: 8080 similar, non-Z80 peripheral device, and Z80 Family peripheral with or without daisy chain.

- On-chip dynamic memory refresh counter.

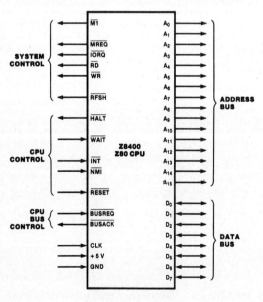

Figure 1. Pin Functions

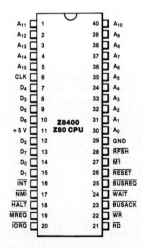

Figure 2a. 40-Pin Dual-In-Line Package (DIP)
Pin Assignments

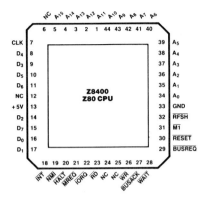

Figure 2b. 44-Pin Chip Carrier Pin Assignments

GENERAL DESCRIPTION

The Z80, Z80A, Z80B, and Z80H CPUs are third-generation single-chip microprocessors with exceptional computational power. They offer higher system throughput and more efficient memory utilization than comparable second- and third-generation microprocessors. The internal registers contain 208 bits of read/write memory that are accessible to the programmer. These registers include two sets of six general-purpose registers which may be used individually as either 8-bit registers or as 16-bit register pairs. In addition, there are two sets of accumulator and flag registers. A group of "Exchange" instructions makes either set of main or alternate registers accessible to the programmer. The alternate set allows operation in foreground-background mode or it may be reserved for very fast interrupt response.

The Z80 also contains a Stack Pointer, Program Counter, two index registers, a Refresh register (counter), and an Interrupt register. The CPU is easy to incorporate into a system since it requires only a single +5V power source. All output signals are fully decoded and timed to control standard memory or peripheral circuits; the CPU is supported by an extensive family of peripheral controllers. The internal block diagram (Figure 3) shows the primary functions of the Z80 processors. Subsequent text provides more detail on the Z80 I/O controller family, registers, instruction set, interrupts and daisy chaining, and CPU timing.

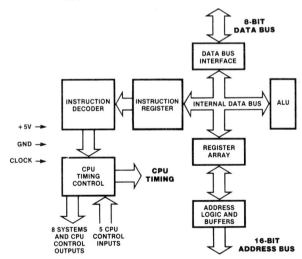

Figure 3. Z80 CPU Block Diagram

Z80 MICROPROCESSOR FAMILY

The Zilog Z80 microprocessor is the central element of a comprehensive microprocessor product family. This family works together in most applications with minimum requirements for additional logic, facilitating the design of efficient and cost-effective microcomputer-based systems.

Zilog has designed five components to provide extensive support for the Z80 microprocessor. These are:

■ The PIO (Parallel Input/Output) operates in both data-byte I/O transfer mode (with handshaking) and in bit mode (without handshaking). The PIO may be configured to interface with standard parallel peripheral devices such as printers, tape punches, and keyboards.

■ The CTC (Counter/Timer Circuit) features four programmable 8-bit counter/timers, each of which has an 8-bit prescaler. Each of the four channels may be configured to operate in either counter or timer mode.

■ The DMA (Direct Memory Access) controller provides dual port data transfer operations and the ability to terminate data transfer as a result of a pattern match.

■ The SIO (Serial Input/Output) controller offers two channels. It is capable of operating in a variety of programmable modes for both synchronous and asynchronous communication, including Bi-Synch and SDLC.

■ The DART (Dual Asynchronous Receiver/Transmitter) device provides low cost asynchronous serial communication. It has two channels and a full modem control interface.

Z80 CPU REGISTERS

Figure 4 shows three groups of registers within the Z80 CPU. The first group consists of duplicate sets of 8-bit registers: a principal set and an alternate set (designated by ′ [prime], e.g., A′). Both sets consist of the Accumulator Register, the Flag Register, and six general-purpose registers. Transfer of data between these duplicate sets of registers is accomplished by use of "Exchange" instructions. The result is faster response to interrupts and easy, efficient implementation of such versatile pro-

gramming techniques as background-foreground data processing. The second set of registers consists of six registers with assigned functions. These are the I (Interrupt Register), the R (Refresh Register), the IX and IY (Index Registers), the SP (Stack Pointer), and the PC (Program Counter). The third group consists of two interrupt status flip-flops, plus an additional pair of flip-flops which assists in identifying the interrupt mode at any particular time. Table 1 provides further information on these registers.

MAIN REGISTER SET

ALTERNATE REGISTER SET

A ACCUMULATOR	F FLAG REGISTER	A′ ACCUMULATOR	F′ FLAG REGISTER
B GENERAL PURPOSE	C GENERAL PURPOSE	B′ GENERAL PURPOSE	C′ GENERAL PURPOSE
D GENERAL PURPOSE	E GENERAL PURPOSE	D′ GENERAL PURPOSE	E′ GENERAL PURPOSE
H GENERAL PURPOSE	L GENERAL PURPOSE	H′ GENERAL PURPOSE	L′ GENERAL PURPOSE

◄──── 8 BITS ────►

◄──── 16 BITS ────►

IX INDEX REGISTER	
IY INDEX REGISTER	
SP STACK POINTER	
PC PROGRAM COUNTER	
I INTERRUPT VECTOR	R MEMORY REFRESH

◄──── 8 BITS ────►

INTERRUPT FLIP-FLOPS STATUS

IFF₁   IFF₂

0 = INTERRUPTS DISABLED
1 = INTERRUPTS ENABLED

STORES IFF1
DURING $\overline{NMI}$
SERVICE

INTERRUPT MODE FLIP-FLOPS

IMFₐ	IMFᵦ	
0	0	INTERRUPT MODE 0
0	1	NOT USED
1	0	INTERRUPT MODE 1
1	1	INTERRUPT MODE 2

Figure 4. CPU Registers

Z80 CPU REGISTERS (Continued)

Table 1. Z80 CPU Registers

Register		Size (Bits)	Remarks
A, A'	Accumulator	8	Stores an operand or the results of an operation.
F, F'	Flags	8	See Instruction Set.
B, B'	General Purpose	8	Can be used separately or as a 16-bit register with C.
C, C'	General Purpose	8	See B, above.
D, D'	General Purpose	8	Can be used separately or as a 16-bit register with E.
E, E'	General Purpose	8	See D, above.
H, H'	General Purpose	8	Can be used separately or as a 16-bit register with L.
L, L'	General Purpose	8	See H, above.

			Note: The (B,C), (D,E), and (H,L) sets are combined as follows:
			  B — High byte C — Low byte
			  D — High byte E — Low byte
			  H — High byte L — Low byte

I	Interrupt Register	8	Stores upper eight bits of memory address for vectored interrupt processing.
R	Refresh Register	8	Provides user-transparent dynamic memory refresh. Automatically incremented and placed on the address bus during each instruction fetch cycle.
IX	Index Register	16	Used for indexed addressing.
IY	Index Register	16	Used for indexed addressing
SP	Stack Pointer	16	Holds address of the top of the stack. See Push or Pop in instruction set.
PC	Program Counter	16	Holds address of next instruction.
IFF_1-IFF_2	Interrupt Enable	Flip-Flops	Set or reset to indicate interrupt status (see Figure 4).
IMFa-IMFb	Interrupt Mode	Flip-Flops	Reflect Interrupt mode (see Figure 4).

INTERRUPTS: GENERAL OPERATION

The CPU accepts two interrupt input signals: $\overline{NMI}$ and $\overline{INT}$. The $\overline{NMI}$ is a non-maskable interrupt and has the highest priority. $\overline{INT}$ is a lower priority interrupt and it requires that interrupts be enabled in software in order to operate. $\overline{INT}$ can be connected to multiple peripheral devices in a wired-OR configuration.

The Z80 has a single response mode for interrupt service for the non-maskable interrupt. The maskable interrupt, $\overline{INT}$, has three programmable response modes available. These are:

■ Mode 0 — similar to the 8080 microprocessor.

■ Mode 1 — Peripheral Interrupt service, for use with non-8080/Z80 systems.

■ Mode 2 — a vectored interrupt scheme, usually daisy-chained, for use with Z80 Family and compatible peripheral devices.

The CPU services interrupts by sampling the $\overline{NMI}$ and $\overline{INT}$ signals at the rising edge of the last clock of an instruction. Further interrupt service processing depends upon the type of interrupt that was detected. Details on interrupt responses are shown in the CPU Timing Section.

Non-Maskable Interrupt ($\overline{NMI}$). The nonmaskable interrupt cannot be disabled by program control and therefore will be accepted at all times by the CPU. $\overline{NMI}$ is usually reserved for servicing only the highest priority type interrupts, such as that for orderly shutdown after power failure has been detected. After recognition of the $\overline{NMI}$ signal (providing $\overline{BUSREQ}$ is not active), the CPU jumps to restart location 0066H. Normally, software starting at this address contains the interrupt service routine.

Maskable Interrupt ($\overline{INT}$). Regardless of the interrupt mode set by the user, the Z80 response to a maskable interrupt input follows a common timing cycle. After the interrupt has been detected by the CPU (provided that interrupts are enabled and $\overline{BUSREQ}$ is not active) a special interrupt processing cycle begins. This is a special fetch ($\overline{M1}$) cycle in which $\overline{IORQ}$ becomes active rather than $\overline{MREQ}$, as in a normal $\overline{M1}$ cycle. In addition, this special $\overline{M1}$ cycle is automatically extended by two $\overline{WAIT}$ states, to allow for the time required to acknowledge the interrupt request.

Mode 0 Interrupt Operation. This mode is similar to the 8080 microprocessor interrupt service procedures. The interrupting device places an instruction on the data bus. This is normally a Restart instruction, which will initiate a call to the selected one of eight restart locations in page zero of memory. Unlike the 8080, the Z80 CPU responds to the Call instruction with only one interrupt acknowledge cycle followed by two memory read cycles.

Mode 1 Interrupt Operation. Mode 1 operation is very similar to that for the $\overline{NMI}$. The principal difference is that the Mode 1 interrupt has only one restart location, 0038H.

Mode 2 Interrupt Operation. This interrupt mode has been designed to utilize most effectively the capabilities of the Z80 microprocessor and its associated peripheral family. The interrupting peripheral device selects the starting address of the interrupt service routine. It does this by placing an 8-bit vector on the data bus during the interrupt acknowledge cycle. The CPU forms a pointer using this byte as the lower 8 bits and the contents of the I register as the upper 8 bits. This points to an entry in a table of addresses for interrupt service routines. The CPU then jumps to the routine at that address. This flexibility in selecting the interrupt service routine address allows the peripheral device to use several different types of service routines. These routines may be located at any available location in memory. Since the interrupting device supplies the low-order byte of the 2-byte vector, bit 0 (A_0) must be a zero.

Interrupt Priority (Daisy Chaining and Nested Interrupts). The interrupt priority of each peripheral device is determined by its physical location within a daisy-chain configuration. Each device in the chain has an interrupt enable input line (IEI) and an interrupt enable output line (IEO), which is fed to the next lower priority device. The first device in the daisy chain has its IEI input hardwired to a High

level. The first device has highest priority, while each succeeding device has a corresponding lower priority. This arrangement permits the CPU to select the highest priority interrupt from several simultaneously interrupting peripherals.

The interrupting device disables its IEO line to the next lower priority peripheral until it has been serviced. After servicing, its IEO line is raised, allowing lower priority peripherals to demand interrupt servicing.

The Z80 CPU will nest (queue) any pending interrupts or interrupts received while a selected peripheral is being serviced.

Interrupt Enable/Disable Operation. Two flip-flops, IFF_1 and IFF_2, referred to in the register description, are used to signal the CPU interrupt status. Operation of the two flip-flops is described in Table 2. For more details, refer to the *Z80 CPU Technical Manual* (03-0029-01) and *Z80 Assembly Language Programming Manual* (03-0002-01).

Table 2. State of Flip-Flops

Action	IFF_1	IFF_2	Comments
CPU Reset	0	0	Maskable interrupt INT disabled
DI instruction execution	0	0	Maskable interrupt INT disabled
EI instruction execution	1	1	Maskable interrupt INT enabled
LD A,I instruction execution	•	•	$IFF_2 \rightarrow$ Parity flag
LD A,R instruction execution	•	•	$IFF_2 \rightarrow$ Parity flag
Accept NMI	0	IFF_1	$IFF_1 \rightarrow IFF_2$ (Maskable interrupt INT disabled)
RETN instruction execution	IFF_2	•	$IFF_2 \rightarrow IFF_1$ at completion of an NMI service routine.

INSTRUCTION SET

The Z80 microprocessr has one of the most powerful and versatile instruction sets available in any 8-bit microprocessor. It includes such unique operations as a block move for fast, efficient data transfers within memory, or between memory and I/O. It also allows operations on any bit in any location in memory.

The following is a summary of the Z80 instruction set which shows the assembly language mnemonic, the operation, the flag status, and gives comments on each instruction. For an explanation of flag notations and symbols for mnemonic tables, see the Symbolic Notations section which follows these tables. The *Z80 CPU Technical Manual* (03-0029-01), the *Programmer's Reference Guide* (03-0012-03), and *Assembly Language Programming Manual* (03-0002-01) contain significantly more details for programming use.

The instructions are divided into the following categories:

□ 8-bit loads

□ 16-bit loads

□ Exchanges, block transfers, and searches

□ 8-bit arithmetic and logic operations

□ General-purpose arithmetic and CPU control

□ 16-bit arithmetic operations

□ Rotates and shifts

□ Bit set, reset, and test operations

□ Jumps

□ Calls, returns, and restarts

□ Input and output operations

A variety of addressing modes are implemented to permit efficient and fast data transfer between various registers, memory locations, and input/output devices. These addressing modes include:

□ Immediate

□ Immediate extended

□ Modified page zero

□ Relative

□ Extended

□ Indexed

□ Register

□ Register indirect

□ Implied

□ Bit

8-BIT LOAD GROUP

Mnemonic	Symbolic Operation	S	Z	Flags H	P/V	N	C	Opcode 76	543	210	Hex	No. of Bytes	No. of M Cycles	No. of T States	Comments	
LD r, r'	r ← r'	•	•	X	•	X	•	•	•	01	r	r'		1	1	4	r, r'	Reg.
LD r, n	r ← n	•	•	X	•	X	•	•	•	00	r	110		2	2	7	000	B
									← n →						001	C
LD r, (HL)	r ← (HL)	•	•	X	•	X	•	•	•	01	r	110		1	2	7	010	D
LD r, (IX + d)	r ← (IX + d)	•	•	X	•	X	•	•	•	11	011	101	DD	3	5	19	011	E
									01	r	110					100	H
									← d →						101	L
LD r, (IY + d)	r ← (IY + d)	•	•	X	•	X	•	•	•	11	111	101	FD	3	5	19	111	A
									01	r	110						
									← d →							
LD (HL), r	(HL) ← r	•	•	X	•	X	•	•	•	01	110	r		1	2	7		
LD (IX + d), r	(IX + d) ← r	•	•	X	•	X	•	•	•	11	011	101	DD	3	5	19		
									01	110	r						
									← d →							
LD (IY + d), r	(IY + d) ← r	•	•	X	•	X	•	•	•	11	111	101	FD	3	5	19		
									01	110	r						
									← d →							
LD (HL), n	(HL) ← n	•	•	X	•	X	•	•	•	00	110	110	36	2	3	10		
									← n →							
LD (IX + d), n	(IX + d) ← n	•	•	X	•	X	•	•	•	11	011	101	DD	4	5	19		
									00	110	110	36					
									← d →							
									← n →							

8-BIT LOAD GROUP (Continued)

Mnemonic	Symbolic Operation	S	Z	H	P/V	N	C	76	543	210	Hex	No. of Bytes	No. of M Cycles	No. of T States	Comments
LD (IY + d), n	(IY + d) ← n	•	•	X	• X	•	• •	11	111	101	FD	4	5	19	
								00	110	110	36				
					← d →										
					← n →										
LD A, (BC)	A ← (BC)	•	•	X	• X	•	• •	00	001	010	0A	1	2	7	
LD A, (DE)	A ← (DE)	•	•	X	• X	•	• •	00	011	010	1A	1	2	7	
LD A, (nn)	A ← (nn)	•	•	X	• X	•	• •	00	111	010	3A	3	4	13	
					← n →										
					← n →										
LD (BC), A	(BC) ← A	•	•	X	• X	•	• •	00	000	010	02	1	2	7	
LD (DE), A	(DE) ← A	•	•	X	• X	•	• •	00	010	010	12	1	2	7	
LD (nn), A	(nn) ← A	•	•	X	• X	•	• •	00	110	010	32	3	4	13	
					← n →										
					← n →										
LD A, I	A ← I	‡	‡	X	0 X	IFF	0 •	11	101	101	ED	2	2	9	
								01	010	111	57				
LD A, R	A ← R	‡	‡	X	0 X	IFF	0 •	11	101	101	ED	2	2	9	
								01	011	111	5F				
LD I, A	I ← A	•	•	X	• X	•	• •	11	101	101	ED	2	2	9	
								01	000	111	47				
LD R, A	R ← A	•	•	X	• X	•	• •	11	101	101	ED	2	2	9	
								01	001	111	4F				

NOTE: IFF, the content of the interrupt enable flip-flop, (IFF_2), is copied into the P/V flag.

16-BIT LOAD GROUP

Mnemonic	Symbolic Operation	S	Z	H	P/V	N	C	76	543	210	Hex	No. of Bytes	No. of M Cycles	No. of T States	Comments
LD dd, nn	dd ← nn	•	•	X	• X	•	• •	00	dd0	001		3	3	10	dd Pair
					← n →										00 BC
					← n →										01 DE
LD IX, nn	IX ← nn	•	•	X	• X	•	• •	11	011	101	DD	4	4	14	10 HL
								00	100	001	21				11 SP
					← n →										
					← n →										
LD IY, nn	IY ← nn	•	•	X	• X	•	• •	11	111	101	FD	4	4	14	
								00	100	001	21				
					← n →										
					← n →										
LD HL, (nn)	H ← (nn + 1)	•	•	X	• X	•	• •	00	101	010	2A	3	5	16	
	L ← (nn)				← n →										
					← n →										
LD dd, (nn)	dd_H ← (nn + 1)	•	•	X	• X	•	• •	11	101	101	ED	4	6	20	
	dd_L ← (nn)							01	dd1	011					
					← n →										
					← n →										

NOTE: $(PAIR)_H$, $(PAIR)_L$ refer to high order and low order eight bits of the register pair respectively. e.g., BC_L = C, AF_H = A.

16-BIT LOAD GROUP (Continued)

Mnemonic	Symbolic Operation	S	Z		H		P/V	N	C	76	543	210	Hex	No. of Bytes	No. of M Cycles	No. of T States	Comments
LD IX, (nn)	$IX_H \leftarrow (nn+1)$ $IX_L \leftarrow (nn)$	•	•	X	•	X	•	•	•	11 00 ←n→ ←n→	011 101	101 010	DD 2A	4	6	20	
LD IY, (nn)	$IY_H \leftarrow (nn+1)$ $IY_L \leftarrow (nn)$	•	•	X	•	X	•	•	•	11 00 ←n→ ←n→	111 101	101 010	FD 2A	4	6	20	
LD (nn), HL	$(nn+1) \leftarrow H$ $(nn) \leftarrow L$	•	•	X	•	X	•	•	•	00 ←n→ ←n→	100	010	22	3	5	16	
LD (nn), dd	$(nn+1) \leftarrow dd_H$ $(nn) \leftarrow dd_L$	•	•	X	•	X	•	•	•	11 01 ←n→ ←n→	101 dd0	101 011	ED	4	6	20	
LD (nn), IX	$(nn+1) \leftarrow IX_H$ $(nn) \leftarrow IX_L$	•	•	X	•	X	•	•	•	11 00 ←n→ ←n→	011 100	101 010	DD 22	4	6	20	
LD (nn), IY	$(nn+1) \leftarrow IY_H$ $(nn) \leftarrow IY_L$	•	•	X	•	X	•	•	•	11 00 ←n→ ←n→	111 100	101 010	FD 22	4	6	20	
LD SP, HL	$SP \leftarrow HL$	•	•	X	•	X	•	•	•	11	111	001	F9	1	1	6	
LD SP, IX	$SP \leftarrow IX$	•	•	X	•	X	•	•	•	11 11	011 111	101 001	DD F9	2	2	10	
LD SP, IY	$SP \leftarrow IY$	•	•	X	•	X	•	•	•	11 11	111 111	101 001	FD F9	2	2	10	
PUSH qq	$(SP-2) \leftarrow qq_L$ $(SP-1) \leftarrow qq_H$ $SP \rightarrow SP-2$	•	•	X	•	X	•	•	•	11	qq0	101		1	3	11	qq Pair 00 BC 01 DE 10 HL 11 AF
PUSH IX	$(SP-2) \leftarrow IX_L$ $(SP-1) \leftarrow IX_H$ $SP \rightarrow SP-2$	•	•	X	•	X	•	•	•	11 11	011 100	101 101	DD E5	2	4	15	
PUSH IY	$(SP-2) \leftarrow IY_L$ $(SP-1) \leftarrow IY_H$ $SP \rightarrow SP-2$	•	•	X	•	X	•	•	•	11 11	111 100	101 101	FD E5	2	4	15	
POP qq	$qq_H \leftarrow (SP+1)$ $qq_L \leftarrow (SP)$ $SP \rightarrow SP+2$	•	•	X	•	X	•	•	•	11	qq0	001		1	3	10	
POP IX	$IX_H \leftarrow (SP+1)$ $IX_L \leftarrow (SP)$ $SP \rightarrow SP+2$	•	•	X	•	X	•	•	•	11 11	011 100	101 001	DD E1	2	4	14	
POP IY	$IY_H \leftarrow (SP+1)$ $IY_L \leftarrow (SP)$ $SP \rightarrow SP+2$	•	•	X	•	X	•	•	•	11 11	111 100	101 001	FD E1	2	4	14	

NOTE: (PAIR)$_H$, (PAIR)$_L$ refer to high order and low order eight bits of the register pair respectively, e.g., $BC_L = C$, $AF_H = A$.

EXCHANGE, BLOCK TRANSFER, BLOCK SEARCH GROUPS

Mnemonic	Symbolic Operation	S	Z	Flags H	P/V	N	C	Opcode 76	543	210	Hex	No. of Bytes	No. of M Cycles	No. of T States	Comments
EX DE, HL	DE ↔ HL	•	•	X	• X	•	•	•	11	101	011	EB	1	1	4	
EX AF, AF'	AF ↔ AF'	•	•	X	• X	•	•	•	00	001	000	08	1	1	4	
EXX	BC ↔ BC'	•	•	X	• X	•	•	•	11	011	001	D9	1	1	4	Register bank
	DE ↔ DE'															and auxiliary
	HL ↔ HL'															register bank
																exchange
EX (SP), HL	H ↔ (SP + 1)	•	•	X	• X	•	•	•	11	100	011	E3	1	5	19	
	L ↔ (SP)															
EX (SP), IX	IX$_H$ ↔ (SP + 1)	•	•	X	• X	•	•	•	11	011	101	DD	2	6	23	
	IX$_L$ ↔ (SP)								11	100	011	E3				
EX (SP), IY	IY$_H$ ↔ (SP + 1)	•	•	X	• X	•	•	•	11	111	101	FD	2	6	23	
	IYL ↔ (SP)								11	100	011	E3				
LDI	(DE) ← (HL)	•	•	X	0	X	①‡ 0	•	11	101	101	ED	2	4	16	Load (HL) into
	DE ← DE + 1								10	100	000	A0				(DE), increment
	HL ← HL + 1															the pointers and
	BC ← BC − 1															decrement the
																byte counter
																(BC)
LDIR	(DE) ← (HL)	•	•	X	0	X	②0 0	•	11	101	101	ED	2	5	21	If BC ≠ 0
	DE ← DE + 1								10	110	000	B0	2	4	16	If BC = 0
	HL ← HL + 1															
	BC ← BC − 1															
	Repeat until															
	BC = 0															
LDD	(DE) ← (HL)	•	•	X	0	X	①‡ 0	•	11	101	101	ED	2	4	16	
	DE ← DE − 1								10	101	000	A8				
	HL ← HL − 1															
	BC ← BC − 1															
LDDR	(DE) ← (HL)	•	•	X	0	X	②0 0	•	11	101	101	ED	2	5	21	If BC ≠ 0
	DE ← DE − 1								10	111	000	B8	2	4	16	If BC = 0
	HL ← HL − 1															
	BC ← BC − 1															
	Repeat until															
	BC = 0															
CPI	A − (HL)	‡	‡	X	③‡	X	①‡ 1	•	11	101	101	ED	2	4	16	
	HL ← HL + 1								10	100	001	A1				
	BC ← BC − 1															

NOTE: ① P/V flag is 0 if the result of BC − 1 = 0, otherwise P/V = 1.
         ② P/V flag is 0 only at completion of instruction.
         ③ Z flag is 1 if A = HL , otherwise Z = 0.

EXCHANGE, BLOCK TRANSFER, BLOCK SEARCH GROUPS (Continued)

Mnemonic	Symbolic Operation	S	Z	H	P/V	N	C	76	543	210	Hex	No. of Bytes	No. of M Cycles	No. of T States	Comments
CPIR	A − (HL)	↕	↕③	X	↕	X①↕	1	•	11	101	101	ED	2	5	21	If BC ≠ 0 and A ≠ (HL)
	HL ← HL + 1								10	110	001	B1	2	4	16	If BC = 0 or A = (HL)
	BC ← BC − 1															
	Repeat until															
	A = (HL) or															
	BC = 0															
CPD	A − (HL)	↕	↕③	X	↕	X①↕	1	•	11	101	101	ED	2	4	16	
	HL ← HL − 1								10	101	001	A9				
	BC ← BC − 1															
CPDR	A − (HL)	↕	↕③	X	↕	X①↕	1	•	11	101	101	ED	2	5	21	If BC ≠ 0 and A ≠ (HL)
	HL ← HL − 1								10	111	001	B9	2	4	16	If BC = 0 or ·A = (HL)
	BC ← BC − 1															
	Repeat until															
	A = (HL) or															
	BC = 0															

NOTE: ① P/V flag is 0 if the result of BC − 1 = 0, otherwise P/V = 1.
        ② P/V flag is 0 only at completion of instruction.
        ③ Z flag is 1 if A = (HL), otherwise Z = 0.

8-BIT ARITHMETIC AND LOGICAL GROUP

Mnemonic	Symbolic Operation	S	Z	H	P/V	N	C	76	543	210	Hex	No. of Bytes	No. of M Cycles	No. of T States	Comments
ADD A, r	A ← A + r	↕	↕	X	↕	X V	0	↕	10	[000]	r		1	1	4	r Reg.
ADD A, n	A ← A + n	↕	↕	X	↕	X V	0	↕	11	[000]	110		2	2	7	000 B
										← n →						001 C
																010 D
ADD A, (HL)	A ← A + (HL)	↕	↕	X	↕	X V	0	↕	10	[000]	110		1	2	7	011 E
ADD A, (IX + d)	A ← A + (IX + d)	↕	↕	X	↕	X V	0	↕	11	011	101	DD	3	5	19	100 H
									10	[000]	110					101 L
										← d →						111 A
ADD A, (IY + d)	A ← A + (IY + d)	↕	↕	X	↕	X V	0	↕	11	111	101	FD	3	5	19	
									10	[000]	110					
										← d →						
ADC A, s	A ← A + s + CY	↕	↕	X	↕	X V	0	↕	[001]							s is any of r, n,
SUB s	A ← A − s	↕	↕	X	↕	X V	1	↕	[010]							(HL), (IX + d),
SBC A, s	A ← A − s − CY	↕	↕	X	↕	X V	1	↕	[011]							(IY + d) as
AND s	A ← A ∧ s	↕	↕	X	1	X P	0	0	[100]							shown for ADD
OR s	A ← A ∨ s	↕	↕	X	0	X P	0	0	[110]							instruction. The
XOR s	A ← A ⊕ s	↕	↕	X	0	X P	0	0	[101]							indicated bits
CP s	A − s	↕	↕	X	↕	X V	1	↕	[111]							replace the [000] in the ADD set above.

8-BIT ARITHMETIC AND LOGICAL GROUP (Continued)

Mnemonic	Symbolic Operation	S	Z		H		P/V	N	C	76	543	210	Hex	No. of Bytes	No. of M Cycles	No. of T States	Comments
INC r	r←r+1	‡	‡	X	‡	X	V	0	•	00	r	[100]		1	1	4	
INC (HL)	(HL)← (HL)+1	‡	‡	X	‡	X	V	0	•	00	110	[100]		1	3	11	
INC (IX+d)	(IX+d)← (IX+d)+1	‡	‡	X	‡	X	V	0	•	11	011	101	DD	3	6	23	
										00	110	[100]					
										←d→							
INC (IY+d)	(IY+d)← (IY+d)+1	‡	‡	X	‡	X	V	0	•	11	111	101	FD	3	6	23	
										00	110	[100]					
										←d→							
DEC m	m←m−1	‡	‡	X	‡	X	V	1	•			[101]					

NOTE: m is any of r, (HL), (IX+d), (IY+d) as shown for INC. DEC same format and states as INC. Replace [100] with [101] in opcode.

GENERAL-PURPOSE ARITHMETIC AND CPU CONTROL GROUPS

Mnemonic	Symbolic Operation	S	Z		H		P/V	N	C	76	543	210	Hex	No. of Bytes	No. of M Cycles	No. of T States	Comments
DAA	@	‡	‡	X	‡	X	P	•	‡	00	100	111	27	1	1	4	Decimal adjust accumulator.
CPL	A←Ā	•	•	X	1	X	•	1	•	00	101	111	2F	1	1	4	Complement accumulator (one's complement).
NEG	A←0−A	‡	‡	X	‡	X	V	1	‡	11	101	101	ED	2	2	8	Negate acc. (two's complement).
										01	000	100	44				
CCF	CY←CȲ	•	•	X	X	X	•	0	‡	00	111	111	3F	1	1	4	Complement carry flag.
SCF	CY←1	•	•	X	0	X	•	0	1	00	110	111	37	1	1	4	Set carry flag.
NOP	No operation	•	•	X	•	X	•	•	•	00	000	000	00	1	1	4	
HALT	CPU halted	•	•	X	•	X	•	•	•	01	110	110	76	1	1	4	
DI ★	IFF←0	•	•	X	•	X	•	•	•	11	110	011	F3	1	1	4	
EI ★	IFF←1	•	•	X	•	X	•	•	•	11	111	011	FB	1	1	4	
IM 0	Set interrupt mode 0	•	•	X	•	X	•	•	•	11	101	101	ED	2	2	8	
										01	000	110	46				
IM 1	Set interrupt mode 1	•	•	X	•	X	•	•	•	11	101	101	ED	2	2	8	
										01	010	110	56				
IM 2	Set interrupt mode 2	•	•	X	•	X	•	•	•	11	101	101	ED	2	2	8	
										01	011	110	5E				

NOTES: @ converts accumulator content into packed BCD following add or subtract with packed BCD operands.
IFF indicates the interrupt enable flip-flop.
CY indicates the carry flip-flop.
★ indicates interrupts are not sampled at the end of EI or DI.

16-BIT ARITHMETIC GROUP

Mnemonic	Symbolic Operation	S	Z		H		P/V	N	C	76	543	210	Hex	No. of Bytes	No. of M Cycles	No. of T States	Comments	
ADD HL, ss	HL ← HL+ss	•	•	X	X	X	•	0	‡	00	ss1	001		1	3	11	ss	Reg.
																	00	BC
ADC HL, ss	HL ←																01	DE
	HL+ss+CY	‡	‡	X	X	X	V	0	‡	11	101	101	ED	2	4	15	10	HL
										01	ss1	010					11	SP
SBC HL, ss	HL ←																	
	HL−ss−CY	‡	‡	X	X	X	V	1	‡	11	101	101	ED	2	4	15		
										01	ss0	010						
ADD IX, pp	IX ← IX+pp	•	•	X	X	X	•	0	‡	11	011	101	DD	2	4	15	pp	Reg.
										01	pp1	001					00	BC
																	01	DE
																	10	IX
																	11	SP
ADD IY, rr	IY ← IY+rr	•	•	X	X	X	•	0	‡	11	111	101	FD	2	4	15	rr	Reg.
										00	rr1	001					00	BC
INC ss	ss ← ss+1	•	•	X	•	X	•	•	•	00	ss0	011		1	1	6	01	DE
INC IX	IX ← IX+1	•	•	X	•	X	•	•	•	11	011	101	DD	2	2	10	10	IY
										00	100	011	23				11	SP
INC IY	IY ← IY+1	•	•	X	•	X	•	•	•	11	111	101	FD	2	2	10		
										00	100	011	23					
DEC ss	ss ← ss−1	•	•	X	•	X	•	•	•	00	ss1	011		1	1	6		
DEC IX	IX ← IX−1	•	•	X	•	X	•	•	•	11	011	101	DD	2	2	10		
										00	101	011	2B					
DEC IY	IY ← IY−1	•	•	X	•	X	•	•	•	11	111	101	FD	2	2	10		
										00	101	011	2B					

ROTATE AND SHIFT GROUP

Mnemonic	Symbolic Operation	S	Z		H		P/V	N	C	76	543	210	Hex	No. of Bytes	No. of M Cycles	No. of T States	Comments
RLCA	[CY] ← [7 ← 0] ← (A)	•	•	X	0	X	•	0	‡	00	000	111	07	1	1	4	Rotate left circular accumulator.
RLA	[CY] ← [7 ← 0] (A)	•	•	X	0	X	•	0	‡	00	010	111	17	1	1	4	Rotate left accumulator.
RRCA	[7 → 0] → [CY] (A)	•	•	X	0	X	•	0	‡	00	001	111	0F	1	1	4	Rotate right circular accumulator.
RRA	[7 → 0] → [CY] (A)	•	•	X	0	X	•	0	‡	00	011	111	1F	1	1	4	Rotate right accumulator.

ROTATE AND SHIFT GROUP (Continued)

Mnemonic	Symbolic Operation	S	Z	H	P/V	N	C	76	543	210	Hex	No. of Bytes	No. of M Cycles	No. of T States	Comments
RLC r		↕	↕ X 0 X		P	0•↕	11	001	011	CB	2	2	8	Rotate left circular register r.
							00	[000]	r					
RLC (HL)		↕	↕ X 0 X		P	0 ↕	11	001	011	CB	2	4	15	r Reg.
							00	000	110					000 B
														001 C
RLC (IX + d)		↕	↕ X 0 X		P	0 ↕	11	011	101	DD	4	6	23	010 D
	r,(HL),(IX + d),(IY + d)						11	001	011	CB				011 E
							← d →							001 H
							00	[000]	110					101 L
														111 A
RLC (IY + d)		↕	↕ X 0 X		P	0 ↕	11	111	101	FD	4	6	23	
							11	001	011	CB				
							← d →							Instruction format and
							00	[000]	110					states are as
RL m		↕	↕ X 0 X		P	0 ↕		[010]						shown for
	m = r,(HL,(IX + d),(IY + d)													RLCs. To form
RRC m		↕	↕ X 0 X		P	0 ↕		[001]						new opcode replace [000]
	m = r,(HL),(IX + d),(IY + d)													or RLCs with
RR m		↕	↕ X 0 X		P	0 ↕		[011]						shown code.
	m = r,(HL),(IX + d),(IY + d)													
SLA m		↕	↕ X 0 X		P	0 ↕		[100]						
	m = r,(HL),(IX + d),(IY + d)													
SRA m		↕	↕ X 0 X		P	0 ↕		[101]						
	m = r,(HL),(IX + d),(IY + d)													
SRL m		↕	↕ X 0 X		P	0 ↕		[111]						
	m = r,(HL),(IX + d),(IY + d)													
RLD		↕	↕ X 0 X		P	0 •	11	101	101	ED	2	5	18	Rotate digit left and right between the accumulator and location (HL).
							01	101	111	6F				
RRD		↕	↕ X 0 X		P	0 •	11	101	101	ED	2	5	18	The content of the upper half of the accumulator is unaffected.
							01	100	111	67				

BIT SET, RESET AND TEST GROUP

Mnemonic	Symbolic Operation	S	Z	H	P/V	N	C	76	543	210	Hex	No. of Bytes	No. of M Cycles	No. of T States
BIT b, r	$Z \leftarrow \overline{r_b}$	X	↕	1	X	0	•	11	001	011	CB	2	2	8
								01	b	r				
BIT b, (HL)	$Z \leftarrow \overline{(HL)_b}$	X	↕	1	X	0	•	11	001	011	CB	2	3	12
								01	b	110				
BIT b, (IX+d)	$Z \leftarrow \overline{(IX+d)_b}$	X	↕	1	X	0	•	11	011	101	DD	4	5	20
								11	001	011	CB			
									← d →					
								01	b	110				
BIT b, (IY+d)	$Z \leftarrow \overline{(IY+d)_b}$	X	↕	1	X	0	•	11	111	101	FD	4	5	20
								11	001	011	CB			
									← d →					
								01	b	110				
SET b, r	$r_b \leftarrow 1$	•	•	X	•	•	•	11	001	011	CB	2	2	8
								[11]	b	r				
SET b, (HL)	$(HL)_b \leftarrow 1$	•	•	X	•	•	•	11	001	011	CB	2	4	15
								[11]	b	110				
SET b, (IX+d)	$(IX+d)_b \leftarrow 1$	•	•	X	•	•	•	11	011	101	DD	4	6	23
								11	001	011	CB			
									← d →					
								[11]	b	110				
SET b, (IY+d)	$(IY+d)_b \leftarrow 1$	•	•	X	•	•	•	11	111	101	FD	4	6	23
								11	001	011	CB			
									← d →					
								[11]	b	110				
RES b, m	$m_b \leftarrow 0$ $m \equiv r, (HL),$ $(IX+d), (IY+d)$	•	•	X	•	•	•	[10]						

Comments

r	Reg.		b	Bit Tested
000	B		000	0
001	C		001	1
010	D		010	2
011	E		011	3
100	H		100	4
101	L		101	5
111	A		110	6
			111	7

(RES b, m comments) To form new opcode replace [11] of SET b, s with [10]. Flags and time states for SET instruction.

NOTE: The notation m_b indicates location m, bit b (0 to 7).

JUMP GROUP

Mnemonic	Symbolic Operation	S	Z	H	P/V	N	C	76	543	210	Hex	No. of Bytes	No. of M Cycles	No. of T States	Comments
JP nn	PC ← nn	•	•	X	• X	•	•	11	000	011	C3	3	3	10	cc Condition
								← n →							000 NZ (non-zero)
								← n →							001 Z (zero)
JP cc, nn	If condition cc is true PC←nn, otherwise continue	•	•	X	• X	•	•	11	cc	010		3	3	10	010 NC (non-carry)
								← n →							011 C (carry)
								← n →							100 PO (parity odd)
															101 PE (parity even)
JR e	PC ← PC + e	•	•	X	• X	•	•	00	011	000	18	2	3	12	110 P (sign positive)
								← e − 2 →							111 M (sign negative)
JR C, e	If C = 0, continue	•	•	X	• X	•	•	00	111	000	38	2	2	7	If condition not met.
	If C = 1, PC ← PC + e											2	3	12	If condition is met.
JR NC, e	IF C = 1, continue	•	•	X	• X	•	•	00	110	000	30	2	2	7	If condition not met.
	If C = 0, PC ← PC + e								← e − 2 →				2	3	12	If condition is met.
JP Z, e	If Z = 0 continue	•	•	X	• X	•	•	00	101	000	28	2	2	7	If condition not met.
	If Z = 1, PC ← PC + e								← e − 2 →				2	3	12	If condition is met.
JR NZ, e	If Z = 1, continue	•	•	X	• X	•	•	00	100	000	20	2	2	7	If condition not met.
	If Z = 0, PC ← PC + e								← e − 2 →				2	3	12	If condition is met.
JP (HL)	PC ← HL	•	•	X	• X	•	•	11	101	001	E9	1	1	4	
JP (IX)	PC ← IX	•	•	X	• X	•	•	11	011	101	DD	2	2	8	
								11	101	001	E9				
JP (IY)	PC ← IY	•	•	X	• X	•	•	11	111	101	FD	2	2	8	
								11	101	001	E9				
DJNZ, e	B ← B − 1 If B = 0, continue	•	•	X	• X	•	•	00	010	000	10	2	2	8	If B = 0
	If B≠0, PC ← PC + e								← e − 2 →				2	3	13	If B≠0.

NOTES: e represents the extension in the relative addressing mode.

e is a signal two's complement number in the range < − 126, 129 >.

e − 2 in the opcode provides an effective address of pc + e as PC is incremented by 2 prior to the addition of e.

CALL AND RETURN GROUP

Mnemonic	Symbolic Operation	S	Z	H	P/V	N	C	76	543	210	Hex	No. of Bytes	No. of M Cycles	No. of T States	Comments
CALL nn	$(SP-1) \leftarrow PC_H$	•	•	X	•	X	•	11	001	101	CD	3	5	17	
	$(SP-2) \leftarrow PC_L$								←n→						
	$PC \leftarrow nn,$								←n→						
CALL cc,nn	If condition cc is false continue, otherwise same as CALL nn	•	•	X	•	X	•	11	cc	100		3	3	10	If cc is false.
									←n→						
									←n→			3	5	17	If cc is true.
RET	$PC_L \leftarrow (SP)$	•	•	X	•	X	•	11	001	001	C9	1	3	10	
	$PC_H \leftarrow (SP+1)$														
RET cc	If condition cc is false continue, otherwise same as RET	•	•	X	•	X	•	11	cc	000		1	1	5	If cc is false.
												1	3	11	If cc is true.
RETI	Return from interrupt	•	•	X	•	X	•	11	101	101	ED	2	4	14	
								01	001	101	4D				
RETN[1]	Return from non-maskable interrupt	•	•	X	•	X	•	11	101	101	ED	2	4	14	
								01	000	101	45				
RST p	$(SP-1) \leftarrow PC_H$	•	•	X	•	X	•	11	t	111		1	3	11	
	$(SP-2) \leftarrow PC_L$														
	$PC_H \leftarrow 0$														
	$PC_L \leftarrow p$														

cc	Condition
000	NZ (non-zero)
001	Z (zero)
010	NC (non-carry)
011	C (carry)
100	PO (parity odd)
101	PE (parity even)
110	P (sign positive)
111	M (sign negative)

t	p
000	00H
001	08H
010	10H
011	18H
100	20H
101	28H
110	30H
111	38H

NOTE: [1]RETN loads $IFF_2 \rightarrow IFF_1$

INPUT AND OUTPUT GROUP

Mnemonic	Symbolic Operation	S	Z	H	P/V	N	C	76	543	210	Hex	No. of Bytes	No. of M Cycles	No. of T States	Comments
IN A, (n)	$A \leftarrow (n)$	•	•	X	•	X	•	11	011	01	DB	2	3	11	n to $A_0 \sim A_7$ Acc. to $A_8 \sim A_{15}$
IN r, (C)	$r \leftarrow (C)$ if r = 110 only the flags will be affected	↕	↕	X	↕	P	0	11 01	101 r	101 000	ED	2	3	12	C to $A_0 \sim A_7$ B to $A_8 \sim A_{15}$
INI	$(HL) \leftarrow (C)$ $B \leftarrow B-1$ $HL \leftarrow HL+1$	X	↕ ①	X	X	X	1	11 10	101 100	101 010	ED A2	2	4	16	C to $A_0 \sim A_7$ B to $A_8 \sim A_{15}$
INIR	$(HL) \leftarrow (C)$ $B \leftarrow B-1$ $HL \leftarrow HL+1$ Repeat until B = 0	X	1 ②	X	X	X	1	11 10	101 110	101 010	ED B2	2 2	5 (If B≠0) 4 (If B = 0)	21 16	C to $A_0 \sim A_7$ B to $A_8 \sim A_{15}$
IND	$(HL) \leftarrow (C)$ $B \leftarrow B-1$ $HL \leftarrow HL-1$	X	↕ ①	X	X	X	1	11 10	101 101	101 010	ED AA	2	4	16	C to $A_0 \sim A_7$ B to $A_8 \sim A_{15}$
INDR	$(HL) \leftarrow (C)$ $B \leftarrow B-1$ $HL \leftarrow HL-1$ Repeat until B = 0	X	1 ②	X	X	X	1	11 10	101 111	101 010	ED BA	2 2	5 (If B≠0) 4 (If B = 0)	21 16	C to $A_0 \sim A_7$ B to $A_8 \sim A_{15}$
OUT (n), A	$(n) \leftarrow A$	•	•	X	•	X	•	11	010	011	D3	2	3	11	n to $A_0 \sim A_7$ Acc. to $A_8 \sim A_{15}$
OUT (C), r	$(C) \leftarrow r$	•	•	X	•	X	•	11 01	101 r	101 001	ED	2	3	12	C to $A_0 \sim A_7$ B to $A_8 \sim A_{15}$
OUTI	$(C) \leftarrow (HL)$ $B \leftarrow B-1$ $HL \leftarrow HL+1$	X	↕ ①	X	X	X	1	11 10	101 100	101 011	ED A3	2	4	16	C to $A_0 \sim A_7$ B to $A_8 \sim A_{15}$
OTIR	$(C) \leftarrow (HL)$ $B \leftarrow B-1$ $HL \leftarrow HL+1$ Repeat until B = 0	X	1 ②	X	X	X	1	11 10	101 110	101 011	ED B3	2 2	5 (If B≠0) 4 (If B = 0)	21 16	C to $A_0 \sim A_7$ B to $A_8 \sim A_{15}$
OUTD	$(C) \leftarrow (HL)$ $B \leftarrow B-1$ $HL \leftarrow HL-1$	X	↕ ①	X	X	X	1	11 10	101 101	101 011	ED AB	2	4	16	C to $A_0 \sim A_7$ B to $A_8 \sim A_{15}$
OTDR	$(C) \leftarrow (HL)$ $B \leftarrow B-1$ $HL \leftarrow HL-1$ Repeat until B = 0	X	1 ②	X	X	X	1	11 10	101 111	101 011	ED	2 2	5 (If B≠0) 4 (If B = 0)	21 16	C to $A_0 \sim A_7$ B to $A_8 \sim A_{15}$

NOTES: ① If the result of B − 1 is zero, the Z flag is set; otherwise it is reset.
② Z flag is set upon instruction completion only.

SUMMARY OF FLAG OPERATION

Instructions	D7 S	Z		H		P/V	N	D0 C	Comments
ADD A, s; ADC A, s	‡	‡	X	‡	X	V	0	‡	8-bit add or add with carry.
SUB s; SBC A, s; CP s; NEG	‡	‡	X	‡	X	V	1	‡	8-bit subtract, subtract with carry, compare and negate accumulator.
AND s	‡	‡	X	1	X	P	0	0	Logical operation.
OR s, XOR s	‡	‡	X	0	X	P	0	0	Logical operation.
INC s	‡	‡	X	‡	X	V	0	•	8-bit increment.
DEC s	‡	‡	X	‡	X	V	1	•	8-bit decrement.
ADD DD, ss	•	•	X	X	X	•	0	‡	16-bit add.
ADC HL, ss	‡	‡	X	X	X	V	0	‡	16-bit add with carry.
SBC HL, ss	‡	‡	X	X	X	V	1	‡	16-bit subtract with carry.
RLA; RLCA; RRA; RRCA	•	•	X	0	X	•	0	‡	Rotate accumulator.
RL m; RLC m; RR m; RRC m; SLA m; SRA m; SRL m	‡	‡	X	0	X	P	0	‡	Rotate and shift locations.
RLD; RRD	‡	‡	X	0	X	P	0	•	Rotate digit left and right.
DAA	‡	‡	X	‡	X	P	•	‡	Decimal adjust accumulator.
CPL	•	•	X	1	X	•	1	•	Complement accumulator.
SCF	•	•	X	0	X	•	0	1	Set carry.
CCF	•	•	X	X	X	•	0	‡	Complement carry.
IN r (C)	‡	‡	X	0	X	P	0	•	Input register indirect.
INI; IND; OUTI; OUTD	X	‡	X	X	X	X	1	•	Block input and output. Z = 1 if B ≠ 0, otherwise Z = 0.
INIR; INDR; OTIR; OTDR	X	1	X	X	X	X	1	•	Block input and output. Z = 1 if B ≠ 0, otherwise Z = 0.
LDI; LDD	X	X	X	0	X	‡	0	•	Block transfer instructions. P/V = 1 if BC ≠ 0, otherwise P/V = 0.
LDIR; LDDR	X	X	X	0	X	0	0	•	Block transfer instructions. P/V = 1 if BC ≠ 0, otherwise P/V = 0.
CPI; CPIR; CPD; CPDR	X	‡	X	X	X	‡	1	•	Block search instructions. Z = 1 if A = (HL), otherwise Z = 0. P/V = 1 if BC ≠ 0, otherwise P/V = 0.
LD A; I, LD A, R	‡	‡	X	0	X	IFF	0	•	IFF, the content of the interrupt enable flip-flop, (IFF₂), is copied into the P/V flag.
BIT b, s	X	‡	X	1	X	X	0	•	The state of bit b of location s is copied into the Z flag.

SYMBOLIC NOTATION

Symbol	Operation
S	Sign flag. S = 1 if the MSB of the result is 1.
Z	Zero flag. Z = 1 if the result of the operation is 0.
P/V	Parity or overflow flag. Parity (P) and overflow (V) share the same flag. Logical operations affect this flag with the parity of the result while arithmetic operations affect this flag with the overflow of the result. If P/V holds parity: P/V = 1 if the result of the operation is even; P/V = 0 if result is odd. If P/V holds overflow, P/V = 1 if the result of the operation produced an overflow. If P/V does not hold overflow, P/V = 0.
H*	Half-carry flag. H = 1 if the add or subtract operation produced a carry into, or borrow from, bit 4 of the accumulator.
N*	Add/Subtract flag. N = 1 if the previous operation was a subtract.
C	Carry/Link flag. C = 1 if the operation produced a carry from the MSB of the operand or result.

Symbol	Operation
‡	The flag is affected according to the result of the operation.
•	The flag is unchanged by the operation.
0	The flag is reset by the operation.
1	The flag is set by the operation.
X	The flag is indeterminate.
V	P/V flag affected according to the overflow result of the operation.
P	P/V flag affected according to the parity result of the operation.
r	Any one o the CPU registers A, B, C, D, E, H, L.
s	Any 8-bit location for all the addressing modes allowed for the particular instruction.
ss	Any 16-bit location for all the addressing modes allowed for that instruction.
ii	Any one of the two index registers IX or IY.
R	Refresh counter.
n	8-bit value in range < 0, 255 >.
nn	16-bit value in range < 0, 65535 >.

*H and N flags are used in conjunction with the decimal adjust instruction (DAA) to properly correct the result into packed BCD format following addition or subtraction using operands with packed BCD format.

PIN DESCRIPTIONS

A_0-A_{15}. *Address Bus* (output, active High, 3-state). A_0-A_{15} form a 16-bit address bus. The Address Bus provides the address for memory data bus exchanges (up to 64K bytes) and for I/O device exchanges.

BUSACK. *Bus Acknowledge* (output, active Low). Bus Acknowledge indicates to the requesting device that the CPU address bus, data bus, and control signals MREQ, IORQ, RD, and WR have entered their high-impedance states. The external circuitry can now control these lines.

BUSREQ. *Bus Request* (input, active Low). Bus Request has a higher priority than NMI and is always recognized at the end of the current machine cycle. BUSREQ forces the CPU address bus, data bus, and control signals MREQ, IORQ, RD, and WR to go to a high-impedance state so that other devices can control these lines. BUSREQ is normally wired-OR and requires an external pullup for these applications. Extended BUSREQ periods due to extensive DMA operations can prevent the CPU from properly refreshing dynamic RAMs.

D_0-D_7. *Data Bus* (input/output, active High, 3-state). D_0-D_7 constitute an 8-bit bidirectional data bus, used for data exchanges with memory and I/O.

Halt. *Halt State* (output, active Low). HALT indicates that the CPU has executed a Halt instruction and is awaiting either a nonmaskable or a maskable interrupt (with the mask enabled) before operation can resume. While halted, the CPU executes NOPs to maintain memory refresh.

INT. *Interrupt Request* (input, active Low). Interrupt Request is generated by I/O devices. The CPU honors a request at the end of the current instruction if the internal software-controlled interrupt enable flip-flop (IFF) is enabled. INT is normally wired-OR and requires an external pullup for these applications.

IORQ. *Input/Output Request* (output, active Low, 3-state). IORQ indicates that the lower half of the address bus holds a valid I/O address for an I/O read or write operation. IORQ is also generated concurrently with M1 during an interrupt acknowledge cycle to indicate that an interrupt response vector can be placed on the data bus.

M1. *Machine Cycle One* (output, active Low). M1, together with MREQ, indicates that the current machine cycle is the opcode fetch cycle of an instruction execution. M1, together with IORQ, indicates an interrupt acknowledge cycle.

MREQ. *Memory Request* (output, active Low, 3-state). MREQ indicates that the address bus holds a valid address for a memory read or memory write operation.

NMI. *Non-Maskable Interrupt* (input, negative edge-triggered). NMI has a higher priority than INT. NMI is always recognized at the end of the current instruction, independent of the status of the interrupt enable flip-flop, and automatically forces the CPU to restart at location 0066H.

RD. *Read* (output, active Low, 3-state). RD indicates that the CPU wants to read data from memory or an I/O device. The addressed I/O device or memory should use this signal to gate data onto the CPU data bus.

RESET. *Reset* (input, active Low). RESET initializes the CPU as follows: it resets the interrupt enable flip-flop, clears the PC and Registers I and R, and sets the interrupt status to Mode 0. During reset time, the address and data bus go to a high-impedance state, and all control output signals go to the inactive state. Note that RESET must be active for a minimum of three full clock cycles before the reset operation is complete.

RFSH. *Refresh* (output, active Low). RFSH, together with MREQ, indicates that the lower seven bits of the system's address bus can be used as a refresh address to the system's dynamic memories.

WAIT. *Wait* (input, active Low). WAIT indicates to the CPU that the addressed memory or I/O devices are not ready for a data transfer. The CPU continues to enter a Wait state as long as this signal is active. Extended WAIT periods can prevent the CPU from refreshing dynamic memory properly.

WR. *Write* (output, active Low, 3-state). WR indicates that the CPU data bus holds valid data to be stored at the addressed memory or I/O location.

CPU TIMING

The Z80 CPU executes instructions by proceeding through a specific sequence of operations:

■ Memory read or write

■ I/O device read or write

■ Interrupt acknowledge

The basic clock period is referred to as a T time or cycle, and three or more T cycles make up a machine cycle (M1, M2 or M3 for instance). Machine cycles can be extended either by the CPU automatically inserting one or more Wait states or by the insertion of one or more Wait states by the user.

Instruction Opcode Fetch. The CPU places the contents of the Program Counter (PC) on the address bus at the start of the cycle (Figure 5). Approximately one-half clock cycle later, MREQ goes active. When active, RD indicates that the memory data can be enabled onto the CPU data bus.

The CPU samples the WAIT input with the falling edge of clock state T2. During clock states T3 and T4 of an M1 cycle, dynamic RAM refresh can occur while the CPU starts decoding and executing the instruction. When the Refresh Control signal becomes active, refreshing of dynamic memory can take place.

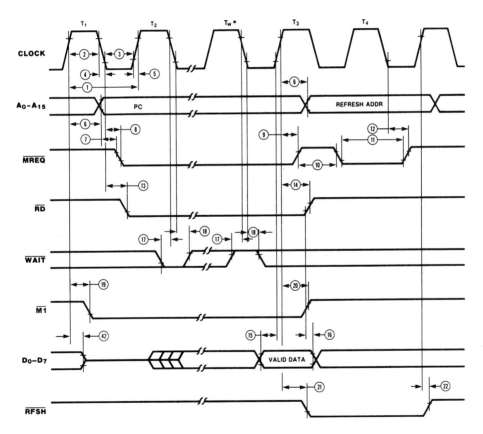

* Tw = Wait cycle added when necessary for slow ancilliary devices.

Figure 5. Instruction Opcode Fetch

Memory Read or Write Cycles. Figure 6 shows the timing of memory read or write cycles other than an opcode fetch ($\overline{M1}$) cycle. The $\overline{MREQ}$ and $\overline{RD}$ signals function exactly as in the fetch cycle. In a memory write cycle, $\overline{MREQ}$ also becomes active when the address bus is stable. The $\overline{WR}$ line is active when the data bus is stable, so that it can be used directly as an R/$\overline{W}$ pulse to most semiconductor memories.

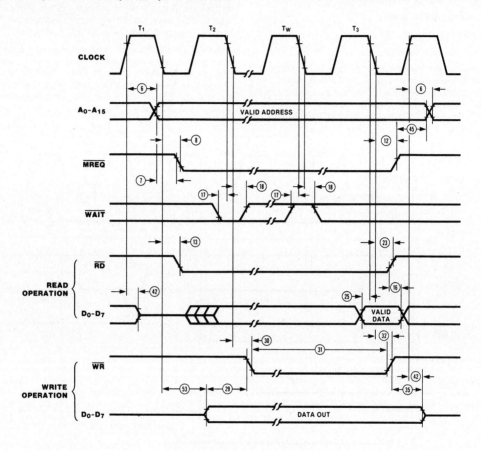

Figure 6. Memory Read or Write Cycles

Input or Output Cycles. Figure 7 shows the timing for an I/O read or I/O write operation. During I/O operations, the CPU automatically inserts a single Wait state (T_{WA}). This extra Wait state allows sufficient time for an I/O port to decode the address from the port address lines.

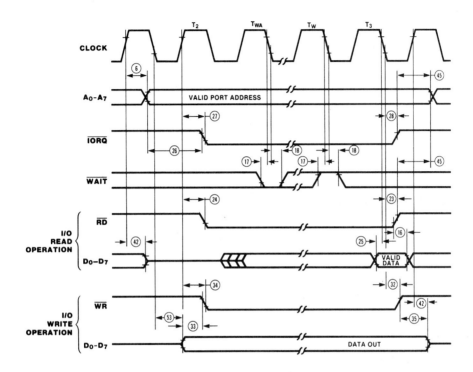

T_{WA} = One wait cycle automatically inserted by CPU.

Figure 7. Input or Output Cycles

Interrupt Request/Acknowledge Cycle. The CPU samples the interrupt signal with the rising edge of the last clock cycle at the end of any instruction (Figure 8). When an interrupt is accepted, a special $\overline{M1}$ cycle is generated. During this $\overline{M1}$ cycle, $\overline{IORQ}$ becomes active (instead of $\overline{MREQ}$) to indicate that the interrupting device can place an 8-bit vector on the data bus. The CPU automatically adds two Wait states to this cycle.

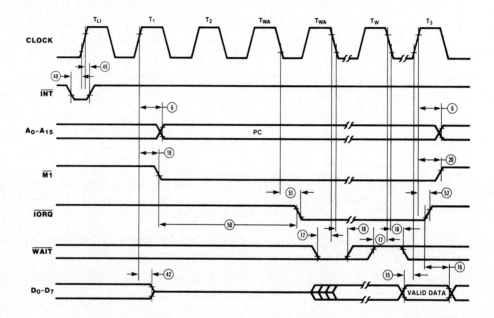

NOTES: 1) T_{LI} = Last state of any instruction cycle.
        2) T_{WA} = Wait cycle automatically inserted by CPU.

Figure 8. Interrupt Request/Acknowledge Cycle

Non-Maskable Interrupt Request Cycle. $\overline{\text{NMI}}$ is sampled at the same time as the maskable interrupt input $\overline{\text{INT}}$ but has higher priority and cannot be disabled under software control. The subsequent timing is similar to that of a normal memory read operation except that data put on the bus by the memory is ignored. The CPU instead executes a restart (RST) operation and jumps to the $\overline{\text{NMI}}$ service routine located at address 0066H (Figure 9).

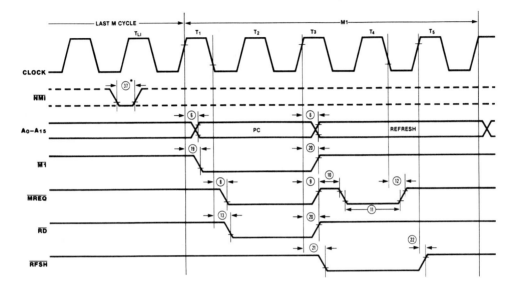

*Although $\overline{\text{NMI}}$ is an asynchronous input, to guarantee its being recognized on the following machine cycle, $\overline{\text{NMI}}$'s falling edge must occur no later than the rising edge of the clock cycle preceding the last state of any instruction cycle (T_{LI}).

Figure 9. Non-Maskable Interrupt Request Operation

Bus Request/Acknowledge Cycle. The CPU samples BUSREQ with the rising edge of the last clock period of any machine cycle (Figure 10). If BUSREQ is active, the CPU sets its address, data, and MREQ, IORQ, RD, and WR lines to a high-impedance state with the rising edge of the next clock pulse. At that time, any external device can take control of these lines, usually to transfer data between memory and I/O devices.

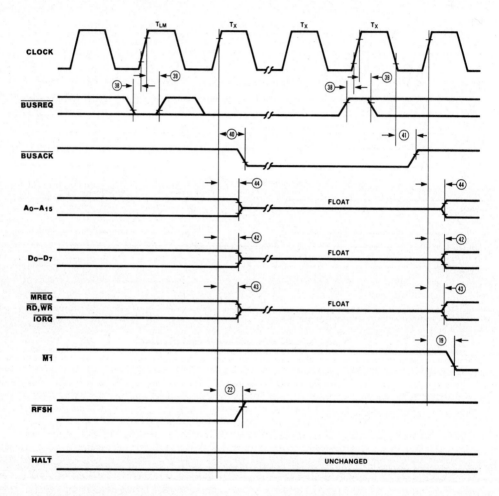

NOTES: 1) T_LM = Last state of any M cycle.
2) T_X = An arbitrary clock cycle used by requesting device.

Figure 10. Z-BUS Request/Acknowledge Cycle

Halt Acknowledge Cycle. When the CPU receives a HALT instruction, it executes NOP states until either an $\overline{\text{INT}}$ or $\overline{\text{NMI}}$ input is received. When in the Halt state, the $\overline{\text{HALT}}$ output is active and remains so until an interrupt is received (Figure 11). INT will also force a Halt exit.

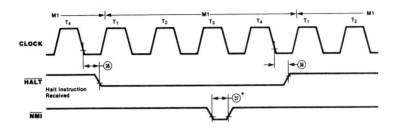

*Although $\overline{\text{NMI}}$ is an asynchronous input, to guarantee its being recognized on the following machine cycle, $\overline{\text{MNI}}$'s falling edge must occur no later than the rising edge of the clock cycle preceding the last state of any instruction cycle (T_{LI}).

Figure 11. Halt Acknowledge Cycle

Reset Cycle. $\overline{\text{RESET}}$ must be active for at least three clock cycles for the CPU to properly accept it. As long as $\overline{\text{RESET}}$ remains active, the address and data buses float, and the control outputs are inactive. Once $\overline{\text{RESET}}$ goes inactive, two internal T cycles are consumed before the CPU resumes normal processing operation. RESET clears the PC register, so the first opcode fetch will be to location 0000H (Figure 12).

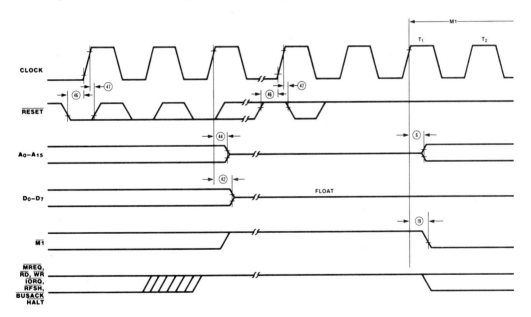

Figure 12. Reset Cycle

AC CHARACTERISTICS†

Number	Symbol	Parameter	Z80 CPU Min	Z80 CPU Max	Z80A CPU Min	Z80A CPU Max	Z80B CPU Min	Z80B CPU Max	Z80H CPU Min	Z80H CPU Max
1	TcC	Clock Cycle Time	400*		250*		165*		125*	
2	TwCh	Clock Pulse Width (High)	180	2000	110	2000	65	2000	55	2000
3	TwCl	Clock Pulse Width (Low)	180	2000	110	2000	65	2000	55	2000
4	TfC	Clock Fall Time		30		30		20		10
5	TrC	Clock Rise Time		30		30		20		10
6	TdCr(A)	Clock ↑ to Address Valid Delay		145		110		90		80
7	TdA(MREQf)	Address Valid to $\overline{MREQ}$ ↓ Delay	125*		65*		35*		20*	
8	TdCf(MREQf)	Clock ↓ to $\overline{MREQ}$ ↓ Delay		100		85		70		60
9	TdCr(MREQr)	Clock ↑ to $\overline{MREQ}$ ↑ Delay		100		85		70		60
10	TwMREQh	$\overline{MREQ}$ Pulse Width (High)	170*		110*		65*		45*	
11	TwMREQl	$\overline{MREQ}$ Pulse Width (Low)	360*		220*		135*		100*	
12	TdCf(MREQr)	Clock ↓ to $\overline{MREQ}$ ↑ Delay		100		85		70		60
13	TdCf(RDf)	Clock ↓ to $\overline{RD}$ ↓ Delay		130		95		80		70
14	TdCr(RDr)	Clock ↑ to $\overline{RD}$ ↑ Delay		100		85		70		60
15	TsD(Cr)	Data Setup Time to Clock ↑	50		35		30		30	
16	ThD(RDr)	Data Hold Time to $\overline{RD}$ ↑		0		0		0		0
17	TsWAIT(Cf)	$\overline{WAIT}$ Setup Time to Clock ↓	70		70		60		50	
18	ThWAIT(Cf)	$\overline{WAIT}$ Hold Time after Clock ↓		0		0		0		0
19	TdCr(M1f)	Clock ↑ to $\overline{M1}$ ↓ Delay		130		100		80		70
20	TdCr(M1r)	Clock ↑ to $\overline{M1}$ ↑ Delay		130		100		80		70
21	TdCr(RFSHf)	Clock ↑ to $\overline{RFSH}$ ↓ Delay		180		130		110		95
22	TdCr(RFSHr)	Clock ↑ to $\overline{RFSH}$ ↑ Delay		150		120		100		85
23	TdCf(RDr)	Clock ↓ to $\overline{RD}$ ↑ Delay		110		85		70		60
24	TdCr(RDf)	Clock ↑ to $\overline{RD}$ ↓ Delay		100		85		70		60
25	TsD(Cf)	Data Setup to Clock ↓ during M_2, M_3, M_4, or M_5 Cycles	60		50		40		30	
26	TdA(IORQf)	Address Stable prior to $\overline{IORQ}$ ↓	320*		180*		110*		75*	
27	TdCr(IORQf)	Clock ↑ to $\overline{IORQ}$ ↓ Delay		90		75		65		55
28	TdCf(IORQr)	Clock ↓ to $\overline{IORQ}$ ↑ Delay		110		85		70		60
29	TdD(WRf)	Data Stable prior to $\overline{WR}$ ↓	190*		80*		25*		5*	
30	TdCf(WRf)	Clock ↓ to $\overline{WR}$ ↓ Delay		90		80		70		60
31	TwWR	$\overline{WR}$ Pulse Width	360*		220*		135*		100*	
32	TdCf(WRr)	Clock ↓ to $\overline{WR}$ ↑ Delay		100		80		70		60
33	TdD(WRf)	Data Stable prior to $\overline{WR}$ ↓	20*		-10*		-55*		55*	
34	TdCr(WRf)	Clock ↑ to $\overline{WR}$ ↓ Delay		80		65		60		55
35	TdWRr(D)	Data Stable from $\overline{WR}$ ↑	120*		60*		30*		15*	
36	TdCf(HALT)	Clock ↓ to $\overline{HALT}$ ↑ or ↓		300		300		260		225
37	TwNMI	$\overline{NMI}$ Pulse Width	80		80		70		60*	
38	TsBUSREQ(Cr)	$\overline{BUSREQ}$ Setup Time to Clock ↑	80		50		50		40	

*For clock periods other than the minimums shown, calculate parameters using the table on the following page. Calculated values above assumed TrC = TfC = 20 ns.

†Units in nanoseconds (ns).

AC CHARACTERISTICS† (Continued)

Number	Symbol	Parameter	Z80 CPU Min	Z80 CPU Max	Z80A CPU Min	Z80A CPU Max	Z80B CPU Min	Z80B CPU Max	Z80H CPU Min	Z80H CPU Max
39	ThBUSREQ(Cr)	BUSREQ Hold Time after Clock ↑	0		0		0		0	
40	TdCr(BUSACKf)	Clock ↑ to BUSACK ↓ Delay		120		100		90		80
41	TdCf(BUSACKr)	Clock ↓ to BUSACK ↑ Delay		110		100		90		80
42	TdCr(Dz)	Clock ↑ to Data Float Delay		90		90		80		70
43	TdCr(CTz)	Clock ↑ to Control Outputs Float Delay (MREQ, IORQ, RD, and WR)		110		80		70		60
44	TdCr(Az)	Clock ↑ to Address Float Delay		110		90		80		70
45	TdCTr(A)	MREQ ↑, IORQ ↑, RD ↑, and WR ↑ to Address Hold Time	160*		80*		35*		20*	
46	TsRESET(Cr)	RESET to Clock ↑ Setup Time	90		60		60		45	
47	ThRESET(Cr)	RESET to Clock ↑ Hold Time		0		0		0		0
48	TsINTf(Cr)	INT to Clock ↑ Setup Time	80		80		70		55	
49	ThINTr(Cr)	INT to Clock ↑ Hold Time		0		0		0		0
50	TdM1f(IORQf)	M1 ↓ to IORQ ↓ Delay	920*		565*		365*		270*	
51	TdCf(IORQf)	Clock ↓ to IORQ ↓ Delay		110		85		70		60
52	TdCf(IORQr)	Clock ↑ IORQ ↑ Delay		100		85		70		60
53	TdCf(D)	Clock ↓ to Data Valid Delay		230		150		130		115

*For clock periods other than the minimums shown, calculate parameters using the following table. Calculated values above assumed TrC = TfC = 20 ns.
†Units in nanoseconds (ns).

FOOTNOTES TO AC CHARACTERISTICS

Number	Symbol	General Parameter	Z80	Z80A	Z80B	Z80H
1	TcC	TwCh + TwCl + TrC + TfC				
7	TdA(MREQf)	TwCh + TfC	− 75	− 65	− 50	− 45
10	TwMREQh	TwCh + TfC	− 30	− 20	− 20	− 20
11	TwMREQl	TcC	− 40	− 30	− 30	− 25
26	TdA(IORQf)	TcC	− 80	− 70	− 55	− 50
29	TdD(WRf)	TcC	− 210	− 170	− 140	− 120
31	TwWR	TcC	− 40	− 30	− 30	− 25
33	TdD(WRf)	TwCl + TrC	− 180	− 140	− 140	− 120
35	TdWRr(D)	TwCl + TrC	− 80	− 70	− 55	− 50
45	TdCTr(A)	TwCl + TrC	− 40	− 50	− 50	− 45
50	TdM1f(IORQf)	2TcC + TwCh + TfC	− 80	− 65	− 50	− 45

AC Test Conditions:
V_{IH} = 2.0 V V_{OH} = 1.5 V
V_{IL} = 0.8 V V_{OL} = 1.5 V
V_{IHC} = V_{CC} −0.6 V   FLOAT = ±0.5 V
V_{ILC} = 0.45 V

ABSOLUTE MAXIMUM RATINGS

Voltages on all pins with respect to ground . . .0.3V to +7V
Operating Ambient
 Temperature . . . . .See Ordering Information
Storage Temperature . . . .−65°C to +150°C

Stresses greater than those listed under Absolute Maximum Ratings may cause permanent damage to the device. This is a stress rating only; operation of the device at any condition above these indicated in the operational sections of these specifications is not implied. Exposure to absolute maximum rating conditions for extended periods may affect device reliability.

STANDARD TEST CONDITIONS

The DC Characteristics and Capacitance sections below apply for the following standard test conditions, unless otherwise noted. All voltages are referenced to GND (0V). Positive current flows into the referenced pin.

Available operating temperature ranges are:

- S = 0°C to +70°C, +4.75V ⩽ V_{CC} ⩽ +5.25V

- E = −40°C to +85°C, +4.75V ⩽ V_{CC} ⩽ +5.25V

- M = −55°C to +125°C, +4.5V ⩽ V_{CC} ⩽ +5.25V

The Ordering Information section lists temperature ranges and product numbers. Package drawings are in the Package Information section in this book. Refer to the Literature List for additional documentation.

All ac parameters assume a load capacitance of 100 pf. Add 15 ns delay for each 50 pf increase in load up to a maximum of 200 pf for the data bus. AC timing measurements are referenced to 1.5 volts (except for clock, which is referenced to the 10% and 90% points).

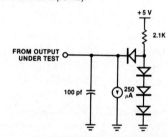

DC CHARACTERISTICS
All parameters are tested unless otherwise noted.

Symbol	Parameter	Min	Max	Unit	Test Condition
V_{ILC}	Clock Input Low Voltage	−0.3	0.45	V	
V_{IHC}	Clock Input High Voltage	V_{CC} − .6	V_{CC} + .3	V	
V_{IL}	Input Low Voltage	−0.3	0.8	V	
V_{IH}	Input High Voltage	2.0[1]	V_{CC}	V	
V_{OL}	Output Low Voltage		0.4	V	I_{OL} = 2.0 mA
V_{OH}	Output High Voltage	2.4[1]		V	I_{OH} = −250 μA
I_{CC}	Power Supply Current		200	mA	Note 3
I_{LI}	Input Leakage Current		10	μA	V_{IN} = 0 to V_{CC}
I_{LO}	3-State Output Leakage Current in Float	−10	10[2]	μA	V_{OUT} = 0.4 to V_{CC}

1. For military grade parts, refer to the Z80 Military Electrical Specification.
2. A_{15}-A_0, D_7-D_0, $\overline{MREQ}$, $\overline{IORQ}$, $\overline{RD}$, and $\overline{WR}$.
3. Measurements made with outputs floating.

CAPACITANCE
Guaranteed by design and characterization.

Symbol	Parameter	Min	Max	Unit
C_{CLOCK}	Clock Capacitance		35	pf
C_{IN}	Input Capacitance		5	pf
C_{OUT}	Output Capacitance		15	pf

NOTES:
 T_A = 25°C, f = 1 MHz.
 Unmeasured pins returned to ground.

ORDERING INFORMATION

Z80 CPU, 2.5 MHz

40-pin DIP	44-pin LCC	44-pin PCC
Z8400 PS	Z8400 LM*	Z8400 VS†
Z8400 CS	Z8400 LMB*†	
Z8400 PE		
Z8400 CE		
Z8400 CM*		
Z8400 CMB*		
Z8400 CMJ*		

Z80B CPU, 6.0 MHz

40-pin DIP	44-pin PCC
Z8400B PS	Z8400B VS†
Z8400B CS	
Z8400B PE	

Z80H CPU, 8.0 MHz

40-pin DIP	44-pin PCC
Z8400H PS	Z8400H VS†

Z80A CPU, 4.0 MHz

40-pin DIP	44-pin LCC	44-pin PCC
Z8400A PS	Z8400A LM*	Z8400A VS†
Z8400A CS	Z8400A LMB*†	
Z8400A PE		
Z8400A CE		
Z8400A CM*		
Z8400A CMB*		
Z8400A CMJ*		

Codes

First letter is for package; second letter is for temperature.

C = Ceramic DIP
P = Plastic DIP
L = Ceramic LCC
V = Plastic PCC

R = Protopack
T = Low Profile Protopack
DIP = Dual-In-Line Package
LCC = Leadless Chip Carrier
PCC = Plastic Chip Carrier (Leaded)

TEMPERATURE
S = 0°C to +70°C
E = −40°C to +85°C
M* = −55°C to +125°C

FLOW
B = 883 Class B
J = JAN 38510 Class B

*For Military Orders, refer to the Military Section.
†Available soon.

APPENDIX C: DATA SHEET FOR THE INTEL 8255A PROGRAMMABLE PERIPHERAL INTERFACE

8255A/8255A-5
PROGRAMMABLE PERIPHERAL INTERFACE

- **MCS-85™ Compatible 8255A-5**
- **24 Programmable I/O Pins**
- **Completely TTL Compatible**
- **Fully Compatible with Intel® Micro-processor Families**
- **Improved Timing Characteristics**

- **Direct Bit Set/Reset Capability Easing Control Application Interface**
- **40-Pin Dual In-Line Package**
- **Reduces System Package Count**
- **Improved DC Driving Capability**

The Intel® 8255A is a general purpose programmable I/O device designed for use with Intel® microprocessors. It has 24 I/O pins which may be individually programmed in 2 groups of 12 and used in 3 major modes of operation. In the first mode (MODE 0), each group of 12 I/O pins may be programmed in sets of 4 to be input or output. In MODE 1, the second mode, each group may be programmed to have 8 lines of input or output. Of the remaining 4 pins, 3 are used for hand-shaking and interrupt control signals. The third mode of operation (MODE 2) is a bidirectional bus mode which uses 8 lines for a bidirectional bus, and 5 lines, borrowing one from the other group, for handshaking.

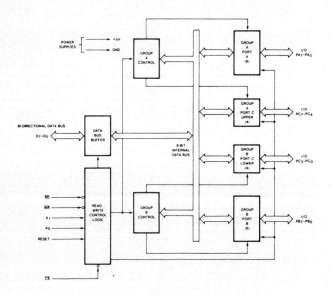

Figure 1. 8255A Block Diagram

Figure 2. Pin Configuration

8255A FUNCTIONAL DESCRIPTION

General

The 8255A is a programmable peripheral interface (PPI) device designed for use in Intel® microcomputer systems. Its function is that of a general purpose I/O component to interface peripheral equipment to the microcomputer system bus. The functional configuration of the 8255A is programmed by the system software so that normally no external logic is necessary to interface peripheral devices or structures.

Data Bus Buffer

This 3-state bidirectional 8-bit buffer is used to interface the 8255A to the system data bus. Data is transmitted or received by the buffer upon execution of input or output instructions by the CPU. Control words and status information are also transferred through the data bus buffer.

Read/Write and Control Logic

The function of this block is to manage all of the internal and external transfers of both Data and Control or Status words. It accepts inputs from the CPU Address and Control busses and in turn, issues commands to both of the Control Groups.

(CS)

Chip Select. A "low" on this input pin enables the commuinction between the 8255A and the CPU.

(RD)

Read. A "low" on this input pin enables the 8255A to send the data or status information to the CPU on the data bus. In essence, it allows the CPU to "read from" the 8255A.

(WR)

Write. A "low" on this input pin enables the CPU to write data or control words into the 8255A.

(A₀ and A₁)

Port Select 0 and Port Select 1. These input signals, in conjunction with the RD and WR inputs, control the selection of one of the three ports or the control word registers. They are normally connected to the least significant bits of the address bus (A_0 and A_1).

8255A BASIC OPERATION

A_1	A_0	$\overline{RD}$	$\overline{WR}$	$\overline{CS}$	INPUT OPERATION (READ)
0	0	0	1	0	PORT A ⇒ DATA BUS
0	1	0	1	0	PORT B ⇒ DATA BUS
1	0	0	1	0	PORT C ⇒ DATA BUS
					OUTPUT OPERATION (WRITE)
0	0	1	0	0	DATA BUS ⇒ PORT A
0	1	1	0	0	DATA BUS ⇒ PORT B
1	0	1	0	0	DATA BUS ⇒ PORT C
1	1	1	0	0	DATA BUS ⇒ CONTROL
					DISABLE FUNCTION
X	X	X	X	1	DATA BUS ⇒ 3-STATE
1	1	0	1	0	ILLEGAL CONDITION
X	X	1	1	0	DATA BUS ⇒ 3-STATE

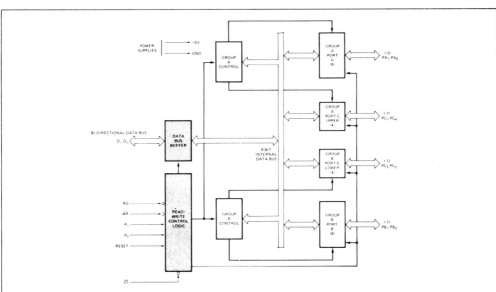

Figure 3. 8255A Block Diagram Showing Data Bus Buffer and Read/Write Control Logic Functions

(RESET)

Reset. A "high on this input clears the control register and all ports (A, C, C) are set to the input mode.

Group A and Group B Controls

The functional configuration of each port is programmed by the systems software. In essence, the CPU "outputs" a control word to the 8255A. The control word contains information such as "mode", "bit set", "bit reset", etc., that initializes the functional configuration of the 8255A.

Each of the Control blocks (Group A and Group B) accepts "commands" from the Read/Write Control Logic, receives "control words" from the internal data bus and issues the proper commands to its associated ports.

    Control Group A – Port A and Port C upper (C7-C4)
    Control Group B – Port B and Port C lower (C3-C0)

The Control Word Register can **Only** be written into. No Read operation of the Control Word Register is allowed.

Ports A, B, and C

The 8255A contains three 8-bit ports (A, B, and C). All can be configured in a wide variety of functional characteristics by the system software but each has its own special features or "personality" to further enhance the power and flexibility of the 8255A.

Port A. One 8-bit data output latch/buffer and one 8-bit data input latch.

Port B. One 8-bit data input/output latch/buffer and one 8-bit data input buffer.

Port C. One 8-bit data output latch/buffer and one 8-bit data input buffer (no latch for input). This port can be divided into two 4-bit ports under the mode control. Each 4-bit port contains a 4-bit latch and it can be used for the control signal outputs and status signal inputs in conjunction with ports A and B.

PIN CONFIGURATION

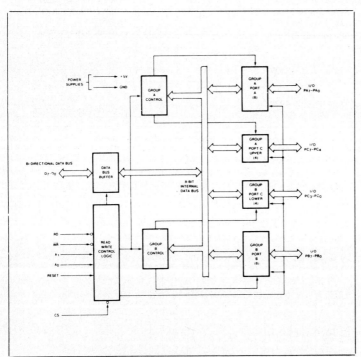

PIN NAMES

D_7 - D_0	DATA BUS (BI DIRECTIONAL)
RESET	RESET INPUT
CS	CHIP SELECT
RD	READ INPUT
WR	WRITE INPUT
A0, A1	PORT ADDRESS
PA7-PA0	PORT A (BIT)
PB7-PB0	PORT B (BIT)
PC7-PC0	PORT C (BIT)
V_{CC}	+5 VOLTS
GND	0 VOLTS

Figure 4. 8225A Block Diagram Showing Group A and Group B Control Functions

8255A OPERATIONAL DESCRIPTION

Mode Selection

There are three basic modes of operation that can be selected by the system software:

Mode 0 — Basic Input/Output
Mode 1 — Strobed Input/Output
Mode 2 — Bi-Directional Bus

When the reset input goes "high" all ports will be set to the input mode (i.e., all 24 lines will be in the high impedance state). After the reset is removed the 8255A can remain in the input mode with no additional initialization required. During the execution of the system program any of the other modes may be selected using a single output instruction. This allows a single 8255A to service a variety of peripheral devices with a simple software maintenance routine.

The modes for Port A and Port B can be separately defined, while Port C is divided into two portions as required by the Port A and Port B definitions. All of the output registers, including the status flip-flops, will be reset whenever the mode is changed. Modes may be combined so that their functional definition can be "tailored" to almost any I/O structure. For instance; Group B can be programmed in Mode 0 to monitor simple switch closings or display computational results, Group A could be programmed in Mode 1 to monitor a keyboard or tape reader on an interrupt-driven basis.

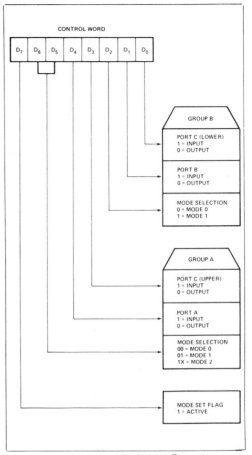

Figure 6. Mode Definition Format

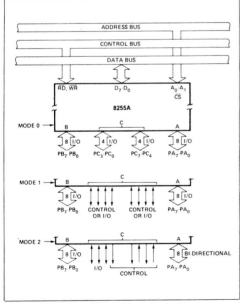

**Figure 5. Basic Mode Definitions
and Bus Interface**

The mode definitions and possible mode combinations may seem confusing at first but after a cursory review of the complete device operation a simple, logical I/O approach will surface. The design of the 8255A has taken into account things such as efficient PC board layout, control signal definition vs PC layout and complete functional flexibility to support almost any peripheral device with no external logic. Such design represents the maximum use of the available pins.

Single Bit Set/Reset Feature

Any of the eight bits of Port C can be Set or Reset using a single OUTput instruction. This feature reduces software requirements in Control-based applications.

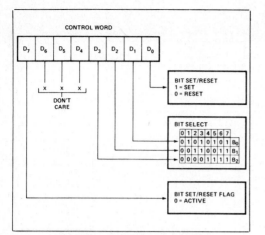

Figure 7. Bit Set/Reset Format

When Port C is being used as status/control for Port A or B, these bits can be set or reset by using the Bit Set/Reset operation just as if they were data output ports.

Interrupt Control Functions

When the 8255A is programmed to operate in mode 1 or mode 2, control signals are provided that can be used as interrupt request inputs to the CPU. The interrupt request signals, generated from port C, can be inhibited or enabled by setting or resetting the associated INTE flip-flop, using the bit set/reset function of port C.

This function allows the Programmer to disallow or allow a specific I/O device to interrupt the CPU without affecting any other device in the interrupt structure.

INTE flip-flop definition:

(BIT-SET) — INTE is SET — Interrupt enable
(BIT-RESET) — INTE is RESET — Interrupt disable

Note: All Mask flip-flops are automatically reset during mode selection and device Reset.

Operating Modes

MODE 0 (Basic Input/Output). This functional configuration provides simple input and output operations for each of the three ports. No "handshaking" is required, data is simply written to or read from a specified port.

Mode 0 Basic Functional Definitions:

- Two 8-bit ports and two 4-bit ports.
- Any port can be input or output.
- Outputs are latched.
- Inputs are not latched.
- 16 different Input/Output configurations are possible in this Mode.

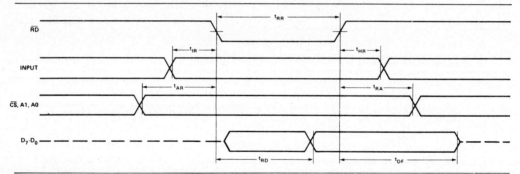

MODE 0 (Basic Input)

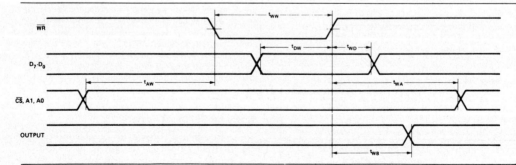

MODE 0 (Basic Output)

MODE 0 Port Definition

A		B		GROUP A			GROUP B	
D_4	D_3	D_1	D_0	PORT A	PORT C (UPPER)	#	PORT B	PORT C (LOWER)
0	0	0	0	OUTPUT	OUTPUT	0	OUTPUT	OUTPUT
0	0	0	1	OUTPUT	OUTPUT	1	OUTPUT	INPUT
0	0	1	0	OUTPUT	OUTPUT	2	INPUT	OUTPUT
0	0	1	1	OUTPUT	OUTPUT	3	INPUT	INPUT
0	1	0	0	OUTPUT	INPUT	4	OUTPUT	OUTPUT
0	1	0	1	CUTPUT	INPUT	5	OUTPUT	INPUT
0	1	1	0	OUTPUT	INPUT	6	INPUT	OUTPUT
0	1	1	1	OUTPUT	INPUT	7	INPUT	INPUT
1	0	0	0	INPUT	OUTPUT	8	OUTPUT	OUTPUT
1	0	0	1	INPUT	OUTPUT	9	OUTPUT	INPUT
1	0	1	0	INPUT	OUTPUT	10	INPUT	OUTPUT
1	0	1	1	INPUT	OUTPUT	11	INPUT	INPUT
1	1	0	0	INPUT	INPUT	12	OUTPUT	OUTPUT
1	1	0	1	INPUT	INPUT	13	OUTPUT	INPUT
1	1	1	0	INPUT	INPUT	14	INPUT	CUTPUT
1	1	1	1	INPUT	INPUT	15	INPUT	INPUT

MODE 0 Configurations

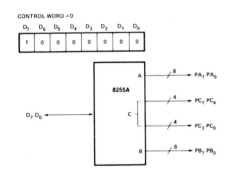

CONTROL WORD #0

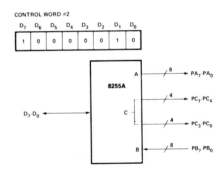

CONTROL WORD #2

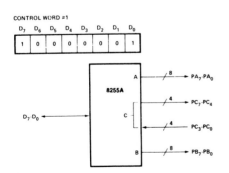

CONTROL WORD #1

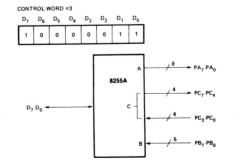

CONTROL WORD #3

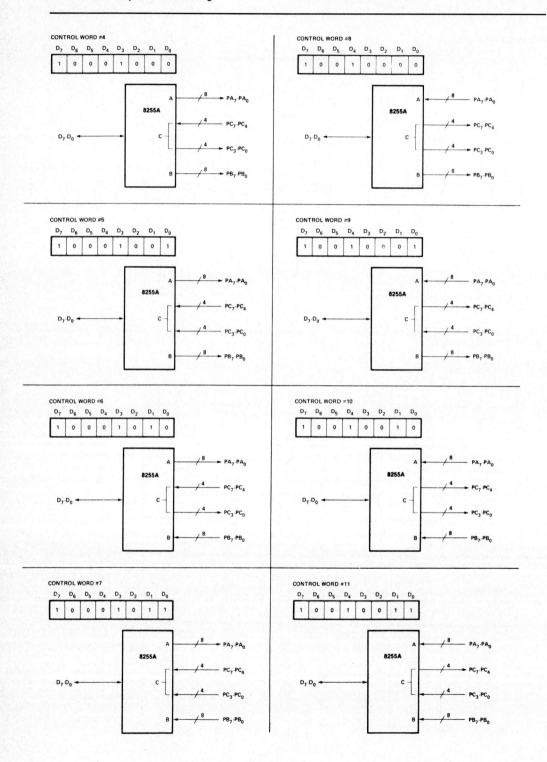

CONTROL WORD #4

D_7	D_6	D_5	D_4	D_3	D_2	D_1	D_0
1	0	0	0	1	0	0	0

CONTROL WORD #8

D_7	D_6	D_5	D_4	D_3	D_2	D_1	D_0
1	0	0	1	0	0	0	0

CONTROL WORD #5

D_7	D_6	D_5	D_4	D_3	D_2	D_1	D_0
1	0	0	0	1	0	0	1

CONTROL WORD #9

D_7	D_6	D_5	D_4	D_3	D_2	D_1	D_0
1	0	0	1	0	0	0	1

CONTROL WORD #6

D_7	D_6	D_5	D_4	D_3	D_2	D_1	D_0
1	0	0	0	1	0	1	0

CONTROL WORD #10

D_7	D_6	D_5	D_4	D_3	D_2	D_1	D_0
1	0	0	1	0	0	1	0

CONTROL WORD #7

D_7	D_6	D_5	D_4	D_3	D_2	D_1	D_0
1	0	0	0	1	0	1	1

CONTROL WORD #11

D_7	D_6	D_5	D_4	D_3	D_2	D_1	D_0
1	0	0	1	0	0	1	1

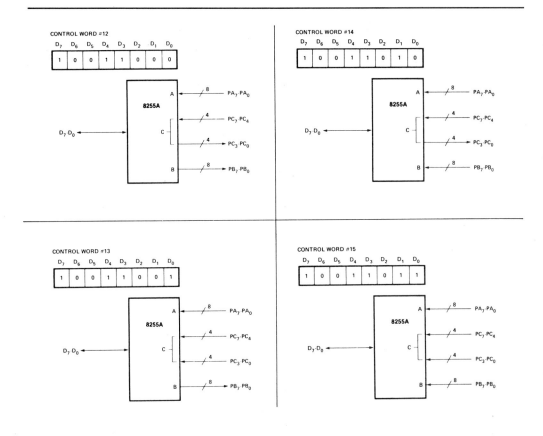

Operating Modes

MODE 1 (Strobed Input/Output). This functional configuration provides a means for transferring I/O data to or from a specified port in conjunction with strobes or "handshaking" signals. In mode 1, port A and Port B use the lines on port C to generate or accept these "handshaking" signals.

Mode 1 Basic Functional Definitions:

• Two Groups (Group A and Group B)
• Each group contains one 8-bit data port and one 4-bit control/data port.
• The 8-bit data port can be either input or output. Both inputs and outputs are latched.
• The 4-bit port is used for control and status of the 8-bit data port.

Input Control Signal Definition

STB (Strobe Input). A "low" on this input loads data into the input latch.

IBF (Input Buffer Full F/F)

A "high" on this output indicates that the data has been loaded into the input latch; in essence, an acknowledgement. IBF is set by STB input being low and is reset by the rising edge of the RD input.

INTR (Interrupt Request)

A "high" on this output can be used to interrupt the CPU when an input device is requesting service. INTR is set by the $\overline{STB}$ is a "one", IBF is a "one" and INTE is a "one". It is reset by the falling edge of $\overline{RD}$. This procedure allows an input device to request service from the CPU by simply strobing its data into the port.

INTE A

Controlled by bit set/reset of PC_4.

INTE B

Controlled by bit set/reset of PC_2.

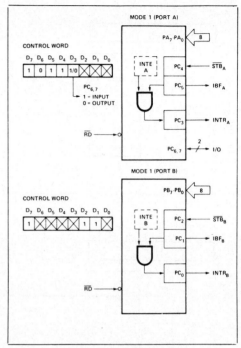

Figure 8. MODE 1 Input

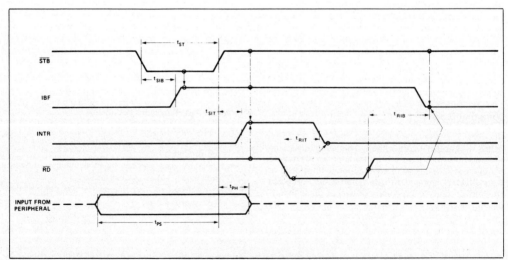

Figure 9. MODE 1 (Strobed Input)

Output Control Signal Definition

__OBF (Output Buffer Full F/F).__ The OBF output will go "low" to indicate that the CPU has written data out to the specified port. The OBF F/F will be set by the rising edge of the WR input and reset by ACK Input being low.

__ACK (Acknowledge Input).__ A "low" on this input informs the 8255A that the data from port A or B has been accepted. In essence, a response from the peripheral device indicating that it has received the data output by the CPU.

__INTR (Interrupt Request).__ A "high" on this output can be used to interrupt the CPU when an output device has accepted data transmitted by the CPU. INTR is set when ACK is a "one", OBF is a "one" and INTE is a "one". It is reset by the falling edge of WR.

    INTE A

    Controlled by bit set/reset of PC_6.

    INTE B

    Controlled by bit set/reset of PC_2.

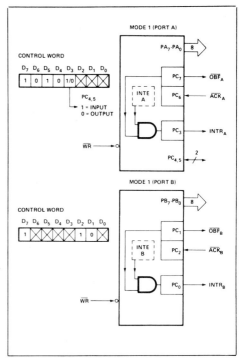

Figure 10. MODE 1 Output

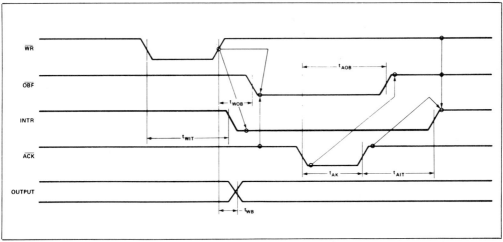

Figure 11. Mode 1 (Strobed Output)

Combinations of MODE 1

Port A and Port B can be individually defined as input or output in Mode 1 to support a wide variety of strobed I/O applications.

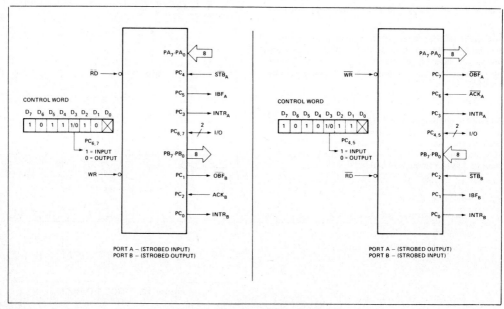

Figure 12. Combinations of MODE 1

Operating Modes

MODE 2 (Strobed Bidirectional Bus I/O). This functional configuration provides a means for communicating with a peripheral device or structure on a single 8-bit bus for both transmitting and receiving data (bidirectional bus I/O). "Handshaking" signals are provided to maintain proper bus flow discipline in a similar manner to MODE 1. Interrupt generation and enable/disable functions are also available.

MODE 2 Basic Functional Definitions:
- Used in Group A only.
- One 8-bit, bi-directional bus Port (Port A) and a 5-bit control Port (Port C).
- Both inputs and outputs are latched.
- The 5-bit control port (Port C) is used for control and status for the 8-bit, bi-directional bus port (Port A).

Bidirectional Bus I/O Control Signal Definition

INTR (Interrupt Request). A high on this output can be used to interrupt the CPU for both input or output operations.

Output Operations

$\overline{\text{OBF}}$ **(Output Buffer Ful).** The OBF output will go "low" to indicate that the CPU has written data out to port A.

$\overline{\text{ACK}}$ **(Acknowledge).** A "low" on this input enables the tri-state output buffer of port A to send out the data. Otherwise, the output buffer will be in the high impedance state.

INTE 1 (The INTE Flip-Flop Associated with OBF). Controlled by bit set/reset of PC_6.

Input Operations

$\overline{\text{STB}}$ **(Strobe Input)**

$\overline{\text{STB}}$ **(Strobe Input).** A "low" on this input loads data into the input latch.

IBF (Input Buffer Full F/F). A "high" on this output indicates that data has been loaded into the input latch.

INTE 2 (The INTE Flip-Flop Associated with IBF). Controlled by bit set/reset of PC_4.

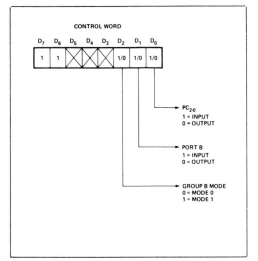

Figure 13. MODE Control Word

Figure 14. MODE 2

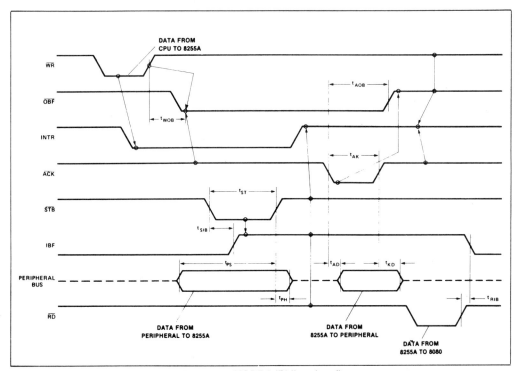

Figure 15. MODE 2 (Bidirectional)

NOTE: Any sequence where $\overline{WR}$ occurs before $\overline{ACK}$ and $\overline{STB}$ occurs before $\overline{RD}$ is permissible.
   (INTR = IBF · $\overline{MASK}$ · $\overline{STB}$ · $\overline{RD}$ + $\overline{OBF}$ · $\overline{MASK}$ · $\overline{ACK}$ · $\overline{WR}$)

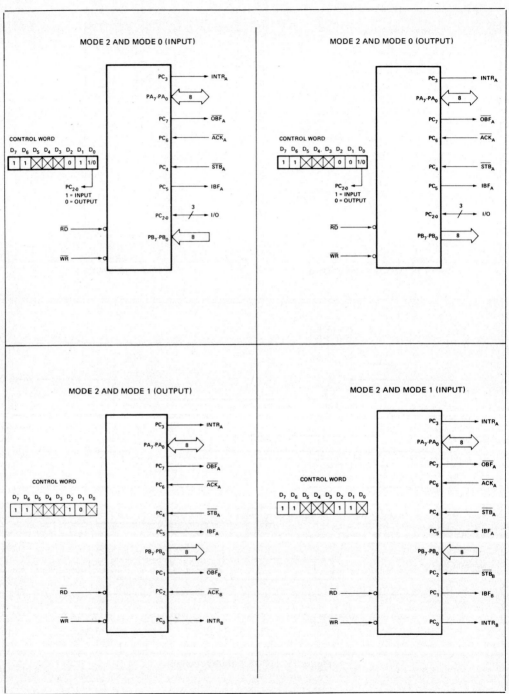

Figure 16. MODE ¼ Combinations

Mode Definition Summary

	MODE 0		MODE 1		MODE 2
	IN	OUT	IN	OUT	GROUP A ONLY
PA$_0$	IN	OUT	IN	OUT	◄——►
PA$_1$	IN	OUT	IN	OUT	◄——►
PA$_2$	IN	OUT	IN	OUT	◄——►
PA$_3$	IN	OUT	IN	OUT	◄——►
PA$_4$	IN	OUT	IN	OUT	◄——►
PA$_5$	IN	OUT	IN	OUT	◄——►
PA$_6$	IN	OUT	IN	OUT	◄——►
PA$_7$	IN	OUT	IN	OUT	◄——►
PB$_0$	IN	OUT	IN	OUT	——
PB$_1$	IN	OUT	IN	OUT	——
PB$_2$	iN	OUT	IN	OUT	——
PB$_3$	IN	OUT	IN	OUT	——
PB$_4$	IN	OUT	IN	OUT	——
PB$_5$	IN	OUT	IN	OUT	——
PB$_6$	IN	OUT	IN	OUT	——
PB$_7$	IN	OUT	IN	OUT	——
PC$_0$	IN	OUT	INTR$_B$	INTR$_B$	I/O
PC$_1$	IN	OUT	IBF$_B$	$\overline{OBF}_B$	I/O
PC$_2$	IN	OUT	$\overline{STB}_B$	$\overline{ACK}_B$	I/O
PC$_3$	IN	OUT	INTR$_A$	INTR$_A$	INTR$_A$
PC$_4$	IN	OUT	$\overline{STB}_A$	I/O	$\overline{STB}_A$
PC$_5$	IN	OUT	IBF$_A$	I/O	IBF$_A$
PC$_6$	IN	OUT	I/O	$\overline{ACK}_A$	$\overline{ACK}_A$
PC$_7$	IN	OUT	I/O	$\overline{OBF}_A$	$\overline{OBF}_A$

(MODE 2 lower bracket: MODE 0 OR MODE 1 ONLY)

Special Mode Combination Considerations

There are several combinations of modes when not all of the bits in Port C are used for control or status. The remaining bits can be used as follows:

If Programmed as Inputs —
All input lines can be accessed during a normal Port C read.

If Programmed as Outputs —
Bits in C upper (PC$_7$-PC$_4$) must be individually accessed using the bit set/reset function.

Bits in C lower (PC$_3$-PC$_0$) can be accessed using the bit set/reset function or accessed as a threesome by writing into Port C.

Source Current Capability on Port B and Port C

Any set of **eight** output buffers, selected randomly from Ports B and C can source 1mA at 1.5 volts. This feature allows the 8255 to directly drive Darlington type drivers and high-voltage displays that require such source current.

Reading Port C Status

In Mode 0, Port C transfers data to or from the peripheral device. When the 8255 is programmed to function in Modes 1 or 2, Port C generates or accepts "hand-shaking" signals with the peripheral device. Reading the contents of Port C allows the programmer to test or verify the "status" of each peripheral device and change the program flow accordingly.

There is no special instruction to read the status information from Port C. A normal read operation of Port C is executed to perform this function.

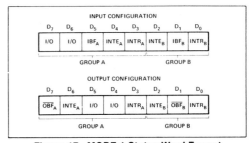

Figure 17. MODE 1 Status Word Format

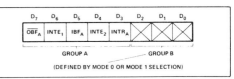

Figure 18. MODE 2 Status Word Format

APPLICATIONS OF THE 8255A

The 8255A is a very powerful tool for interfacing peripheral equipment to the microcomputer system. It represents the optimum use of available pins and is flexible enough to interface almost any I/O device without the need for additional external logic.

Each peripheral device in a microcomputer system usually has a "service routine" associated with it. The routine manages the software interface between the device and the CPU. The functional definition of the 8255A is programmed by the I/O service routine and becomes an extension of the system software. By examining the I/O devices interface characteristics for both data transfer and timing, and matching this information to the examples and tables in the detailed operational description, a control word can easily be developed to initialize the 8255A to exactly "fit" the application. Figures 19 through 25 present a few examples of typical applications of the 8255A.

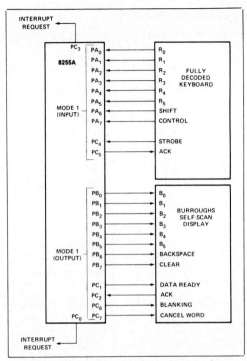

Figure 20. Keyboard and Display Interface

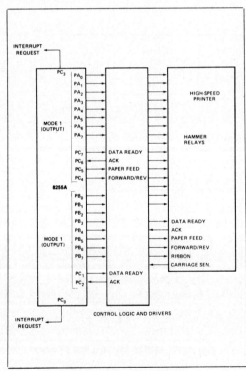

Figure 19. Printer Interface

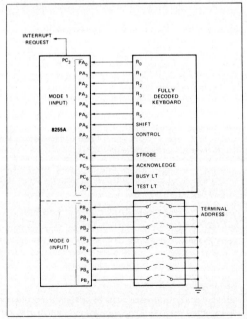

Figure 21. Keyboard and Terminal Address Interface

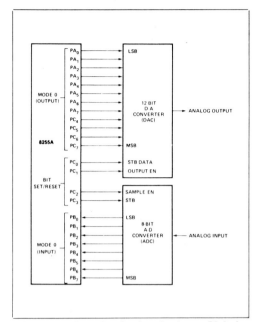

Figure 22. Digital to Analog, Analog to Digital

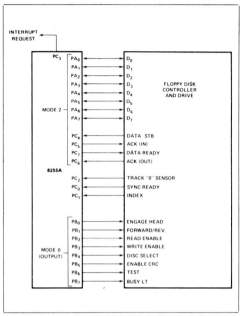

Figure 23. Basic CRT Controller Interface

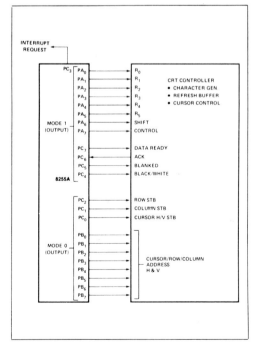

Figure 24. Basic Floppy Disc Interface

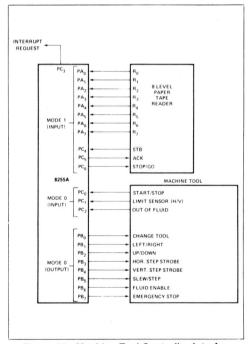

Figure 25. Machine Tool Controller Interface

ABSOLUTE MAXIMUM RATINGS*

Ambient Temperature Under Bias. . . . . 0°C to 70°C
Storage Temperature . . . . −65°C to +150°C
Voltage on Any Pin
　With Respect to Ground. . . . . −0.5V to +7V
Power Dissipation . . . . 1 Watt

NOTICE: Stresses above those listed under "Absolute Maximum Ratings" may cause permanent damage to the device. This is a stress rating only and functional operation of the device at these or any other conditions above those indicated in the operational sections of this specification is not implied. Exposure to absolute maximum rating conditions for extended periods may affect device reliability.

D.C. CHARACTERISTICS   (T_A = 0°C to 70°C, V_{CC} = +5V ± 5%, GND = 0V)

Symbol	Parameter	Min.	Max.	Unit	Test Conditions
V_{IL}	Input Low Voltage	−0.5	0.8	V	
V_{IH}	Input High Voltage	2.0	V_{CC}	V	
V_{OL} (DB)	Output Low Voltage (Data Bus)		0.45	V	I_{OL} = 2.5mA
V_{OL}(PER)	Output Low Voltage (Peripheral Port)		0.45	V	I_{OL} = 1.7mA
V_{OH}(DB)	Output High Voltage (Data Bus)	2.4		V	I_{OH} = −400μA
V_{OH}(PER)	Output High Voltage (Peripheral Port)	2.4		V	I_{OH} = −200μA
I_{DAR}[1]	Darlington Drive Current	−1.0	−4.0	mA	R_{EXT} = 750Ω; V_{EXT} = 1.5V
I_{CC}	Power Supply Current		120	mA	
I_{IL}	Input Load Current		±10	μA	V_{IN} = V_{CC} to 0V
I_{OFL}	Output Float Leakage		±10	μA	V_{OUT} = V_{CC} to .45V

NOTE:
1. Available on any 8 pins from Port B and C.

CAPACITANCE   (T_A = 25°C, V_{CC} = GND = 0V)

Symbol	Parameter	Min.	Typ.	Max.	Unit	Test Conditions
C_{IN}	Input Capacitance			10	pF	fc = 1MHz
$C_{I/O}$	I/O Capacitance			20	pF	Unmeasured pins returned to GND

A.C. CHARACTERISTICS   (T_A = 0°C to 70°C, V_{CC} = +5V ± 5%, GND = 0V)

Bus Parameters

READ

Symbol	Parameter	8255A		8255A-5		Unit
		Min.	Max.	Min.	Max.	
t_{AR}	Address Stable Before READ	0		0		ns
t_{RA}	Address Stable After READ	0		0		ns
t_{RR}	READ Pulse Width	300		300		ns
t_{RD}	Data Valid From READ[1]		250		200	ns
t_{DF}	Data Float After READ	10	150	10	100	ns
t_{RV}	Time Between READs and/or WRITEs	850		850		ns

A.C. CHARACTERISTICS (Continued)
WRITE

Symbol	Parameter	8255A		8255A-5		Unit
		Min.	Max.	Min.	Max.	
t_{AW}	Address Stable Before WRITE	0		0		ns
t_{WA}	Address Stable After WRITE	20		20		ns
t_{WW}	WRITE Pulse Width	400		300		ns
t_{DW}	Data Valid to WRITE (T.E.)	100		100		ns
t_{WD}	Data Valid After WRITE	30		30		ns

OTHER TIMINGS

Symbol	Parameter	8255A		8255A-5		Unit
		Min.	Max.	Min.	Max.	
t_{WB}	WR = 1 to Output[1]		350		350	ns
t_{IR}	Peripheral Data Before RD	0		0		ns
t_{HR}	Peripheral Data After RD	0		0		ns
t_{AK}	ACK Pulse Width	300		300		ns
t_{ST}	STB Pulse Width	500		500		ns
t_{PS}	Per. Data Before T.E. of STB	0		0		ns
t_{PH}	Per. Data After T.E. of STB	180		180		ns
t_{AD}	ACK = 0 to Output[1]		300		300	ns
t_{KD}	ACK = 1 to Output Float	20	250	20	250	ns
t_{WOB}	WR = 1 to OBF = 0[1]		650		650	ns
t_{AOB}	ACK = 0 to OBF = 1[1]		350		350	ns
t_{SIB}	STB = 0 to IBF = 1[1]		300		300	ns
t_{RIB}	RD = 1 to IBF = 0[1]		300		300	ns
t_{RIT}	RD = 0 to INTR = 0[1]		400		400	ns
t_{SIT}	STB = 1 to INTR = 1[1]		300		300	ns
t_{AIT}	ACK = 1 to INTR = 1[1]		350		350	ns
t_{WIT}	WR = 0 to INTR = 0[1,3]		450		450	ns

NOTES:
1. Test Conditions: C_L = 150 pF.
2. Period of Reset pulse must be at least 50μs during or after power on. Subsequent Reset pulse can be 500 ns min.
3. INTR↑ may occur as early as $\overline{WR}$↓.

A.C. TESTING INPUT, OUTPUT WAVEFORM

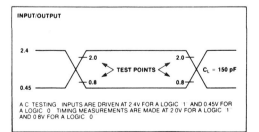

A C TESTING INPUTS ARE DRIVEN AT 2 4V FOR A LOGIC 1 AND 0 45V FOR
A LOGIC 0 TIMING MEASUREMENTS ARE MADE AT 2 0V FOR A LOGIC 1
AND 0 8V FOR A LOGIC 0

A.C. TESTING LOAD CIRCUIT

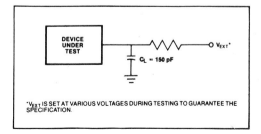

*V_{EXT} IS SET AT VARIOUS VOLTAGES DURING TESTING TO GUARANTEE THE SPECIFICATION.

WAVEFORMS

MODE 0 (BASIC INPUT)

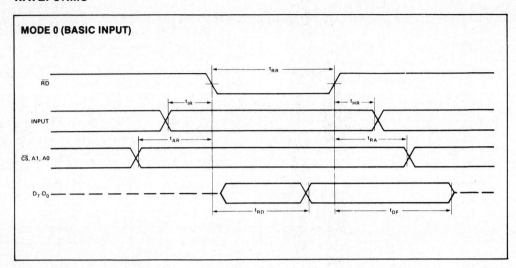

MODE 0 (BASIC OUTPUT)

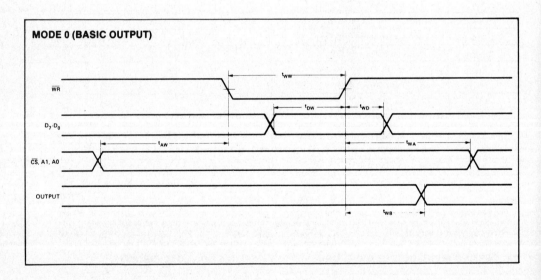

WAVEFORMS (Continued)

MODE 1 (STROBED INPUT)

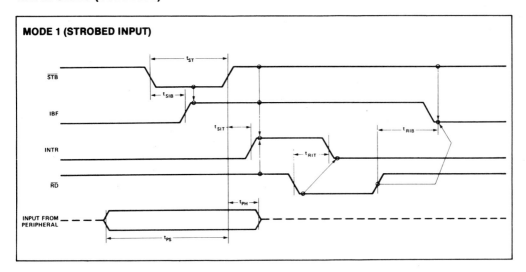

MODE 1 (STROBED OUTPUT)

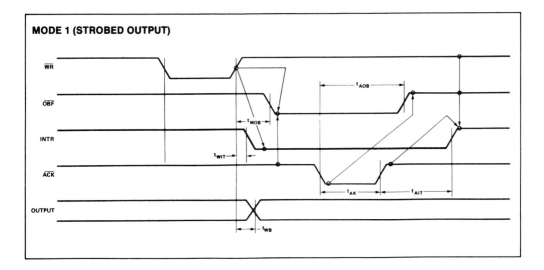

WAVEFORMS (Continued)

MODE 2 (BIDIRECTIONAL)

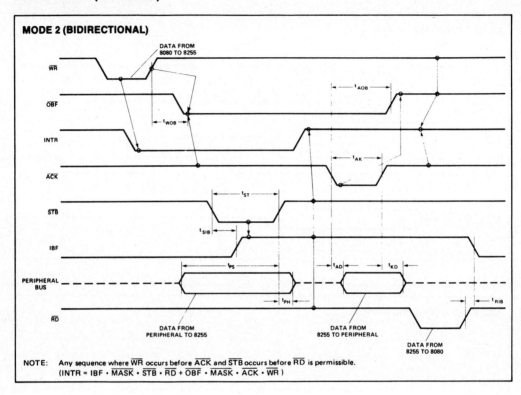

NOTE: Any sequence where $\overline{WR}$ occurs before $\overline{ACK}$ and $\overline{STB}$ occurs before $\overline{RD}$ is permissible.
(INTR = IBF $\cdot$ $\overline{MASK}$ $\cdot$ $\overline{STB}$ $\cdot$ $\overline{RD}$ + $\overline{OBF}$ $\cdot$ $\overline{MASK}$ $\cdot$ $\overline{ACK}$ $\cdot$ $\overline{WR}$)

WRITE TIMING

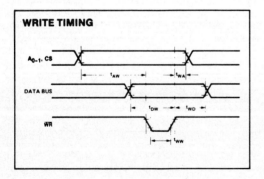

READ TIMING

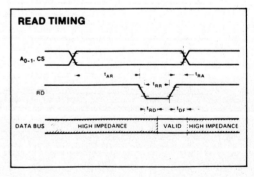

APPENDIX D: DATA SHEET FOR THE ZILOG Z80® PI0 PARALLEL INPUT/OUTPUT CONTROLLER

Z8420 Z80® PIO
Parallel Input/Output
Controller

Zilog

Product
Specification

April 1985

FEATURES

■ Provides a direct interface between Z80 microcomputer systems and peripheral devices.

■ Two ports with interrupt-driven handshake for fast response.

■ Four programmable operating modes: Output, Input, Bidirectional (Port A only), and Bit Control

■ Programmable interrupts on peripheral status conditions.

■ Standard Z80 Family bus-request and prioritized interrupt-request daisy chains implemented without external logic.

■ The eight Port B outputs can drive Darlington transistors (1.5 mA at 1.5V).

GENERAL DESCRIPTION

The Z80 PIO Parallel I/O Circuit is a programmable, dual-port device that provides a TTL-compatible interface between peripheral devices and the Z80 CPU (Figures 1 and 2). The CPU configures the Z80 PIO to interface with a wide range of peripheral devices with no other external logic. Typical peripheral devices that are compatible with the Z80 PIO include most keyboards, paper tape readers and punches, printers, and PROM programmers.

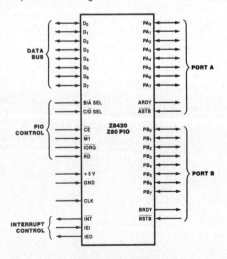

Figure 1. Pin Functions

Figure 2a. 40-pin Dual-In-Line Package (DIP),
Pin Assignments

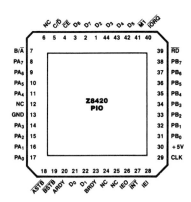

**Figure 2b. 44-pin Chip Carrier,
Pin Assignments**

One characteristic of the Z80 peripheral controllers that separates them from other interface controllers is that all data transfer between the peripheral device and the CPU is accomplished under interrupt control. Thus, the interrupt logic of the PIO permits full use of the efficient interrupt capabilities of the Z80 CPU during I/O transfers. All logic necessary to implement a fully nested interrupt structure is included in the PIO (Figure 3).

Another feature of the PIO is the ability to interrupt the CPU upon occurrence of specified status conditions in the peripheral device. For example, the PIO can be programmed to interrupt if any specified peripheral alarm conditions should occur. This interrupt capability reduces the time the processor must spend in polling peripheral status.

The Z80 PIO interfaces to peripherals via two independent general-purpose I/O ports, designated Port A and Port B. Each port has eight data bits and two handshake signals, Ready and Strobe, which control data transfer. The Ready output indicates to the peripheral that the port is ready for a data transfer. Strobe is an input from the peripheral that indicates when a data transfer has occurred.

Operating Modes. The Z80 PIO ports can be programmed to operate in four modes: Output (Mode 0), Input (Mode 1), Bidirectional (Mode 2) and Bit Control (Mode 3).

Either Port A or Port B can be programmed to output data in Mode 0. Both ports have output registers that are individually addressed by the CPU; data can be written to either port at any time. When data is written to a port, an active Ready output indicates to the external device that data is available at the associated port and is ready for transfer to the external device. After the data transfer, the external device responds with an active Strobe input, which generates an interrupt, if enabled.

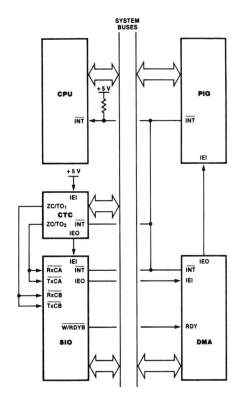

Figure 3. PIO in a Typical Z80 Family Environment

Either Port A or Port B can be programmed to input data in Mode 1. Each port has an input register addressed by the CPU. When the CPU reads data from a port, the PIO sets the Ready signal, which is detected by the external device. The external device then places data on the I/O lines and strobes the I/O port, which latches the data into the Port Input Register, resets Ready, and triggers the Interrupt Request, if enabled. The CPU can read the input data at any time, which again sets Ready.

Mode 2 is bidirectional and uses only Port A, plus the interrupts and handshake signals from both ports. Port B must be set to Mode 3 and masked off from generating interrupts. In operation, Port A is used for both data input and output. Output operation is similar to Mode 0 except that data is allowed out onto the Port A bus only when $\overline{ASTB}$ is Low. For input, operation is similar to Mode 1, except that the data input uses the Port B handshake signals and the Port B interrupt, if enabled.

Both ports can be used in Mode 3. In this mode, the individual bits are defined as either input or output bits. This provides up to eight separate, individually defined bits for each port. During operation, Ready and Strobe are not used. Instead, an interrupt is generated if the condition of one input changes, or if all inputs change. The requirements for generating an interrupt are defined during the programming operation; the active level is specified as either High or Low, and the logic condition is specified as either one input active (OR) or all inputs active (AND). For example, if the port is programmed for active Low inputs and the logic function is AND, then all inputs at the specified port must go Low to generate an interrupt.

Data outputs are controlled by the CPU and can be written or changed at any time.

■ Individual bits can be masked off.

■ The handshake signals are not used in Mode 3; Ready is held Low, and Strobe is disabled.

■ When using the Z80 PIO interrupts, the Z80 CPU interrupt mode must be set to Mode 2.

INTERNAL STRUCTURE

The internal structure of the Z80 PIO consists of a Z80 CPU bus interface, internal control logic, Port A I/O logic, Port B I/O logic, and interrupt control logic (Figure 4). The CPU bus interface logic allows the Z80 PIO to interface directly to the Z80 CPU with no other external logic. The internal control logic synchronizes the CPU data bus to the peripheral device interfaces (Port A and Port B). The two I/O ports (A and B) are virtually identical and are used to interface directly to peripheral devices.

Port Logic. Each port contains separate input and output registers, handshake control logic, and the control registers shown in Figure 5. All data transfers between the peripheral unit and the CPU use the data input and output registers. The handshake logic associated with each port controls the data transfers through the input and the output registers. The mode control register (two bits) selects one of the four programmable operating modes.

The Bit Control mode (Mode 3) uses the remaining registers. The input/output control register specifies which of the eight data bits in the port are to be outputs and enables these bits; the remaining bits are inputs. The mask register and the mask control register govern Mode 3 interrupt conditions. The mask register specifies which of the bits in the port are active and which are masked or inactive.

The mask control register specifies two conditions: first, whether the active state of the input bits is High or Low, and second, whether an interrupt is generated when any one unmasked input bit is active (OR condition) or if the interrupt is generated when *all* unmasked input bits are active (AND condition).

Interrupt Control Logic. The interrupt control logic section handles all CPU interrupt protocol for nested-priority interrupt structures. Any device's physical location in a daisy-chain configuration determines its priority. Two lines (IEI and IEO) are provided in each PIO to form this daisy chain. The device closest to the CPU has the highest priority. Within a PIO, Port A interrupts have higher priority than those of Port B. In the byte input, byte output, or bidirectional modes, an interrupt can be generated whenever the peripheral requests a new byte transfer. In the bit control mode, an interrupt can be generated when the peripheral status matches a programmed value. The PIO provides for complete control of nested interrupts. That is, lower priority devices may not interrupt higher priority devices that have not had their interrupt service routines completed by the CPU. Higher priority devices may interrupt the servicing of lower priority devices.

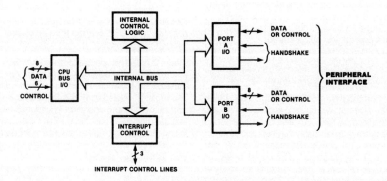

Figure 4. Block Diagram

If the CPU (in interrupt Mode 2) accepts an interrupt, the interrupting device must provide an 8-bit interrupt vector for the CPU. This vector forms a pointer to a location in memory where the address of the interrupt service routine is located. The 8-bit vector from the interrupting device forms the least significant eight bits of the indirect pointer while the I Register in the CPU provides the most significant eight bits of the pointer. Each port (A and B) has an independent interrupt vector. The least significant bit of the vector is automatically set to 0 within the PIO because the pointer must point to two adjacent memory locations for a complete 16-bit address.

Unlike the other Z80 peripherals, the PIO does not enable interrupts immediately after programming. It waits until $\overline{M1}$ goes Low (e.g., during an opcode fetch). This condition is unimportant in the Z80 environment but might not be if another type of CPU is used.

The PIO decodes the RETI (Return From Interrupt) instruction directly from the CPU data bus so that each PIO in the system knows at all times whether it is being serviced by the CPU interrupt service routine. No other communication with the CPU is required.

CPU Bus I/O Logic. The CPU bus interface logic interfaces the Z80 PIO directly to the Z80 CPU, so no external logic is necessary. For large systems, however, address decoders and/or buffers may be necessary.

Internal Control Logic. This logic receives the control words for each port during programming and, in turn, controls the operating functions of the Z80 PIO. The control logic synchronizes the port operations, controls the port mode, port addressing, selects the read/write function, and issues appropriate commands to the ports and the interrupt logic. The Z80 PIO does not receive a write input from the CPU; instead, the $\overline{RD}$, $\overline{CE}$, C/$\overline{D}$ and $\overline{IORQ}$ signals internally generate the write input.

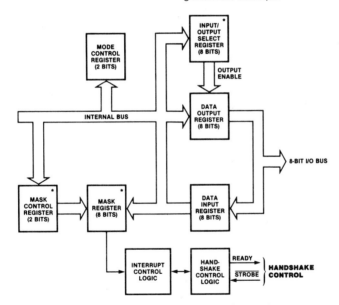

*Used in the bit mode only to allow generation of an interrupt if the peripheral I/O pins go to the specified state.

Figure 5. Typical Port I/O Block Diagram

PROGRAMMING

Mode 0, 1, or 2. (Input, Output, or Bidirectional). Programming a port for Mode 0, 1, or 2 requires at least one, and up to three, control words per port. These words are:

Mode Control Word (Figure 6). Selects the port operating mode. This word is required and may be written at any time.

Interrupt Vector Word (Figure 7). The Z80 PIO is designed for use with the Z80 CPU in interrupt Mode 2. This word must be programmed if interrupts are to be used.

Interrupt Control Word (Figure 9) or *Interrupt Disable Word* (Figure 11). Controls the enable or disable of the PIO interrupt function.

Mode 3 (Bit Control). Programming a port for Mode 3 requires at least two, and up to four, control words.

Mode Control Word (Figure 6). Selects the port operating mode. This word is required and may be written at any time.

I/O Register Control Word (Figure 8). When Mode 3 is selected, the Mode Control Word must be followed by the I/O Control Word. This word configures the I/O control register, which defines which port lines are inputs or outputs. This word is required.

Interrupt Vector Word (Figure 7). The Z80 PIO is designed for use with the Z80 CPU in interrupt Mode 2. This word must be programmed if interrupts are to be used.

Interrupt Control Word. In Mode 3, handshake is not used. Interrupts are generated as a logic function of the input signal levels. The interrupt control word sets the logic conditions and the logic levels required for generating an interrupt. Two logic conditions or functions are available: AND (if all input bits change to the active level, an interrupt is triggered), and OR (if any one of the input bits changes to the active level, an interrupt is triggered). Bit D_5 sets the logic function, as shown in Figure 9. The active level of the input bits can be set either High or Low. The active level is controlled by Bit D_5.

Mask Control Word. This word sets the mask control register, allowing any unused bits to be masked off. If any bits are to be masked, then D_4 must be set. When D_4 is set, the next word written to the port must be a mask control word (Figure 10).

Interrupt Disable Word. This control word can be used to enable or disable a port interrupt. It can be used without changing the rest of the interrupt control word (Figure 11).

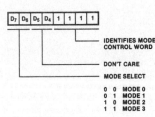

Figure 6. Mode Control Word

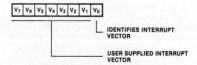

Figure 7. Interrupt Vector Word

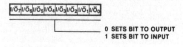

Figure 8. I/O Register Control Word

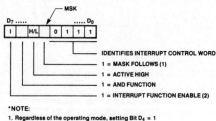

*NOTE:
1. Regardless of the operating mode, setting Bit D_4 = 1 causes any pending interrupts to be cleared.
2. The port interrupt is not enabled until the interrupt function enable is followed by an active $\overline{M1}$.

Figure 9. Interrupt Control Word

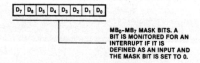

Figure 10. Mask Control Word

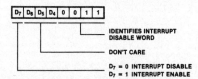

Figure 11. Interrupt Disable Word

PIN DESCRIPTION

PA$_0$-PA$_7$. *Port A Bus* (bidirectional, 3-state). This 8-bit bus transfers data, status, or control information between Port A of the PIO and a peripheral device. PA$_0$ is the least significant bit of the Port A data bus.

ARDY. *Register A Ready* (output, active High). The meaning of this signal depends on the mode of operation selected for Port A as follows:

Output Mode. This signal goes active to indicate that the Port A output register has been loaded and the peripheral data bus is stable and ready for transfer to the peripheral device.

Input Mode. This signal is active when the Port A input register is empty and ready to accept data from the peripheral device.

Bidirectional Mode. This signal is active when data is available in the Port A output register for transfer to the peripheral device. In this mode, data is not placed on the Port A data bus, unless $\overline{ASTB}$ is active.

Control Mode. This signal is disabled and forced to a Low state.

$\overline{ASTB}$. *Port A Strobe Pulse From Peripheral Device* (input, active Low). The meaning of this signal depends on the mode of operation selected for Port A as follows:

Output Mode. The positive edge of this strobe is issued by the peripheral to acknowledge the receipt of data made available by the PIO.

Input Mode. The strobe is issued by the peripheral to load data from the peripheral into the Port A input register. Data is loaded into the PIO when this signal is active.

Bidirectional Mode. When this signal is active, data from the Port A output register is gated onto the Port A bidirectional data bus. The positive edge of the strobe acknowledges the receipt of the data.

Control Mode. The strobe is inhibited internally.

PB$_0$-PB$_7$. *Port B Bus* (bidirectional, 3-state). This 8-bit bus transfers data, status, or control information between Port B and a peripheral device. The Port B data bus can supply 1.5 mA at 1.5V to drive Darlington transistors. PB$_0$ is the least significant bit of the bus.

B/$\overline{A}$. *Port B or A Select* (input, High = B). This pin defines which port is accessed during a data transfer between CPU and the PIO. A Low on this pin selects Port A; a High selects Port B. Often address bit A$_0$ from the CPU is used for this selection function.

BRDY. *Register B Ready* (output, active High). This signal is similar to ARDY, except that in the Port A bidirectional mode this signal is High when the Port A input register is empty and ready to accept data from the peripheral device.

$\overline{BSTB}$. *Port B Strobe Pulse From Peripheral Device* (input, active Low). This signal is similar to $\overline{ASTB}$, except that in the Port A bidirectional mode this signal strobes data from peripheral device into the Port A input register.

C/$\overline{D}$. *Control or Data Select* (input, High = C). This pin defines the type of data transfer to be performed between the CPU and the PIO. A High on this pin during a CPU write to the PIO causes the Z80 data bus to be interpreted as a *command* for the port selected by the B/$\overline{A}$ Select line. A Low on this pin means that the Z80 data bus is being used to transfer data between the CPU and the PIO. Often address bit A$_1$ from the CPU is used for this function.

$\overline{CE}$. *Chip Enable* (input, active Low). A Low on this pin enables the PIO to accept command or data inputs from the CPU during a write cycle or to transmit data to the CPU during a read cycle. This signal is generally decoded from four I/O port numbers for Ports A and B, data, and control.

CLK. *System Clock* (input). The Z80 PIO uses the standard single-phase Z80 system clock.

D$_0$-D$_7$. *Z80 CPU Data Bus* (bidirectional, 3-state). This bus is used to transfer all data and commands between the Z80 CPU and the Z80 PIO. D$_0$ is the least significant bit.

IEI. *Interrupt Enable In* (input, active High). This signal is used to form a priority-interrupt daisy chain when more than one interrupt driven device is being used. A High level on this pin indicates that no other devices of higher priority are being serviced by a CPU interrupt service routine.

IEO. *Interrupt Enable Out* (output, active High). The IEO signal is the other signal required to form a daisy chain priority scheme. It is High only if IEI is High and the CPU is not servicing an interrupt from this PIO. Thus this signal blocks lower priority devices from interrupting while a higher priority device is being serviced by its CPU interrupt service routine.

$\overline{INT}$. *Interrupt Request* (output, open drain, active Low). When $\overline{INT}$ is active the Z80 PIO is requesting an interrupt from the Z80 CPU.

$\overline{IORQ}$. *Input/Output Request* (input from Z80 CPU, active Low). $\overline{IORQ}$ is used in conjunction with B/$\overline{A}$, C/$\overline{D}$, $\overline{CE}$, and $\overline{RD}$ to transfer commands and data between the Z80 CPU and the Z80 PIO. When $\overline{CE}$, $\overline{RD}$, and $\overline{IORQ}$ are active, the port addressed by B/$\overline{A}$ transfers data to the CPU (a read operation). Conversely, when $\overline{CE}$ and $\overline{IORQ}$ are active but $\overline{RD}$ is not, the port addressed by B/$\overline{A}$ is written into from the CPU with either data or control information, as specified by C/$\overline{D}$. Also, if $\overline{IORQ}$ and $\overline{M1}$ are active simultaneously, the CPU is acknowledging an interrupt; the interrupting port automatically places its interrupt vector on the CPU data bus if it is the highest priority device requesting an interrupt.

M1. *Machine Cycle* (input from CPU, active Low). This signal is used as a sync pulse to control several internal PIO operations. When both the $\overline{M1}$ and $\overline{RD}$ signals are active, the Z80 CPU is fetching an instruction from memory. Conversely, when both $\overline{M1}$ and $\overline{IORQ}$ are active, the CPU is acknowledging an interrupt. In addition, $\overline{M1}$ has two other functions within the Z80 PIO: it synchronizes the PIO

interrupt logic; when $\overline{M1}$ occurs without an active $\overline{RD}$ or IORQ signal, the PIO is reset.

$\overline{RD}$. *Read Cycle Status* (input from Z80 CPU, active Low). If $\overline{RD}$ is active, or an I/O operation is in progress, $\overline{RD}$ is used with B/$\overline{A}$, C/$\overline{D}$, $\overline{CE}$, and $\overline{IORQ}$ to transfer data from the Z80 PIO to the Z80 CPU.

TIMING

The following timing diagrams show typical timing in a Z80 CPU environment. For more precise specifications refer to the composite ac timing diagram.

Write Cycle. Figure 12 illustrates the timing for programming the Z80 PIO or for writing data to one of its ports. The PIO does not receive a specific write signal; it internally generates its own from the lack of an active $\overline{RD}$ signal.

Read Cycle. Figure 13 illustrates the timing for reading the data input from an external device to one of the Z80 PIO ports.

Output Mode (Mode 0). An output cycle (Figure 14) is always started by the execution of an output instruction by the CPU. The $\overline{WR}$* pulse from the CPU latches the data from the CPU data bus into the selected port's output register. The $\overline{WR}$* pulse sets the Ready flag after a Low-going edge of CLK, indicating data is available. Ready stays active until the positive edge of the strobe line is received, indicating that data was taken by the peripheral. The positive edge of the strobe pulse generates an $\overline{INT}$ if the interrupt enable flip-flop has been set and if this device has the highest priority.

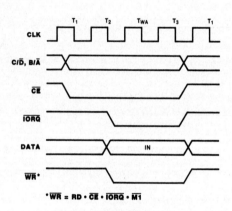

*$\overline{WR}$ = RD · $\overline{CE}$ · $\overline{IORQ}$ · $\overline{M1}$

Figure 12. Write Cycle Timing

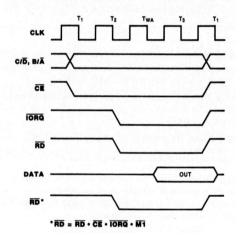

*$\overline{RD}$ = $\overline{RD}$ · $\overline{CE}$ · $\overline{IORQ}$ · $\overline{M1}$

Figure 13. Read Cycle Timing

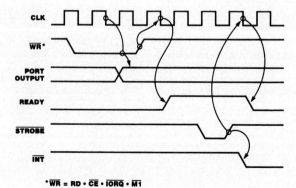

*$\overline{WR}$ = RD · $\overline{CE}$ · $\overline{IORQ}$ · $\overline{M1}$

Figure 14. Mode 0 Output Timing

Input Mode (Mode 1). When STROBE goes from Low to High, data is latched into the selected port input register (Figure 15). While STROBE is Low, the input data latches are transparent. The next rising edge of STROBE activates INT, if Interrupt Enable is set and this is the highest-priority requesting device. The following falling edge of CLK resets Ready to an inactive state, indicating that the input register is full and cannot accept any more data until the CPU completes a read. When a read is complete, the positive edge of RD sets Ready at the next Low-going transition of CLK. At this time new data can be loaded into the PIO.

Bidirectional Mode (Mode 2). This is a combination of Modes 0 and 1 using all four handshake lines and the eight Port A I/O lines (Figure 16). Port B must be set to the bit mode and its inputs must be masked. The Port A handshake lines are used for output control and the Port B lines are used for input control. If interrupts occur, Port A's vector will be used during port output and Port B's will be used during port input. Data is allowed out onto the Port A bus only when ASTB is Low. The rising edge of this strobe can be used to latch the data into the peripheral.

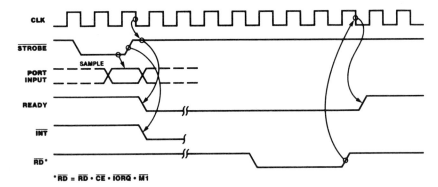

*RD = RD • CE • IORQ • M1

Figure 15. Mode 1 Input Timing

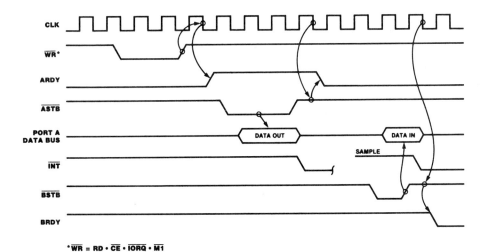

*WR = RD • CE • IORQ • M1

Figure 16. Mode 2 Bidirectional Timing

Bit Control Mode (Mode 3). The bit mode does not utilize the handshake signals, and a normal port write or port read can be executed at any time. When writing, the data is latched into the output registers with the same timing as the output mode.

When reading (Figure 17) the PIO, the data returned to the CPU is composed of output register data from those port data lines assigned as outputs and input register data from those port data lines assigned as inputs. The input register contains data that was present immediately prior to the falling edge of $\overline{RD}$. An interrupt is generated if interrupts from the port are enabled and the data on the port data lines satisfy the logical equation defined by the 8-bit mask and 2-bit mask control registers. However, if Port A is programmed in bidirectional mode, Port B does not issue an interrupt in bit mode and must therefore be polled.

Interrupt Acknowledge Timing. During $\overline{M1}$ time, peripheral controllers are inhibited from changing their interrupt enable status, permitting the Interrupt Enable signal to ripple through the daisy chain. The peripheral with IEI High and IEO Low during $\overline{INTACK}$ places a preprogrammed 8-bit interrupt vector on the data bus at this time (Figure 18). IEO is held Low until a Return From

Interrupt (RETI) instruction is executed by the CPU while IEI is High. The 2-byte RETI instruction is decoded internally by the PIO for this purpose.

Return From Interrupt Cycle. If a Z80 peripheral has no interrupt pending and is not under service, then its IEO = IEI. If it has an interrupt under service (i.e., it has already interrupted and received an interrupt acknowledge) then its IEO is always Low, inhibiting lower priority devices from interrupting. If it has an interrupt pending which has not yet been acknowledged, IEO is Low unless an "ED" is decoded as the first byte of a 2-byte opcode (Figure 19). In this case, IEO goes High until the next opcode byte is decoded, whereupon it goes Low again. If the second byte of the opcode was a "4D," then the opcode was an RETI instruction.

After an "ED" opcode is decoded, only the peripheral device which has interrupted and is currently under service has its IEI High and its IEO Low. This device is the highest-priority device in the daisy chain that has received an interrupt acknowledge. All other peripherals have IEI = IEO. If the next opcode byte decoded is "4D," this peripheral device resets its "interrupt under service" condition.

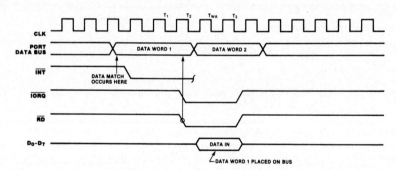

Figure 17. Mode 3 Bit Control Mode Timing, Bit Mode Read

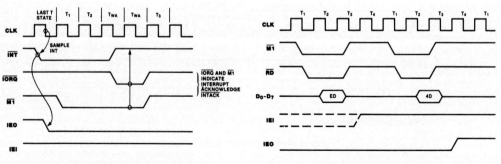

Figure 18. Interrupt Acknowledge Timing   **Figure 19. Return From Interrupt**

AC TIMING DIAGRAM

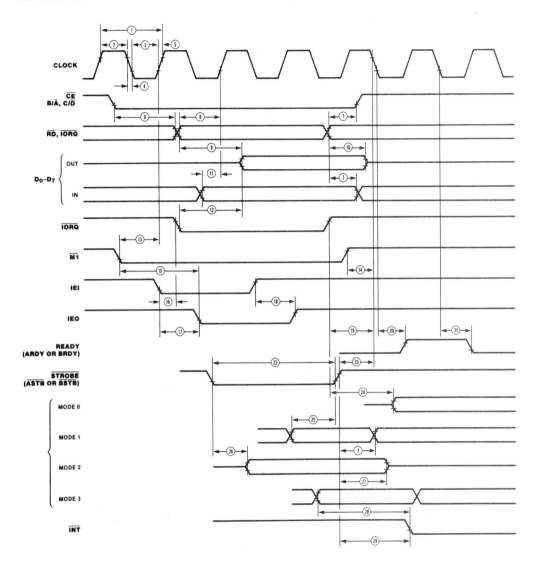

AC CHARACTERISTICS†

Number	Symbol	Parameter	Z-80 PIO* Min	Z-80 PIO* Max	Z-80A PIO* Min	Z-80A PIO* Max	Z-80B PIO* Min	Z-80B PIO* Max	Notes
1	TcC	Clock Cycle Time	400	[1]	250	[1]	165	[1]	
2	TwCh	Clock Width (High)	170	2000	105	2000	65	2000	
3	TwC1	Clock Width (Low)	170	2000	105	2000	65	2000	
4	TfC	Clock Fall Time		30		30		20	
5	TrC	Clock Rise Time		30		30		20	
6	TsCS(RI)	$\overline{CE}$, B/$\overline{A}$, C/$\overline{D}$ to $\overline{RD}$, $\overline{IORQ}$ ↓ Setup Time	50		50		50		[6]
7	Th	Any Hold Times for Specified Setup Time	0		0		0	0	
8	TsRI(C)	$\overline{RD}$, $\overline{IORQ}$ to Clock ↑ Setup Time	115		115		70		
9	TdRI(DO)	$\overline{RD}$, $\overline{IORQ}$ ↓ to Data Out Delay		430		380		300	[2]
10	TdRI(DOs)	$\overline{RD}$, $\overline{IORQ}$ ↑ to Data Out Float Delay		160		110		70	
11	TsDI(C)	Data In to Clock ↑ Setup Time	50		50		40		CL = 50 pf
12	TdIO(DOI)	$\overline{IORQ}$ ↓ to Data Out Delay (INTACK Cycle)		340		160		120	[3]
13	TsM1(Cr)	$\overline{M1}$ ↓ to Clock ↑ Setup Time	210		90		70		
14	TsM1(Cf)	$\overline{M1}$ ↑ to Clock ↓ Setup Time ($\overline{M1}$ Cycle)	0		0		0		[8]
15	TdM1(IEO)	$\overline{M1}$ ↓ to IEO ↓ Delay (Interrupt Immediately Preceding $\overline{M1}$ ↓)		300		190		100	[5,7]
16	TsIEI(IO)	IEI to $\overline{IORQ}$ ↓ Setup Time (INTACK Cycle)	140		140		100		[7]
17	TdIEI(IEOf)	IEI ↓ to IEO ↓ Delay		190		130		120	[5] CL = 50 pf
18	TdIEI(IEOr)	IEI ↑ to IEO ↑ Delay (after ED Decode)		210		160		150	[5]
19	TcIO(C)	$\overline{IORQ}$ ↑ to Clock ↓ Setup Time (To Activate READY on Next Clock Cycle)	220		200		170		
20	TdC(RDYr)	Clock ↓ to READY ↑ Delay		200		190		170	[5] CL = 50 pf
21	TdC(RDYf)	Clock ↓ to READY ↓ Delay		150		140		120	[5]
22	TwSTB	$\overline{STROBE}$ Pulse Width	150		150		120		[4]
23	TsSTB(C)	$\overline{STROBE}$ ↑ to Clock ↓ Setup Time (To Activate READY on Next Clock Cycle)	220		220		150		[5]
24	TdIO(PD)	$\overline{IORQ}$ ↑ to PORT DATA Stable Delay (Mode 0)		200		180		160	[5]
25	TsPD(STB)	PORT DATA to $\overline{STROBE}$ ↑ Setup Time (Mode 1)	260		230		190		
26	TdSTB(PD)	$\overline{STROBE}$ ↓ to PORT DATA Stable (Mode 2)		230		210		180	[5]
27	TdSTB(PDr)	$\overline{STROBE}$ ↑ to PORT DATA Float Delay (Mode 2)		200		180		160	CL = 50 pf
28	TdPD(INT)	PORT DATA Match to $\overline{INT}$ ↓ Delay (Mode 3)		540		490		430	
29	TdSTB(INT)	$\overline{STROBE}$ ↑ to $\overline{INT}$ ↓ Delay		490		440		350	

NOTES:
[1] TcC = TwCh + TwCl + TrC + TfC.
[2] Increase TdRI(DO) by 10 ns for each 50 pf increase in load up to 200 pf max.
[3] Increase TdIO(DOI) by 10 ns for each 50 pf, increase in loading up to 200 pf max.
[4] For Mode 2: TwSTB > TsPD(STB).
[5] Increase these values by 2 ns for each 10 pf increase in loading up to 100 pf max.
[6] TsCS(RI) may be reduced. However, the time subtracted from TsCS(RI) will be added to TdRI(DO).
* $\overline{M1}$ must be active for a minimum of two clock cycles to reset the PIO.
† Units in nanoseconds (ns).

ABSOLUTE MAXIMUM RATINGS

Voltages on all pins with respect
to GND . . . . –0.3V to +7V
Operating Ambient
Temperature . . . . See Ordering Information
Storage Temperature . . . . –65°C to +150°C

Stresses greater than those listed under Absolute Maximum Ratings may cause permanent damage to the device. This is a stress rating only; operation of the device at any condition above those indicated in the operational sections of these specifications is not implied. Exposure to absolute maximum rating conditions for extended periods may affect device reliability.

STANDARD TEST CONDITIONS

The DC characteristics and capacitance sections listed below apply for the following standard test conditions, unless otherwise noted. All voltages are referenced to GND (0V). Positive current flows into the referenced pin.

Available operating temperature ranges are:

- S = 0°C to +70°C, +4.75V ≤ V_{CC} ≤ +5.25V

- E = –40°C to +85°C, +4.75V ≤ V_{CC} ≤ +5.25V

- M = –55°C to +125°C, +4.5V ≤ V_{CC} ≤ +5.5V

The Ordering Information section lists package temperature ranges and product numbers. Package drawings are in the Package Information section. Refer to the Literature List for additional documentation.

All ac parameters assume a load capacitance of 100 pf max.

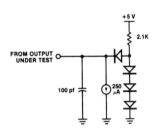

DC CHARACTERISTICS

Symbol	Parameter	Min	Max	Unit	Test Condition
V_{ILC}	Clock Input Low Voltage	–0.3	+0.45	V	
V_{IHC}	Clock Input High Voltage	V_{CC} – 0.6	V_{CC} + 0.3	V	
V_{IL}	Input Low Voltage	–0.3	+0.8	V	
V_{IH}	Input High Voltage	+2.0	V_{CC}	V	
V_{OL}	Output Low Voltage		+0.4	V	I_{OL} = 2.0 mA
V_{OH}	Output High Voltage	+2.4		V	I_{OH} = –250 μA
I_{LI}	Input Leakage Current		±10	μA	V_{IN} = 0 to V_{CC}
I_{LO}	3-State Output Leakage Current in Float		±10	μA	V_{OUT} = 0.4V to V_{CC}
I_{CC}	Power Supply Current		100	mA	
I_{OHD}	Darlington Drive Current	–1.5		mA	V_{OH} = 1.5V
	Port B Only				R_{EXT} = 390 Ω

Over specified temperature and voltage range.

CAPACITANCE

Symbol	Parameter	Min	Max	Unit
C	Clock Capacitance		10	pf
C_{IN}	Input Capacitance		5	pf
C_{OUT}	Output Capacitance		15	pf

Over specified temperature range; f = 1 MHz.
Unmeasured pins returned to ground.

ORDERING INFORMATION

Z80 PIO, 2.5 MHz

40-pin DIP	44-pin LCC
Z8420 PS	Z8420 LM*
Z8420 CS	Z8420 LMB*†
Z8420 PE	
Z8420 CE	
Z8420 CM*	
Z8420 CMB*	

Z80B PIO, 6.0 MHz

40-pin DIP
Z8420B PS
Z8420B CS

Z80A PIO, 4.5 MHz

40-pin DIP	44-pin LCC
Z8420A PS	Z8420A LM*
Z8420A CS	Z8420A LMB*†
Z8420A PE	
Z8420A CE	
Z8420A CM*	
Z8420A CMB*	

Codes

First letter is for package; second letter is for temperature.

C	= Ceramic DIP	R	= Protopack
P	= Plastic DIP	T	= Low Profile Protopack
L	= Ceramic LCC	DIP	= Dual-In-Line Package
V	= Plastic PCC	LCC	= Leadless Chip Carrier
		PCC	= Plastic Chip Carrier (Leaded)

TEMPERATURE
S = 0°C to +70°C
E = −40°C to +85°C
M*= −55°C to +125°C

FLOW
B = 883 Class B

Example: PS is a plastic DIP, 0°C to +70°C.

†Available soon.
*For Military Orders, contact your local Zilog Sales Office for Military Electrical Specifications.

APPENDIX E: DATA SHEET FOR THE INTEL 8251A PROGRAMMABLE COMMUNICATION INTERFACE

8251A
PROGRAMMABLE COMMUNICATION INTERFACE

- Synchronous and Asynchronous Operation
- Synchronous 5–8 Bit Characters; Internal or External Character Synchronization; Automatic Sync Insertion
- Asynchronous 5–8 Bit Characters; Clock Rate—1, 16 or 64 Times Baud Rate; Break Character Generation; 1, 1½, or 2 Stop Bits; False Start Bit Detection; Automatic Break Detect and Handling
- Synchronous Baud Rate—DC to 64K Baud

- Asynchronous Baud Rate—DC to 19.2K Baud
- Full-Duplex, Double-Buffered Transmitter and Receiver
- Error Detection—Parity, Overrun and Framing
- Compatible with an Extended Range of Intel Microprocessors
- 28-Pin DIP Package
- All Inputs and Outputs are TTL Compatible
- Single +5V Supply
- Single TTL Clock

The Intel® 8251A is the enhanced version of the industry standard, Intel 8251 Universal Synchronous/Asynchronous Receiver/Transmitter (USART), designed for data communications with Intel's microprocessor families such as MCS-68, 80, 85, and iAPX-86, 88. The 8251A is used as a peripheral device and is programmed by the CPU to operate using virtually any serial data transmission technique presently in use (including IBM "bi-sync"). The USART accepts data characters from the CPU in parallel format and then converts them into a continuous serial data stream for transmission. Simultaneously, it can receive serial data streams and convert them into parallel data characters for the CPU. The USART will signal the CPU whenever it can accept a new character for transmission or whenever it has received a character for the CPU. The CPU can read the complete status of the USART at any time. These include data transmission errors and control signals such as SYNDET, TxEMPTY. The chip is fabricated using N-channel silicon gate technology.

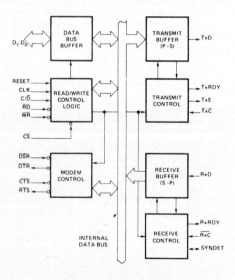

Figure 1. Block Diagram

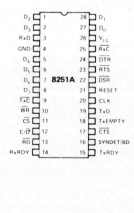

Figure 2. Pin Configuration

FEATURES AND ENHANCEMENTS

The 8251A is an advanced design of the industry standard USART, the Intel® 8251. The 8251A operates with an extended range of Intel microprocessors and maintains compatibility with the 8251. Familiarization time is minimal because of compatibility and involves only knowing the additional features and enhancements, and reviewing the AC and DC specifications of the 8251A.

The 8251A incorporates all the key features of the 8251 and has the following additional features and enhancements:

- 8251A has double-buffered data paths with separate I/O registers for control, status, Data In, and Data Out, which considerably simplifies control programming and minimizes CPU overhead.
- In asynchronous operations, the Receiver detects and handles "break" automatically, relieving CPU of this task.
- A refined Rx initialization prevents the Receiver from starting when in "break" state, preventing unwanted interrupts from a disconnected USART.
- At the conclusion of a transmission, TxD line will always return to the marking state unless SBRK is programmed.
- Tx Enable logic enhancement prevents a Tx Disable command from halting transmission until all data previously written has been transmitted. The logic also prevents the transmitter from turning off in the middle of a word.
- When External Sync Detect is programmed, Internal Sync Detect is disabled, and an External Sync Detect status is provided via a flip-flop which clears itself upon a status read.
- Possibility of false sync detect is minimized by ensuring that if double character sync is programmed, the characters be contiguously detected and also by clearing the Rx register to all ones whenever Enter Hunt command is issued in Sync mode.
- As long as the 8251A is not selected, the $\overline{RD}$ and $\overline{WR}$ do not affect the internal operation of the device.
- The 8251A Status can be read at any time but the status update will be inhibited during status read.
- The 8251A is free from extraneous glitches and has enhanced AC and DC characteristics, providing higher speed and better operating margins.
- Synchronous Baud rate from DC to 64K.

FUNCTIONAL DESCRIPTION

General

The 8251A is a Universal Synchronous/Asynchronous Receiver/Transmitter designed for a wide range of Intel microcomputers such as 8048, 8080, 8085, 8086 and 8088. Like other I/O devices in a microcomputer system, its functional configuration is programmed by the system's software for maximum flexibility. The 8251A can support most serial data techniques in use, including IBM "bi-sync."

In a communication environment an interface device must convert parallel format system data into serial format for transmission and convert incoming serial format data into parallel system data for reception. The interface device must also delete or insert bits or characters that are functionally unique to the communication technique. In essence, the interface should appear "transparent" to the CPU, a simple input or output of byte-oriented system data.

Data Bus Buffer

This 3-state, bidirectional, 8-bit buffer is used to interface the 8251A to the system Data Bus. Data is transmitted or received by the buffer upon execution of INput or OUTput instructions of the CPU. Control words, Command words and Status information are also transferred through the Data Bus Buffer. The Command Status, Data-In and Data-Out registers are separate, 8-bit registers communicating with the system bus through the Data Bus Buffer.

This functional block accepts inputs from the system Control bus and generates control signals for overall device operation. It contains the Control Word Register and Command Word Register that store the various control formats for the device functional definition.

RESET (Reset)

A "high" on this input forces the 8251A into an "Idle" mode. The device will remain at "Idle" until a new set of control words is written into the 8251A to program its functional definition. Minimum RESET pulse width is 6 t_{CY} (clock must be running).

A command reset operation also puts the device into the "Idle" state.

CLK (Clock)

The CLK input is used to generate internal device timing and is normally connected to the Phase 2 (TTL) output of the Clock Generator. No external inputs or outputs are referenced to CLK but the frequency of CLK must be greater than 30 times the Receiver or Transmitter data bit rates.

$\overline{WR}$ (Write)

A "low" on this input informs the 8251A that the CPU is writing data or control words to the 8251A.

$\overline{RD}$ (Read)

A "low" on this input informs the 8251A that the CPU is reading data or status information from the 8251A.

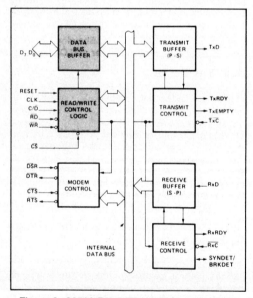

Figure 3. 8251A Block Diagram Showing Data Bus Buffer and Read/Write Logic Functions

C/$\overline{D}$	$\overline{RD}$	$\overline{WR}$	$\overline{CS}$	
0	0	1	0	8251A DATA ⇒ DATA BUS
0	1	0	0	DATA BUS ⇒ 8251A DATA
1	0	1	0	STATUS ⇒ DATA BUS
1	1	0	0	DATA BUS ⇒ CONTROL
X	1	1	0	DATA BUS ⇒ 3-STATE
X	X	X	1	DATA BUS ⇒ 3-STATE

C/$\overline{D}$ (Control/Data)

This input, in conjunction with the $\overline{WR}$ and $\overline{RD}$ inputs, informs the 8251A that the word on the Data Bus is either a data character, control word or status information.

1 = CONTROL/STATUS; 0 = DATA.

$\overline{CS}$ (Chip Select)

A "low" on this input selects the 8251A. No reading or writing will occur unless the device is selected. When $\overline{CS}$ is high, the Data Bus is in the float state and $\overline{RD}$ and $\overline{WR}$ have no effect on the chip.

Modem Control

The 8251A has a set of control inputs and outputs that can be used to simplify the interface to almost any modem. The modem control signals are general purpose in nature and can be used for functions other than modem control, if necessary.

$\overline{DSR}$ (Data Set Ready)

The $\overline{DSR}$ input signal is a general-purpose, 1-bit inverting input port. Its condition can be tested by the CPU using a Status Read operation. The $\overline{DSR}$ input is normally used to test modem conditions such as Data Set Ready.

$\overline{DTR}$ (Data Terminal Ready)

The $\overline{DTR}$ output signal is a general-purpose, 1-bit inverting output port. It can be set "low" by programming the appropriate bit in the Command Instruction word. The $\overline{DTR}$ output signal is normally used for modem control such as Data Terminal Ready.

$\overline{RTS}$ (Request to Send)

The $\overline{RTS}$ output signal is a general-purpose, 1-bit inverting output port. It can be set "low" by programming the appropriate bit in the Command Instruction word. The $\overline{RTS}$ output signal is normally used for modem control such as Request to Send.

$\overline{CTS}$ (Clear to Send)

A "low" on this input enables the 8251A to transmit serial data if the Tx Enable bit in the Command byte is set to a "one." If either a Tx Enable off or $\overline{CTS}$ off condition occurs while the Tx is in operation, the Tx will transmit all the data in the USART, written prior to Tx Disable command before shutting down.

Transmitter Buffer

The Transmitter Buffer accepts parallel data from the Data Bus Buffer, converts it to a serial bit stream, inserts the appropriate characters or bits (based on the communication technique) and outputs a composite serial stream of data on the TxD output pin on the falling edge of $\overline{\text{TxC}}$. The transmitter will begin transmission upon being enabled if $\overline{\text{CTS}}$ = 0. The TxD line will be held in the marking state immediately upon a master Reset or when Tx Enable or $\overline{\text{CTS}}$ is off or the transmitter is empty.

Transmitter Control

The Transmitter Control manages all activities associated with the transmission of serial data. It accepts and issues signals both externally and internally to accomplish this function.

TxRDY (Transmitter Ready)

This output signals the CPU that the transmitter is ready to accept a data character. The TxRDY output pin can be used as an interrupt to the system, since it is masked by TxEnable; or, for Polled operation, the CPU can check TxRDY using a Status Read operation. TxRDY is automatically reset by the leading edge of $\overline{\text{WR}}$ when a data character is loaded from the CPU.

Note that when using the Polled operation, the TxRDY status bit is *not* masked by TxEnable, but will only indicate the Empty/Full Status of the Tx Data Input Register.

TxE (Transmitter Empty)

When the 8251A has no characters to send, the TxEMPTY output will go "high." It resets upon receiving a character from the CPU if the transmitter is enabled. TxEMPTY remains low when the transmitter is disabled even if it is actually empty. TxEMPTY can be used to indicate the end of a transmission mode, so that the CPU "knows" when to "turn the line around" in the half-duplex operational mode.

In the Synchronous mode, a "high" on this output indicates that a character has not been loaded and the SYNC character or characters are about to be or are being transmitted automatically as "fillers." TxEMPTY does not go low when the SYNC characters are being shifted out.

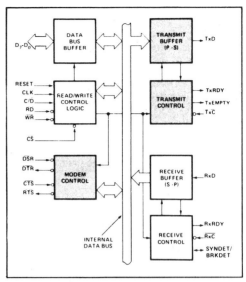

Figure 4. 8251A Block Diagram Showing Modem and Transmitter Buffer and Control Functions

$\overline{\text{TxC}}$ (Transmitter Clock)

The Transmitter Clock controls the rate at which the character is to be transmitted. In the Synchronous transmission mode, the Baud Rate (1x) is equal to the $\overline{\text{TxC}}$ frequency. In Asynchronous transmission mode, the baud rate is a fraction of the actual $\overline{\text{TxC}}$ frequency. A portion of the mode instruction selects this factor; it can be 1, 1/16 or 1/64 the $\overline{\text{TxC}}$.

For Example:

If Baud Rate equals 110 Baud,
$\overline{\text{TxC}}$ equals 110 Hz in the 1x mode.
$\overline{\text{TxC}}$ equals 1.72 kHz in the 16x mode.
$\overline{\text{TxC}}$ equals 7.04 kHz in the 64x mode.

The falling edge of $\overline{\text{TxC}}$ shifts the serial data out of the 8251A.

Receiver Buffer

The Receiver accepts serial data, converts this serial input to parallel format, checks for bits or characters that are unique to the communication technique and sends an "assembled" character to the CPU. Serial data is input to RxD pin, and is clocked in on the rising edge of $\overline{\text{RxC}}$.

Receiver Control

This functional block manages all receiver-related activities which consists of the following features.

The RxD initialization circuit prevents the 8251A from mistaking an unused input line for an active low data line in the "break condition." Before starting to receive serial characters on the RxD line, a valid "1" must first be detected after a chip master Reset. Once this has been determined, a search for a valid low (Start bit) is enabled. This feature is only active in the asynchronous mode, and is only done once for each master Reset.

The False Start bit detection circuit prevents false starts due to a transient noise spike by first detecting the falling edge and then strobing the nominal center of the Start bit (RxD = low).

Parity error detection sets the corresponding status bit.

The Framing Error status bit is set if the Stop bit is absent at the end of the data byte (asynchronous mode).

RxRDY (Receiver Ready)

This output indicates that the 8251A contains a character that is ready to be input to the CPU. RxRDY can be connected to the interrupt structure of the CPU or, for polled operation, the CPU can check the condition of RxRDY using a Status Read operation.

RxEnable, when off, holds RxRDY in the Reset Condition. For Asynchronous mode, to set RxRDY, the Receiver must be enabled to sense a Start Bit and a complete character must be assembled and transferred to the Data Output Register. For Synchronous mode, to set RxRDY, the Receiver must be enabled and a character must finish assembly and be transferred to the Data Output Register.

Failure to read the received character from the Rx Data Output Register prior to the assembly of the next Rx Data character will set overrun condition error and the previous character will be written over and lost. If the Rx Data is being read by the CPU when the internal transfer is occurring, overrun error will be set and the old character will be lost.

$\overline{\text{RxC}}$ (Receiver Clock)

The Receiver Clock controls the rate at which the character is to be received. In Synchronous Mode, the Baud Rate (1x) is equal to the actual frequency of $\overline{\text{RxC}}$. In Asynchronous Mode, the Baud Rate is a fraction of the actual $\overline{\text{RxC}}$ frequency. A portion of the mode instruction selects this factor: 1, 1/16 or 1/64 the $\overline{\text{RxC}}$.

For example:

Baud Rate equals 300 Baud, if
$\overline{\text{RxC}}$ equals 300 Hz in the 1x mode;
$\overline{\text{RxC}}$ equals 4800 Hz in the 16x mode;
$\overline{\text{RxC}}$ equals 19.2 kHz in the 64x mode.

Baud Rate equals 2400 Baud, if
$\overline{\text{RxC}}$ equals 2400 Hz in the 1x mode;
$\overline{\text{RxC}}$ equals 38.4 kHz in the 16x mode;
$\overline{\text{RxC}}$ equals 153.6 kHz in the 64x mode.

Data is sampled into the 8251A on the rising edge of $\overline{\text{RxC}}$.

NOTE: In most communications systems, the 8251A will be handling both the transmission and reception operations of a single link. Consequently, the Receive and Transmit Baud Rates will be the same. Both $\overline{\text{TxC}}$ and $\overline{\text{RxC}}$ will require identical frequencies for this operation and can be tied together and connected to a single frequency source (Baud Rate Generator) to simplify the interface.

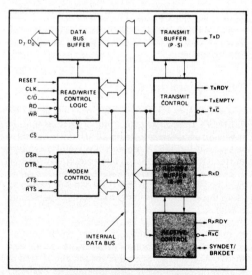

Figure 5. 8251A Block Diagram Showing Receiver Buffer and Control Functions

SYNDET (SYNC Detect/BRKDET Break Detect)

This pin is used in Synchronous Mode for SYNDET and may be used as either input or output, programmable through the Control Word. It is reset to output mode low upon RESET. When used as an output (internal Sync mode), the SYNDET pin will go "high" to indicate that the 8251A has located the SYNC character in the Receive mode. If the 8251A is programmed to use double Sync characters (bi-sync), then SYNDET will go "high" in the middle of the last bit of the second Sync character. SYNDET is automatically reset upon a Status Read operation.

When used as an input (external SYNC detect mode), a positive going signal will cause the 8251A to start assembling data characters on the rising edge of the next $\overline{RxC}$. Once in SYNC, the "high" input signal can be removed. When External SYNC Detect is programmed, Internal SYNC Detect is disabled.

BREAK (Async Mode Only)

This output will go high whenever the receiver remains low through two consecutive stop bit sequences (including the start bits, data bits, and parity bits). Break Detect may also be read as a Status bit. It is reset only upon a master chip Reset or Rx Data returning to a "one" state.

DETAILED OPERATION DESCRIPTION

General

The complete functional definition of the 8251A is programmed by the system's software. A set of control words must be sent out by the CPU to initialize the 8251A to support the desired communications format. These control words will program the: BAUD RATE, CHARACTER LENGTH, NUMBER OF STOP BITS, SYNCHRONOUS or ASYNCHRONOUS OPERATION, EVEN/ODD/OFF PARITY, etc. In the Synchronous Mode, options are also provided to select either internal or external character synchronization.

Once programmed, the 8251A is ready to perform its communication functions. The TxRDY output is raised "high" to signal the CPU that the 8251A is ready to receive a data character from the CPU. This output (TxRDY) is reset automatically when the CPU writes a character into the 8251A. On the other hand, the 8251A receives serial data from the MODEM or I/O device. Upon receiving an entire character, the RxRDY output is raised "high" to signal the CPU that the 8251A has a complete character ready for the CPU to fetch. RxRDY is reset automatically upon CPU data read operation.

The 8251A cannot begin transmission until the Tx Enable (Transmitter Enable) bit is set in the Command Instruction and it has received a Clear To Send ($\overline{CTS}$) input. The TxD output will be held in the marking state upon Reset.

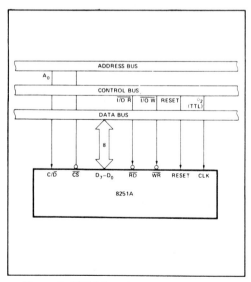

Figure 6. 8251A Interface to 8080 Standard System Bus

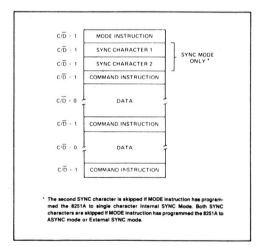

* The second SYNC character is skipped if MODE instruction has programmed the 8251A to single character Internal SYNC Mode. Both SYNC characters are skipped if MODE instruction has programmed the 8251A to ASYNC mode or External SYNC mode.

Figure 7. Typical Data Block

Programming the 8251A

Prior to starting data transmission or reception, the 8251A must be loaded with a set of control words generated by the CPU. These control signals define the complete functional definition of the 8251A and must immediately follow a Reset operation (internal or external).

The control words are split into two formats:

1. Mode Instruction
2. Command Instruction

Mode Instruction

This instruction defines the general operational characteristics of the 8251A. It must follow a Reset operation (internal or external). Once the Mode Instruction has been written into the 8251A by the CPU, SYNC characters or Command Instructions may be written.

Command Instruction

This instruction defines a word that is used to control the actual operation of the 8251A.

Both the Mode and Command Instructions must conform to a specified sequence for proper device operation (see Figure 7). The Mode Instruction must be written immediately following a Reset operation, prior to using the 8251A for data communication.

All control words written into the 8251A after the Mode Instruction will load the Command Instruction. Command Instructions can be written into the 8251A at any time in the data block during the operation of the 8251A. To return to the Mode Instruction format, the master Reset bit in the Command Instruction word can be set to initiate an internal Reset operation which automatically places the 8251A back into the Mode Instruction format. Command Instructions must follow the Mode Instructions or Sync characters.

Mode Instruction Definition

The 8251A can be used for either Asynchronous or Synchronous data communication. To understand how the Mode Instruction defines the functional operation of the 8251A, the designer can best view the device as two separate components, one Asynchronous and the other Synchronous, sharing the same package. The format definition can be changed only after a master chip Reset. For explanation purposes the two formats will be isolated.

NOTE: When parity is enabled it is not considered as one of the data bits for the purpose of programming the word length. The actual parity bit received on the Rx Data line cannot be read on the Data Bus. In the case of a programmed character length of less than 8 bits, the least significant Data Bus bits will hold the data; unused bits are "don't care" when writing data to the 8251A, and will be "zeros" when reading the data from the 8251A.

Asynchronous Mode (Transmission)

Whenever a data character is sent by the CPU the 8251A automatically adds a Start bit (low level) followed by the data bits (least significant bit first), and the programmed number of Stop bits to each character. Also, an even or odd Parity bit is inserted prior to the Stop bit(s), as defined by the Mode Instruction. The character is then transmitted as a serial data stream on the TxD output. The serial data is shifted out on the falling edge of $\overline{TxC}$ at a rate equal to 1, 1/16, or 1/64 that of the $\overline{TxC}$, as defined by the Mode Instruction. BREAK characters can be continuously sent to the TxD if commanded to do so.

When no data characters have been loaded into the 8251A the TxD output reamins "high" (marking) unless a Break (continuously low) has been programmed.

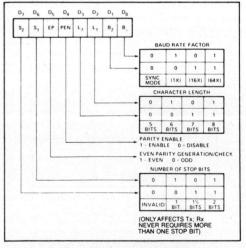

Figure 8. Mode Instruction Format, Asynchronous Mode

Asynchronous Mode (Receive)

The RxD line is normally high. A falling edge on this line triggers the beginning of a START bit. The validity of this START bit is checked by again strobing this bit at its nominal center (16X or 64X mode only). If a low is detected again, it is a valid START bit, and the bit counter will start counting. The bit counter thus locates the center of the data bits, the parity bit (if it exists) and the stop bits. If parity error occurs, the parity error flag is set. Data and parity bits are sampled on the RxD pin with the rising edge of $\overline{RxC}$. If a low level is detected as the STOP bit, the Framing Error flag will be set. The STOP bit signals the end of a character. Note that the *receiver* requires only *one* stop bit, regardless of the number of stop bits programmed. This character is then loaded into the parallel I/O buffer of the 8251A. The RxRDY pin is raised to signal the CPU that a character is ready to be fetched. If a previous character has not been fetched by the CPU, the present character replaces it in the I/O buffer, and the OVERRUN Error flag is raised (thus the previous character is lost). All of the error flags can be reset by an Error Reset Instruction. The occurrence of any of these errors will not affect the operation of the 8251A.

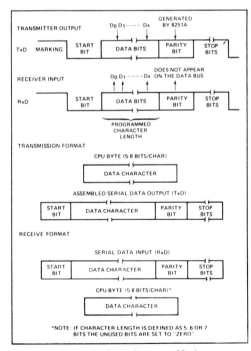

Figure 9. Asynchronous Mode

Synchronous Mode (Transmission)

The TxD output is continuously high until the CPU sends its first character to the 8251A which usually is a SYNC character. When the $\overline{CTS}$ line goes low, the first character is serially transmitted out. All characters are shifted out on the falling edge of $\overline{TxC}$. Data is shifted out at the same rate as the $\overline{TxC}$.

Once transmission has started, the data stream at the TxD output must continue at the $\overline{TxC}$ rate. If the CPU does not provide the 8251A with a data character before the 8251A Transmitter Buffers become empty, the SYNC characters (or character if in single SYNC character mode) will be automatically inserted in the TxD data stream. In this case, the TxEMPTY pin is raised high to signal that the 8251A is empty and SYNC characters are being sent out. TxEMPTY does not go low when the SYNC is being shifted out (see figure below). The TxEMPTY pin is internally reset by a data character being written into the 8251A.

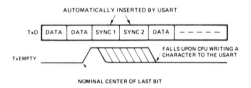

Synchronous Mode (Receive)

In this mode, character synchronization can be internally or externally achieved. If the SYNC mode has been programmed, ENTER HUNT command should be included in the first command instruction word written. Data on the RxD pin is then sampled on the rising edge of $\overline{RxC}$. The content of the Rx buffer is compared at every bit boundary with the first SYNC character until a match occurs. If the 8251A has been programmed for two SYNC characters, the subsequent received character is also compared; when both SYNC characters have been detected, the USART ends the HUNT mode and is in character synchronization. The SYNDET pin is then set high, and is reset automatically by a STATUS READ. If parity is programmed, SYNDET will not be set until the middle of the parity bit instead of the middle of the last data bit.

In the external SYNC mode, synchronization is achieved by applying a high level on the SYNDET pin, thus forcing the 8251A out of the HUNT mode. The high level can be removed after one $\overline{RxC}$ cycle. An ENTER HUNT command has no effect in the synchronous mode of operation.

Parity error and overrun error are both checked in the same way as in the Asynchronous Rx mode. Parity is checked when not in Hunt, regardless of whether the Receiver is enabled or not.

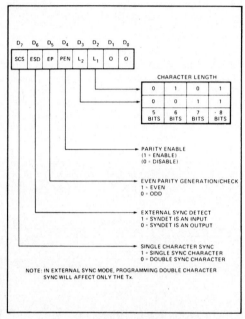

Figure 10. Mode Instruction Format, Synchronous Mode

The CPU can command the receiver to enter the HUNT mode if synchronization is lost. This will also set all the used character bits in the buffer to a "one," thus preventing a possible false SYNDET caused by data that happens to be in the Rx Buffer at ENTER HUNT time. Note that the SYNDET F/F is reset at each Status Read, regardless of whether internal or external SYNC has been programmed. This does not cause the 8251A to return to the HUNT mode. When in SYNC mode, but not in HUNT, Sync Detection is still functional, but only occurs at the "known" word boundaries. Thus, if one Status Read indicates SYNDET and a second Status Read also indicates SYNDET, then the programmed SYNDET characters have been received since the previous Status Read. (If double character sync has been programmed, then both sync characters have been contiguously received to gate a SYNDET indication.) When external SYNDET mode is selected, internal Sync Detect is disabled, and the SYNDET F/F may be set at any bit boundary.

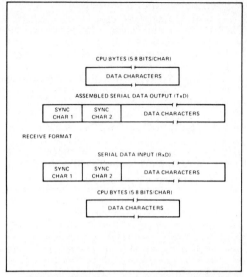

Figure 11. Data Format, Synchronous Mode

COMMAND INSTRUCTION DEFINITION

Once the functional definition of the 8251A has been programmed by the Mode Instruction and the sync characters are loaded (if in Sync Mode) then the device is ready to be used for data communication. The Command Instruction controls the actual operation of the selected format. Functions such as: Enable Transmit/Receive, Error Reset and Modem Controls are provided by the Command Instruction.

Once the Mode Instruction has been written into the 8251A and Sync characters inserted, if necessary, then all further "control writes" (C/D = 1) will load a Command Instruction. A Reset Operation (internal or external) will return the 8251A to the Mode Instruction format.

Note: Internal Reset on Power-up

When power is first applied, the 8251A may come up in the Mode, Sync character or Command format. To guarantee that the device is in the Command Instruction format before the Reset command is issued, it is safest to execute the worst-case initialization sequence (sync mode with two sync characters). Loading three 00Hs consecutively into the device with C/D̄ = 1 configures sync operation and writes two dummy 00H sync characters. An Internal Reset command (40H) may then be issued to return the device to the "Idle" state.

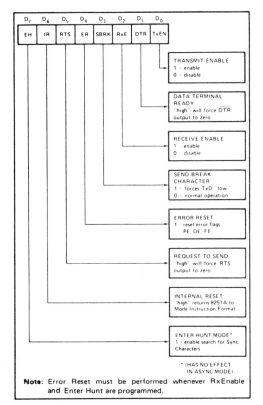

Figure 12. Command Instruction Format

STATUS READ DEFINITION

In data communication systems it is often necessary to examine the "status" of the active device to ascertain if errors have occurred or other conditions that require the processor's attention. The 8251A has facilities that allow the programmer to "read" the status of the device at any time during the functional operation. (Status update is inhibited during status read.)

A normal "read" command is issued by the CPU with $C/\overline{D} = 1$ to accomplish this function.

Some of the bits in the Status Read Format have identical meanings to external output pins so that the 8251A can be used in a completely polled or interrupt-driven environment. TxRDY is an exception.

Note that status update can have a maximum delay of 28 clock periods from the actual event affecting the status.

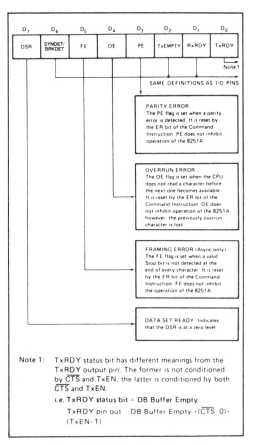

Figure 13. Status Read Format

APPLICATIONS OF THE 8251A

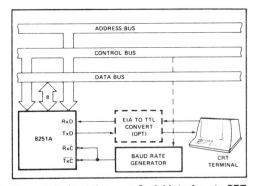

Figure 14. Asynchronous Serial Interface to CRT Terminal, DC—9600 Baud

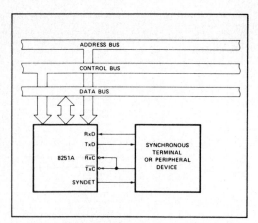

Figure 15. Synchronous Interface to Terminal or Peripheral Device

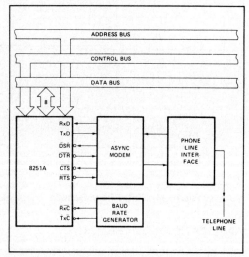

Figure 16. Asynchronous Interface to Telephone Lines

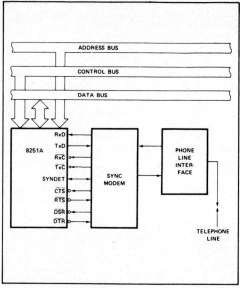

Figure 17. Synchronous Interface to Telephone Lines

ABSOLUTE MAXIMUM RATINGS*

Ambient Temperature Under Bias .... 0°C to 70°C
Storage Temperature .... −65°C to +150°C
Voltage On Any Pin
  With Respect To Ground .... −0.5V to +7V
Power Dissipation .... 1 Watt

NOTICE: Stresses above those listed under "Absolute Maximum Ratings" may cause permanent damage to the device. This is a stress rating only and functional operation of the device at these or any other conditions above those indicated in the operational sections of this specification is not implied. Exposure to absolute maximum rating conditions for extended periods may affect device reliability.

D.C. CHARACTERISTICS (T_A = 0°C to 70°C, V_{CC} = 5.0V ±5%, GND = 0V)

Symbol	Parameter	Min.	Max.	Unit	Test Conditions
V_{IL}	Input Low Voltage	−0.5	0.8	V	
V_{IH}	Input High Voltage	2.0	V_{CC}	V	
V_{OL}	Output Low Voltage		0.45	V	I_{OL} = 2.2 mA
V_{OH}	Output High Voltage	2.4		V	I_{OL} = −400 μA
I_{OFL}	Output Float Leakage		±10	μA	V_{OUT} = V_{CC} TO 0.45V
I_{IL}	Input Leakage		±10	μA	V_{IN} = V_{CC} TO 0.45V
I_{CC}	Power Supply Current		100	mA	All Outputs = High

CAPACITANCE (T_A = 25°C, V_{CC} = GND = 0V)

Symbol	Parameter	Min.	Max.	Unit	Test Conditions
C_{IN}	Input Capacitance		10	pF	fc = 1MHz
$C_{I/O}$	I/O Capacitance		20	pF	Unmeasured pins returned to GND

A.C. CHARACTERISTICS (T_A = 0°C to 70°C, V_{CC} = 5.0V ±5%, GND = 0V)
Bus Parameters (Note 1)
READ CYCLE

Symbol	Parameter	Min.	Max.	Unit	Test Conditions
t_{AR}	Address Stable Before READ ($\overline{CS}$, C/$\overline{D}$)	0		ns	Note 2
t_{RA}	Address Hold Time for READ ($\overline{CS}$, C/$\overline{D}$)	0		ns	Note 2
t_{RR}	READ Pulse Width	250		ns	
t_{RD}	Data Delay from READ		200	ns	3, C_L = 150 pF
t_{DF}	READ to Data Floating	10	100	ns	

WRITE CYCLE

Symbol	Parameter	Min.	Max.	Unit	Test Condtions
t_{AW}	Address Stable Before WRITE	0		ns	
t_{WA}	Address Hold Time for WRITE	0		ns	
t_{WW}	WRITE Pulse Width	250		ns	
t_{DW}	Data Set-Up Time for WRITE	150		ns	
t_{WD}	Data Hold Time for WRITE	20		ns	
t_{RV}	Recovery Time Between WRITES	6		t_{CY}	Note 4

A.C. CHARACTERISTICS (Continued)

OTHER TIMINGS

Symbol	Parameter	Min.	Max.	Unit	Test Conditions
t_{CY}	Clock Period	320	1350	ns	Notes 5, 6
$t_\emptyset$	Clock High Pulse Width	120	$t_{CY}-90$	ns	
$t_{\overline{\emptyset}}$	Clock Low Pulse Width	90		ns	
t_R, t_F	Clock Rise and Fall Time		20	ns	
t_{DTx}	TxD Delay from Falling Edge of $\overline{TxC}$		1	μs	
f_{Tx}	Transmitter Input Clock Frequency 1x Baud Rate 16x Baud Rate 64x Baud Rate	DC DC DC	64 310 615	kHz kHz kHz	
t_{TPW}	Transmitter Input Clock Pulse Width 1x Baud Rate 16x and 64x Baud Rate	12 1		t_{CY} t_{CY}	
t_{TPD}	Transmitter Input Clock Pulse Delay 1x Baud Rate 16x and 64x Baud Rate	15 3		t_{CY} t_{CY}	
f_{Rx}	Receiver Input Clock Frequency 1x Baud Rate 16x Baud Rate 64x Baud Rate	DC DC DC	64 310 615	kHz kHz kHz	
t_{RPW}	Receiver Input Clock Pulse Width 1x Baud Rate 16x and 64x Baud Rate	12 1		t_{CY} t_{CY}	
t_{RPD}	Receiver Input Clock Pulse Delay 1x Baud Rate 16x and 64x Baud Rate	15 3		t_{CY} t_{CY}	
t_{TxRDY}	TxRDY Pin Delay from Center of Last Bit		8	t_{CY}	Note 7
$t_{TxRDY\ CLEAR}$	TxRDY ↓ from Leading Edge of $\overline{WR}$		400	ns	Note 7
t_{RxRDY}	RxRDY Pin Delay from Center of Last Bit		26	t_{CY}	Note 7
$t_{RxRDY\ CLEAR}$	RxRDY ↓ from Leading Edge of $\overline{RD}$		400	ns	Note 7
t_{IS}	Internal SYNDET Delay from Rising Edge of $\overline{RxC}$		26	t_{CY}	Note 7
t_{ES}	External SYNDET Set-Up Time After Rising Edge of $\overline{RxC}$	18		t_{CY}	Note 7
$t_{TxEMPTY}$	TxEMPTY Delay from Center of Last Bit	20		t_{CY}	Note 7
t_{WC}	Control Delay from Rising Edge of WRITE (TxEn, $\overline{DTR}$, $\overline{RTS}$)	8		t_{CY}	Note 7
t_{CR}	Control to READ Set-Up Time ($\overline{DSR}$, $\overline{CTS}$)	20		t_{CY}	Note 7

A.C. CHARACTERISTICS (Continued)

NOTES:
1. AC timings measured V_{OH} = 2.0 V_{OL} = 2.0, V_{OL} = 0.8, and with load circuit of Figure 1.
2. Chip Select (CS) and Command/Data (C/D) are considered as Addresses.
3. Assumes that Address is valid before $R_D\downarrow$.
4. This recovery time is for Mode Initialization only. Write Data is allowed only when TxRDY = 1. Recovery Time between Writes for Asynchronous Mode is 8 t_{CY} and for Synchronous Mode is 16 t_{CY}.
5. The TxC and RxC frequencies have the following limitations with respect to CLK: For 1x Baud Rate, f_{Tx} or $f_{Rx} \leqslant 1/(30\ t_{CY})$:
   For 16x and 64x Baud Rate, f_{Tx} or $f_{Rx} \leqslant 1/(4.5\ t_{CY})$.
6. Reset Pulse Width = 6 t_{CY} minimum; System Clock must be running during Reset.
7. Status update can have a maximum delay of 28 clock periods from the event affecting the status.

TYPICAL Δ OUTPUT DELAY VS. Δ CAPACITANCE (pF)

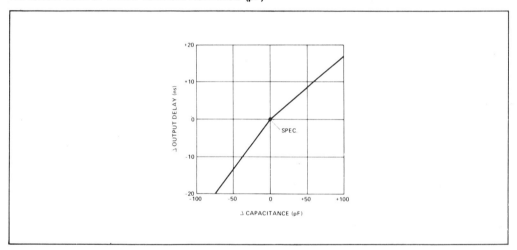

A.C. TESTING INPUT, OUTPUT WAVEFORM

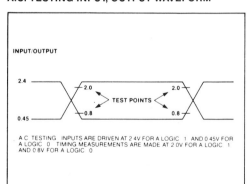

A.C. TESTING LOAD CIRCUIT

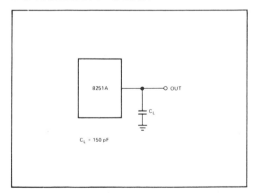

WAVEFORMS

SYSTEM CLOCK INPUT

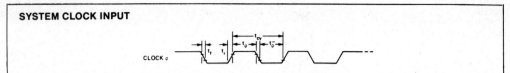

TRANSMITTER CLOCK AND DATA

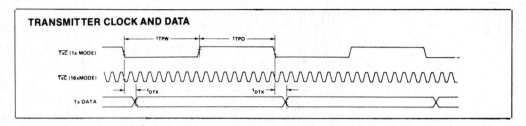

RECEIVER CLOCK AND DATA

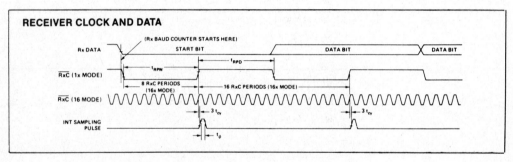

WRITE DATA CYCLE (CPU → USART)

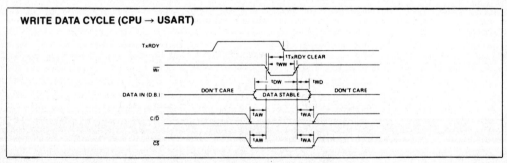

READ DATA CYCLE (CPU ← USART)

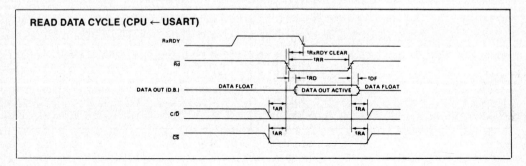

WAVEFORMS (Continued)

WRITE CONTROL OR OUTPUT PORT CYCLE (CPU → USART)

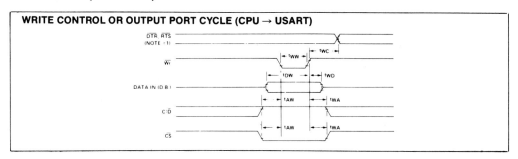

READ CONTROL OR INPUT PORT (CPU ← USART)

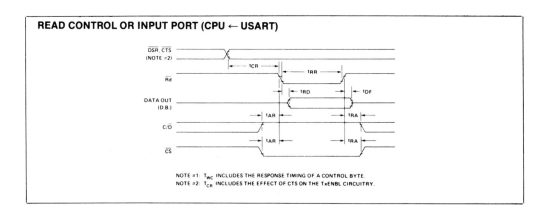

NOTE #1: T$_{WC}$ INCLUDES THE RESPONSE TIMING OF A CONTROL BYTE.
NOTE #2: T$_{CR}$ INCLUDES THE EFFECT OF CTS ON THE TxENBL CIRCUITRY.

TRANSMITTER CONTROL AND FLAG TIMING (ASYNC MODE)

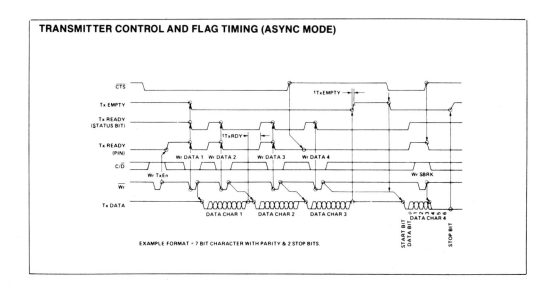

EXAMPLE FORMAT = 7 BIT CHARACTER WITH PARITY & 2 STOP BITS.

WAVEFORMS (Continued)

RECEIVER CONTROL AND FLAG TIMING (ASYNC MODE)

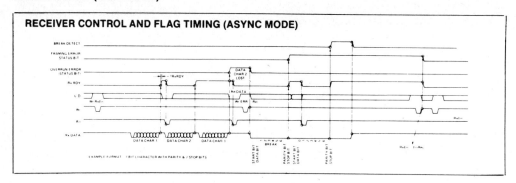

TRANSMITTER CONTROL AND FLAG TIMING (SYNC MODE)

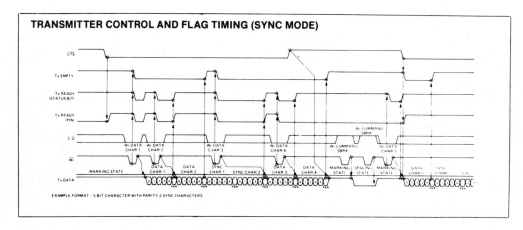

RECEIVER CONTROL AND FLAG TIMING (SYNC MODE)

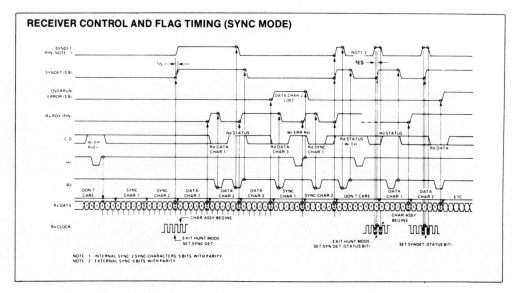

APPENDIX F: DATA SHEET FOR THE ZILOG SCC SERIAL COMMUNICATIONS CONTROLLER

Z8530 SCC Serial Communications Controller

Zilog

Product Specification

April 1985

Features

- Two independent, 0 to 1.5M bit/second, full-duplex channels, each with a separate crystal oscillator, baud rate generator, and Digital Phase-Locked Loop for clock recovery.

- Multi-protocol operation under program control; programmable for NRZ, NRZI, or FM data encoding.

- Asynchronous mode with five to eight bits and one, one and one-half, or two stop bits per character; programmable clock factor; break detection and generation; parity, overrun, and framing error detection.

- Synchronous mode with internal or external character synchronization on one or two

synchronous characters and CRC generation and checking with CRC-16 or CRC-CCITT preset to either 1s or 0s.

- SDLC/HDLC mode with comprehensive frame-level control, automatic zero insertion and deletion, I-field residue handling, abort generation and detection, CRC generation and checking, and SDLC Loop mode operation.

- Local Loopback and Auto Echo modes.

- 1.544M bit/second T1 digital trunk compatible version available.

General Description

The Z8530 SCC Serial Communications Controller is a dual-channel, multi-protocol data communications peripheral designed for use with conventional non-multiplexed buses. The SCC functions as a serial-to-parallel, parallel-to-serial converter/controller. The SCC can be software-configured to satisfy a wide variety of serial communications applications. The device contains a variety of new, sophisticated internal functions including on-chip baud rate generators, Digital Phase-Locked Loops, and crystal oscillators that dramatically reduce the need for external logic.

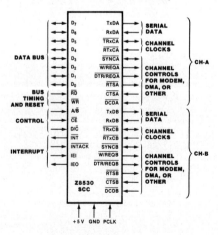

Figure 1. Pin Functions

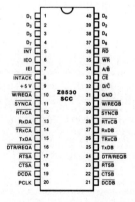

Figure 2a. 40-pin Dual-In-Line Package (DIP),
Pin Assignments

General Description (Continued)

The SCC handles asynchronous formats, Synchronous byte-oriented protocols such as IBM Bisync, and Synchronous bit-oriented protocols such as HDLC and IBM SDLC. This versatile device supports virtually any serial data transfer application (cassette, diskette, tape drives, etc.).

The device can generate and check CRC codes in any Synchronous mode and can be programmed to check data integrity in various modes. The SCC also has facilities for modem controls in both channels. In applications where these controls are not needed, the modem controls can be used for general-purpose I/O.

The Z-Bus daisy-chain interrupt hierarchy is also supported—as is standard for Zilog peripheral components.

The Z8530 SCC is packaged in a 40-pin ceramic DIP and a 44-pin chip carrier.

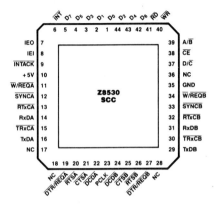

Figure 2b. 44-pin Chip Carrier. Pin Assignments

Pin Description

The following section describes the pin functions of the SCC. Figures 1 and 2 detail the respective pin functions and pin assignments.

A/B̄. *Channel A/Channel B Select* (input). This signal selects the channel in which the read or write operation occurs.

C̄Ē. *Chip Enable* (input, active Low). This signal selects the SCC for a read or write operation.

C̄TSA, C̄TSB. *Clear To Send* (inputs, active Low). If these pins are programmed as Auto Enables, a Low on the inputs enables the respective transmitters. If not programmed as Auto Enables, they may be used as general-purpose inputs. Both inputs are Schmitt-trigger buffered to accommodate slow rise-time inputs. The SCC detects pulses on these inputs and can interrupt the CPU on both logic level transitions.

D/C̄. *Data/Control Select* (input). This signal defines the type of information transferred to or from the SCC. A High means data is transferred; a Low indicates a command.

D̄CDA, D̄CDB. *Data Carrier Detect* (inputs, active Low). These pins function as receiver enables if they are programmed for Auto Enables; otherwise they may be used as general-purpose input pins. Both pins are Schmitt-trigger buffered to accomodate slow rise-time signals. The SCC detects pulses on these pins and can interrupt the CPU on both logic level transitions.

D₀-D₇. *Data Bus* (bidirectional, 3-state). These lines carry data and commands to and from the SCC.

D̄TR/R̄EQA, D̄TR/R̄EQB. *Data Terminal Ready/Request* (outputs, active Low). These outputs follow the state programmed into the DTR bit. They can also be used as general-purpose outputs or as Request lines for a DMA controller.

IEI. *Interrupt Enable In* (input, active High). IEI is used with IEO to form an interrupt daisy chain when there is more than one interrupt-driven device. A High IEI indicates that no other higher priority device has an interrupt under service or is requesting an interrupt.

IEO. *Interrupt Enable Out* (output, active High). IEO is High only if IEI is High and the CPU is not servicing an SCC interrupt or the SCC is not requesting an interrupt (Interrupt Acknowledge cycle only). IEO is connected to the next lower priority device's IEI input and thus inhibits interrupts from lower priority devices.

ĪNT. *Interrupt Request* (output, open-drain, active Low). This signal is activated when the SCC requests an interrupt.

ĪNTACK. *Interrupt Acknowledge* (input, active Low). This signal indicates an active Interrupt Acknowledge cycle. During this cycle, the SCC interrupt daisy chain settles. When R̄D becomes active, the SCC places an interrupt vector on the data bus (if IEI is High). ĪNTACK is latched by the rising edge of PCLK.

PCLK. *Clock* (input). This is the master SCC clock used to synchronize internal signals PCLK is a TTL level signal.

R̄D. *Read* (input, active Low). This signal indicates a read operation and when the SCC is selected, enables the SCC's bus drivers. During the Interrupt Acknowledge cycle, this signal gates the interrupt vector onto the bus if the SCC is the highest priority device requesting an interrupt.

RxDA, RxDB. *Receive Data* (inputs, active High). These input signals receive serial data at standard TTL levels.

R̄TxCA, R̄TxCB. *Receive/Transmit Clocks* (inputs, active Low). These pins can be programmed in several different modes of operation. In each channel, R̄TxC may supply the receive clock, the transmit clock, the clock for the baud rate generator, or the clock for the Digital Phase-Locked Loop. These pins can also be programmed for use with the respective S̄YNC pins as a crystal oscillator. The receive clock may be 1, 16, 32, or 64 times the data rate in Asynchronous modes.

R̄TSA, R̄TSB. *Request To Send* (outputs, active Low). When the Request To Send (RTS) bit in Write Register 5 (Figure 11) is set, the R̄TS signal goes Low. When the RTS bit is reset in the Asynchronous mode and Auto

Pin Description (Continued)

Enable is on, the signal goes High after the transmitter is empty. In Synchronous mode or in Asynchronous mode with Auto Enable off, the RTS pin strictly follows the state of the RTS bit. Both pins can be used as general-purpose outputs.

SYNCA, SYNCB. *Synchronization* (inputs or outputs, active Low). These pins can act either as inputs, outputs, or part of the crystal oscillator circuit. In the Asynchronous Receive mode (crystal oscillator option not selected), these pins are inputs similar to $\overline{CTS}$ and $\overline{DCD}$. In this mode, transitions on these lines affect the state of the Synchronous/Hunt status bits in Read Register 0 (Figure 10) but have no other function.

In External Synchronization mode with the crystal oscillator not selected, these lines also act as inputs. In this mode, $\overline{SYNC}$ must be driven Low two receive clock cycles after the last bit in the synchronous character is received. Character assembly begins on the rising edge of the receive clock immediately preceding the activation of $\overline{SYNC}$.

In the Internal Synchronization mode (Monosync and Bisync) with the crystal oscillator not selected, these pins act as outputs and are active only during the part of the receive clock cycle in which synchronous characters are recognized. The synchronous condition is not latched, so these outputs are active each time a synchronization pattern is recognized (regardless of character boundaries). In SDLC mode, these pins act as outputs and are valid on receipt of a flag.

TxDA, TxDB. *Transmit Data* (outputs, active High). These output signals transmit serial data at standard TTL levels.

TRxCA, TRxCB. *Transmit/Receive Clocks* (inputs or outputs, active Low). These pins can be programmed in several different modes of operation. $\overline{TRxC}$ may supply the receive clock or the transmit clock in the input mode or supply the output of the Digital Phase-Locked Loop, the crystal oscillator, the baud rate generator, or the transmit clock in the output mode.

WR. *Write* (input, active Low). When the SCC is selected, this signal indicates a write operation. The coincidence of $\overline{RD}$ and $\overline{WR}$ is interpreted as a reset.

W/REQA, W/REQB. *Wait/Request* (outputs, open-drain when programmed for a Wait function, driven High or Low when programmed for a Request function). These dual-purpose outputs may be programmed as Request lines for a DMA controller or as Wait lines to synchronize the CPU to the SCC data rate. The reset state is Wait.

Functional Description

The functional capabilities of the SCC can be described from two different points of view: as a data communications device, it transmits and receives data in a wide variety of data communications protocols; as a microprocessor peripheral, the SCC offers valuable features such as vectored interrupts, polling, and simple handshake capability.

Data Communications Capabilities. The SCC provides two independent full-duplex channels programmable for use in any common Asynchronous or Synchronous data-communication protocol. Figure 3 and the following description briefly detail these protocols.

Asynchronous Modes. Transmission and reception can be accomplished independently on each channel with five to eight bits per character, plus optional even or odd parity. The transmitters can supply one, one-and-a-half, or two stop bits per character and can provide a break output at any time. The receiver break-detection logic interrupts the CPU both at the start and at the end of a received break. Reception is protected from spikes by a transient spike-rejection

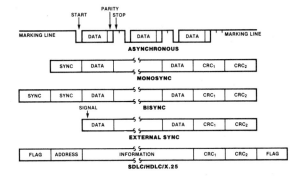

Figure 3. Some SCC Protocols

Functional Description (Continued)

mechanism that checks the signal one-half a bit time after a Low level is detected on the receive data input (RxDA or RxDB in Figure 1). If the Low does not persist (as in the case of a transient), the character assembly process does not start.

Framing errors and overrun errors are detected and buffered together with the partial character on which they occur. Vectored interrupts allow fast servicing or error conditions using dedicated routines. Furthermore, a built-in checking process avoids the interpretation of a framing error as a new start bit: a framing error results in the addition of one-half a bit time to the point at which the search for the next start bit begins.

The SCC does not require symmetric transmit and receive clock signals—a feature allowing use of the wide variety of clock sources. The transmitter and receiver can handle data at a rate of 1, 1/16, 1/32, or 1/64 of the clock rate supplied to the receive and transmit clock inputs. In Asynchronous modes, the $\overline{\text{SYNC}}$ pin may be programmed as an input used for functions such as monitoring a ring indicator.

Synchronous Modes. The SCC supports both byte-oriented and bit-oriented synchronous communication. Synchronous byte-oriented protocols can be handled in several modes, allowing character synchronization with a 6-bit or 8-bit synchronous character (Monosync), any 12-bit synchronization pattern (Bisync), or with an external synchronous signal. Leading sync characters can be removed without interrupting the CPU.

Five- or 7-bit synchronous characters are detected with 8- or 16-bit patterns in the SCC by overlapping the larger pattern across multiple incoming synchronous characters as shown in Figure 4.

CRC checking for Synchronous byte-oriented modes is delayed by one character time so that the CPU may disable CRC checking on specific characters. This permits the implementation of protocols such as IBM Bisync.

Both CRC-16 ($X^{16} + X^{15} + X^2 + 1$) and CCITT ($X^{16} + X^{12} + X^5 + 1$) error checking polynomials are supported. Either polynomial may be selected in all Synchronous modes. Users may preset the CRC generator and checker to all 1s or all 0s. The SCC also provides a feature that automatically transmits CRC data when no other data is available for transmission. This allows for high speed transmissions under DMA control, with no need for CPU intervention at the end of a message. When there is no data or CRC to send in Synchronous modes, the transmitter inserts 6-, 8-, or 16-bit synchronous characters, regardless of the programmed character length.

The SCC supports Synchronous bit-oriented protocols, such as SDLC and HDLC, by performing automatic flag sending, zero insertion, and CRC generation. A special command can be used to abort a frame in transmission. At the end of a message, the SCC automatically transmits the CRC and trailing flag when the transmitter underruns. The transmitter may also be programmed to send an idle line consisting of continuous flag characters or a steady marking condition.

If a transmit underrun occurs in the middle of a message, an external/status interrupt warns the CPU of this status change so that an abort may be issued. The SCC may also be programmed to send an abort itself in case of an underrun, relieving the CPU of this task. One to eight bits per character can be sent, allowing reception of a message with no prior information about the character structure in the information field of a frame.

The receiver automatically acquires synchronization on the leading flag of a frame in SDLC or HDLC and provides a synchronization signal on the $\overline{\text{SYNC}}$ pin (an interrupt can also be programmed). The receiver can be programmed to search for frames addressed by a single byte (or four bits within a byte) of a user-selected address or to a global broadcast address. In this mode, frames not matching either the user-selected or broadcast address are ignored. The number of address bytes can be extended under software control. For receiving data, an interrupt on the first received character, or an interrupt on every character, or on special condition only (end-of-frame) can be selected. The receiver automatically deletes all 0s inserted by the transmitter during character assembly. CRC is also calculated and is automatically checked to validate frame transmission. At the end of transmission, the status of a received frame is available in the status registers. In SDLC mode, the SCC must be programmed to use the SDLC CRC polynomial, but the generator and checker may be preset to all 1s or all 0s.

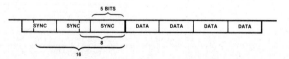

Figure 4. Detecting 5- or 7-Bit Synchronous Characters

Functional Description (Continued)

The CRC is inverted before transmission and the receiver checks against the bit pattern 0001110100001111.

NRZ, NRZI or FM coding may be used in any 1x mode. The parity options available in Asynchronous modes are available in Synchronous modes.

The SCC can be conveniently used under DMA control to provide high speed reception or transmission. In reception, for example, the SCC can interrupt the CPU when the first character of a message is received. The CPU then enables the DMA to transfer the message to memory. The SCC then issues an end-of-frame interrupt and the CPU can check the status of the received message. Thus, the CPU is freed for other service while the message is being received. The CPU may also enable the DMA first and have the SCC interrupt only on end-of-frame. This procedure allows all data to be transferred via the DMA.

SDLC Loop Mode. The SCC supports SDLC Loop mode in addition to normal SDLC. In an SDLC Loop, there is a primary controller station that manages the message traffic flow on the loop and any number of secondary stations. In SDLC Loop mode, the SCC performs the functions of a secondary station while an SCC operating in regular SDLC mode can act as a controller (Figure 5).

A secondary station in an SDLC Loop is always listening to the messages being sent around the loop, and in fact must pass these messages to the rest of the loop by retransmitting them with a one-bit-time delay. The secondary station can place its own message on the loop only at specific times. The controller signals that secondary stations may transmit messages by sending a special character, called an EOP (End Of Poll), around the loop. The EOP character is the bit pattern 11111110. Because of zero insertion during messages, this bit pattern is unique and easily recognized.

When a secondary station has a message to transmit and recognizes an EOP on the line, it

changes the last binary 1 of the EOP to a 0 before transmission. This has the effect of turning the EOP into a flag sequence. The secondary station now places its message on the loop and terminates the message with an EOP. Any secondary stations further down the loop with messages to transmit can then append their messages to the message of the first secondary station by the same process. Any secondary stations without messages to send merely echo the incoming messages and are prohibited from placing messages on the loop (except upon recognizing an EOP).

SDLC Loop mode is a programmable option in the SCC. NRZ, NRZI, and FM coding may all be used in SDLC Loop mode.

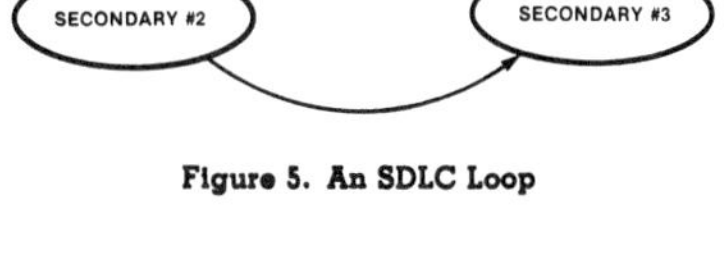

Baud Rate Generator. Each channel in the SCC contains a programmable baud rate generator. Each generator consists of two 8-bit time constant registers that form a 16-bit time constant, a 16-bit down counter, and a flip-flop on the output producing a square wave. On startup, the flip-flop on the output is set in a High state, the value in the time constant register is loaded into the counter, and the counter starts counting down. The output of the baud rate generator toggles upon reaching 0, the value in the time constant register is loaded into the counter, and the process is repeated. The time constant may be changed at any time, but the new value does not take effect until the next load of the counter.

The output of the baud rate generator may be used as either the transmit clock, the receive clock, or both. It can also drive the Digital Phase-Locked Loop (see next section).

If the receive clock or transmit clock is not programmed to come from the $\overline{TRxC}$ pin, the output of the baud rate generator may be echoed out via the $\overline{TRxC}$ pin.

The following formula relates the time constant to the baud rate (the baud rate is in bits/second and the BR clock period is in seconds):

$$\text{baud rate} = \frac{1}{2\,(\text{time constant} + 2) \times (\text{BR clock period})}$$

Digital Phase-Locked Loop. The SCC contains a Digital Phase-Locked-Loop (DPLL) to recover clock information from a data stream with NRZI or FM encoding. The DPLL is driven by a clock that is nominally 32 (NRZI) or 16 (FM) times the data rate. The DPLL uses this clock, along with the data stream, to construct a clock for the data. This clock may then be used as the SCC receive clock, the transmit clock, or both.

For NRZI encoding, the DPLL counts the 32x clock to create nominal bit times. As the 32x clock is counted, the DPLL is searching the

Figure 5. An SDLC Loop

Functional Description (Continued)

incoming data stream for edges (either 1 to 0 or 0 to 1). Whenever an edge is detected, the DPLL makes a count adjustment (during the next counting cycle), producing a terminal count closer to the center of the bit cell.

For FM encoding, the DPLL still counts from 0 to 31, but with a cycle corresponding to two bit times. When the DPLL is locked, the clock edges in the data stream should occur between counts 15 and 16 and between counts 31 and 0. The DPLL looks for edges only during a time centered on the 15 to 16 counting transition.

The 32x clock for the DPLL can be programmed to come from either the $\overline{RTxC}$ input or the output of the baud rate generator. The DPLL output may be programmed to be echoed out of the SCC via the $\overline{TRxC}$ pin (if this pin is not being used as an input).

Data Encoding. The SCC may be programmed to encode and decode the serial data in four different ways (Figure 6). In NRZ encoding, a 1 is represented by a High level and a 0 is represented by a Low level. In NRZI encoding, a 1 is represented by no change in level and a 0 is represented by a change in level. In FM1 (more properly, bi-phase mark), a transition occurs at the beginning of every bit cell. A 1 is represented by an additional transition at the center of the bit cell and a 0 is represented by no additional transition at the center of the bit cell. In FM0 (bi-phase space), a transition occurs at the beginning of every bit cell. A 0 is represented by an additional transition at the center of the bit cell, and a 1 is represented by no additional transition at the center of the bit cell. In addition to these four methods, the SCC can be used to decode Manchester (bi-phase level) data by using the DPLL in the FM mode and programming the receiver for NRZ data. Manchester encoding always produces a transition at the center of the bit cell. If the transition is 0 to 1, the bit is a 0. If the transition is 1 to 0, the bit is a 1.

Auto Echo and Local Loopback. The SCC is capable of automatically echoing everything it receives. This feature is useful mainly in Asynchronous modes, but works in Synchronous and SDLC modes as well. In Auto Echo mode, TxD is RxD. Auto Echo mode can be used with NRZI or FM encoding with no additional delay, because the data stream is not decoded before retransmission. In Auto Echo mode, the $\overline{CTS}$ input is ignored as a transmitter enable (although transitions on this input can still cause interrupts if programmed to do so). In this mode, the transmitter is actually bypassed and the programmer is responsible for disabling transmitter interrupts and WAIT/REQUEST on transmit.

The SCC is also capable of local loopback. In this mode TxD is RxD, just as in Auto Echo mode. However, in Local Loopback mode, the internal transmit data is tied to the internal receive data and RxD is ignored (except to be echoed out via TxD). The $\overline{CTS}$ and $\overline{DCD}$ inputs are also ignored as transmit and receive enables. However, transitions on these inputs can still cause interrupts. Local Loopback works in Asynchronous, Synchronous and SDLC modes with NRZ, NRZI or FM coding of the data stream.

I/O Interface Capabilities. The SCC offers the choice of Polling, Interrupt (vectored or nonvectored), and Block Transfer modes to transfer data, status, and control information to and from the CPU. The Block Transfer mode can be implemented under CPU or DMA control.

Polling. All interrupts are disabled. Three status registers in the SCC are automatically updated whenever any function is performed. For example, end-of-frame in SDLC mode sets a bit in one of these status registers. The idea behind polling is for the CPU to periodically read a status register until the register contents indicate the need for data to be transferred. Only one register needs to be

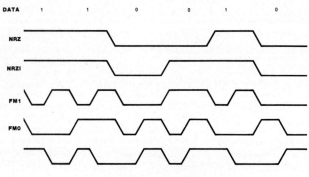

Figure 6. Data Encoding Methods

read; depending on its contents, the CPU either writes data, reads data, or continues. Two bits in the register indicate the need for data transfer. An alternative is a poll of the Interrupt Pending register to determine the source of an interrupt. The status for both channels resides in one register.

Interrupts. When an SCC responds to an Interrupt Acknowledge signal ($\overline{\text{INTACK}}$) from the CPU, an interrupt vector may be placed on the data bus. This vector is written in WR2 and may be read in RR2A or RR2B (Figures 10 and 11).

To speed interrupt response time, the SCC can modify three bits in this vector to indicate status. If the vector is read in Channel A, status is never included; if it is read in Channel B, status is always included.

Each of the six sources of interrupts in the SCC (Transmit, Receive, and External/Status interrupts in both channels) has three bits associated with the interrupt source: Interrupt Pending (IP), Interrupt Under Service (IUS), and Interrupt Enable (IE). Operation of the IE bit is straightforward. If the IE bit is set for a given interrupt source, then that source can request interrupts. The exception is when the MIE (Master Interrupt Enable) bit in WR9 is reset and no interrupts may be requested. The IE bits are write only.

The other two bits are related to the interrupt priority chain (Figure 7). As a microprocessor peripheral, the SCC may request an interrupt only when no higher priority device is requesting one, e.g., when IEI is High. If the device in question requests an interrupt, it pulls down $\overline{\text{INT}}$. The CPU then responds with $\overline{\text{INTACK}}$, and the interrupting device places the vector on the data bus.

In the SCC, the IP bit signals a need for interrupt servicing. When an IP bit is 1 and the IEI input is High, the $\overline{\text{INT}}$ output is pulled Low, requesting an interrupt. In the SCC, if the IE bit is not set by enabling interrupts, then the IP for that source can never be set. The IP bits are readable in RR3A.

The IUS bits signal that an interrupt request is being serviced. If an IUS is set, all interrupt sources of lower priority in the SCC and external to the SCC are prevented from requesting interrupts. The internal interrupt sources are inhibited by the state of the internal daisy chain, while lower priority devices are inhibited by the IEO output of the SCC being pulled Low and propagated to subsequent peripherals. An IUS bit is set during an Interrupt Acknowledge cycle if there are no higher priority devices requesting interrupts.

There are three types of interrupts: Transmit, Receive, and External/Status. Each interrupt type is enabled under program control with Channel A having higher priority than Channel B, and with Receiver, Transmit, and External/Status interrupts prioritized in that order within each channel. When the Transmit interrupt is enabled, the CPU is interrupted when the transmit buffer becomes empty. (This implies that the transmitter must have had a data character written into it so that it can become empty.) When enabled, the receiver can interrupt the CPU in one of three ways:

- Interrupt on First Receive Character or Special Receive Condition.

- Interrupt on All Receive Characters or Special Receive Condition.

- Interrupt on Special Receive Condition Only.

Interrupt on First Character or Special Condition and Interrupt on Special Condition Only are typically used with the Block Transfer mode. A Special Receive Condition is one of the following: receiver overrun, framing error in Asynchronous mode, end-of-frame in SDLC mode and, optionally, a parity error. The Special Receive Condition interrupt is different from an ordinary receive character available interrupt only in the status placed in the vector during the Interrupt Acknowledge cycle. In Interrupt on First Receive Character, an interrupt can occur from Special Receive Conditions any time after the first receive character interrupt.

The main function of the External/Status interrupt is to monitor the signal transitions of the $\overline{\text{CTS}}$, $\overline{\text{DCD}}$, and $\overline{\text{SYNC}}$ pins; however, an

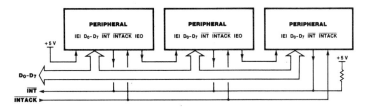

Figure 7. Interrupt Schedule

Functional Description (Continued)

External/Status interrupt is also caused by a Transmit Underrun condition, or a zero count in the baud rate generator, or by the detection of a Break (Asynchronous mode), Abort (SDLC mode) or EOP (SDLC Loop mode) sequence in the data stream. The interrupt caused by the Abort or EOP has a special feature allowing the SCC to interrupt when the Abort or EOP sequence is detected or terminated. This feature facilitates the proper termination of the current message, correct initialization of the next message, and the accurate timing of the Abort condition in external logic in SDLC mode. In SDLC Loop mode, this feature allows secondary stations to recognize the wishes of the primary station to regain control of the loop during a poll sequence.

CPU/DMA Block Transfer. The SCC provides a Block Transfer mode to accommodate CPU block transfer functions and DMA controllers. The Block Transfer mode uses the $\overline{\text{WAIT}}$/$\overline{\text{REQUEST}}$ output in conjunction with the Wait/Request bits in WR1. The $\overline{\text{WAIT}}$/$\overline{\text{REQUEST}}$ output can be defined under software control as a $\overline{\text{WAIT}}$ line in the CPU Block Transfer mode or as a $\overline{\text{REQUEST}}$ line in the DMA Block Transfer mode.

To a DMA controller, the SCC $\overline{\text{REQUEST}}$ output indicates that the SCC is ready to transfer data to or from memory. To the CPU, the $\overline{\text{WAIT}}$ line indicates that the SCC is not ready to transfer data, thereby requesting that the CPU extend the I/O cycle. The $\overline{\text{DTR}}$/$\overline{\text{REQUEST}}$ line allows full-duplex operation under DMA control.

Architecture

The SCC internal structure includes two full-duplex channels, two baud rate generators, internal control and interrupt logic, and a bus interface to a nonmultiplexed bus. Associated with each channel are a number of read and write registers for mode control and status information, as well as logic necessary to interface to modems or other external devices (Figure 8).

The logic for both channels provides formats, synchronization, and validation for data transferred to and from the channel interface. The modem control inputs are monitored by the control logic under program control. All of the modem control signals are general-purpose in nature and can optionally be used for functions other than modem control.

The register set for each channel includes ten control (write) registers, two sync-character (write) registers, and four status (read) registers. In addition, each baud rate generator has two (read/write) registers for holding the time constant that determines the baud rate. Finally, associated with the interrupt logic is a write register for the interrupt vector accessible through either channel, a

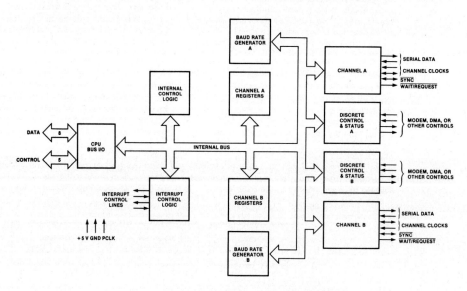

Figure 8. Block Diagram of SCC Architecture

Architecture
(Continued)

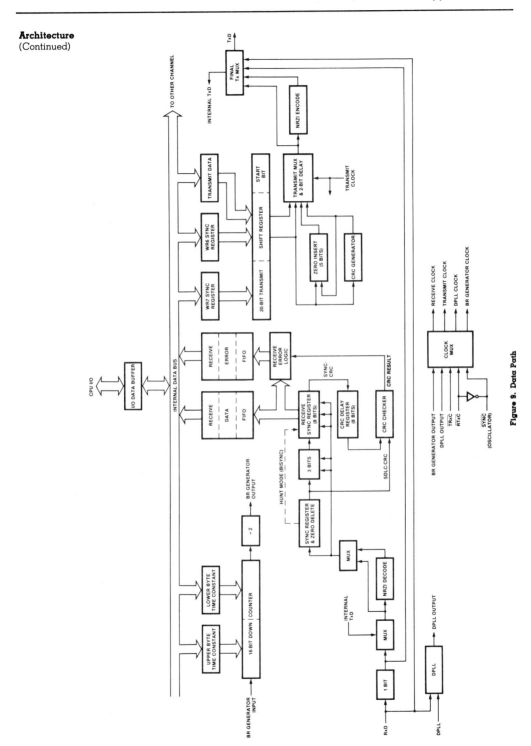

Figure 9. Data Path

Architecture (Continued)

write only Master Interrupt Control register and three read registers: one containing the vector with status infomation (Channel B only), one containing the vector without status (Channel A only), and one containing the Interrupt Pending bits (Channel A only).

The registers for each channel are designated as follows:

WR0–WR15 — Write Registers 0 through 15.

RR0–RR3, RR10, RR12, RR13, RR15 — Read Registers 0 through 3, 10, 12, 13, 15.

Table 1 lists the functions assigned to each read or write register. The SCC contains only one WR2 and WR9, but they can be accessed by either channel. All other registers are paired (one for each channel).

Data Path. The transmit and receive data path illustrated in Figure 9 is identical for both channels. The receiver has three 8-bit buffer registers in an FIFO arrangement, in addition to the 8-bit receive shift register. This scheme creates additional time for the CPU to service an interrupt at the beginning of a block of high speed data. Incoming data is routed through one of several paths (data or CRC) depending on the selected mode (the character length in Asynchronous modes also determines the data path).

The transmitter has an 8-bit Transmit Data buffer register loaded from the internal data bus and a 20-bit Transmit Shift register that can be loaded either from the synchronous character registers or from the Transmit Data register. Depending on the operational mode, outgoing data is routed through one of four main paths before it is transmitted from the Transmit Data output (TxD)

Read Register Functions

RR0	Transmit/Receive buffer status and External status
RR1	Special Receive Condition status
RR2	Modified interrupt vector (Channel B only) Unmodified interrupt vector (Channel A only)
RR3	Interrupt Pending bits (Channel A only)
RR8	Receive buffer
RR10	Miscellaneous status
RR12	Lower byte of baud rate generator time constant
RR13	Upper byte of baud rate generator time constant
RR15	External/Status interrupt information

Write Register Functions

WR0	CRC initialize, initialization commands for the various modes, Register Pointers
WR1	Transmit/Receive interrupt and data transfer mode definition
WR2	Interrupt vector (accessed through either channel)
WR3	Receive parameters and control
WR4	Transmit/Receive miscellaneous parameters and modes
WR5	Transmit parameters and controls
WR6	Sync characters or SDLC address field
WR7	Sync character or SDLC flag
WR8	Transmit buffer
WR9	Master interrupt control and reset (accessed through either channel)
WR10	Miscellaneous transmitter/receiver control bits
WR11	Clock mode control
WR12	Lower byte of baud rate generator time constant
WR13	Upper byte of baud rate generator time constant
WR14	Miscellaneous control bits
WR15	External/Status interrupt control

Table 1. Read and Write Register Functions

Programming

The SCC contains 13 write registers in each channel that are programmed by the system separately to configure the functional personality of the channels.

In the SCC, register addressing is direct for the data registers only, which are selected by a High on the D/$\overline{\text{C}}$ pin. In all other cases (with the exception of WR0 and RR0), programming the write registers requires two write operations and reading the read registers requires both a write and a read operation. The first write is to WR0 and contains three bits that point to the selected register. The second write is the actual control word for the selected register, and if the second operation is read,

the selected read register is accessed. All of the registers in the SCC, including the data registers, may be accessed in this fashion. The pointer bits are automatically cleared after the read or write operation so that WR0 (or RR0) is addressed again.

The system program first issues a series of commands to initialize the basic mode of operation. This is followed by other commands to qualify conditions within the selected mode. For example, the Asynchronous mode, character length, clock rate, number of stop bits, even or odd parity might be set first. Then the interrupt mode would be set, and finally, receiver or transmitter enable.

Read Registers. The SCC contains eight read registers (actually nine, counting the receive buffer (RR8) in each channel). Four of these may be read to obtain status information (RR0, RR1, RR10, and RR15). Two registers (RR12 and RR13) may be read to learn the baud rate generator time constant. RR2 contains either the unmodified interrupt vector (Channel A) or the vector modified by status information

(Channel B). RR3 contains the Interrupt Pending (IP) bits (Channel A). Figure 10 shows the formats for each read register.

The status bits of RR0 and RR1 are carefully grouped to simplify status monitoring; e.g., when the interrupt vector indicates a Special Receive Condition interrupt, all the appropriate error bits can be read from a single register (RR1).

Read Register 0

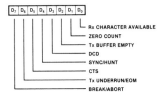

Read Register 1

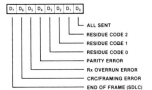

Read Register 2

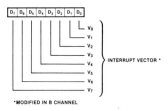

Read Register 3

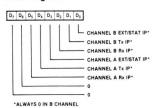

Read Register 10

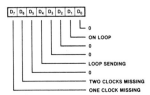

Read Register 12

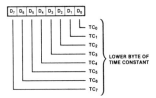

Read Register 13

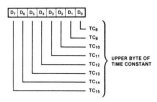

Read Register 15

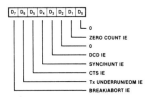

Figure 10. Read Register Bit Functions

Programming (Continued)

Write Registers. The SCC contains 13 write registers (14 counting WR8, the transmit buffer) in each channel. These write registers are programmed separately to configure the functional "personality" of the channels. In addition, there are two registers (WR2 and WR9) shared by the two channels that may be accessed through either of them. WR2 contains the interrupt vector for both channels, while WR9 contains the interrupt control bits. Figure 11 shows the format of each write register.

Write Register 0

D_7	D_6	D_5	D_4	D_3	D_2	D_1	D_0

0	0	0	REGISTER 0
0	0	1	REGISTER 1
0	1	0	REGISTER 2
0	1	1	REGISTER 3
1	0	0	REGISTER 4
1	0	1	REGISTER 5
1	1	0	REGISTER 6
1	1	1	REGISTER 7
0	0	0	REGISTER 8
0	0	1	REGISTER 9
0	1	0	REGISTER 10
0	1	1	REGISTER 11
1	0	0	REGISTER 12
1	0	1	REGISTER 13
1	1	0	REGISTER 14
1	1	1	REGISTER 15

0	0	0	NULL CODE
0	0	1	POINT HIGH
0	1	0	RESET EXT/STAT INTERRUPTS
0	1	1	SEND ABORT (SDLC)
1	0	0	ENABLE INT ON NEXT Rx CHARACTER
1	0	1	RESET TxINT PENDING
1	1	0	ERROR RESET
1	1	1	RESET HIGHEST IUS

0	0	NULL CODE
0	1	RESET Rx CRC CHECKER
1	0	RESET Tx CRC GENERATOR
1	1	RESET Tx UNDERRUN/EOM LATCH

*WITH POINT HIGH COMMAND

Write Register 1

D_7	D_6	D_5	D_4	D_3	D_2	D_1	D_0

- EXT INT ENABLE
- Tx INT ENABLE
- PARITY IS SPECIAL CONDITION

0	0	Rx INT DISABLE
0	1	Rx INT ON FIRST CHARACTER OR SPECIAL CONDITION
1	0	INT ON ALL Rx CHARACTERS OR SPECIAL CONDITION
1	1	Rx INT ON SPECIAL CONDITION ONLY

- WAIT/DMA REQUEST ON RECEIVE/TRANSMIT
- WAIT/DMA REQUEST FUNCTION
- WAIT/DMA REQUEST ENABLE

Write Register 2

D_7	D_6	D_5	D_4	D_3	D_2	D_1	D_0

- V_0
- V_1
- V_2
- V_3 — INTERRUPT VECTOR
- V_4
- V_5
- V_6
- V_7

Write Register 3

D_7	D_6	D_5	D_4	D_3	D_2	D_1	D_0

- Rx ENABLE
- SYNC CHARACTER LOAD INHIBIT
- ADDRESS SEARCH MODE (SDLC)
- Rx CRC ENABLE
- ENTER HUNT MODE
- AUTO ENABLES

0	0	Rx 5 BITS/CHARACTER
0	1	Rx 7 BITS/CHARACTER
1	0	Rx 6 BITS/CHARACTER
1	1	Rx 8 BITS/CHARACTER

Write Register 4

D_7	D_6	D_5	D_4	D_3	D_2	D_1	D_0

- PARITY ENABLE
- PARITY EVEN/ODD

0	0	SYNC MODES ENABLE
0	1	1 STOP BIT/CHARACTER
1	0	1½ STOP BITS/CHARACTER
1	1	2 STOP BITS/CHARACTER

0	0	8 BIT SYNC CHARACTER
0	1	16 BIT SYNC CHARACTER
1	0	SDLC MODE (01111110 FLAG)
1	1	EXTERNAL SYNC MODE

0	0	X1 CLOCK MODE
0	1	X16 CLOCK MODE
1	0	X32 CLOCK MODE
1	1	X64 CLOCK MODE

Write Register 5

D_7	D_6	D_5	D_4	D_3	D_2	D_1	D_0

- Tx CRC ENABLE
- RTS
- SDLC/CRC-16
- Tx ENABLE
- SEND BREAK

0	0	Tx 5 BITS (OR LESS)/CHARACTER
0	1	Tx 7 BITS/CHARACTER
1	0	Tx 6 BITS/CHARACTER
1	1	Tx 8 BITS/CHARACTER

- DTR

Write Register 6

D_7	D_6	D_5	D_4	D_3	D_2	D_1	D_0

$SYNC_7$	$SYNC_6$	$SYNC_5$	$SYNC_4$	$SYNC_3$	$SYNC_2$	$SYNC_1$	$SYNC_0$	MONOSYNC, 8 BITS
$SYNC_1$	$SYNC_0$	$SYNC_5$	$SYNC_4$	$SYNC_3$	$SYNC_2$	$SYNC_1$	$SYNC_0$	MONOSYNC, 6 BITS
$SYNC_7$	$SYNC_6$	$SYNC_5$	$SYNC_4$	$SYNC_3$	$SYNC_2$	$SYNC_1$	$SYNC_0$	BISYNC, 16 BITS
$SYNC_3$	$SYNC_2$	$SYNC_1$	$SYNC_0$	1	1	1	1	BISYNC, 12 BITS
ADR_7	ADR_6	ADR_5	ADR_4	x	ADR_2	ADR_1	ADR_0	SDLC
ADR_7	ADR_6	ADR_5	ADR_4	x	x	x	x	SDLC (ADDRESS RANGE)

Figure 11. Write Register Bit Functions

Programming
(Continued)

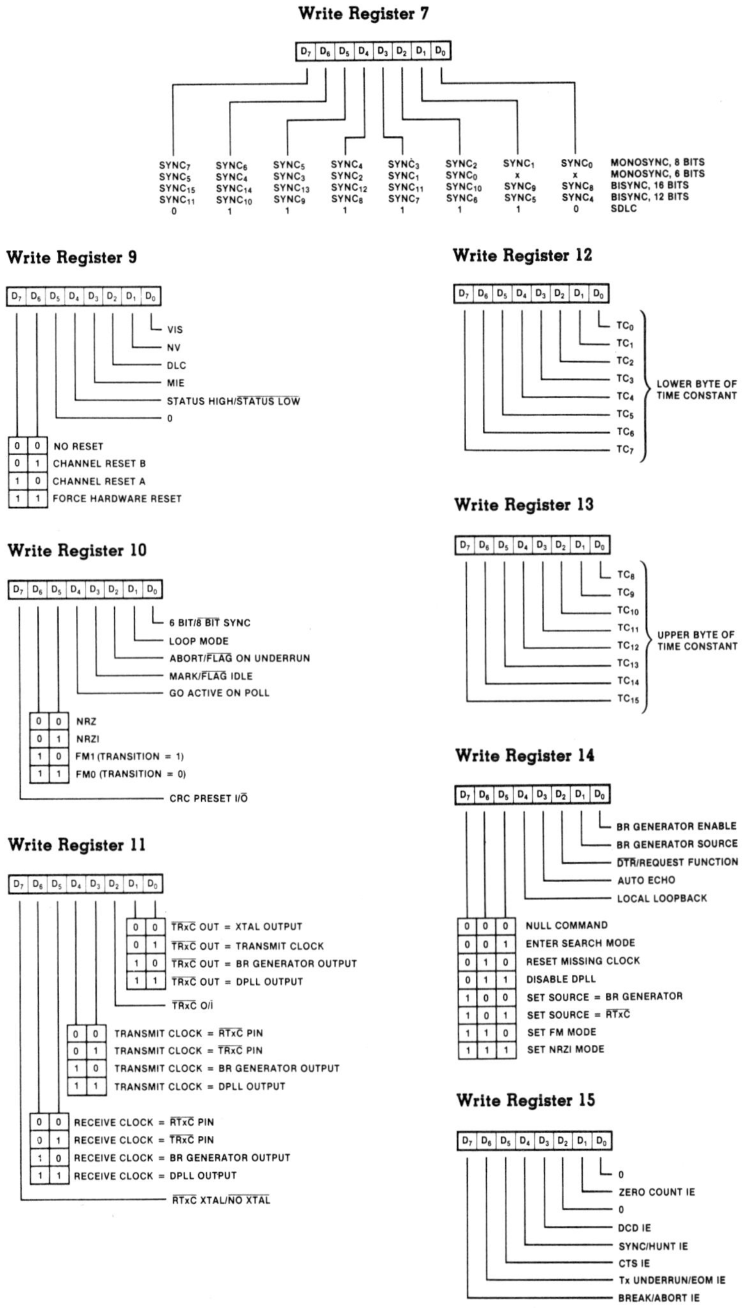

Write Register 7

SYNC7	SYNC6	SYNC5	SYNC4	SYNC3	SYNC2	SYNC1	SYNC0	MONOSYNC, 8 BITS
SYNC5	SYNC4	SYNC3	SYNC2	SYNC1	SYNC0	x	x	MONOSYNC, 6 BITS
SYNC15	SYNC14	SYNC13	SYNC12	SYNC11	SYNC10	SYNC9	SYNC8	BISYNC, 16 BITS
SYNC11	SYNC10	SYNC9	SYNC8	SYNC7	SYNC6	SYNC5	SYNC4	BISYNC, 12 BITS
0	1	1	1	1	1	1	0	SDLC

Write Register 9

- VIS
- NV
- DLC
- MIE
- STATUS HIGH/STATUS LOW
- 0

0	0	NO RESET
0	1	CHANNEL RESET B
1	0	CHANNEL RESET A
1	1	FORCE HARDWARE RESET

Write Register 10

- 6 BIT/8 BIT SYNC
- LOOP MODE
- ABORT/FLAG ON UNDERRUN
- MARK/FLAG IDLE
- GO ACTIVE ON POLL

0	0	NRZ
0	1	NRZI
1	0	FM1 (TRANSITION = 1)
1	1	FM0 (TRANSITION = 0)

- CRC PRESET I/O

Write Register 11

0	0	TRxC OUT = XTAL OUTPUT
0	1	TRxC OUT = TRANSMIT CLOCK
1	0	TRxC OUT = BR GENERATOR OUTPUT
1	1	TRxC OUT = DPLL OUTPUT

TRxC O/I

0	0	TRANSMIT CLOCK = RTxC PIN
0	1	TRANSMIT CLOCK = TRxC PIN
1	0	TRANSMIT CLOCK = BR GENERATOR OUTPUT
1	1	TRANSMIT CLOCK = DPLL OUTPUT

0	0	RECEIVE CLOCK = RTxC PIN
0	1	RECEIVE CLOCK = TRxC PIN
1	0	RECEIVE CLOCK = BR GENERATOR OUTPUT
1	1	RECEIVE CLOCK = DPLL OUTPUT

RTxC XTAL/NO XTAL

Write Register 12

- TC0
- TC1
- TC2
- TC3
- TC4 LOWER BYTE OF TIME CONSTANT
- TC5
- TC6
- TC7

Write Register 13

- TC8
- TC9
- TC10
- TC11
- TC12 UPPER BYTE OF TIME CONSTANT
- TC13
- TC14
- TC15

Write Register 14

- BR GENERATOR ENABLE
- BR GENERATOR SOURCE
- DTR/REQUEST FUNCTION
- AUTO ECHO
- LOCAL LOOPBACK

0	0	0	NULL COMMAND
0	0	1	ENTER SEARCH MODE
0	1	0	RESET MISSING CLOCK
0	1	1	DISABLE DPLL
1	0	0	SET SOURCE = BR GENERATOR
1	0	1	SET SOURCE = RTxC
1	1	0	SET FM MODE
1	1	1	SET NRZI MODE

Write Register 15

- 0
- ZERO COUNT IE
- 0
- DCD IE
- SYNC/HUNT IE
- CTS IE
- Tx UNDERRUN/EOM IE
- BREAK/ABORT IE

Figure 11. Write Register Bit Functions (Continued)

Timing   The SCC generates internal control signals from $\overline{WR}$ and $\overline{RD}$ that are related to PCLK. Since PCLK has no phase relationship with $\overline{WR}$ and $\overline{RD}$, the circuitry generating these internal control signals must provide time for metastable conditions to disappear. This gives rise to a recovery time related to PCLK. The recovery time applies only between bus transactions involving the SCC. The recovery time required for proper operation is specified from the rising edge of $\overline{WR}$ or $\overline{RD}$ in the first trans-action involving the SCC to the falling edge of $\overline{WR}$ or $\overline{RD}$ in the second transaction involving the SCC. This time must be at least 6 PCLK cycles plus 200 ns.

Read Cycle Timing. Figure 12 illustrates Read cycle timing. Addresses on $A/\overline{B}$ and $D/\overline{C}$ and the status on $\overline{INTACK}$ must remain stable throughout the cycle. If $\overline{CE}$ falls after $\overline{RD}$ falls or if it rises before $\overline{RD}$ rises, the effective $\overline{RD}$ is shortened.

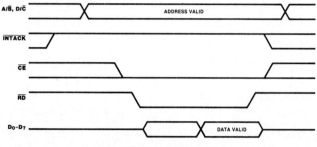

Figure 12. Read Cycle Timing

Write Cycle Timing. Figure 13 illustrates Write cycle timing. Addresses on $A/\overline{B}$ and $D/\overline{C}$ and the status on $\overline{INTACK}$ must remain stable throughout the cycle. If $\overline{CE}$ falls after $\overline{WR}$ falls or if it rises before $\overline{WR}$ rises, the effective $\overline{WR}$ is shortened.

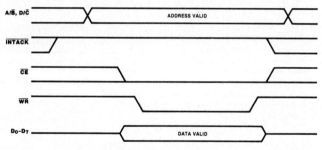

Figure 13. Write Cycle Timing

Interrupt Acknowledge Cycle Timing. Figure 14 illustrates Interrupt Acknowledge cycle timing. Between the time $\overline{INTACK}$ goes Low and the falling edge of $\overline{RD}$, the internal and external IEI/IEO daisy chains settle. If there is an interrupt pending in the SCC and IEI is High when $\overline{RD}$ falls, the Acknowledge cycle is intended for the SCC. In this case, the SCC may be programmed to respond to $\overline{RD}$ Low by placing its interrupt vector on D_0-D_7 and it then sets the appropriate Interrupt-Under-Service latch internally.

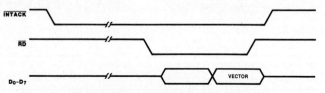

Figure 14. Interrupt Acknowledge Cycle Timing

Absolute Maximum Ratings

Voltages on all pins with respect
  to GND . . . . -0.3V to $+7.0$V
Operating Ambient
  Temperature . . . . See Ordering Information
Storage Temperature . . . . $-65\,°C$ to $+150\,°C$

Stresses greater than those listed under Absolute Maximum Ratings may cause permanent damage to the device. This is a stress rating only; operation of the device at any condition above those indicated in the operational sections of these specifications is not implied. Exposure to absolute maximum rating conditions for extended periods may affect device reliability.

Standard Test Conditions

The DC characteristics and capacitance section below apply for the following standard test conditions, unless otherwise noted. All voltages are referenced to GND. Positive current flows into the referenced pin.

Standard conditions are as follows:

- $+4.75\ V \leq V_{CC} \leq +5.25\ V$
- $GND = 0\ V$
- T_A as specified in Ordering Information

The Ordering Information section lists temperature ranges and product numbers. Package drawings are in the Package Information section in this book. Refer to the Literature List for additional documentation.

All ac parameters assume a load capacitance of 50 pf max.

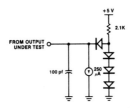

Figure 15. Standard Test Load

Figure 16. Open-Drain Test Load

DC Characteristics

Symbol	Parameter	Min	Max	Unit	Condition
V_{IH}	Input High Voltage	2.0	$V_{CC}+0.3$	V	
V_{IL}	Input Low Voltage	-0.3	0.8	V	
V_{OH}	Output High Voltage	2.4		V	$I_{OH} = -250\ \mu A$
V_{OL}	Output Low Voltage		0.4	V	$I_{OL} = +2.0\ mA$
I_{IL}	Input Leakage		± 10.0	μA	$0.4 \leq V_{IN} \leq +2.4V$
I_{OL}	Output Leakage		± 10.0	μA	$0.4 \leq V_{OUT} \leq +2.4V$
I_{CC}	V_{CC} Supply Current		250	mA	

$V_{CC} = 5\ V \pm 5\%$ unless otherwise specified, over specified temperature range.

Capacitance

Symbol	Parameter	Min	Max	Unit	Test Condition
C_{IN}	Input Capacitance		10	pF	
C_{OUT}	Output Capacitance		15	pF	
$C_{I/O}$	Bidirectional Capacitance		20	pF	

$f = 1\ MHz$, over specified temperature range.
Unmeasured pins returned to ground.

Read and Write Timing

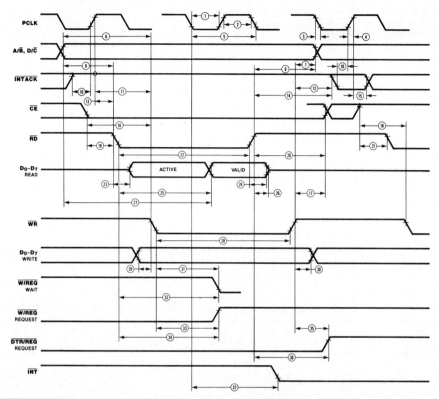

No.	Symbol	Parameter	4 MHz Min	4 MHz Max	6 MHz Min	6 MHz Max	Notes*†
1	TwPCl	PCLK Low Width	105	2000	70‡	1000	
2	TwPCh	PCLK High Width	105	2000	70‡	1000	
3	TfPC	PCLK Fall Time		20		10	
4	TrPC	PCLK Rise Time		20		15	
5	TcPC	PCLK Cycle Time	250	4000	165°	2000	
6	TsA(WR)	Address to $\overline{WR}$ ↓ Setup Time	80		80		
7	ThA(WR)	Address to $\overline{WR}$ ↑ Hold Time	0		0		
8	TsA(RD)	Address to $\overline{RD}$ ↓ Setup Time	80		80		
9	ThA(RD)	Address to $\overline{RD}$ ↑ Hold Time	0		0		
10	TsIA(PC)	$\overline{INTACK}$ to PCLK ↑ Setup Time	0		0		
11	TsIAi(WR)	$\overline{INTACK}$ to $\overline{WR}$ ↓ Setup Time	200		160		1
12	ThIA(WR)	$\overline{INTACK}$ to $\overline{WR}$ ↑ Hold Time	0		0		
13	TsIAi(RD)	$\overline{INTACK}$ to $\overline{RD}$ ↓ Setup Time	200		160		1
14	ThIA(RD)	$\overline{INTACK}$ to $\overline{RD}$ ↑ Hold Time	0		0		
15	ThIA(PC)	$\overline{INTACK}$ to PCLK ↑ Hold Time	100		100		
16	TsCEl(WR)	$\overline{CE}$ Low to $\overline{WR}$ ↓ Setup Time	0		0		
17	ThCE(WR)	$\overline{CE}$ to $\overline{WR}$ ↑ Hold Time	0		0		
18	TsCEh(WR)	$\overline{CE}$ High to $\overline{WR}$ ↓ Setup Time	100		70		
19	TsCEl(RD)	$\overline{CE}$ Low to $\overline{RD}$ ↓ Setup Time	0		0		1
20	ThCE(RD)	$\overline{CE}$ to $\overline{RD}$ ↑ Hold Time	0		0		1
21	TsCEh(RD)	$\overline{CE}$ High to $\overline{RD}$ ↓ Setup Time	100		70		1
22	TwRDl	$\overline{RD}$ Low Width	390		250		1
23	TdRD(DRA)	$\overline{RD}$ ↓ to Read Data Active Delay	0		0		
24	TdRDr(DR)	$\overline{RD}$ ↑ to Read Data Not Valid Delay	0		0		
25	TdRDf(DR)	$\overline{RD}$ ↓ to Read Data Valid Delay		250		180	
26	TdRD(DRz)	$\overline{RD}$ ↑ to Read Data Float Delay		70		45	2

NOTES:
1. Parameter does not apply to Interrupt Acknowledge transactions.
2. Float delay is defined as the time required for a ± 0.5 V change in the output with a maximum dc load and minimum ac load.

* Timings are preliminary and subject to change.
† Units in nanoseconds (ns).
‡ Parameter equals 64 ns for Z8530A SL436 version compatible with T1 operation.
° Parameter equals 153 ns for Z8530A SL436 version compatible with T1 operation.

Interrupt Acknowledge Timing

Reset Timing

Cycle Timing

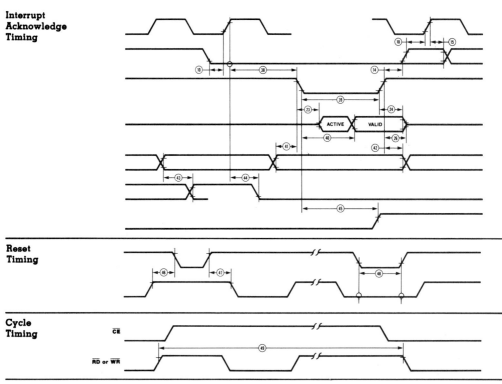

No.	Symbol	Parameter	4 MHz Min	4 MHz Max	6 MHz Min	6 MHz Max	Notes*†
27	TdA(DR)	Address Required Valid to Read Data Valid Delay		590		420	
28	TwWRl	$\overline{WR}$ Low Width	390		250		
29	TsDW(WR)	Write Data to $\overline{WR}$ ↓ Setup Time	0		0		
30	ThDW(WR)	Write Data to $\overline{WR}$ ↑ Hold Time	0		0		
31	TdWR(W)	$\overline{WR}$ ↓ to Wait Valid Delay		240		200	4
32	TdRD(W)	$\overline{RD}$ ↓ to Wait Valid Delay		240		200	4
33	TdWRf(REQ)	$\overline{WR}$ ↓ to $\overline{W/REQ}$ Not Valid Delay		240		200	
34	TdRDf(REQ)	$\overline{RD}$ ↓ to $\overline{W/REQ}$ Not Valid Delay		240		200	
35	TdWRr(REQ)	$\overline{WR}$ ↑ to $\overline{DTR/REQ}$ Not Valid Delay		5TcPC +300		5TcPC +250	
36	TdRDr(REQ)	$\overline{RD}$ ↑ to $\overline{DTR/REQ}$ Not Valid Delay		5TcPC +300		5TcPC +250	
37	TdPC(INT)	PCLK ↓ to $\overline{INT}$ Valid Delay		500		500	4
38	TdIAi(RD)	$\overline{INTACK}$ to $\overline{RD}$ ↓ (Acknowledge) Delay	250		250		5
39	TwRDA	$\overline{RD}$ (Acknowledge) Width	285		250		
40	TdRDA(DR)	$\overline{RD}$ ↓ (Acknowledge) to Read Data Valid Delay		190		180	
41	TsIEI(RDA)	IEI to $\overline{RD}$ ↓ (Acknowledge) Setup Time	120		100		
42	ThIEI(RDA)	IEI to $\overline{RD}$ ↑ (Acknowledge) Hold Time	0		0		
43	TdIEI(IEO)	IEI to IEO Delay Time		120		100	
44	TdPC(IEO)	PCLK ↑ to IEO Delay		250		250	
45	TdRDA(INT)	$\overline{RD}$ ↓ to $\overline{INT}$ Inactive Delay		500		500	4
46	TdRD(WRQ)	$\overline{RD}$ ↑ to $\overline{WR}$ ↓ Delay for No Reset	30		15		
47	TdWRQ(RD)	$\overline{WR}$ ↑ to $\overline{RD}$ ↓ Delay for No Reset	30		30		
48	TwRES	$\overline{WR}$ and $\overline{RD}$ Coincident Low for Reset	250		250		
49	Trc	Valid Access Recovery Time	6TcPC +200		6TcPC +130		3

NOTES:
3. Parameter applies only between transactions involving the SCC.
4. Open-drain output, measured with open-drain test load.
5. Parameter is system dependent. For any SCC in the daisy chain, TdIAi(RD) must be greater than the sum of TdPC(IEO) for the highest priority device in the daisy chain, TsIEI(RDA)

for the SCC, and TdIEIf(IEO) for each device separating them in the daisy chain.
* Timings are preliminary and subject to change.
† Units in nanoseconds (ns).

**General
Timing**

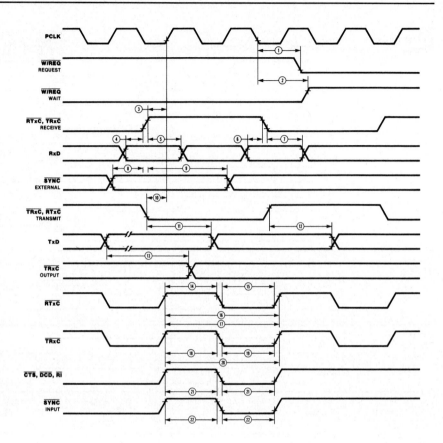

No.	Symbol	Parameter	4 MHz Min	4 MHz Max	6 MHz Min	6 MHz Max	Notes*†
1	TdPC(REQ)	PCLK ↓ to $\overline{\text{W}/\text{REQ}}$ Valid Delay		250		250	
2	TdPC(W)	PCLK ↓ to Wait Inactive Delay		350		350	
3	TsRXC(PC)	$\overline{\text{RxC}}$ ↑ to PCLK ↑ Setup Time (PCLK ÷ 4 case only)	80	TwPC1	70	TwPC1	1,4
4	TsRXD(RXCr)	RxD to $\overline{\text{RxC}}$ ↑ Setup Time (X1 Mode)	0		0		1
5	ThRXD(RXCr)	RxD to $\overline{\text{RxC}}$ ↑ Hold Time (X1 Mode)	150		150		1
6	TsRXD(RXCf)	RxD to $\overline{\text{RxC}}$ ↓ Setup Time (X1 Mode)	0		0		1,5
7	ThRXD(RXCf)	RxD to $\overline{\text{RxC}}$ ↓ Hold Time (X1 Mode)	150		150		1,5
8	TsSY(RXC)	$\overline{\text{SYNC}}$ to $\overline{\text{RxC}}$ ↑ Setup Time	−200		−200		1
9	ThSY(RXC)	$\overline{\text{SYNC}}$ to $\overline{\text{RxC}}$ ↑ Hold Time	3TcPC +200		3TcPC +200		1
10	TsTXC(PC)	$\overline{\text{TxC}}$ ↓ to PCLK ↑ Setup Time	0		0		2,4
11	TdTXCf(TXD)	$\overline{\text{TxC}}$ ↓ to TxD Delay (X1 Mode)		300		230	2
12	TdTXCr(TXD)	$\overline{\text{TxC}}$ ↓ to TxD Delay (X1 Mode)		300		230	2,5
13	TdTXD(TRX)	TxD to $\overline{\text{TRxC}}$ Delay (Send Clock Echo)		200		200	
14	TwRTXh	$\overline{\text{RTxC}}$ High Width	180		180		6
15	TwRTX1	$\overline{\text{RTxC}}$ Low Width	180		180		6
16	TcRTX	$\overline{\text{RTxC}}$ Cycle Time	400		400		6
17	TcRTXX	Crystal Oscillator Period	250	1000	250	1000	3
18	TwTRXh	$\overline{\text{TRxC}}$ High Width	180		180		6
19	TwTRX1	$\overline{\text{TRxC}}$ Low Width	180		180		6
20	TcTRX	$\overline{\text{TRxC}}$ Cycle Time	400		400		6
21	TwEXT	$\overline{\text{DCD}}$ or $\overline{\text{CTS}}$ Pulse Width	200		200		
22	TwSY	$\overline{\text{SYNC}}$ Pulse Width	200		200		

NOTES:
1. RxC is $\overline{\text{RTxC}}$ or $\overline{\text{TRxC}}$, whichever is supplying the receive clock.
2. $\overline{\text{TxC}}$ is $\overline{\text{TRxC}}$ or $\overline{\text{RTxC}}$, whichever is supplying the transmit clock.
3. Both $\overline{\text{RTxC}}$ and $\overline{\text{SYNC}}$ have 30 pF capacitors to ground connected to them.
4. Parameter applies only if the data rate is one-fourth the PCLK rate. In all other cases, no phase relationship between $\overline{\text{RxC}}$ and PCLK or $\overline{\text{TxC}}$ and PCLK is required.

5. Parameter applies only to FM encoding/decoding.
6. Parameter applies only for transmitter and receiver; DPLL and baud rate generator timing requirements are identical to chip PCLK requirements.
* Timings are preliminary and subject to change.
† Units in nanoseconds (ns).

System Timing

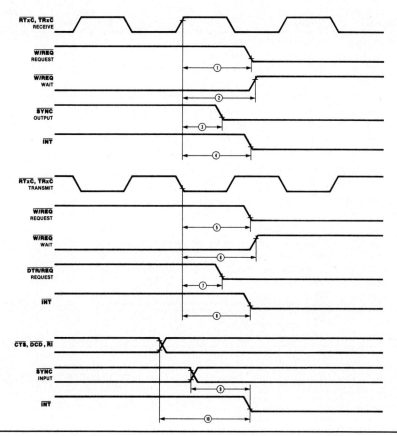

No.	Symbol	Parameter	4 MHz Min	4 MHz Max	6 MHz Min	6 MHz Max	Notes*†
1	TdRXC(REQ)	$\overline{RxC}$ ↑ to $\overline{W/REQ}$ Valid Delay	8	12	8	12	2
2	TdRXC(W)	$\overline{RxC}$ ↑ to Wait Inactive Delay	8	12	8	12	1,2
3	TdRXC(SY)	$\overline{RxC}$ ↑ to $\overline{SYNC}$ Valid Delay	4	7	4	7	2
4	TdRXC(INT)	$\overline{RxC}$ ↑ to $\overline{INT}$ Valid Delay	10	16	10	16	1,2
5	TdTXC(REQ)	$\overline{TxC}$ ↓ to $\overline{W/REQ}$ Valid Delay	5	8	5	8	3
6	TdTXC(W)	$\overline{TxC}$ ↓ to Wait Inactive Delay	5	8	5	8	1,3
7	TdTXC(DRQ)	$\overline{TxC}$ ↓ to $\overline{DTR/REQ}$ Valid Delay	4	7	4	7	3
8	TdTXC(INT)	$\overline{TxC}$ ↓ to $\overline{INT}$ Valid Delay	6	10	6	10	1,3
9	TdSY(INT)	$\overline{SYNC}$ Transition to $\overline{INT}$ Valid Delay	2	6	2	6	1
10	TdEXT(INT)	$\overline{DCD}$ or $\overline{CTS}$ Transition to $\overline{INT}$ Valid Delay	2	6	2	6	1

NOTES:
1. Open-drain output, measured with open-drain test load.
2. $\overline{RxC}$ is $\overline{RTxC}$ or $\overline{TRxC}$, whichever is supplying the receive clock.
3. $\overline{TxC}$ is $\overline{TRxC}$ or $\overline{RTxC}$, whichever is supplying the transmit clock.

* Timings are preliminary and subject to change.
† Units equal to TcPC.

ORDERING INFORMATION

Z8530 SCC, 4.0 MHz

40-pin DIP	**44-pin LCC**	**44-pin PCC**
Z8530 PS	Z8530 LM*	Z8530 VS
Z8530 CS	Z8530 LMB*†	
Z8530 PE		
Z8530 CE		
Z8530 CM*		
Z8530 CMB*		

Z8530A SCC, 6.0 MHz

40-pin DIP	**44-pin LCC**	**44-pin PCC**
Z8530A PS	Z8530A LM*	Z8530A VS
Z8530A CS	Z8530A LMB*†	
Z8530A PE		
Z8530A CE		
Z8530A CM*		
Z8530A CMB*		

Z8530A SCC, 6.5 MHz—T1 Compatible

40-pin DIP	**44-pin PCC**
Z8530A PS SL436	Z8530A VS SL436
Z8530A CS SL436	

Codes

First letter is for package; second letter is for temperature.

C = Ceramic DIP
P = Plastic DIP
L = Ceramic LCC
V = Plastic PCC

R = Protopack
T = Low Profile Protopack
DIP = Dual-In-Line Package
LCC = Leadless Chip Carrier
PCC = Plastic Chip Carrier (Leaded)

TEMPERATURE
S = 0°C to +70°C
E = -40°C to +85°C
M* = -55°C to +125°C

FLOW
B = 883 Class B

Example: PS is a plastic DIP, 0°C to +70°C.

†Available soon.
*For Military Orders, contact your local Zilog Sales Office for Military Electrical Specifications.

Index

ACK signal (PPI), 98–100,144
ADC (*see* Analog to digital converters)
Address decoding, 14–15
Addressing modes, 55–7
  bit, 57
  combined, 57
  immediate, 55
  immediate extended, 55
  implied, 55
  indexed, 57
  modified page zero, 56
  register, 56
  register indirect, 56
  relative, 56
Alternate register set, 33, 61
Analog to digital converters (ADC), 16–18, 20–2
  accuracy, 21
  coding format, 22
  ramp and comparator, 17
  resolution, 20
  simultaneous, 16
  speed of conversion, 21
  successive approximations, 17
Arithmetic logic unit (ALU), 11, 28–32
  flags, 29–32
ARDY signal (PIO), 172
ASCII code, 5, 255–6
Assembler, 68–71
  comment field, 70
  directives, 70
  label field, 68
  opcode field, 69
  operand field, 69
ASTB signal (PIO), 172

Baud rate, 219
BCD (*see* Binary coded decimal numbers)
Binary coded decimal numbers, 4–6, 31–2
Bit set–reset (PPI), 101–4
  control word format, 102
BRDY signal (PIO), 172
BSTB signal (PIO), 172
BUFOUT system routine, 72
Bus acknowledge cycle, 49–50
Bus request cycle, 49–50
Buses, 10–11

Carry flag, 29
Central processing unit (CPU), 7
Clock circuit, 231
Clock (T) cycles, 41–3
Control unit, 12, 35–7
CTS signal (RS 232–C), 213–5

DAC (*see* Digital to analog converters)
Data bus, 10
DCD signal (RS 232–C), 213–5
DCE (Data Communication Equipment), 212
DEFB assembler directive, 71
DEFM assembler directive, 71
DEFW assembler directive, 71
Digital to analog converters (DAC), 18–22
  accuracy, 21
  coding format, 22
  R–2R ladder, 19–20
  resolution, 20
  speed of conversion, 21
DSR signal (RS 232–C), 213–4
DTE (Data Terminal Equipment), 212
DTR signal (RS 232–C), 213–4

EI instruction, 140, 144
END assembler directive, 71
EQU assembler directive, 70

Fetch–execute cycle, 35–7
Flag register, 29–32
  carry flag, 29
  half carry flag, 31
  parity/overflow flag, 30
  sign flag, 30
  subtract flag, 31
  zero flag, 30
Full–duplex communication, 212

Half carry flag, 31
Half–duplex communication, 212
Hexadecimal numbers, 4–5

IBF flag (PPI), 97, 143
IEI signal (PIO), 179–81
IEO signal (PIO), 179–81
IM0 instruction, 135, 138
IM1 instruction, 135, 138

IM2 instruction, 135, 138
Index registers, 32, 35
Input/output devices, 16
Input/output machine cycle, 47–8
Instruction register, 7, 36
Instructions (Z80), 57–68
  CPU control, 67–8
  data processing, 62–4
    arithmetic, 62–3
    logical, 63–4
    rotate and shift, 64
  data transfer, 57–62
    block search, 62
    block transfer, 61–2
    exchange, 61
    load memory, 57–8
    load register, 57–8
    stack, 59–61
  input/output, 66
  test and branch, 64–6
    call and return, 66
    conditional jump, 65
    unconditional jump, 64–5
INT timing diagram, 135
INTE flip–flop (PPI), 144
Interrupt register, 35
Interrupt software, 145–9
  CPU and PPI initialization, 146–7
  interrupt service routine, 148–9
Interrupts, 133–42
  INT timing diagram, 135
  modes, 135, 138
  NMI timing diagram, 141
  Z80 interrupt request line (INT), 134–6
  Z80 non–maskable interrupt (NMI), 140–2
INTR signal (PPI), 144

Machine (M) cycles, 41
Memory, 12–16
  access time, 242–6
  address decoding, 14–16
  dynamic RAM, 35
  external organization, 14
  random access, 13, 242–6
  read cycle, 45–7
  read only, 13, 242–6
  read–write, 13
  static RAM, 35
  write cycle, 45–7
Memory read cycle, 45–7, 243–6
Memory refresh register (Z80), 35
Memory write cycle, 45–7, 243–6
Microcomputers, 6–8
Microcontrol store, 36
Microprocessor, 8–12
  ALU, 11–12

  buses, 10–11
  control unit, 12, 35–7
  CPU, 7
  input/output devices, 16
  registers, 8–10
    alternate, 33, 61
    general, 32
    index, 32, 35
    instruction, 7, 36
    program counter, 7, 32
    stack pointer, 32–5, 59–60
Multi–level interrupts, 137–8, 183–6
  using PPI, 137–8
  using Z80 PIO, 183–6

NMI timing diagram, 141
Number systems, 1–6
  BCD, 4–6, 31–2
  binary to decimal conversion, 1
  decimal to binary conversion, 1–2
  hexadecimal, 4–5
  negative numbers, 2–4
  octal, 4–6
  1's complement, 3–4
  2's complement, 3–4

OBF flag (PPI), 98, 143
Octal numbers, 4–6
1's complement, 3–4
Opcode fetch machine cycle, 43–5
ORG assembler directive, 70
Overflow flag, 30

Parity flag, 30
PCI (*see* Programmable communication
  interface)
PIO (*see* Z80 PIO)
Program counter, 7, 32
Programmable Communication Interface,
  216–24
  block diagram, 217
  command instruction, 222–3
  data sheet, 325–42
  microprocessor interface, 216–8
  mode instruction, 221
  modem control, 218–9
  programming, 220–1
  receive buffer and control, 220
  status register, 223–4
  transmit buffer and control, 219
  TTL to RS 232–C level shifting, 248
Programmable Peripheral Interface, 88–106,
  133–49, 247–9
  acknowledge (ACK) signal, 98, 144
  addressing, 91–2
  basic I/O, 89–91

bit set–reset, 101–4
  control word format, 102
block diagram, 89
buffering, 247
data sheet, 289–310
handshaking I/O, 94–5
input buffer full (IBF) flag, 97, 143
interrupt enable flip–flop (INTE), 144
interrupt handling, 142–5
interrupt request (INTR), 144
mode control word, 90
mode 0, 89–90
mode 1, 96–8
  interrupts, 142–5
  strobed input, 96–7
  strobed output, 98
mode 2, 98–101
  bi–directional, input, 100
  bi–directional, output, 100–1
  output buffer full (OBF) flag, 98, 144
  pin allocations, 104–5
  strobe (STB) signal, 97, 143
  unconditional I/O, 92–3
PPI (*see* Programmable peripheral interface)

RAM (Random access memory), 13, 242–6
  interfacing to Z80, 242–6
Registers, 8–10
  hold time, 9
  propagation delay, 9
  set–up time, 9
  shift registers, 9
  Z80, 32–5
Reset circuit, 240–1
RETI instruction, 140
ROM (Read–only memory), 13, 242–6
  access time, 243
  interfacing to Z80, 242–6
RS 232–C interface standard, 211–6
  CTS (clear to send), 213–5
  DCD (data carrier detect), 213–5
  DCE (data communications equipment), 212
  DSR (data set ready), 213–4
  DTE (data terminal equipment), 212
  DTR (data terminal ready), 212, 214
  RTS (request to send), 213–5
  RxD (receive data), 214
  serial transmission format, 212
  terminal to computer connection, 215
  timing diagram, 214
  TXD (transmit data), 214
RTS signal (RS 232–C), 213–5
RxD signal (RS 232–C), 214

SCC (*see* Serial communications controller)
Serial communications controller, 224–30

baud rate generator, 224–5
command bits, 225
data sheet, 343–65
initialization, 226–9
mode bits, 225
registers, 225–6
status information, 229–30
Shift register, 9
Sign flag, 30
Simplex communication, 212
Stack pointer register, 32–5, 59–60
Stand–alone system, 238–49
STB signal (PPI), 97, 143
Subroutines, 33–5
Subtract flag, 31

Table of interrupt vectors, 138–40, 184–5
Three–state buffer, 10–11
TTYIN system routine, 72
TTYOUT system routine, 72
TTYST system routine, 72
2's complement, 3–4
TxD signal (RS 232–C), 214

UART, 216
USART, 216

V24, 211

Wait states, 41, 45–8, 245–6
  circuit for generating, 246

Zero flag, 30
Z80, 28–50, 54–75, 133–42, 238–46
  address bus, 38
  addressing modes, 55–7
  alternate register set, 33, 61
  ALU, 11, 28–32
  control bus, 38–40
  data bus, 38
  data sheet, 257–88
  general purpose registers, 32
  index registers, 32, 35
  instruction set, 57–68
  interrupt mode 0, 135, 138
  interrupt mode 1, 135, 138
  interrupt mode 2, 135, 138
  interrupt register, 35
  interrupts, 133–42
    interrupt request line (INT), 134–6
    non–maskable interrupt (NMI), 140–2
  memory refresh register, 35
  pin descriptions, 37–41
  program counter, 7, 32
  return from interrupt, 140

stack pointer, 32–5, 59–60
Z80 PIO, 169–92
  basic I/O, 176–8
  bi–directional timing diagram, 174
  block diagram, 170
  control words, 177–83
    input/output select, 177
    interrupt, 181
    interrupt disable, 182
    interrupt vector, 179
    mask, 183
    mode, 177
  data sheet, 311–24
  hardware reset, 241–2
  input timing diagram, 173
  internal registers, 175–6
    data, 176
    input/output select, 176
    mask, 176
    mask control, 176
    mode control, 175–6
  interrupt control section, 171

interrupt driven I/O, 178–83
interrupt timing diagram, 180
microprocessor interface, 169–71
mode 0 – output, 172, 182
mode 1 – input, 173, 182
mode 2 – bi–directional, 173, 182
mode 3 – bit control, 173, 182
multi–level interrupts, 183–6
output timing diagram, 173
peripheral interface, 172
  ready line (ARDY, BRDY), 172–4
  strobe line (ASTB, BSTB), 172–4
port operation, 174–6
priority daisy chain, 179
registers, 175–6
  data input, 176
  data output, 176
  input/output select, 176
  mask, 176
  mask control, 176
  mode control, 175–6
return from interrupt timing diagram, 181